THE HANDBOOK OF DIALECTICAL BEHAVIOR THERAPY

THE HANDBOOK OF DIALECTICAL BEHAVIOR THERAPY

THEORY, RESEARCH, AND EVALUATION

Edited by

JAMIE BEDICS

California Lutheran University, Thousand Oaks, CA, United States

ELSEVIER

ACADEMIC PRESS

An imprint of Elsevier

Academic Press is an imprint of Elsevier
125 London Wall, London EC2Y 5AS, United Kingdom
525 B Street, Suite 1650, San Diego, CA 92101, United States
50 Hampshire Street, 5th Floor, Cambridge, MA 02139, United States
The Boulevard, Langford Lane, Kidlington, Oxford OX5 1GB, United Kingdom

Notices
Knowledge and best practice in this field are constantly changing. As new research and experience broaden our understanding, changes in research methods, professional practices, or medical treatment may become necessary.

Practitioners and researchers must always rely on their own experience and knowledge in evaluating and using any information, methods, compounds, or experiments described herein. In using such information or methods they should be mindful of their own safety and the safety of others, including parties for whom they have a professional responsibility.

To the fullest extent of the law, neither the Publisher nor the authors, contributors, or editors, assume any liability for any injury and/or damage to persons or property as a matter of products liability, negligence or otherwise, or from any use or operation of any methods, products, instructions, or ideas contained in the material herein.

British Library Cataloguing-in-Publication Data
A catalogue record for this book is available from the British Library

Library of Congress Cataloging-in-Publication Data
A catalog record for this book is available from the Library of Congress

ISBN: 978-0-12-816384-9

For Information on all Academic Press publications
visit our website at https://www.elsevier.com/books-and-journals

Publisher: Nikki Levy
Editorial Project Manager: Barbara Makinster
Production Project Manager: Omer Mukthar
Cover Designer: Matthew Limbert

Typeset by MPS Limited, Chennai, India

Contents

Contents

III

SPECIFIC SETTINGS AND POPULATIONS

IV
FUTURE DIRECTIONS

List of contributors

Joan R. Asarnow Psychiatry and Biobehavioral Sciences, UCLA, Los Angeles, CA, United States

Autumn Askew University of Minnesota, Minneapolis, MN, United States

Kalina N. Babeva Psychiatry and Behavioral Medicine, Seattle Children's Hospital, Seattle, WA, United States; Psychiatry and Biobehavioral Sciences, UCLA, Los Angeles, CA, United States

Jamie D. Bedics California Lutheran University, Thousand Oaks, CA, United States

Michele S. Berk Department of Psychiatry and Behavioral Sciences, Division of Child and Adolescent Psychiatry, Stanford University, Stanford, CA, United States

Lisa S. Bolden UCLA David Geffen School of Medicine Health Sciences at Harbor UCLA Medical Center, Torrance, CA, United States

Adam Carmel Department of Psychiatry and Behavioral Sciences, University of Washington at Harborview Medical Center, Seattle, WA, United States

Alexander L. Chapman Department of Psychology, Simon Fraser University, Vancouver, BC, Canada

Carla D. Chugani Department of Pediatrics, University of Pittsburgh, Pittsburgh, PA, United States

Kate Comtois Department of Psychiatry and Behavioral Sciences, University of Washington, WA, United States

Suzanne E. Decker VA Connecticut Health Care System, West Haven, CT, United States; Yale School of Medicine, New Haven, CT, United States

Christopher R. DeCou Department of Psychiatry and Behavioral Sciences, University of Washington at Harborview Medical Center, Seattle, WA, United States

Elizabeth Dexter-Mazza Mazza Consulting, Seattle, Washington, United States

Jesse Dzombak University of Minnesota, Minneapolis, MN, United States

Olivia Fitzpatrick Psychology Department, Harvard University, Cambridge, MA, United States

Erin Gallagher University of Minnesota, Minneapolis, MN, United States

Lizbeth Gaona California Baptist University, College of Behavioral and Social Sciences, Riverside, CA, United States

Nora Gerardi Cognitive & Behavioral Consultants, White Plains, NY, United States

Marianne Goodman James J. Peters Veterans Administration Medical Center, The Bronx, NY, United States; Icahn School of Medicine at Mount Sinai, New York, NY, United States

Rebekah Halpert Department of Psychiatry, New York Presbyterian-Columbia University Medical Center, NY, United States

Ann F. Haynos University of Minnesota, Minneapolis, MN, United States

Dorian A. Hunter The Seattle Clinic LLC, Seattle, WA, United States

Jacqueline K. Krychiw Department of Psychology, Hofstra University, Hempstead, NY, United States

Sara J. Landes Central Arkansas Veterans Healthcare System, Little Rock, AR, United States; University of Arkansas for Medical Sciences, Little Rock, AR, United States

Anne R. Limowski Department of Psychology, Hofstra University, Hempstead, NY, United States

Elizabeth R. LoTempio The Seattle Clinic LLC, Seattle, WA, United States

James J. Mazza Mazza Consulting, Seattle, Washington, United States

Sacha A. McBain Central Arkansas Veterans Healthcare System, Little Rock, AR, United States; University of Arkansas for Medical Sciences, Little Rock, AR, United States

Lynn McFarr UCLA David Geffen School of Medicine at Harbor-UCLA Medical Center, Torrance, CA, United States

Holly McKinley Minneapolis VA, Minneapolis, MN, United States

Laura L. Meyers Orlando VA Medical Center, Orlando, FL, United States

Jared D. Michonski The Seattle Clinic LLC, Seattle, WA, United States

Erin M. Miga The Seattle Clinic LLC, Seattle, WA, United States

Alec L. Miller Cognitive & Behavioral Consultants, White Plains, NY, United States

Lynnaea Owens Department of Psychology, Simon Fraser University, Vancouver, BC, Canada

Francheska Perepletchikova Weill Cornell Medicine, White Plains, NY, United States

Jill H. Rathus Department of Psychology, Long Island University-Post, Brookville, NY, United States

Rachael K. Richter Department of Pediatrics, University of Pittsburgh, Pittsburgh, PA, United States

Nicholas L. Salsman School of Psychology, Xavier University, Cincinnati, OH, United States

Ashley M. Smith Boston Medical Center, Boston, MA, United States

Brandy N. Smith VA Palo Alto Veterans Health Care System, Menlo Park, CA, United States

Angela Page Spears James J. Peters Veterans Administration Medical Center, The Bronx, NY, United States

Kaylee Stewart Boston Medical Center, Boston, MA, United States

Sarah R. Sullivan James J. Peters Veterans Administration Medical Center, The Bronx, NY, United States

Sarah E. Valentine Department of Psychiatry, Boston University School of Medicine, Boston, MA, United States; Boston Medical Center, Boston, MA, United States

Erin F. Ward-Ciesielski Department of Psychology, Hofstra University, Hempstead, NY, United States

Kristin P. Wyatt Department of Psychiatry & Behavioral Sciences, Duke University Medical Center, Durham, NC, United States

Preface

A quote attributed to George Wilhelm Friedrich Hegel says "The learner always begins by finding fault, but the scholar sees the positive merit in everything." The quote is relevant to this book in several ways. As a learner, a student, we continually seek to improve our understanding of the world around us. We strive for change and ask ourselves questions such as "What have we missed?" and "What is next?" In doing so, we find fault. During these times, we can, however, advance too quickly and seek change in an ill-informed manner. As a scholar, we similarly seek to improve our understanding of the world. We strive for understanding through a comprehensive and detailed review of an accumulated body of literature. We ask ourselves questions such as "What have we done?" and "How have we done it?" In doing so, we find and acknowledge the positive merit in the work that has been accomplished. We can, however, progress too slowly or wrongly accept a conclusion that is deserving of further attention. It is through a balance of questioning and understanding, change and acceptance, that a field of study can advance.

The primary motivation for this edited book is to highlight the varied and significant advances made in the scientific study of dialectical behavior therapy (DBT). DBT began with the singular goal of improving the lives of those experiencing so much pain that they considered suicide as a solution to their problems. DBT was also developed with a unique focus on the personal experience of those diagnosed with borderline personality disorder (BPD). The resulting treatment was a multimodal, comprehensive intervention rooted in the traditions of cognitive-behavioral therapy, Zen meditation, and dialectical philosophy. Individually, the strategies and techniques that made up DBT were quite familiar to most psychotherapists. They consisted of foundational approaches to psychotherapy, including behavioral, cognitive, Rogerian, Gestalt, and mindfulness as well as the latest advances in the assessment and management of suicidal behavior. When taken together, however, the resulting treatment was something quite new. Linehan's use of an overarching dialectical framework, to carefully balance and structure the aforementioned therapies, centered around the fundamental dialectic of acceptance and change, and guided by the phenomenological experience of those diagnosed with BPD was both innovative and groundbreaking.

Since its inception, DBT has expanded in both application and method of delivery. It is fair to say that there is no longer a single "DBT" but many "DBTs" that exist as part of a larger family of treatments. DBT has been modified to fit particular settings and to meet the needs of specific demographic groups and diagnostic populations. Returning to the initial quote, it is clear there has been a lot of changes in our thinking and application of DBT. The goal of this text is to provide a comprehensive understanding of the areas where DBT has shown growth. In each chapter, I have asked the contributing authors to address the questions "What have we done?" and "How have we done it?" In their areas of expertise the authors have focused on the details of the research methodology including the variations in how DBT has been delivered, the consistency or inconsistency in outcomes across studies, and the overall replicability of the findings. In doing so the authors demonstrate the positive merit in the existing evidence-base supporting the diverse family of interventions falling under the broad heading of DBT. At the same time, they show the significant potential for growth in each area for future research.

The first section of this book includes four chapters that cover several foundational topics in DBT. In Chapter 1, History and overview of dialectical behavior therapy, Erin F. Ward-Ciesielski, Anne R. Limowski, and Jacqueline K. Krychiw provide a thorough history of the development of DBT, including its core philosophical and scientific foundations. In Chapter 2, The therapeutic alliance and therapeutic relationship in dialectical behavior therapy, myself and Holly McKinley review the unique and critical role of the therapeutic alliance and therapeutic relationship in DBT. Chapter 3, Mechanisms of change in dialectical behavior therapy, by Alexander L. Chapman and Lynnaea Owens, discusses the hypothesized mechanisms of change in DBT and the evidence in support of their impact. Lastly, in Chapter 4, Accreditation, adherence, and training in dialectical behavior therapy: data review and practical applications, Erin M. Miga, Elizabeth R. LoTempio, Jared D. Michonski, and Dorian A. Hunter provide a detailed and comprehensive review of the various methods for learning DBT, including the process of becoming certified in DBT.

The second section of this book is focused on the empirical evidence surrounding unique *Clinical Populations*. In Chapter 5, Efficacy of dialectical behavior therapy in the treatment of suicidal behavior, Christopher R. DeCou and Adam Carmel provide a review of the evidence in support of the efficacy and effectiveness of DBT for the treatment of suicidal behavior. Chapter 6, Eating disorders, by Autumn Askew, Erin Gallagher, Jesse Dzombak, and Ann F. Haynos, reviews the quantitative evidence in support of DBT for the treatment of eating disorders. In Chapter 7, Dialectical behavior therapy for individuals with substance use problems: theoretical adaptations and empirical evidence, Nicholas L. Salsman reviews the empirical literature surrounding the treatment of substance use and substance disorders in DBT. Chapter 8, Dialectical behavior therapy for adolescents: a review of the research, and Chapter 9, Clinical illustration of the dialectical behavior therapy for preadolescent children: addressing primary targets, have a focus on the application of DBT to youth. Chapter 8, Dialectical behavior therapy for adolescents: a review of the research, by Jill Rathus, Alec Miller, Michele Berk, and Rebekah Halpert, evaluates the extensive development of DBT for the treatment of adolescents. In Chapter 9, Clinical illustration of the dialectical behavior therapy for preadolescent children: addressing primary targets, Francheska Perepletchikova presents an adaptation of DBT for children and provides a detailed clinical illustration that demonstrates how families can be incorporated into the treatment.

The third section of this book has its focus on *Clinical Settings* of DBT. In Chapter 10, Research of dialectical behavior therapy in schools, Alec L. Miller, Nora Gerardi, James J. Mazza, and Elizabeth Dexter-Mazza review the various applications of DBT to school settings. Chapter 11, Dialectical behavior therapy in college counseling centers, by Carla D. Chugani, Kristin P. Wyatt, and Rachael K. Richter, takes a careful look at the evidence surrounding the benefit of adapting DBT for university and college counseling centers. In Chapter 12, Dialectical behavior therapy research and program evaluation in the Department of Veterans Affairs, Sara J. Landes, Suzanne E. Decker, Sacha A. McBain, Marianne Goodman, Brandy N. Smith, Sarah R. Sullivan, Angela Page Spears, and Laura L. Meyers review the significant effort taken to disseminate, implement, and evaluate DBT in the Department of Veterans Affairs. Chapter 13, Dialectical behavior therapy stepped care for hospitals, by Kalina Babeva, Olivia Fitzpatrick, and Joan Asarnow, present a novel stepped care model of DBT developed for a hospital setting. Chapter 14, DBT−ACES in a multicultural community mental health setting: implications for clinical practice, by Lisa S. Bolden, Lizbeth Gaona, Lynn McFarr, and Kate Comtois, review a unique approach to DBT focused on clients who have already completed one year of DBT. The chapter is unique in its emphasis on incorporating various models of cultural understanding to improve the delivery of DBT. Lastly, in Chapter 15, A review of the empirical evidence for DBT skills training as a stand-alone intervention, Sarah E. Valentine, Ashley M. Smith, and Kaylee Stewart provide a review of the overall effectiveness and efficacy of DBT skills as a stand-alone intervention. In the final chapter, I provide concluding statements based upon my review of the core chapters in light of the scientific principles of replicability and reproducibility as a method of advancing the science of DBT.

I would like to thank all the chapter contributors for their effort and energy in providing thorough, open, and honest reflections on the advancement of the study in their areas of expertise related to DBT. The amount of work put into these chapters was significant and reflects the passion and creativity of the larger DBT community. I would also like to thank all those at Elsevier for their support and patience in the process of developing this text. Finally, I would like to thank Dr. Marsha Linehan for her graciousness and support in my early academic career.

Jamie Bedics

SECTION I

Overview

CHAPTER

1

History and overview of dialectical behavior therapy

Erin F. Ward-Ciesielski, Anne R. Limowski and Jacqueline K. Krychiw

Department of Psychology, Hofstra University, Hempstead, NY, United States

> Borderline patients are so numerous that most practitioners must treat at least one. They present with severe problems and intense misery. They are difficult to treat successfully. It is no wonder that many mental health clinicians are feeling overwhelmed and inadequate and are in search of a treatment that promises some relief (Linehan, 1993, p. 3).

Dialectical behavior therapy (DBT) is an intensive, comprehensive, multimodal psychosocial intervention developed by Marsha Linehan originally for the treatment of chronically suicidal individuals. Built on cognitive, behavioral, and mindfulness-based techniques, DBT incorporates principles of behaviorism, Zen philosophy, and Christian contemplative prayer within an overarching framework of dialectics. The treatment's primary aim is to help clients develop a "life worth living" so that suicidal behaviors are no longer necessary. DBT was developed in response to the problems encountered when applying standard behavioral principles and social learning theories to chronically suicidal individuals who often met criteria for borderline personality disorder (BPD) and presented with complex, high-risk, and multidiagnostic problems (Linehan, 1981).

History of dialectical behavior therapy

DBT was developed in the late 1970s and 1980s when no empirically supported treatments existed for individuals struggling with suicidal and

The Handbook of Dialectical Behavior Therapy
DOI: https://doi.org/10.1016/B978-0-12-816384-9.00001-4

other self-injurious behaviors. Linehan herself was trained in behavior therapy, which was considered the "gold-standard" intervention in the 1980s for most clinical disorders; however, like many other clinicians, Linehan struggled to treat the complex problems of chronically suicidal individuals. These clients tended to present with a variety of urgent concerns that could not be adequately addressed by treatment manuals, which were usually limited in scope to a single clinical disorder.

The first draft of Linehan's treatment manual focused primarily on decreasing suicidal behaviors (Linehan & Wilks, 2015), but DBT's target population eventually became merged with BPD. In fact, life-threatening behaviors are so ubiquitous among individuals with BPD that suicide and self-injury have been referred to as the "behavioral specialty" of BPD (Gunderson, 1984). Prevalence rates for suicidal and nonsuicidal self-injurious behaviors are high among individuals with BPD. Estimates at the time indicated that approximately three quarters of clients with BPD had engaged in at least one act of self-injury in their lifetime (Clarkin, Widiger, Frances, Hurt, & Gilmore, 1983; Cowdry, Pickar, & Davies, 1985) and the suicide rate among clients with BPD was approximately 9% (Kroll, Carey, & Sines, 1985; Paris, Brown, & Nowlis, 1987; Stone, 1989). Soloff, Lis, Kelly, Cornelius, and Ulrich (1994) estimate that 75% of clients who meet criteria for BPD have attempted suicide, with an average of 3.4 attempts per person. Notably, more recent estimates of the prevalence of suicidal behaviors in individuals with BPD continue to underscore this crucial clinical overlap (Black, Blum, Pfohl, & Hale, 2004; Paris, 2008). In the first randomized controlled trial (RCT) of DBT, Linehan sought to study the most severely suicidal people she could recruit from local hospitals. However, because federal grant funding required treatment research to specify a diagnosis, her sample comprised women with BPD (Linehan, Armstrong, Suarez, Allmon, & Heard, 1991), and thus this demographic became the main population described in the first edition of DBT manual, *Cognitive-Behavioral Treatment of Borderline Personality Disorder* (Linehan, 1993).

DBT was developed during a time when clients with BPD represented an estimated 14%–20% of inpatients (Widiger & Frances, 1989; Widiger & Weissman, 1991) and 8%–11% of outpatients (Kroll et al., 1981; Modestin, Abrecht, Tschaggelar, & Hoffman, 1997; Widiger & Frances, 1989) but utilized approximately 40% of mental health resources (Koerner & Dimeff, 2007). When DBT was first introduced in the literature (Linehan, 1987), the only treatments for self-injurious behaviors and BPD were pharmacological or psychoanalytic in nature. These treatments were not very effective, as chronically suicidal individuals demonstrated high rates of treatment failure (Perry & Cooper, 1985; Tucker, Bauer, Wagner, Harlam, & Sher, 1987). Yet, the life-threatening behaviors of these individuals posed an ethical dilemma.

On the one hand, involuntary psychiatric hospitalization was legally required for individuals who were at imminent risk of inflicting significant bodily harm to themselves. On the other, clients with BPD required frequent rehospitalization shortly after discharge (sometimes called the "revolving door" problem), which seemed to indicate that they did not benefit from inpatient treatment. In addition, in outpatient psychotherapy, clients with BPD engaged in interpersonal behaviors that interfered with effective delivery of treatment, as discussed in the next section. To address these challenges, DBT was developed out of an iterative process of trial-and-error application of behavior therapy interventions, and clinical observations and feedback (Linehan & Wilks, 2015; Lungu & Linehan, 2017). Until DBT, no empirically based psychosocial treatment offered a consolidated, hierarchical treatment approach appropriate for addressing the "crisis-of-the-week" presentation typical of these cases (Koerner & Dimeff, 2007), while simultaneously managing suicide risk. Linehan's treatment filled an important gap in clinical practice for chronically suicidal clients exhibiting life-threatening behaviors.

Challenges encountered in the development of dialectical behavior therapy

As with any new intervention, the development of DBT involved several challenges. Much like other clinicians, Linehan originally sought to apply standard behavior therapy to chronically suicidal clients (many of whom she would ultimately realize met criteria for BPD). However, the consequence of employing a change-focused treatment was that it was experienced as invalidating and clients withdrew from treatment, attacked the therapist, or both (Dimeff & Linehan, 2001). It was clear that, although behavior therapy sought to provide relief by focusing on changing client behavior, clients interpreted this as a lack of understanding by the therapist who, if they really understood the magnitude and severity of the suffering, would realize that change is not possible. By contrast, when an entirely acceptance-based approach was attempted—where the therapist focused instead on providing ample validation and support for the difficulties clients were experiencing—this was also experienced as invalidating (Heard & Linehan, 1994). In this case, clients pointed out that they already knew their lives were unbearable, they did not need the therapist to point that out—they needed help. This clear tension between the opposite poles of change and acceptance underlies the core dialectic in DBT. Linehan recognized that a treatment entirely focused on either change or acceptance-based strategies was not able to both acknowledge where clients are and the difficulties with which they are dealing *and* help them to get out of those unbearable situations and into lives they want to live. The introduction of dialectics and a range of treatment strategies (discussed later) were intended to facilitate a more balanced, flexible approach to incorporating change and acceptance within a single treatment.

Another challenge presented was the realization that these clients often experience a range of crises and that the highest priority problems change quickly between or even within a single session (Koerner & Dimeff, 2007). Week to week, clients may be dealing with impending eviction, acute suicidal urges or self-injurious behaviors, an abusive romantic relationship, and the loss of a job. In addition, in a single session, a client may bring up self-injury during the previous week, drug or alcohol use relapse, a fight at work, and wanting to quit therapy. Well-meaning therapists may be tempted to work on the most pressing crisis at any given time; however, the result is a disjointed and inconsistent treatment that does not enable long-term focused attention on overarching deficits and targets. In fact, this approach may inadvertently reinforce therapists for focusing on nonlife-threatening issues in favor of highly stressful ones and result in less attention paid to the highest risk problems. Two aspects of DBT are designed to address this challenge: diary cards and the treatment target hierarchy. Weekly diary cards enable the client to track both ongoing behaviors of interest (e.g., emotions, urges for self-injury or suicide, fights, and drug use) and skills use. The therapist uses the diary card at the beginning of the session to obtain a snapshot view of the previous week to help guide how time in the session will be spent. This helps ensure high-risk targets are not overlooked if a new crisis is the most pressing issue on the client's mind. In addition, as described in more detail later, the specific targets are arranged in a hierarchy of importance to help therapists prioritize a range of ongoing issues.

A third challenge was that often clients unintentionally reinforced ineffective therapist behaviors. For example, a client who has limited emotion regulation skills may lash out in anger when a therapist encourages them to describe a painful emotional experience (e.g., sadness) in session. That reaction might then, understandably, decrease the likelihood that the therapist would encourage emotional description in the future. Unfortunately, many of the difficulties these clients have require the therapist to persist, despite being punished for doing so—or being reinforced for less effective or even iatrogenic behaviors. Take, for example, a client who calls her therapist after having cut herself after a fight with her partner. The therapist might want to provide support, empathy, and validation for the emotional pain that led to the self-injury; however, providing these types of reactions immediately following self-injury could inadvertently serve as a strong reinforcer for self-injurious behavior. Thus the more therapeutic response in this situation is to remain cooler and assess the severity of the injury in a matter-of-fact way (e.g., is medical intervention needed) before quickly ending the call. These seemingly counterintuitive responses and therapists' difficulty maintaining them throughout their work with high-risk clients resulted in the need for a therapist consultation team. As described in more detail later, the therapist consultation team is intended to help therapists maintain fidelity to the treatment and all of its components. Therapists can use this team to obtain the reinforcement and support they need to continue engaging in therapeutic behaviors for which they may be punished in session as well as for maintaining contingencies (i.e., the 24-hour rule which dictates that therapists will not provide between-session contact for 24 hours after a target behavior occurs) when doing so can lead to intense therapist anxiety and distress.

Overview of the major philosophical aspects of dialectical behavior therapy

To address the shortcomings of prior interventions for suicidal individuals with BPD, DBT development was guided by the integration of several philosophical ideologies. This section reviews many of these theoretical underpinnings, namely, the biosocial theory, behaviorism, acceptance, and how the overarching theme of dialectics aims to balance the strengths and weaknesses of each of these philosophies.

The biosocial theory

Linehan relied in part on her personal experience with receiving treatment at a psychiatric facility to guide the creation of DBT (Carey, 2011). Specifically, she sought to develop a nonpejorative model to understand and explain BPD to guide effective therapy in a way that was consistent with empirical findings. Through her clinical work and research, she observed that individuals with BPD have a high sensitivity to emotional stimuli, experience more intense emotional reactions, and return to their emotional baseline more slowly than other clients. In essence, individuals with BPD struggle with emotion dysregulation, which was initially conceptualized as the product of emotional vulnerability and an inability to regulate intense emotions (Linehan, 1993). Thus the behaviors that make up diagnostic criteria for BPD serve to regulate these intense emotions and/or are a consequence of dysregulation. In this way, emotion dysregulation is the core feature of BPD, and therefore a critical target of DBT.

To highlight this important characteristic, Linehan (1993) proposed the biosocial theory that postulates that emotion dysregulation results from a biological predisposition to intense emotions which, when evoked, are made worse by specific experiences in the social environment (i.e., invalidation). This "poorness of fit" between the susceptible individual and their dysfunctional environment creates further dysregulation. Importantly, an invalidating environment does not provide individuals with the opportunity to learn how to properly label or regulate their emotions. Individuals are often told to control their emotions and solve their problems, rather than being taught how to do so. Second, this simplistic response to solving life's various challenges does not teach individuals how to tolerate distress and develop realistic goals and beliefs. Third, clients learn that it is only through escalating their emotional displays (e.g., threatening suicide) that they receive a response from others in their environment, which reinforces these extreme behaviors and often ignores or punishes clients' direct communication of emotions. As a result, individuals vacillate between emotional inhibition and extreme emotional arousal. Lastly, such an environment does not teach individuals to trust their own private experiences (e.g., thoughts, emotions) but rather promotes the internalization of invalidation. The biosocial theory, which acknowledges the biological and environmental etiologies of BPD through a nonjudgmental framework, is the central guiding principle of DBT.

Behavioral and social learning theories

The early stages of DBT treatment development were also guided by a theoretical framework comprising behaviorism (Skinner, 1974), social learning theory (Bandura, 1977), and the social behavioral model of personality (Staats & Staats, 1963). Behaviorism is a theory of learning based on the idea that all behaviors are the result of continuous "stimulus–response" transactions (operant conditioning; Skinner, 1974). Specifically, this model posits that all behavior is caused by external stimuli and can be explained without the need to consider internal mental states or consciousness. Alternatively, social learning theory and the social behavioral model of personality extend principles of behaviorism by integrating both behavioral and cognitive theories of learning. The social learning theory posits individuals can acquire behaviors through observation, imitation, and modeling (Bandura, 1977). The social behavioral model of personality suggests that a person's internal experiences can be explained through observable behaviors. Much like behaviorism, these social learning theories highlight the importance of consequences in determining whether or not an individual will engage in a particular behavior. Important aspects of social psychology (Mischel, 1973), and cognitive behavioral principles (Goldfried & Davison, 1976; Wilson & O'Leary, 1980), were also incorporated into early interventions. Taken together, the initial treatment aimed at reducing suicidal behaviors was principle-driven, rather than protocol-driven (Harned, Banawan, & Lynch, 2006), and focused on promoting effective problem-solving strategies to reduce the problematic behaviors exhibited by many individuals with BPD (Linehan & Wilks, 2015). In particular, treatment revolved around completing behavioral chain analyses of problem behaviors to better understand the variables that appeared to prompt and maintain them (Robins, 2002).

Acceptance-based philosophies

As discussed previously, the change-focused approaches that rest on these theories were perceived as invalidating by suicidal individuals, prompting Linehan to search for approaches that focused solely on acceptance without the ulterior goal of change. Eastern (Zen Buddhist practices) and Western (Christian contemplative prayer teachings) principles were used as guidance for this novel treatment approach. The foundation of Buddhism is characterized by several "truths" that propose human suffering is created by attachment. Thus individuals practicing Zen are encouraged to let go of ideas about what they think reality "should" be and, instead, gain liberation through means of acceptance, self-validation, and tolerance of their experiences (Robins, 2002). Zen practices suggest that this path of enlightenment is a process of disentangling one's self from their body, feelings, thoughts, and consciousness. Alternatively, Christian contemplative prayer underscores the practice of fully opening one's mind and heart to God and is described as an interior transformation (Aitken, 1982; Jager, 2005). Central to both ideologies is the concept of radically accepting the present moment, without attempting to change it (Linehan & Wilks, 2015). Early attempts to integrate aspects of these acceptance-based philosophies into treatment with suicidal individuals involved encouraging clients to practice meditation. However, most clients found it very difficult to sit with their experience and often became dysregulated (Lungu & Linehan, 2017). At this time, meditation was not part of psychotherapy and therefore was perceived as odd, threatening, and somewhat impossible for individuals who already chronically struggled to experience their emotions (Linehan & Wilks, 2015). Instead, an integrative and easily generalized approach was needed.

Consequently, Zen and contemplative prayer teachings were converted into behavioral skills that could be learned by both clients and therapists. Considering the difficulty of implementing a treatment based on several philosophies to a range of suicidal clients with varying religious/spiritual backgrounds, religious and/or spiritual undertones of the practices were also removed. Thus the term "mindfulness (i.e., focusing on the present moment in a nonjudgmental manner)," derived from the work of Langer (1989) and Hahn (1976), was used to describe the skills that were transformed from Zen, while the skills transformed from contemplative practices were classified as "reality acceptance skills" inspired by the work of May (1987).

The dialectical philosophy

Although acceptance-based strategies were helpful in addressing the shortcomings of change-oriented strategies, treatment that focused only on warmth and acceptance was ineffective in reducing the dangerous behaviors that initially brought clients to treatment. Linehan ultimately sought a synthesis between change and acceptance, and dialectics became the overarching framework that organized these two opposing strategies. Dialectics is the philosophical concept that opposing views and/or strategies can be integrated throughout a treatment to keep both therapist and client from becoming "stuck" in extreme positions (Linehan, 1993). It was necessary to accept clients and their actions fully in the moment, while simultaneously pushing for change. However, this "dance" was challenging for many clients because the encouragement of acceptance pushed them to tolerate their distress in the moment, rather than attempt to get rid of or change it. One stylistic strategy that increased the effectiveness of treatment was using irreverent, confrontational comments to facilitate movement throughout treatment (Linehan, 1993). Linehan noticed that she and her clients were often on "opposite ends of a teeter-totter" (Linehan, 1993, p. 30) continuously moving to regain balance. Taken together, a framework that allowed for opposing views and/or strategies (i.e., change and acceptance) to be employed throughout the course of treatment was needed. As a result, the philosophical concept of dialectics was adopted.

As a worldview, dialectical philosophy extends back thousands of years (Bopp & Weeks, 1984; Kaminstein, 1987), although it is most often associated with Marxist socioeconomic principles (Neacsiu, Ward-Ciesielski, & Linehan, 2012). Dialectics involves three important stages that occur continuously throughout treatment. First, an initial proposition or statement (thesis) takes place. Subsequently, the negation of the initial proposition occurs, which involves a contradiction or "antithesis." Lastly, the synthesis of thesis and antithesis occurs, which, in essence, negates the negation. From a dialectical point of view, the push for change and problem-solving in treatment is effective through means of validation and acceptance (Neacsiu et al., 2012). Thus the dialectical theme of DBT is accepting clients where they are by acknowledging they are doing the best they can and, at the same time, pushing them to do better (Lynch, Chapman, Rosenthal, Kuo, & Linehan, 2006).

The foundation of dialectical philosophy is characterized by three main principles: (1) interrelatedness, (2) polarity, and (3) continuous change (Linehan, 1993). First, interrelatedness emphasizes the holistic nature of dialectics. Specifically, one thing cannot exist without the other (Linehan, 1993), everything is the result of a cause and effect relationship, and nothing in the universe can be explained without reference to the transaction of all events with each other (Neacsiu et al., 2012). In DBT, this concept is depicted by asking clients what is being left out; truth is not perceived as absolute within a dialectical philosophy, but is instead constantly evolving (Linehan, 1993; Robins, Schmidt, & Linehan, 2004). Second, polarity highlights that reality is not stationary but rather comprises opposing forces (thesis and antithesis), the subsequent synthesis of which results in another set of novel opposing forces. Although a dialectical philosophy focuses on the whole, it also acknowledges the complexities that exist within the whole. One way this concept is translated into DBT is through the mindfulness skill of "wise mind," which is the synthesis between "emotion mind" and "reasonable mind" (Neacsiu et al., 2012). Lastly, a dialectical framework results in constant change. It is the tension that exists within each system (e.g., the good and bad, parents and children, therapists and clients, and person and environment) that yields transformation. To effectively balance acceptance and change, therapists need to quickly shift from one side of the dialectic to the other so clients do not find themselves stuck on either side (Linehan, 1993). According to Neacsiu et al. (2012), an example of how to maintain this balance during a session might be, "I agree your life is not where you want it to be [acceptance]. So we should work on getting it there. How can you start looking for a job [change]? I know right now it seems like an overwhelming task [acceptance], and what would be one step to take in that direction [change]? Do you have a résumé? [change]" (p. 4).

Dialectical behavior therapy treatment elements

DBT is designed for flexible application depending on the specific clinical presentation of a given client. Unlike protocol-based treatments, there is no structured session-by-session organization to follow (Linehan, 1993). Both long-term and in-the-moment treatment decisions are made based on a set of guiding principles with life-threatening or more severe problems being necessarily addressed first. These treatment targets differ based on the stage of treatment or level of disorder of the client. Furthermore, a range of therapeutic strategies are available to flexibly incorporate acceptance, change, and dialectical interventions and both therapists and clients agree to accept a set of basic assumptions about themselves and the treatment. Each of these aspects (treatment modalities, stages of treatment and treatment targets, treatment strategies, and assumptions) will be outlined in more detail in the following sections.

Treatment modes and targets

All comprehensive treatments address five key functions: (1) enhancing client capabilities, (2) improving client motivation for change, (3) ensuring generalization of new skills and capabilities to all relevant contexts, (4) structuring the environment, and (5) enhancing therapist capabilities and motivation to provide effective treatment (Rizvi, Steffel, & Carson-Wong, 2013). As a comprehensive treatment, DBT comprises four treatment modes: individual therapy, group skills training, between-session coaching, and therapist consultation team. Each mode has a specified set of functions, often overlapping with other modalities to ensure comprehensive treatment and generalization of treatment progress.

Individual therapy

As stated previously, clients receiving DBT are often complex, multi-diagnostic, and high-risk, which necessitates the designation of a single individual as the primary therapist who ultimately oversees the client's entire treatment progression. Thus the primary clinical responsibility in DBT falls to the individual therapist. Within the client–therapist dyad, the individual therapist oversees clinical decision-making, risk and crisis management, and successful integration of the other treatment modes. Individual therapy generally occurs weekly and the specific focus of a given session is organized based on a hierarchy of treatment targets. In order, (1) life-threatening behaviors, (2) therapy-interfering behaviors, and (3) quality-of-life-interfering behaviors are prioritized. Life-threatening behaviors include those that increase risk to the client or the risk of violence against others (e.g., suicide attempts, self-injury). Therapy-interfering behaviors include both client and therapist behaviors that get in the way of achieving goals. For instance, therapy-interfering behavior by the client may include not attending individual or group therapy sessions, using between-session coaching ineffectively, not completing homework, or verbally attacking the therapist during session. Therapy-interfering behavior by the therapist may include arriving late or unprepared to session, failing to deliver the treatment with fidelity, or not seeking consultation or training for issues with which they are unfamiliar. Quality-of-life-interfering behaviors include other severe issues that are interfering with the client gaining behavioral control. For instance, this may include loss of employment, housing concerns, severe psychological disorders [e.g., anxiety, posttraumatic stress disorder (PTSD)], or substance abuse (that is not life-threatening). This organizational hierarchy helps the therapist focus treatment, even if clients are experiencing multiple crises in multiple domains or different crises from week to week. Recognizing the necessity of addressing life-threatening behaviors underscores that DBT is a treatment focused on severe, high-risk client presentations. Similarly, if clients are not attending treatment or are inappropriately engaging in treatment (e.g., overusing or misusing between-session coaching), these problems undermine the dyad's ability to effectively work together toward helping the client build a life worth living. When these higher priority behaviors are under control, then there is time to address other issues that are affecting the client's life. Often quality-of-life issues are those that clients are very motivated to address in treatment, setting up a powerful contingency wherein life-threatening behaviors must be stabilized before treatment can progress to these problems.

Group skills training

Weekly skills training groups are designed to address the primary skills deficits proposed to contribute to suicidal thoughts and behaviors as well as a range of difficulties that comprise the BPD diagnostic presentation (e.g., interpersonal difficulties, emotional lability, and lack of a sense of self). Like individual therapy, group skills training is organized by a hierarchy of targets: (1) therapy-destroying behaviors (e.g., threatening suicide in session); (2) skills acquisition, strengthening, and generalization; and (3) therapy-interfering behaviors (Linehan, 1993). Skills group is organized more like a class than traditional group therapy, emphasizing didactic presentation of information about skills, experiential practice, and homework assignment and review. There are four skill content areas, organized as modules: mindfulness, emotion regulation, distress tolerance, and interpersonal effectiveness. A full dose of skills, in which all modules are covered, typically takes 6 months. In addition to these four modules, self-regulation skills are emphasized throughout skills group. These skills include things such as making plans and commitments, regularly attending appointments, completing out-of-session practice, and engaging in skillful behavior during the group itself.

Between-session coaching

The importance of generalizing skills to all relevant contexts has already been noted in the context of individual therapy and group skills training. The principal mechanism in DBT by which generalization is addressed is between-session coaching. Like an athletic coach who provides consultation mid-game, coaching contact is meant to provide skills-focused problem-solving and intervention when clients are in their real lives, confronted by the problems with which they struggle each day. Rather than waiting until the next therapy session to discuss what skills could have been used or how skills may have been changed or improved, coaching provides real-time intervention and support to facilitate generalization. Coaching is typically provided by the individual therapist. Coaching will vary across therapists, who observe their own limits regarding the specific approach they employ during calls (e.g., how quickly the therapist will respond to a nonemergency call, overnight call expectations).

Importantly, coaching is not intended to serve as additional individual therapy in the sense of lengthy conversations about challenges or to mitigate client's feelings of loneliness, for instance. Calls are usually brief (less than 10 minutes) and structured. For example, a client who is experiencing urges to self-harm may contact her therapist, give a brief description of the present situation (e.g., fight with romantic partner), discuss skills she already tried (e.g., distracting with music), and then be coached by the therapist in a new skill to try (e.g., dunking her face in ice water and then exercising for 20 minutes). Clients are often encouraged to call back if their urges continue (for additional coaching) and/or if they skillfully navigate the situation (for reinforcement), as necessary.

Consistent with behavioral principles, clients are fully oriented to the purpose of coaching and, as needed, shaping procedures are employed to help clients use this resource effectively for in-the-moment skills consultation (e.g., a "24-hour rule" states that between-session contact is suspended for 24 hours after a self-harm behavior occurs). As with individual and group skills treatment modes, between-session coaching is organized according to a hierarchy of targets. For individual therapists providing coaching, this hierarchy includes (1) decreasing suicide crisis behaviors, (2) increasing generalization of skills, and (3) decreasing conflict or distance from the therapist or repairing the therapeutic relationship. For group skills leaders or other therapists who may receiving coaching calls, the principal focus is on decreasing therapy-destroying behaviors (Linehan, 1993).

Therapist consultation team

The treatment of complex and high-risk suicidal clients can easily affect therapists, in their fidelity to the treatment principles, their sense of professional competence and effectiveness, and their potential frustration or burnout. The DBT therapist consultation team is intended to mitigate these potential challenges by serving as "therapy for the therapist." In DBT consultation team meetings, therapists discuss cases, provide consultation and support to one another, and address out-of-town coverage or other practical clinic issues; however, they also address therapist and/or treatment failures, therapist willfulness or "emotion mind" decision-making, and any other issues that may be interfering with therapists providing adherent DBT to their individual and/or group clients. While it is not expected that all therapists on the consultation team will always agree on treatment approaches, the team members agree to incorporate a dialectical philosophy where thesis, antithesis, and synthesis are considered and varied perspectives are discussed.

Ancillary treatment

In addition to the standard DBT modalities, ancillary treatments may also be employed, including pharmacological treatment, marriage and family therapy, or parent training. Importantly, the individual therapist must consider whether any ancillary treatment would be incompatible with DBT (e.g., the skills undermine or contradict DBT skills, new contingencies interfere with DBT contingencies or they encourage or require ineffective behaviors) before encouraging clients to engage in these additional interventions.

Stages of treatment

DBT begins with a pretreatment stage, followed by four possible stages, determined based on the client's level of disorder or dysregulation. Stage 1 is characterized by behavioral dyscontrol, Stage 2 by "quiet desperation" as a result of comorbid psychological disorders, Stage 3 by problems in living, and Stage 4 by a sense of incompleteness (Koerner and Dimeff, 2007).

Pretreatment

The focus of the pretreatment stage is articulating the components of treatment and their functions and rationales, making commitments to the treatment and the relationship, and establishing a collaborative therapeutic relationship. The goal of this stage of treatment is to enable both the client and therapist to enter the treatment voluntarily. Even in situations where clients are mandated to treatment, progression into a later stage of treatment does not begin until the client has committed to the treatment.

Commitment during pretreatment includes establishing agreements for the relevant treatment components and service delivery. For instance, the client may need to agree to work on Stage 1 treatment targets (e.g., life-threatening behaviors), attending individual and group therapy each week, and paying required fees. Different treatment settings may have a range of additional agreements that they may include in this discussion; however, at a minimum, pretreatment agreement will include the targets for the indicated treatment stage and attending the requisite individual and group treatment at the indicated frequency. To facilitate this process, psychoeducation about specific diagnoses (e.g., BPD) and the philosophical framework for DBT (e.g., the biosocial theory) provided during this stage as well. The client and therapist also identify goals that both believe they can work together to achieve. Some of these goals are inherent to the level of disorder (e.g., developing new skills so that suicide is no longer the primary attempt to cope with emotional pain) and some are specific to the individual client (e.g., increasing assertive communication in relationships, reducing trauma-related symptoms). Importantly, pretreatment also involves the therapist making commitments to treatment and the client. For instance, the therapist agrees to work with the client, provide the best treatment possible, and enhance their own skills and obtain consultation, when needed. When both parties make the necessary commitments to the treatment and each other, treatment then progresses to the indicated stage. If either the therapist or client cannot or will not make these commitments, treatment does not progress to another stage. Instead, the therapist may refer the client to a different therapist or treatment setting where the therapist and client believe the client's needs can be better served.

Stage 1

The focus of Stage 1 is behavioral dyscontrol, including high-risk behaviors such as suicide attempts, self-injury, or harm to others. The goal of this stage is to increase behavioral control. The descriptions of individual therapy, group skills training, and between-session coaching provided previously are all based on a Stage 1 client presentation. That is, each of these modes of treatment is provided for clients who are working toward behavioral control. As discussed in the context of individual therapy and group skills training, the targets in Stage 1 are organized hierarchically (i.e., life-threatening behavior, therapy-interfering behavior, quality-of-life-interfering behavior, and behavioral skills deficits) to help the therapist and client organize and focus their work.

Stage 2

The focus of Stage 2 is "quiet desperation" or the more behaviorally controlled exhibition and experience of acute emotional suffering. The goal of this stage is nontraumatic emotional experiencing. Traumatic experiences of sufficient severity to result in cooccurring PTSD diagnoses are common in individuals diagnosed with BPD (e.g., Harned, Rizvi, & Linehan, 2010; Pagura et al., 2010). Historically, Stage 1 has been proposed to require 1 year of DBT before moving forward to Stage 2 where trauma is targeted (Linehan, 1993). However, more recent work by Harned, Korslund, and Linehan (2014) suggests that trauma-focused treatment can be started much earlier and can be safely and effectively incorporated into treatment once serious life-threatening behaviors (e.g., suicide attempts, self-injury) are under control for a shorter period (i.e., 2 months) and sufficient skills are available to help the client move through trauma treatment. This highlights the principle-driven nature of the stages and targets of treatment in DBT wherein different clients will progress through treatment at different rates and once behavioral control is established and maintained, moving on to emotional desperation is appropriate, even if this shift happens relatively quickly in treatment. Furthermore, Harned et al. (2014) have argued that clients receiving DBT may be especially motivated by the opportunity to work on alleviating their trauma symptoms, which makes reducing life-threatening behaviors and learning behavioral skills operant responses to receiving the desired reinforcer more quickly.

Stage 3

The focus of Stage 3 is problems in living. The goal of this stage is to shift these problems to more "ordinary" happiness and unhappiness that facilitates a better quality of life. This may include targeting less severe psychopathology (e.g., anxiety disorders), issues around an eroded sense of self-respect, or other quality-of-life-improving goals the client may have.

Stage 4

The focus of Stage 4 is the remaining "incompleteness" that some clients may experience, even after progressing through the earlier stages. The goal of this stage is a sense of freedom and the capacity to fully experience joy. For many seeking this capacity, treatment may not be the avenue by which it is pursued, but instead they may seek spiritual or other routes to achieve fulfillment and joy (Robins, Zerubavel, Ivanoff, & Linehan, 2018).

Treatment strategies

To effectively address the complex problems and treatment targets described previously, Linehan recognized the need for a range of treatment strategies that therapists could flexibly apply within sessions and across treatment modalities. Many strategies are identified and described in the original DBT treatment manual (Linehan, 1993) and elaborated elsewhere (e.g., Neacsiu et al., 2012; Robins et al., 2018), and these strategies are broadly organized into core strategies (i.e., problem-solving, validation, and dialectical strategies), stylistic strategies, and case management strategies.

Core strategies

Problem-solving

The problem-solving strategies reflect the behavior therapy basis underlying DBT. As such, these strategies can be generally defined as strategies to ensure thorough and functionally grounded assessment and intervention (Linehan, 1993). Behavioral chain analysis, for instance, is a key strategy used to obtain in-depth, moment-by-moment assessment of client's behaviors. This assessment seeks to identify each "link" in the behavioral chain that led to and followed a target behavior (e.g., suicide attempt) by considering emotions, thoughts, and behaviors, as well as consequences that immediately followed the target behavior. By repeatedly conducting behavioral chain analyses, a functional conceptualization of the factors that lead to and maintain target behaviors can be recognized. Furthermore, points of potential intervention, skills deficits, and reinforcing consequences that are maintaining target behaviors can be identified. In addition to assessment, problem-solving strategies include the range of solutions to problems identified during assessment that may be employed in treatment. As with assessment, these change-focused approaches underlie behavior therapy more generally and include behavioral skills training, cognitive restructuring, contingency management, and exposure.

Validation

Validation strategies are the core of DBT acceptance-based strategies. Validation is the acknowledgment and recognition of another person's experiences and an understanding of that person in their own context (Linehan, 1993). Validation can be applied to emotional, behavioral, and cognitive experiences and can be achieved in explicit, verbal ways as well as in functional, nonverbal ones. For instance, for a client struggling to attend a regular therapy appointment at a specific time because of difficulties establishing childcare or transportation, functional validation might involve rescheduling to a more convenient time. That is, the essence of validation is accepting the client where they are in this moment.

In a follow-up to the original treatment manual, Linehan (1997) outlined six levels of verbal, explicit validation that elaborate the key philosophy and rationale for this acceptance-based set of strategies. Validation at level one involves listening and observing by staying awake, alert, and engaged with the client. Validation at levels two and three involve accurately reflecting the client's verbally reported experiences and articulating the client's unstated or unverbalized (e.g., emotional, cognitive) experiences, respectively. Both levels are important in clearly and explicitly acknowledging what a client is saying as well as what they are feeling and thinking. Level four validation acknowledges behavior in the context of previous learning. That is, "Given X has happened, how could behavior Y be otherwise?" (Linehan, 1997). Validation at level five recognizes the validity of behavior in a given moment, as a normative response to a situation. That is, "Anyone would engage in behavior Z in this context." Finally, validation at level six refers to "radical genuineness" or the notion that the client is a valid person, who the therapist believes in, respects, and encourages.

Dialectics

As has been described previously, a dialectical worldview is also an essential philosophical tenet of DBT. In the context of treatment strategies, dialectical strategies serve the function of highlighting dialectical tensions (e.g., opposite perspectives) and modeling dialectical thinking, often to address polarization or "stuckness" in the therapeutic relationship or in a client's thinking or behavior (Linehan, 1993). These dialectical strategies range from encouraging the therapist to articulate opposite or opposing positions (e.g., skills group is experienced as acutely emotionally painful *and* is a crucial part of the treatment that is necessary to get the client to their goals) to extending or taking a more extreme position than the client to push them toward a less extreme position. An example of extending might be if a client says, "I am going to quit treatment because I refuse to go to skills group," for the therapist to say, "If you are sure about ending treatment, we need to figure out your next steps. I will start pulling together referrals for a new therapist for you to work with." The key with this strategy is to take seriously the part of the client's statement that the client does not want taken seriously. Importantly, the goal is not to attack the client, dismiss their statements, or respond sarcastically; instead, the therapist takes the content literally and extends the tension, which results in the client needing to readjust their position to maintain a balance. Other dialectical strategies include using metaphor, playing devil's advocate, and making lemonade out of lemons.

Stylistic strategies

Stylistic strategies include reciprocal and irreverent communication. Reciprocal communication strategies often function to convey acceptance of the client where they are (Linehan, 1993). For instance, being responsive and warmly engaged are reciprocal forms of communication. In addition, employing strategic self-disclosure, for instance in modeling effective use of a skill or a mastery experience where a skill was attempted and needed to be refined to achieve a desired goal, is a common strategy. On the other hand, irreverent communication strategies function to keep the client slightly off balance to facilitate movement and change (Linehan, 1993). The specific strategies include calling the client's bluff, reframing a situation in an unorthodox manner, and using a more confrontational tone. As with the dialectical strategies discussed previously, central to the use of irreverent communication is genuine warmth and compassion for clients, rather than utilizing these strategies to "excuse" antagonistic or sarcastic responses. For example, telling the client that "we have no reason to believe that treatment will work if you are dead" is an unorthodox reframing that may be used in the context of a client who is hopeless about treatment and expressing suicidal urges. The intention of this type of communication strategy is to increase engagement and retention by injecting new or surprising information: things that a client would not expect their therapist to say.

Case management strategies

The final set of treatment strategies involves environmental, consultation-to-the-patient, and supervision or consultation strategies. These explicitly acknowledge that clients live within complex contexts and it may not be possible for all relevant work to be neatly limited to the therapy office or group therapy room. These strategies include both directly intervening in a client's environment (e.g., when cognitively disoriented following a suicide attempt) and acting as a coach or consultant as the client works with others in their own lives (Linehan, 1993). For instance, a consultation-to-the-patient approach might involve the client and therapist practicing interpersonal effectiveness skills to ask the treating psychiatrist to consider a medication change, followed by having a conference call with the client and her psychiatrist during an individual therapy session. This would then allow the client to ask for a change in their medications while the therapist is present to provide coaching and encouragement along the way. A similar approach might be taken if the client has a conflict with a group skills leader wherein the individual therapist may help the client identify and prepare applicable skillful ways to talk to the skills leader, rather than intervening with the skills leader on the client's behalf. This second example also highlights the third set of case management strategies: therapist supervision or consultation. In addition to the description of the therapist consultation team provided previously, these strategies include keeping treatment and consultation team agreements as well as cheerleading and providing dialectical balance for therapists within a consultation team.

Dialectical behavior therapy assumptions

Both DBT therapists and clients acknowledge a set of assumptions about themselves and/or the treatment (Linehan, 1993). These assumptions make explicit some of the key dialectical tensions that arise in treatment and remind therapists and clients to let go of pejorative or judgmental interpretations of one another to maintain a strong therapeutic alliance. They also preclude the need for therapist or client to "prove" their intentions and instead help the dyad to work together from a place of assuming "good" intentions guiding each other's behaviors.

Assumptions about clients

There are several assumptions specific to clients in DBT treatment, some of which have been suggested to apply to clients with BPD specifically, while others are considered to apply to all clients (Linehan, 1993). DBT therapists assume that clients are doing the best they can and want to improve. Evidencing an important dialectical tension, therapists also recognize that clients need to do better, try harder, and be more motivated to change. The effect of both therapist and client acknowledging this dialectical tension is often a reduction in defensiveness or polarization in the therapeutic relationship. Another dialectical assumption is that clients may not have caused all of their own problems, but they have to solve them anyway. While this may not be true in some circumstances for adolescent or child clients, it helps the dyad let go of focusing on who is to "blame" for problems to more effectively move toward problem-solving and acceptance. One further assumption warrants discussion: that clients cannot fail in therapy. For clients who have felt invalidated by their environments and been treated judgmentally, this assumption can have powerful effects. Specifically, highlighting that the behaviors with which they are struggling are the targets of treatment and that if the treatment is not effective, it is not the result of their failure removes the guilt or shame that may result from setbacks or relapses. In addition, this requires therapists to identify their own failures and the limitations of the treatment rather than assuming the client is not trying "hard enough" or is "sabotaging" the treatment.

Assumptions about therapists and therapy

In addition to the assumptions about clients, there are important assumptions about therapists and DBT itself (Neacsiu et al., 2012). As a counterpoint to the abovementioned assumption that clients cannot fail, DBT therapists assume that they can fail and that the treatment can fail, even when they do not. Assumptions also specify that the most caring thing a therapist can do is help clients change in ways that bring them closer to their ultimate goals and that the therapeutic relationship is a real relationship between equals. As highlighted previously, the benefit of these assumptions is often demonstrated in times of polarization or misunderstanding when therapists may utilize a change-focused strategy or encourage skills practice during an emotional crisis, for example. Another key assumption is that the principles of behaviorism (e.g., contingencies) are universal and affect therapists no less than they affect clients. This particular assumption highlights that therapists are also being shaped and influenced by reinforcement and punishment in their work with clients, which often helps to recognize the powerful influence of these contingencies for oneself and for one's clients and underscores the important role that the therapist consultation team plays in helping therapists adhere to the treatment amidst potentially punishing (or nonreinforcing) of effective therapist behaviors.

Research on dialectical behavior therapy

Throughout this book, various chapters provide an in-depth examination of the empirical research on DBT for a range of populations and clinical presentations. Here, we provide a summary of the progression of DBT research, beginning with the earliest clinical efficacy trials and ending with more recent studies conducted in real-world settings.

Research supporting dialectical behavior therapy for borderline personality disorder

The first RCT comparing DBT to a treatment-as-usual (TAU) condition (Linehan et al., 1991) was published shortly after DBT's introduction into the literature (Linehan, 1987). This RCT recruited a sample of chronically suicidal women, many of whom engaged in self-injury and met criteria for BPD. Linehan et al. found that clients who received 12 months of DBT were more likely to remain in treatment, engaged in self-injury less frequently, and made fewer suicide attempts. Furthermore, when participants who received DBT engaged in suicidal behaviors, these behaviors were less severe than those of TAU participants. Participants in the DBT condition also utilized fewer inpatient services. A subsequent RCT replicated support for DBT in reducing suicide attempts, hospitalizations for suicidal ideation, and risk associated with suicide attempts and self-harm (Linehan et al., 2006). Notably, although early efficacy studies relied primarily on samples of females with BPD, several subsequent RCTs broadened the focus to include males with the disorder (Clarkin, Levy, Lenzenweger, & Kernberg, 2007; Feigenbaum et al., 2011; McMain et al., 2009; Pistorello, Fruzzetti, MacLane, Gallop, & Iverson, 2012; Turner, 2000). Almost three decades later, DBT boasts the largest evidence base with dozens of RCTs demonstrating reductions in suicidal and self-harm behaviors, ER visits, and inpatient hospitalizations (e.g., Linehan et al., 1991; Linehan et al., 2006; Van den Bosch, Verheul, Schippers, & van den Brink, 2002;

Verheul et al., 2003). DBT is widely considered a frontline treatment for clients with BPD and for suicidal and self-injurious behaviors.

Notably, some studies (e.g., Clarkin et al., 2007; McMain et al., 2009) have not found significant differences in outcomes between DBT and comparison conditions. Although meta-analyses have been conducted, methodological differences across studies (such as variations in sample characteristics, choice of comparison groups, selection and measurement of outcomes) make definitive interpretations of these findings difficult. Nonetheless, meta-analyses suggest moderate effects for DBT in reducing suicidal and self-harm behaviors (Hawton et al., 2016; Kliem, Kröger, & Kosfelder, 2010). A more detailed review of the efficacy and effectiveness of DBT in treating BPD and suicidal behavior is included in Chapter 5: The efficacy and effectiveness of DBT in the treatment of BPD and suicidal behavior, of this book.

Research on dialectical behavior therapy with other populations

As previously mentioned, DBT is built upon the biosocial theory of BPD as a disorder of chronic and pervasive emotion dysregulation. Although emotion dysregulation is a hallmark feature of BPD, deficits in emotion regulation are widespread among various psychological disorders and have recently been proposed as a transdiagnostic mechanism through which problematic behaviors are maintained (Kring & Sloan, 2010). Thus researchers have evaluated DBT in other clinical populations (e.g., substance use, PTSD) and across specific age-groups (e.g., children, adolescents, older adults). In addition, skills-only treatments (discussed in the next section) have explored the efficacy of DBT for eating disorders, attention deficit hyperactivity disorder (ADHD), and mood disorders.

Linehan et al. (1999, 2002) were the first to study DBT in women with BPD and comorbid substance use disorder. The earlier of these RCTs found that 12-month standard DBT outperformed TAU in treatment completion, reduction of substance use, and improvement on social and global adjustment measures (Linehan et al., 1999). This study also demonstrated the importance of therapist adherence to the DBT manual; DBT therapists who adhered more closely produced better outcomes. The subsequent RCT found that DBT and comprehensive validation therapy plus a 12-step program were equally efficacious in reducing opioid dependence and other psychopathology (Linehan et al., 2002). Chapter 7: Substance use disorders, describes DBT as it has been developed to treat substance use disorders.

While gold-standard treatments for PTSD involve prolonged exposure (PE) to traumatic memories, concerns about safety in conducting this treatment with suicidal populations are common (see Chapter 6: Eating disorders, of this book for a detailed discussion of this adaptation). Thus DBT has also been modified to treat individuals with PTSD. Protocols established for DBT–PTSD or DBT–PE emphasize the appropriate time to begin the PE component, provide guidelines for ongoing suicide risk assessment, and instruct when exposures should be discontinued to permit additional skill-building. With these treatment modifications, multiple studies have found DBT to be efficacious in samples with cooccurring BPD and PTSD (Bohus et al., 2013; Feigenbaum et al., 2011; Harned et al., 2014). Notably, DBT with PE led to larger and more stable improvements than DBT alone (Harned et al., 2014).

In addition to studies applying DBT to other diagnostic groups, researchers have evaluated the treatment in child, adolescent, and older adult samples. For example, a recent RCT of DBT for preadolescent children demonstrated the feasibility and preliminary efficacy of DBT in treating disruptive mood dysregulation disorder (Perepletchikova et al., 2017). Among adolescent populations, DBT has been shown to reduce psychiatric hospitalizations compared to a TAU condition (Rathus & Miller, 2002), self-harm, severity of suicidal ideation, and depression symptoms compared to an enhanced usual care condition (Mehlum et al., 2014), and depressive symptoms among teens with bipolar disorder (Goldstein et al., 2015). Chapter 10, Research of dialectical behavior therapy in schools, and Chapter 11, Dialectical behavior therapy in college counseling centers, respectively, Chapter 8, DBT for adolescents: A review of the research,... detail adaptations of DBT for adolescents and children. Finally, older adults experiencing depression achieved remission faster with DBT plus medication than with medication alone (Lynch, Trost, Salsman, & Linehan, 2007).

Dialectical behavior therapy effectiveness studies

Substantial research conducted in academic research settings supports DBT's efficacy under optimal conditions. Effectiveness studies, by contrast, have examined whether DBT works in less controlled, real-world settings with more representative providers and clients. The first effectiveness RCT was conducted by Koons et al. (2001) who utilized a sample of female veterans with BPD and found that DBT reduced suicidal ideation, depression, and anger compared to TAU. This study also represented the first RCT in which a shortened duration of treatment (i.e., 6 months) was used. Internationally, two studies have been conducted examining DBT in the UK National Health Service. Although one study found no difference in number of days spent in the hospital compared to TAU (Feigenbaum et al., 2011), a later study found that DBT reduced inpatient hospitalizations and self-harm behaviors between the two conditions (Barnicot, Savill, Bhatti, & Priebe, 2014; Priebe et al., 2012). Among male veterans in a US Veterans Affairs hospital, a study by Goodman et al. (2016) found no differences between DBT and TAU. One difference noted is that veterans in the DBT condition utilized more individual mental health services relative to participants in the control condition. Pistorello et al. (2012) conducted an RCT of DBT versus optimized TAU with suicidal university students presenting to a college counseling center. Both conditions offered treatment provided by trainees who were supervised by experts, lasted between 7 and 12 months, and included both individual and group components. Participants in the DBT condition showed greater improvements in suicidality, depression, self-harm, BPD criteria, and quality of life. Finally, support for DBT in improving depression, anxiety, interpersonal functioning, social adjustment, overall psychopathology, and self-harm has been found in a 3-month inpatient adaptation of DBT (Bohus et al., 2004). Readers are referred to Section III of this text for additional information regarding DBT adaptations for specific settings and special populations. Overall, the evidence base supporting the effectiveness of DBT in diverse settings is promising.

Summary

DBT is a comprehensive, evidence-based treatment initially developed to treat complex, multidiagnostic, and high-risk clients, most of whom were chronically suicidal, met criteria for BPD, and whose needs were unaddressed by existing treatments. The challenges encountered in applying standard behavior therapy to these clients resulted in the development of guiding theories and principles, namely, those based on change, acceptance, and dialectics. This synthesis provides therapists and clients with the necessary structure and support to effectively and compassionately work together to build lives that clients want to live, as well as provide clients with skills so that suicidal behaviors are no longer necessary. Decades of research have established DBT as the frontline treatment for BPD, and research also supports its efficacy for other clinical presentations characterized by emotion dysregulation. Furthermore, the potential utility of DBT strategies and modalities for a range of clinical presentations—beyond BPD specifically—has led to additional innovation and application, as is described in detail throughout this book.

References

Aitken, R. (1982). *Taking the path of Zen*. San Francisco: North Point Press.

Bandura, A. (1977). *Social learning theory*. Englewood Cliffs, NJ: Prentice Hall.

Barnicot, K., Savill, M., Bhatti, N., & Priebe, S. (2014). A pragmatic randomized controlled trial of dialectical behaviour therapy: Effects on hospitalisation and post-treatment follow-up. *Psychotherapy and Psychosomatics*, *83*, 192–193. Available from https://doi.org/10.1159/000357365.

Black, D. W., Blum, N., Pfohl, B., & Hale, N. (2004). Suicidal behavior in borderline personality disorder: Prevalence, risk factors, prediction, and prevention. *Journal of Personality Disorders*, *18*(3), 226–239. Available from https://doi.org/10.1521/pedi.18.3.226.35445.

Bohus, M., Dyer, A. S., Priebe, K., Krüger, A., Kleindienst, N., Schmahl, C., ... Steil, R. (2013). Dialectical behaviour therapy for post-traumatic stress disorder after childhood sexual abuse in patients with and without borderline personality disorder: A randomised controlled trial. *Psychotherapy and Psychosomatics*, *82*(4), 221–233. Available from https://doi.org/10.1159/000348451.

Bohus, M., Haaf, B., Simms, T., Limberger, M. F., Schmahl, C., Unckel, C., & Linehan, M. M. (2004). Effectiveness of inpatient dialectical behavioral therapy for borderline personality disorder: A controlled trial. *Behaviour Research and Therapy*, *42*(5), 487–499. Available from https://doi.org/10.1016/S0005-7967(03)00174-8.

Bopp, M., & Weeks, G. (1984). Dialetical metatheory in family therapy. *Family Process*, *23*, 49–61. Available from https://doi.org/10.1111/j.1545-5300.1984.00049.x.

Carey, B. (2011, June 23). Expert on mental illness reveals her own fight. *The New York Times*. Retrieved from http://archive.nytimes.com/www.nytimes.com/2011/06/23/health/23lives.html

Clarkin, J. F., Levy, K. N., Lenzenweger, M. F., & Kernberg, O. F. (2007). Evaluating three treatments for borderline personality disorder: A multiwave study. *American Journal of Psychiatry*, *164*(6), 922–928. Available from https://doi.org/10.1176/ajp.2007.164.6.922.

Clarkin, J. F., Widiger, T. A., Frances, A., Hurt, S. W., & Gilmore, M. (1983). Prototypic typology and the borderline personality disorder. *Journal of Abnormal Psychology*, *92*(3), 263–275. Available from https://doi.org/10.1037/0021-843X.92.3.263.

Cowdry, R. W., Pickar, D., & Davies, R. (1985). Symptoms and EEG findings in the borderline syndrome. *International Journal of Psychiatry in Medicine*, *15*(3), 201–211.

Dimeff, L., & Linehan, M. M. (2001). DBT in a nutshell. *The California Psychologist*, *34*, 10–13.

Feigenbaum, J. D., Fonagy, P., Pilling, S., Jones, A., Wildgoose, A., & Bebbington, P. E. (2011). A real-world study of the effectiveness of DBT in the UK National Health Service. *British Journal of Clinical Psychology*, *51*, 121–141. Available from https://doi.org/10.1111/j.2044-8260.2011.02017.x.

Goldfried, M. R., & Davison, G. C. (1976). *Clinical behavior thearpy*. New York: Holt, Rinehart and Winston.

Goldstein, T. R., Fersch-Podrat, R. K., Rivera, M., Axelson, D. A., Merranko, J., Yu, H., ... Birmaher, B. (2015). Dialectical behavior therapy for adolescents with bipolar disorder: Results from a pilot randomized trial. *Journal of Child and Adolescent Psychopharmacology*, *25*(2), 140–149. Available from https://doi.org/10.1089/cap.2013.0145.

Goodman, M., Banthin, D., Blair, N. J., Mascitelli, K. A., Wilsnack, J., Chen, J., ... New, A. S. (2016). A randomized trial of dialectical behavior therapy in high-risk suicidal veterans. *The Journal of Clinical Psychiatry*, *77*(12), e1591–e1600. Available from https://doi.org/10.4088/JCP.15m10235.

Gunderson, J. G. (1984). *Borderline personality disorder*. Washington, DC: American Psychiatric Press.

Hahn, T. N. (1976). *The miracle of mindfulness*. Boston: Beacon Press.

Harned, M. S., Banawan, S. F., & Lynch, T. R. (2006). Dialectical behavior therapy: An emotion-focused treatment for borderline personality disorder. *Journal of Contemporary Psychotherapy*, *36*, 67–75. Available from https://doi.org/10.1007/s10879-006-9009-x.

Harned, M. S., Korslund, K. E., & Linehan, M. M. (2014). A pilot randomized controlled trial of dialectical behavior therapy with and without the dialectical behavior therapy prolonged exposure protocol for suicidal and self-injuring women with borderline personality disorder and PTSD. *Behavior Research and Therapy, 55*, 7–17. Available from https://doi.org/10.1016/j.brat.2014.01.008.

Harned, M. S., Rizvi, S. L., & Linehan, M. M. (2010). The impact of co-occurring posttraumatic stress disorder on suicidal women with borderline personality disorder. *American Journal of Psychiatry, 167*, 1210–1217.

Hawton, K., Witt, K. G., Taylor., Salisbury, T. L., Arensman, E., Gunnell, D., ... van Heeringen, K. (2016). Psychosocial interventions for self-harm in adults. *The Cochrane Database of Systematic Reviews, 5*, CD012189. Available from https://doi.org/10.1002/14651858.CD012189.

Heard, H. L., & Linehan, M. M. (1994). Dialectical behavior therapy: An integrative approach to the treatment of borderline personality disorder. *Journal of Psychotherapy Integration, 4*(1), 55–82.

Kliem, S., Kröger, C., & Kosfelder, J. (2010). Dialectical behavior therapy for borderline personality disorder: A meta-analysis using mixed-effects modeling. *Journal of Consulting and Clinical Psychology, 78*(6), 936–951. Available from https://doi.org/10.1037/a0021015.

Jager, W. (2005). *Mysticism for modern times: Conversations with Willigis Jager*. Jiguori Publications.

Kaminstein, D. S. (1987). Toward a dialectical metatheory for psychotherapy. *Journal of Contemporary Psychotherapy, 17*, 87–101. Available from https://doi.org/10.1007/BF00946279.

Koerner, K., & Dimeff, L. A. (2007). Overview of dialectical behavior therapy. In K. Koerner, & L. A. Dimeff's (Eds.), *Dialectical behavior therapy in clinical practice: Applications across disorders and settings* (pp. 1–18). New York: The Guilford Press.

Koons, C. R., Robins, C. J., Tweed, J. L., Lynch, T. R., Gonzalez, A. M., Morse, J. Q., ... Bastian, L. A. (2001). Efficacy of dialectical behavior therapy in women veterans with borderline personality disorder. *Behavior Therapy, 32*(2), 371–390. Available from https://doi.org/10.1016/S0005-7894(01)80009-5.

Kring, A. M., & Sloan, D. M. (2010). *Emotion regulation and psychopathology: A transdiagnostic approach to etiology and treatment*. New York: The Guilford Press.

Kroll, J., Sines, L., Martin, K., Lari, S., Pyle, R., & Zander, J. (1981). Borderline personality disorder: Construct validity of the concept. *Archives of General Psychiatry, 38*(9), 1021–1026. Available from https://doi.org/10.1001/archpsyc.1981.01780340073009.

Kroll, J. L., Carey, K. S., & Sines, L. K. (1985). Twenty-year follow-up of borderline personality disorder: A pilot study. In C. Stragass (Ed.), *IV World Congress of biological psychiatry*. New York: Elsevier.

Langer, E.J., Mindfulness, 1989, Merloyd Lawrence Books, Boston.

Linehan, M. M. (1981). A social-behavioral analysis of suicide and parasuicide: Implications for clinical assessment and treatment. In J. F. Clarkin, & H. I. Glazer (Eds.), *Depression: Behavioral and directive intervention strategies* (pp. 229–294). New York: Garland STPM Press.

Linehan, M. M. (1987). Dialectical behavior therapy for borderline personality disorder: Theory and method. *Bulletin of the Menninger Clinic, 51*(3), 261–276.

Linehan, M. M. (1993). *Cognitive-behavioral treatment of borderline personality disorder*. New York: The Guilford Press.

Linehan, M. M. (1997). Validation and psychotherapy. In A. C. Bohart, & L. S. Greenberg (Eds.), *Empathy reconsidered: New directions in psychotherapy* (pp. 353–392). Washington, DC: American Psychological Association.

Linehan, M. M., Armstrong, H. E., Suarez, A., Allmon, D., & Heard, H. L. (1991). Cognitive-behavioral treatment of chronically parasuicidal borderline patients. *Archives of General Psychiatry, 48*(12), 1060–1064.

Linehan, M. M., Comtois, K. A., Murray, A. M., Brown, M. Z., Gallop, R. J., Heard, H. L., ... Lindenboim, N. (2006). Two-year randomized controlled trial and follow-up of dialectical behavior therapy vs therapy by experts for suicidal behaviors and borderline personality disorder. *Archives of General Psychiatry*, *63*(7), 757–766. Available from https://doi.org/10.1001/archpsyc.63.7.757.

Linehan, M. M., Dimeff, L. A., Reynolds, S. K., Comtois, K. A., Welch, S. S., Heagerty, P., & Kivlahan, D. R. (2002). Dialectical behavior therapy versus comprehensive validation therapy plus 12-step for the treatment of opioid dependent women meeting criteria for borderline personality disorder. *Drug and Alcohol Dependence*, *67*(1), 13–26. Available from https://doi.org/10.1016/S0376-8716(02)00011-X.

Linehan, M. M., Schmidt, H., Dimeff, L. A., Craft, J. C., Kanter, J., & Comtois, K. A. (1999). Dialectical behavior therapy for patients with borderline personality disorder and drug-dependence. *American Journal on Addictions*, *8*(4), 279–292. Available from https://doi.org/10.1080/105504999305686.

Linehan, M. M., & Wilks, C. R. (2015). The course and evolution of dialectical behavior therapy. *American Journal of Psychotherapy*, *69*(2), 97–110. Available from https://doi.org/10.1176/appi.psychotherapy.2015.69.2.97.

Lungu, A., & Linehan, M. M. (2017). Dialectical behavior therapy: Overview, characteristics, and future directions. *The science of cognitive behavioral therapy* (pp. 429–459). Academic Press.

Lynch, T. R., Chapman, A. L., Rosenthal, M. Z., Kuo, J. R., & Linehan, M. M. (2006). Mechanisms of change in dialectical behavior therapy: Theoretical and empirical observations. *Journal of Clinical Psychology*, *62*(4), 459–480.

Lynch, T. R., Trost, W. T., Salsman, N., & Linehan, M. M. (2007). Dialectical behavior therapy for borderline personality disorder. *Annual Review of Clinical Psychology*, *3*, 181–205.

May, G. G. (1987). To bear the beams of love: Contemplation and personal growth. *The Way Supplement: Contemplation and the Contemplative Life*, *59*, 24–34.

McMain, S. F., Links, P. S., Gnam, W. H., Guimond, T., Cardish, R. J., Korman, L., & Streiner, D. L. (2009). A randomized trial of dialectical behavior therapy versus general psychiatric management for borderline personality disorder. *American Journal of Psychiatry*, *166*(12), 1365–1374.

Mehlum, L., Tørmoen, A. J., Ramberg, M., Haga, E., Diep, L. M., Laberg, S., ... Grøholt, B. (2014). Dialectical behavior therapy for adolescents with repeated suicidal and self harming behavior: A randomized trial. *Journal of the American Academy of Child & Adolescent Psychiatry*, *53*(10), 1082–1091.

Mischel, W. (1973). Toward a cognitive social learning reconceptualization of personality. *Psychological Review*, *80*(4), 252.

Modestin, J., Abrecht, I., Tschaggelar, W., & Hoffman, H. (1997). Diagnosing borderline: A contribution to the question of its conceptual validity. *Archiv für Psychiatrie und Nervenkrankheiten*, *233*(5), 359–370.

Neacsiu, A. D., Ward-Ciesielski, E. F., & Linehan, M. M. (2012). Emerging approaches to counseling intervention: Dialectical behavior therapy. *The Counseling Psychologist*, *40*(7), 1003–1032.

Pagura, J., Stein, M. B., Bolton, J. M., Cox, B. J., Grant, B., & Sareen, J. (2010). Comorbidity of borderline personality disorder and posttraumatic stress disorder in the US population. *Journal of Psychiatric Research*, *44*(16), 1190–1198.

Paris, J. (2008). *Treatment of borderline personality disorder: A guide to evidence-based practice*. Guilford Press.

Paris, J., Brown, R., & Nowlis, D. (1987). Long-term follow-up of borderline patients in a general hospital. *Comprehensive Psychiatry*, *28*(6), 530–535.

Perepletchikova, F., Nathanson, D., Axelrod, S. R., Merrill, C., Walker, A., Grossman, M., ... Mauer, E. (2017). Randomized clinical trial of dialectical behavior therapy for preadolescent children with disruptive mood dysregulation disorder: Feasibility and outcomes. *Journal of the American Academy of Child & Adolescent Psychiatry, 56*(10), 832–840.

Perry, J. C., & Cooper, S. H. (1985). Psychodynamics, symptoms, and outcome in borderline and antisocial personality disorders and bipolar type II affective disorder. In T. H. McGlashan (Ed.), *The borderline: Current empirical research* (pp. 21–41). Michigan: American Psychiatric Press in Ann Arbor.

Pistorello, J., Fruzzetti, A. E., MacLane, C., Gallop, R., & Iverson, K. M. (2012). Dialectical behavior therapy (DBT) applied to college students: A randomized clinical trial. *Journal of Consulting and Clinical Psychology, 80*(6), 982.

Priebe, S., Bhatti, N., Barnicot, K., Bremner, S., Gaglia, A., Katsakou, C., ... Zinkler, M. (2012). Effectiveness and cost-effectiveness of dialectical behaviour therapy for self harming patients with personality disorder: A pragmatic randomised controlled trial. *Psychotherapy and Psychosomatics, 81*(6), 356–365.

Rathus, J. H., & Miller, A. L. (2002). Dialectical behavior therapy adapted for suicidal adolescents. *Suicide and Life-Threatening Behavior, 32*(2), 146–157.

Rizvi, S. L., Steffel, L. M., & Carson-Wong, A. (2013). An overview of dialectical behavior therapy for professional psychologists. *Professional Psychology: Research and Practice, 44*, 73–80. Available from https://doi.org/10.1037/a0029808.

Robins, C. J. (2002). Zen principles and mindfulness practice in dialectical behavior therapy. *Cognitive and Behavioral Practice, 9*(1), 50–57.

Robins, C. J., Schmidt, H., III, & Linehan, M. M. (2004). Dialectical behavior therapy: Synthesizing radical acceptance with skillful means. In S. C. Hayes, V. M. Follette, & M. M. Linehan (Eds.), *Mindfulness and acceptance: Expanding the cognitive-behavioral tradition* (pp. 30–44). New York: Guilford Press.

Robins, C. J., Zerubavel, N., Ivanoff, A., & Linehan, M. (2018). *Dialectical behavior therapy. Handbook of personality disorders* (pp. 527–540). The Guilford Press.

Skinner, B. F. (1974). *About behaviorism*. New York: Knopf.

Soloff, P. H., Lis, J. A., Kelly, T., Cornelius, J., & Ulrich, R. (1994). Self-mutilation and suicidal behavior in borderline personality disorder. *Journal of Personality Disorders, 8*(4), 257–267.

Staats, A.W., & Staats, C.K. (1963), Complex human behavior: A systematic extension of learning principles, American Psychological Association, Washington, DC.

Stone, M. H. (1989). Long-term follow-up of narcissistic/borderline patients. *Psychiatric Clinics, 12*(3), 621–641.

Tucker, L., Bauer, S. F., Wagner, S., Harlam, D., & Sher, I. (1987). Long-term hospital treatment of borderline patients: A descriptive outcome study. *The American Journal of Psychiatry, 144*, 1443–1448.

Turner, R. M. (2000). Naturalistic evaluation of dialectical behavior therapy-oriented treatment for borderline personality disorder. *Cognitive and Behavioral Practice, 7*(4), 413–419.

Van den Bosch, L. M., Verheul, R., Schippers, G. M., & van den Brink, W. (2002). Dialectical behavior therapy of borderline patients with and without substance use problems: Implementation and long-term effects. *Addictive Behaviors, 27*(6), 911–923.

Verheul, R., Van Den Bosch, L. M., Koeter, M. W., De Ridder, M. A., Stijnen, T., & Van Den Brink, W. (2003). Dialectical behaviour therapy for women with borderline personality disorder: 12-Month, randomised clinical trial in The Netherlands. *The British Journal of Psychiatry, 182*(2), 135–140.

Widiger, T. A., & Frances, A. J. (1989). Epidemiology, diagnosis, and comorbidity of borderline personality disorder. *Review of psychiatry, 8*, 8–24.

Widiger, T. A., & Weissman, M. M. (1991). Epidemiology of borderline personality disorder. *Psychiatric Services, 42*(10), 1015–1021.

Wilson, G. T., & O'Leary, K. D. (1980). *Principles of behavior therapy*. Prentice Hall.

Further reading

Linehan, M. M. (1999). Development, evaluation, and dissemination of effective psychosocial treatments: Levels of disorder, stages of care, and stages of treatment research. In M. D. Glantz, & C. R. Hartel (Eds.), *Drug abuse: Origins & interventions* (pp. 367–394). Washington, DC: American Psychological Association.

Miller, A. L., Rathus, J. H., & Linehan, M. M. (2007). *Dialectical behavior therapy with suicidal adolescents*. New York: Guilford Press.

CHAPTER

2

The therapeutic alliance and therapeutic relationship in dialectical behavior therapy*

Jamie D. Bedics[1] *and Holly McKinley*[2]

[1]California Lutheran University, Thousand Oaks, CA, United States, [2]Minneapolis VA, Minneapolis, MN, United States

The therapeutic alliance and the therapeutic relationship in dialectical behavior therapy

Dialectical behavior therapy (DBT; Linehan, 1993) is a comprehensive, multimodal intervention requiring a high degree of technical skill and proficiency across numerous treatment interventions, including behavioral, cognitive, and Rogerian psychotherapies as well as training in strategies unique to DBT itself. Despite this emphasis on technique, the therapeutic alliance and the therapeutic relationship are thought to be two of the most critical factors contributing to the effectiveness of DBT. According to Linehan, the relationship between the therapist and client reflects a natural dialectic where the relationship acts as both a means through which to make the treatment work while also acting as the therapy itself apart from any technique (pg. 514, Linehan, 1993). The goal of this chapter is to highlight the role of the therapeutic alliance in the individual therapy mode of standard, or comprehensive, DBT (S-DBT; Linehan, 1993). S-DBT is an outpatient therapy consisting of multiple modalities of treatment, including individual therapy, skills training class, telephone consultation, and therapists' participation on a

* Note. Thanks to Katie Patel for assistance in editing.

The Handbook of Dialectical Behavior Therapy
DOI: https://doi.org/10.1016/B978-0-12-816384-9.00002-6

consultation team. The treatment lasts approximately 1-year and was developed to improve the lives of those struggling with suicidal behavior who also met diagnostic criteria for borderline personality disorder (BPD; American Psychiatric Association, 2013).

The first section of this chapter provides a brief introduction to the general literature on the therapeutic alliance. We then discuss the natural dialectic that exists when considering the therapeutic relationship in DBT as both a mechanism of change and also a method of therapy apart from technique. As a mechanism of change, we suggest the therapeutic alliance in DBT can best be conceptualized as a multifaceted construct that advances change through DBT's approach to problem-solving. The areas critical to the therapeutic alliance in DBT as they relate to problem-solving include an agreement on the goals of therapy, a mutual understanding of clients' presenting problems, an agreement on the tasks of therapy, and a commitment to the goals and tasks of treatment. In each of these areas, we emphasize the behavioral actions necessary for the therapist to build an effective alliance. As a method of therapy itself, the therapeutic relationship relies on the therapists' ability to act in accordance with DBT principles to enhance the therapeutic bond through a consistent, nonjudgmental, and flexible manner that balances behaviors of granting autonomy and exerting control. We follow with a review of the limited empirical evidence examining the alliance in DBT. Lastly, we end with a summary and future recommendations for clinical practice and research.

The therapeutic alliance: background and overview

The therapeutic alliance, or alliance, is a construct that attempts to define the collaborative elements of the interpersonal relationship between client and therapist during psychotherapy. The origins of the therapeutic alliance began during a time in psychology when psychoanalytic theory and the use of transference interpretations were dominant (Zetzel, 1956). During this time the alliance was considered a part of the therapeutic relationship and the foundation from which transference interpretations could be made. In this sense the alliance was defined more by what it *was not* rather than what it *was*. Nevertheless, the alliance was considered foundational to the effectiveness of psychotherapy.

Since its inception, the concept of the alliance has grown in at least three ways relevant to the current chapter. First, although frequently referred to and measured as a unitary construct, the alliance is more accurately conceptualized as a multifaceted construct consisting of several areas of emphasis (Bordin, 1976; Greenson, 1965). These areas of emphasis have included an agreement on the goals and tasks of therapy, a commitment to therapy, and the perceived bond between the client and therapist among others (e.g., Horvath & Greenberg, 1989; Marmar, Horowitz, Weiss, & Marziali, 1986). Second, the alliance is considered an active therapeutic ingredient independent from any psychotherapeutic technique (Horvath & Symonds, 1991). Lastly, the alliance is thought to be a common process of change in psychotherapy regardless of theoretical orientation (Wampold & Imel, 2015). Despite its ubiquity across treatments, however, the delivery, timing, frequency, and emphasis placed on each area of the alliance will be uniquely defined by each theoretical model of treatment.

Research on the therapeutic alliance in adult psychotherapy has been fairly robust and in support of the alliance as a mechanism of change in psychotherapy (Crits-Cristoph, Gibbons, & Mukherjee, 2013). The most recent meta-analysis on the association between the alliance and outcome in adult psychotherapy has shown approximately 8% of the variance in outcome can be accounted for by the alliance (Flückiger, Del Re, Wampold, & Horvath, 2018). More importantly, however, the authors noted significant heterogeneity in effect sizes across studies indicating the need for continued research to improve our understanding of how the alliance works in psychotherapy. The authors made several recommendations to enhance research on the alliance, including a greater consideration of the context in which the alliance is delivered during session (e.g. what is being discussed, clinical setting, and population), further refinement in the use of specific measures and scales for assessing the alliance (e.g., focus on the therapeutic bond, commitment, or agreement on goals), an improved consideration of the timing during the course of therapy when the alliance is measured (e.g., early-, mid-, late treatment), and further incorporation of who is rating the alliance during treatment (i.e., therapist, client, independent observer). These points are consistent with the general idea that research on the alliance–outcome association can be improved by incorporating more theoretically derived predictions. In the following section, we describe how the theory of DBT can be used to more fully inform clinical and research practice in the study of the alliance in DBT.

The therapeutic alliance in dialectical behavior therapy

The conceptualization of the therapeutic alliance in DBT has been largely consistent with the advances made in the scientific study of the alliance. The alliance in DBT is understood as both a mechanism that facilitates change as well as a source of healing independent from any technique (Linehan, 1993). In the first part of this section, we describe the therapeutic alliance as a multifaceted construct related to DBT problem-solving and consisting of several areas of emphasis, including (1) an agreement on the goals of therapy, (2) a mutual understanding of clients' problems consistent with DBT philosophy, (3) an agreement on the tasks of therapy, and (4) a commitment to therapy, including the goals and tasks of treatment. We then describe the role of the therapeutic relationship as a source of healing, independent of change techniques, leading to a strong therapeutic bond.

Therapy through the therapeutic relationship: the alliance and problem-solving in dialectical behavior therapy

The core set of strategies for creating change in DBT is referred to as problem-solving strategies (Linehan, 1993). These include the strategies of behavioral analysis, insight, solution analysis, didactic, orienting, and commitment. As a behavioral therapy, these strategies are essential for DBT therapists to master. Briefly, *behavioral analysis* and *insight* both involve the therapists' ongoing assessment of clients' presenting problems as well as the interpretation and highlighting of each problem consistent with DBT theory. The *solution analysis* follows the assessment where therapists and clients brainstorm ways of solving the identified problem. In completing the *didactic* portion of problem-solving, therapists provide psychoeducation surrounding the theoretical model of the selected intervention as well as the empirical basis for the solution(s) selected. Therapists then *orient* the client to how the solution(s) will be delivered and what the expectations are for both the therapist and client in applying the selected strategies. Lastly, therapists can assess their own and their clients' *commitment* to the solution, including an agreement to work, collaborate, and implement the proposed strategies.

DBT's set of problem-solving strategies can be applied at the level of the treatment itself as well as for individual treatment strategies applied for each client. At the level of the treatment itself, and as noted by Linehan (1993), S-DBT can be viewed as a solution in the larger practice of problem-solving for the treatment of BPD. In the case of S-DBT the initial behavioral analysis includes a diagnostic assessment to assess for BPD and the presence of suicidal behavior. In the solution analysis, S-DBT could be selected as one of the many appropriate, evidence-based treatments available given the results of the diagnostic assessment. The didactic portion would involve the therapist providing a review of DBT's theoretical model of BPD and suicidal behavior as well as how the treatment works and its known empirical base. The orientation would include a description of the therapeutic modalities in S-DBT (i.e., individual therapy, skill training, phone coaching, and therapist participation on a treatment team) as well as the time and financial commitment necessary for the completion of the treatment. Lastly, the therapist facilitates the development of a commitment to the treatment as a whole.

In S-DBT, this level of problem-solving, focused on the treatment as a whole, is emphasized during what is referred to as the *pretreatment* phase of S-DBT (Linehan, 1993). The pretreatment stage lasts approximately 1-month and is the time in treatment when both the therapist and client assess the client's fit for treatment. The second application of problem-solving in S-DBT, developed through the rest of this chapter, involves the same set of problem-solving strategies but is applied at the level of individual goals and interventions for each client and occurs continuously throughout treatment.

The alliance and problem-solving in dialectical behavior therapy

The areas of the therapeutic alliance emphasized in S-DBT, and focused on change, can be conceptualized as a collection of behaviors (thoughts, feelings, actions), on the part of the therapist and client, that take place during the application of problem-solving in DBT. In Fig. 2.1, we provide an overview of how we perceive the areas of the therapeutic alliance as matching the strategies of problem-solving in S-DBT. In contrast to a more colloquial understanding of the alliance as something a therapist "has" or "does not have" with a client, DBT places its emphasis on what a therapist and client are expected to "do" in building the alliance during treatment. Such a behavioral emphasis has at least four consequences for the study of the alliance in DBT as a mechanism of change. First, a behavioral understanding of the alliance requires a therapist to clearly communicate expectations surrounding each area of the alliance to both themselves and their clients. Second, the behavioral emphasis has the effect of placing the responsibility of building and maintaining the various areas of the alliance on the therapist. Third, and related to the first two points, any failure to meet expectations in the various areas of the alliance can be subjected to problem-solving by the therapist. Lastly, the most impactful research on the areas of the alliance in DBT will emphasize the assessment and evaluation of therapist behavior at specific times and surrounding particular topics during treatment. In the following sections, we highlight therapist and client behavior expected in each area of the alliance as they relate to problem-solving in DBT.

Agreement on goals of therapy

The treatment goals in S-DBT define the philosophy of the treatment as well as the direction of each individual therapy session (Linehan, 1993).

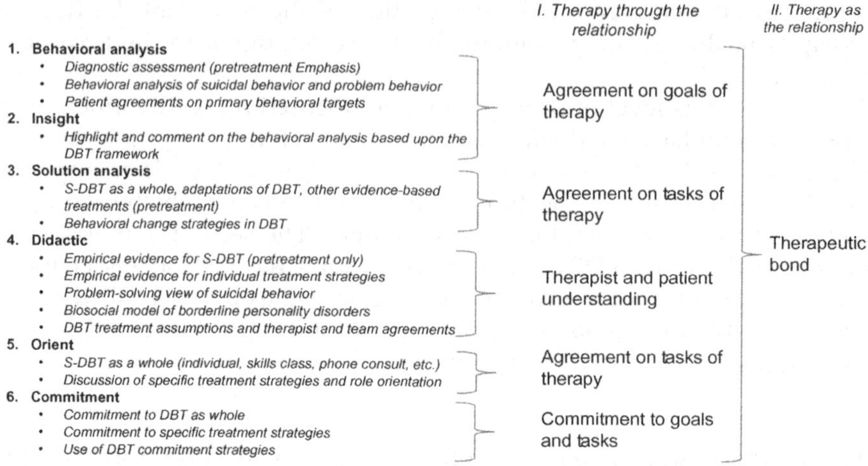

FIGURE 2.1 Facets of the therapeutic alliance during problem-solving in S-DBT. *S-DBT*, Standard dialectical behavior therapy.

In S-DBT, treatment goals are a mixture of those defined by the treatment itself along with those individually tailored to match the goals for the client as determined through ongoing behavioral analysis. Although individual goals can be modified throughout treatment, there are several goals that define the philosophy of DBT and are required throughout treatment. These are described under DBT's patient agreements (Linehan, 1993). The patient agreements consist of the primary behavioral targets in DBT, including a focus on the reduction of suicidal behavior, the treatment of any therapist and client behavior that interferes with the clients' ability to receive the treatment (i.e., therapy-interfering behavior), the reduction of client behavior that interferes with clients' quality of life (i.e., quality-of-life-interfering behavior), and an increase in the clients' use of behavioral skills. The primary behavior targets are organized into a treatment hierarchy with suicidal behavior having the highest priority, followed by therapy-interfering behavior, quality-of-life-interfering behavior, and an increase in behavioral skills.

Suicidal behaviors

A requirement of S-DBT is that clients agree to work toward the reduction and elimination of suicidal behavior. Practically, this means that therapists and clients agree to prioritize their focus of attention in treatment on suicidal behavior whenever there has been, for example, a suicide attempt, occurrence of nonsuicidal self-injury (NSSI), any planning related to suicidal behavior, or an increase in suicidal ideation or suicidal urges beyond baseline. During those weeks, therapists and clients agree to make the circumstances surrounding those moments the first priority in the following session and agree to work toward problem-solving for alternative solutions. What the agreement does not mean, however, is that clients *must* refrain from suicidal behavior in order to continue treatment. Instead, all participants in DBT agree that a life worth living is one that does not include suicidal behavior. Consequently, suicidal behavior is continually monitoring throughout treatment.

Therapy-interfering behavior

In S-DBT, therapists and clients agree that the second priority in treatment is to address any behavior on the part of the therapist or client that interferes with the effective delivery of the treatment to the client. The importance of therapy-interfering behavior is an explicit acknowledgment that the therapy relationship in DBT is a genuine, real relationship, that itself can be subjected to problem-solving. Examples of therapy-interfering behavior include a lack of attention in the therapy, failure to comply with treatment procedures, or a lack of collaboration in the therapeutic relationship (Linehan, 1993). In each instance, it is the therapists' responsibility to clearly assess and problem-solve the behavior perceived as interfering with treatment. Further, DBT takes the position that it is the therapists' responsibility to teach the client to act in ways that are "therapy enhancing" toward treatment goals.

Quality-of-life-interfering behavior and increase in behavioral skills

The majority of client goals in DBT are individually tailored for each client and begin during the initial diagnostic assessment. These goals will typically include the targeting of specific diagnostic categories as well as general problems in living that clients describe as important to them and significantly interfere with the quality of their life (e.g., substance abuse, anxiety disorders, and eating disorders). DBT therapists are typically precise in their understanding of these goals and use techniques such as goal attainment scaling as a method for operationally defining gains and setbacks during treatment (Kiresuk & Sherman, 1968).

DBT is a skills-based, problem-solving treatment. During treatment, therapists and clients agree that their work together will involve learning, practicing, and applying new behavioral skills to all relevant areas of clients' lives. Practically, this assumes clients' participation in the weekly skills training class and the completion of homework assignments between individual therapy sessions.

Understanding the client

Therapist understanding is an area of the therapeutic alliance that attempts to capture the ability of the therapist to empathize, in a non-judgmental manner, with the clients' experience and presenting problems (Gaston, 1991). DBT's clarity around treatment goals not only provides an opportunity for a more collaborative treatment effort but also provides therapists with the opportunity to create a shared understanding of clients' problems based upon the philosophical principles of DBT. The two areas where this shared understanding is most critical are surrounding the topics of suicidal behavior and the diagnosis of BPD. The next two sections describe the DBT approach to demonstrating and creating a mutual understanding of suicidal behavior and the diagnosis of BPD. Although these models are emphasized in the pretreatment stage of DBT, they are taught and reinforced throughout treatment as part of the *didactic* portion of DBT problem-solving.

Suicidal behavior

DBT conceptualizes suicidal behavior as an attempt at problem-solving by the client (Linehan, 1993). Such an understanding is often in contrast to clients' view of suicidal behavior as the problem to be solved. The DBT model instead places suicidal behavior in the context of the larger paradigm of problem-solving. The following is an example of a therapist introducing the problem-solving approach to suicidal behavior:

> T: "In DBT, we consider suicidal behavior, including times when you hurt yourself without the attempt to die, as an attempted solution to a problem. During our time together, we'll make it our priority to better understand the situations and problems in your life that result in you considering suicidal behavior as the solution. They are likely very painful moments and we want to provide you with more effective solutions that will work better for you in the long-run. At the same time, it is important to recognize that therapy takes time and these problems will not change overnight. We want to make sure you can better manage those difficult times, in the short-run, while we work on getting you the life that you want. Does that make sense to you?"

Such an approach validates the problem while at the same time acknowledging and addressing the presence of suicidal behavior as an attempted solution by the client. The abovementioned discussion would naturally lead to the development of a safety plan (e.g., Stanely & Brown, 2012) within the larger framework of problem-solving in DBT (Linehan, Comtois, & Ward-Ciesielski, 2012).

Suicidal behavior as "manipulative" or "attention seeking"

In addition to the emphasis placed on understanding suicidal behavior as an attempt at problem-solving by the client, DBT therapists openly address any pejorative understanding that clients might have about their suicidal behavior. These might include descriptions such as "manipulative," "attention seeking," "a cry for help," or "not a real suicide attempt" among others. Such an understanding of the self can be both painful and a considerable source of self-hate for clients entering treatment. A challenge for the DBT therapist is to correct these judgments while at the same time validating the natural circumstances and contingencies that serve to maintain such behavior.

In the core manual, Linehan (1993) repeatedly notes that functional consequences do not prove "intent," whether conscious or unconscious. In order to facilitate this understanding, DBT therapists might use analogies to better describe the functional relationship between behavior and consequences that challenge a more pejorative understanding of suicidal behavior. For example, a therapist might explain to a client that there is a natural functional relationship between a baby crying and a caregiver providing food (Addis & Martell, 2004). If a baby is consistently fed after crying then a person would expect the baby to cry again when hungry. One would not describe the baby as "manipulative" or "attention seeking" but simply doing what works in the moment. A similar understanding can be applied to clients in DBT where suicidal behavior has worked in particular ways for them (i.e., Brown, Comtois, & Linehan, 2002). Such an understanding validates the fact that problematic behaviors serve a function and can be subjected to problem-solving while at the same time challenging pejorative labels that are antithetical to the philosophy of DBT.

Borderline personality disorder

Similar to suicidal behavior, DBT seeks to transform clients' understanding of the diagnosis of BPD. It is not uncommon for clients entering S-DBT to have some knowledge or awareness of the diagnosis of BPD. DBT adopts the perspective that BPD is simply a collection of behaviors that, when effectively targeted, can be eliminated or managed as to no longer result in sufficient distress to warrant the diagnosis. Consequently, DBT therapists strive to provide an accurate diagnosis of BPD and clearly explain the meaning of the diagnosis to clients. For example, a typical therapist communication would be as follows:

> T: "I would like to give you feedback from the diagnostic interview. Based on the interview, the behavior you described is consistent with the behavior necessary to meet diagnostic criteria for borderline personality disorder. These behaviors include [therapist can list examples from the interview]. The good news is that these are the behaviors that we are most effective at treating. In other words, you are in the right place. Our goal will be to eliminate these behaviors so that you no longer meet criteria for this disorder."

In the abovementioned description, the clinician uses a straightforward and matter-of-fact style in communicating a diagnosis that could hold a great deal of uncertainty for the client and could be the source of much self-hate. The matter-of-fact style of the therapist demonstrates that there is nothing to fear in the name of the disorder. At the same time, it highlights the situational aspects of BPD behaviors that can be corrected and modified versus a dispositional interpretation of BPD as something a person "has."

Biosocial model of borderline personality disorder

Complementary to the discussion of the diagnosis of BPD, DBT therapists provide clients with a model for understanding the development of borderline symptoms called the biosocial model (Crowell, Beauchaine, & Linehan, 2009; Linehan, 1993). In contrast to the symptoms of BPD, the biosocial model describes the emotional experience of clients diagnosed with BPD that are thought to be more stable and temperamental. In this way the biosocial model can speak to the more long-standing elements of clients' experience that can be shaped and modified. The following is a typical description of the biological vulnerability underlying BPD that is communicated to clients during the pre-treatment phase of DBT:

> T: "People who are most suited for DBT often have emotional characteristics that I'd like to describe to you and see if they resonate with your experience. First, people who benefit from DBT often describe themselves as having a high degree of emotional vulnerability. In other words, they might describe themselves as naturally more sensitive to the everyday ups and downs in life. Does that ring true? Second, when problems do arise, they often experience themselves as reacting more intensely than others in similar circumstances. Almost like going from 20-80, on a scale of 0-100, in a split second and during those times acting in ways that are often regretful. Do you find that to be true of you? Lastly, after having reacted, some people have described it taking hours, sometimes days, to come back to their baseline. Does that fit as well?"

The description of BPD highlights the emotional characteristics of BPD that prospective clients often appreciate and find validating. During the course of treatment, therapists continue to tailor this understanding to more precisely fit clients' experience.

In addition to the biological vulnerability, the DBT therapist also explains the hypothesized relationship between the aforementioned biological vulnerability and the clients' social environment. In the core DBT manual, Linehan (1993) described the role of the "invalidating environment" as circumstances when people important to the client might have difficulty understanding the clients' emotional experience and consequently act or react to them in ways that invalidate their emotional experience. A DBT therapist in the pretreatment phase could communicate the following:

> T: "It is common for individuals diagnosed with BPD to not only have the emotional vulnerability we discussed but also have people around them that have trouble understanding such an emotional experience. They might, for example, question your emotional experience, which could leave you doubting yourself and looking to others to know how to feel. Does that ring true? They could also get so upset with your emotional experience that it can become punishing for you to share your emotions. At its worst, you might even come to hate yourself for feeling the way you do as if something is "wrong" with you. Does that resonate? There could be other times when they might, for example, be especially responsive but only when you are under extreme distress. Has that been true? Overall, for a person in such circumstances, they do not learn to label or effectively manage their emotions because they have never been taught how to do so. In fact, it is more likely that they have learned counter-productive ways of managing their emotional experience including ignoring their emotions or only reacting in extremes because that's what worked in the past."

The description of the biosocial model of BPD has become such an essential part of DBT that its instruction has been incorporated into the latest edition of the DBT Skills Training Manual for clients (Linehan, 2015). Therapists routinely, and formally, teach the biosocial model with the hope of providing therapist and client with a new understanding of BPD and related symptomatology.

Dialectical behavior therapy treatment assumptions

In addition to an improved understanding of target behavior, DBT makes several philosophical assumptions about clients diagnosed with BPD and DBT treatment. These assumptions are communicated to clients during the pretreatment stage of S-DBT and reinforced throughout treatment (Linehan, 1993, 2015). The assumptions further provide clients with a new, corrective, understanding of themselves based upon the philosophy of DBT. Similar to the biosocial model of BPD, variations of the following treatment assumptions have been incorporated into the latest revision of the DBT Skills Training Manual (Linehan, 2015). The assumptions are not, however, solely for the benefit of clients. Therapists equally benefit by the frequent reminder of these assumptions during the course of treatment when faced with challenging situations where they might question the "effort," "motivation," or "intent" of clients.

The first assumption is that *clients are doing the best they can* at any given moment. This assumption helps the participants to recall that even in their most frenzied, ineffective moments, people are trying to change for the better. The second assumption is the belief that *clients want to improve*. The assumption is critical given the frequent tendency for therapists and clients to question, for example, clients' motivation and intent in a manner that is not favorable to clients. The third assumption is that *clients need to do better, try harder, and be more motivated to change.* The third assumption balances the first assumption where the first assumption falls along the pole of acceptance and the third captures the pole of change. The fourth assumption is that *clients may not have caused all of their own problems but they have to solve them anyway.* The fifth assumption is that *the lives of DBT clients are unbearable as they are currently being lived.* The assumption serves as a reminder for the participants regarding the severity of the pain experienced in clients' everyday lives. The final three assumptions are more specifically related to the treatment itself. The sixth assumption is that *clients must learn new behaviors in all relevant contexts.* The seventh assumption is that *clients cannot fail in therapy.* Finally, DBT is built on the assumption that *therapists need support.*

Therapist and team consultation agreements

The therapist in S-DBT makes several commitments to their clients and treatment itself that shape their understanding of the treatment (Linehan, 1993). First, DBT therapists do their best to fully engage in the treatment. In doing so, they strive to continually improve their ability to deliver the treatment and guide the clients in learning the behavioral strategies to help clients improve their own lives. An important aspect of this agreement is for therapists to fully participate on a DBT team that supports them in improving their work.

The building of the therapeutic alliance also exists between therapists on the DBT consultation team. A total of six DBT team consultation agreements reflect the philosophical assumptions of DBT as applied to therapists' interaction with each other during the course of treatment (Linehan, 1993). The *dialectical agreement* states that therapists adopt a dialectical philosophy where there is no absolute truth, change is an evolving process, and the revelation of truth occurs through the synthesis of polar positions. The *consultation-to-the-patient agreement* emphasizes the role of team as means of direct support to the therapist in the treatment of their clients. The *consistency agreement* encourages a diversity of opinions on team by highlighting that all therapists do not have to agree with one another. The *observing limits agreement* encourages therapists to be respectful of their own and other team members' limits in providing treatment. The *phenomenological empathy agreement* encourages therapists to take a nonjudgmental stance toward themselves and their clients by assuming that all participants are doing their best and are trying to improve. The *fallibility agreement* states that in principle all therapists are fallible, have made errors, and will continue to make errors.

Pragmatically, one agreement is read each week with the rest being rotated through during the following weeks for the duration of the treatment. On our team, we read one agreement at the beginning of our team meeting, share our immediate reactions and impressions of the agreement read, and then reread the agreement once the entire team has had the opportunity to share. The practice of acting in a manner consistent with these agreements is the responsibility of each team member. During each team meeting, however, a single member of the treatment team takes on the role of *observer*. In the role of observer the person's main responsibility is to bring to the team's awareness of any violations of these agreements. On our team, we also have the observer highlight when any conversation is discussed in a manner consistent with the agreement. In that way, team members are positively reinforced for actualizing the behavior consistent with DBT philosophy.

Agreements on the tasks of therapy

The agreement on the tasks of therapy occurs during the *solution analysis* and *orientation* in problem-solving. During the pretreatment stage the solution analysis is the phase of problem-solving where the therapist and client brainstorm the potential treatment approaches appropriate based upon the initial diagnostic assessment and behavioral analysis. The solution analysis will include specific approaches to delivering DBT, including S-DBT, DBT skills only, or other modifications based upon the needs or limits of the setting or diagnostic population. The solution analysis, at the level of the treatment itself, is not a minor consideration given the diversity of ways DBT can be delivered. Therapists should repeatedly, and deliberately, refer to the exact type of DBT being offered. They can do so by saying "standard DBT," "DBT skills training only," or "DBT-informed behavior therapy." Therapists should avoid the simple statement of "DBT" given the various methods of delivering DBT along with the significant variations in evidence for each method of delivery.

At the level of individual treatment goals, therapists and clients collaboratively generate, evaluate, and select solutions to each targeted problem based on the resulting behavioral analysis (Linehan, 1993). The solutions selected often include a mixture of the four changes strategies in DBT, including skills training, cognitive modification, exposure therapy, and contingency management. The orientation to each individual treatment strategy requires therapists to be clear regarding the expectations for therapists and clients in completing each strategy. For example, one area of S-DBT that requires clear and explicit orientation is phone coaching (Chapman, 2018). Telephone coaching in S-DBT can serve a variety of functions, including the enhancement and repair of the therapeutic relationship, the generalization of skills outside of session, and the facilitation of problem-solving during moments of crisis outside of session (Linehan, 1993). In order to be effective, therapists need to clearly communicate expectations surrounding the use of the telephone, including availability, expected response time, exactly what will be discussed, and how it will be discussed on the phone.

In summary, an agreement on the tasks of therapy, including the choice of the therapy itself, is collaborative and ongoing. Although collaborative, it is the responsibility of therapist to effectively initiate this process of explaining and orienting the client to their role and the therapist's role in delivering the treatment solution.

Commitment to the goals and task of therapy

In the traditional alliance literature, a commitment to therapy has been defined as the clients' and therapists' overall confidence in the treatment as well as their expression of behaviors consistent with such confidence (Gaston, 1991). Treatment commitments in DBT are seen as behavior to be taught and maintained by the therapist (Linehan, 1993). Such a behavioral emphasis in understanding commitment is antithetical to many discussions surrounding commitment to treatment where a client can be described as "acting willfully," "resistant," or not "ready for change." In DBT the responsibility of assessing and supporting a commitment to treatment is placed on the therapist throughout treatment.

As with all the aforementioned areas of the alliance, DBT therapists consider commitment at the level of the treatment as a whole as well as an individual treatment strategy. DBT therapists learn several *commitment strategies* to strengthen client commitment during treatment (Linehan, 1993). These include an analysis of the *pros and cons* of the proposed solutions as well as playing "devil's advocate." Each of these techniques considers the long- and short-term consequences of implementing the solutions selected. A related strategy is to highlight that clients have the freedom to choose the solution they want while at the same time maintaining an absence of alternatives to meet their treatment goals. The idea behind such a strategy is that most people appreciate the freedom to select their own course and will be more likely to demonstrate behavior consistent with their long-term goals when given the choice.

Additional commitment strategies are focused on the therapists' ability to shape commitment behavior toward the agreed-upon goals of treatment. These include "door-in-the-face," "foot-in-the-door," a reminder of prior commitments, shaping procedures, cheerleading, and the assignment of homework (Linehan, 1993). The "door-in-the-face" and "foot-in-the-door" strategies attempt to get the maximum and minimum behavior, respectively, toward the treatment goal. The use of principles of reminding clients of prior commitments, shaping, cheerleading, and specific homework assignments is all focused on motivating client behavior toward successfully meeting the agreed-upon tasks of therapy.

The therapy as the relationship: the therapeutic bond in dialectical behavior therapy

Of all the areas of the therapeutic alliance, the bond between the therapist and client is perhaps the most emblematic of the alliance construct (Crits-Cristoph et al., 2013). The term itself is most often associated with the perceived connection or general "liking" between therapist and client. Such an attachment between therapist and client is thought to be critical in DBT as it can provide a new, corrective, learning experience for the client. Consistent with the prior areas of emphasis on the alliance in DBT, therapists in DBT learn particular strategies that can enhance the bond as well as repair the bond when it is perceived as less than optimal. In both these circumstances the therapeutic relationship in DBT is considered a real, genuine relationship that DBT therapists continually assess, enhance, and improve through problem-solving.

Therapists in DBT seek to optimize the conditions in the therapeutic relationship that maximize the effectiveness of the therapeutic bond. Stylistic communication strategies address the manner, or process, in which the therapist communicates with the client, rather than the content of the therapist's communication (Linehan, 1993). The two styles of communication in DBT are reciprocal communication and irreverent communication. The DBT therapist seeks to balance these two styles, moving between the poles of the vulnerability (i.e., reciprocal communication) and confrontation (i.e., irreverent communication). Reciprocal communication is the mainstay of DBT, and the strategies within this category are thought to be essential to building the therapeutic bond. They include responsiveness, self-disclosure, warm engagement, and genuineness. The special emphasis on therapist self-disclosure in DBT creates an intimacy and warmth in the therapeutic relationship and enhances the "real" relationship created between therapist and client. In contrast to the reciprocal strategies, the irreverence strategies serve the purpose of creating a shift in attention, emotion, or perspective in the room. They can also serve the purpose of moving the session forward to improve the pace of the session defined as the "movement, speed, and flow" of the therapy process. An irreverent communication style can be very matter of fact and confrontational in style and is not the typical mode of interacting with a client. As with any treatment strategy in DBT, the use of irreverence in DBT requires a clear function and purpose with each application. Critical to the effectiveness of the irreverent communication style is that it is surrounded by validation and support provided by the therapist.

Lastly, particular therapist characteristics and skills are thought to build the therapeutic bond in DBT. The core dialectic of DBT is the stance of acceptance versus change (Bedics, Atkins, Comtois, & Linehan, 2012a, 2012b; Shearin & Linehan, 1992). The balance of acceptance and change manifests in the therapeutic relationship as a dance between behavioral expressions of autonomy and control. It creates a relationship in which the client feels accepted but is also expected to change. The second crucial interpersonal position that the therapist must adopt is that of unwavering centeredness versus compassionate flexibility. Along this dimension the therapist finds balance between unwavering consistency in application of the therapy and responsiveness to the client's current experience. The balance between these two poles communicates simultaneously that the therapist believes in the therapy and is attentive to the client as an individual. The final dimension of therapist characteristics is that of nurturing versus benevolent demanding. Nurturing behaviors—coaching, aiding and strengthening the client—create a relationship in which the client understands that they will have support and compassion from the therapist. Nurturing is balanced with the attitude that the client can and must care for themselves. In this way the therapeutic relationship simultaneously is characterized by genuine empathy and support, as well as firm belief in the client's capability to care for themselves.

Research on the therapeutic alliance and relationship in dialectical behavior therapy

Despite the critical nature of the areas of the alliance in S-DBT, there has been little empirical work conducted examining these associations. One study examined the alliance in a subset of clients during a randomized-controlled study of S-DBT versus general psychiatric management (Hirsh, Quilty, Bagby, & McMain, 2012). The authors examined clients' global ratings of the alliance using a measure of the working alliance (Horvath, & Greenberg, 1989). The results showed a positive association between clients' ratings of the alliance with time in treatment regardless of the treatment condition. In other words, clients' ratings of the global alliance increased during treatment for both treatment groups. Similarly, clients' ratings of the global alliance were associated with improvement across both treatments for depression, overall symptomatology, trait anger, impulsive anger, and NSSI. Results were not significant for three outcomes, including borderline symptoms, anger expression, and suicide attempts. In sum, the results provided support of the globally rated alliance for the treatment of BPD regardless of treatment approach.

A unique aspect of the above study was its assessment of therapist ratings of client agreeableness; a trait taken from the five-factor model of personality (Costa & McCrae, 1992). The authors found a significant three-way interaction effect between treatment, therapists' perception of client agreeableness, and time in treatment on the client-rated global alliance for the DBT condition only. In the DBT condition, the more the therapist perceived the client as agreeable (rated at a single time point in treatment and at varying times in treatment), the higher the client rated the global alliance during treatment. The authors then examined whether or not the effect of the therapist-rated agreeableness on posttreatment outcomes was mediated by changes in the working alliance. The authors reported a significant mediation effect for four of the eight outcomes, including depression, BPD symptoms, one measure of anger, and NSSI. Overall, these results showed that therapist's perception of client agreeableness can be meaningfully associated with clients' ratings of the global alliance which could, in turn, impact particular outcomes. Although not mentioned by the authors, an intriguing point from this study was that the clients' personality was rated by the therapists. Consequently, the results potentially highlight the importance of assessing variability in therapists' understanding of clients' in-session behavior during DBT. Once replicated, a more precise understanding of this association could support the importance of therapists' participation on DBT team as improving therapists' understanding of client behavior.

A second study examined the therapeutic alliance in S-DBT compared to a control condition of participants receiving treatment by community nominated experts in the treatment of BPD (Bedics, Atkins, Harned, & Linehan, 2015). In this study the authors utilized a measure of the therapeutic alliance that allows for the assessment of multiple areas of the alliance as reviewed in this chapter (Gaston, 1991). The alliance was rated at 4-month intervals during the course of the year by both therapist and client. Results showed that DBT therapists perceived a greater total alliance regardless of time in treatment. In addition, relative to the control group, DBT therapists reported perceiving a greater agreement on the goals and strategies of therapy early in treatment. The authors suggested this finding might be due to the greater emphasis placed on treatment goals during the pretreatment phase of DBT, although such a variable was not directly assessed.

In examining the association between outcome and areas of the client-rated alliance, the authors found results that were generally consistent with how DBT is expected to work. Overall, increases in clients' ratings of the global alliance were associated with reductions in NSSI in DBT only. Specifically, the areas of alliance associated with reduced NSSI were client-rated commitment and clients' perceptions of therapists' understanding and involvement although the latter only approached significance. Although not tested directly, the authors hypothesized that therapist behavior associated with these areas of the alliance (i.e., commitment to reduce NSSI and an effective expression of understanding surrounding NSSI) might have been related to improvements in clients' ratings of the alliance and outcomes.

In addition to client's ratings of the alliance, the authors also examined therapists' ratings of the alliance. The results showed that therapists' overall positive ratings of the alliance were associated with a decrease in suicide attempts across both treatments. Therapists' ratings of the alliance were not associated with NSSI in DBT. Unexpectedly, results showed a positive association between therapist-rated overall alliance and NSSI in the control condition. In other words, the more positively the therapist perceived the therapeutic alliance, the more their clients reported NSSI in the control condition. The unexpected finding was further unpacked through an analysis of the areas of the alliance emphasized in the study. In this case, therapists in the control condition who rated their clients as more engaged and rated themselves as more understanding of their client had clients who reported greater NSSI. The results are difficult to interpret in the absence of a direct measure of how clients were perceived as "engaged in treatment" or how therapists saw themselves "understanding" their clients. The authors suggested that the results could be interpreted based upon the different theoretical models for understanding BPD across treatments.

Summary and conclusion

The therapeutic alliance in DBT is a multifaceted construct consisting of several areas of emphasis throughout treatment. The areas of the alliance centered around change complement and support the larger framework of problem-solving in DBT. In contrast, the therapeutic bond, as a method of acceptance, can be understood as occurring through therapists' interpersonal style of communication. Current, global, measurements of the alliance provide little to advance the rich and complex, theory-driven hypotheses regarding the therapeutic alliance, and therapeutic relationship in DBT. In addition, these global measures can detract from the behavioral, action-defined, emphasis that DBT places on its understanding of the therapeutic alliance.

Clinically, clinicians could improve their work by considering each area of the alliance as it is developed throughout treatment. Statements such as "Did we reach an agreement on the treatment hierarchy?" (Agreement of Goals), "Did I communicate how the treatment hierarchy will be addressed in session?" (Agreement on Tasks), "Did I adequately express and communicate the biosocial model of understanding to my client's problems?" (Understanding), "How am I enhancing the client's motivation and commitment to reducing suicidal behavior?" (Commitment), and "Did I balance control with warmth and freedom in this session?" (Therapeutic Bond) could serve as effective reminders to therapists' of their responsibility to create and maintain the various areas of the alliance.

Similarly, the most impactful research will begin to examine the association between therapists' behavior, self-reported ratings of each area of the alliance, and outcome. Substantive research questions are those that most closely parallel those that clinicians would ask of themselves during treatment. For example, a simple analysis of the variation in use of commitment strategies and their association to commitment to treatment, treatment goals, and treatment retention would be a valuable research question. Additional areas of the alliance could be subject to experimental manipulation. For example, a group of participants could be randomly assigned to hear a biosocial model of suicidal behavior versus a nonbehavioral model and examine its effect on the sense of being understood by the therapist. The effect of such a manipulation, along with its reversal, would provide an important first step in evaluating the impact of therapist technique on an area of the alliance which could then be linked to symptomatic outcomes. In addition, although we linked the therapeutic bond with the interpersonal style of the therapist, no such empirical base exists although we hope such a topic would be worthwhile in future work.

References

Addis, M., & Martell, C. (2004). Overcoming depression one step at a time: The new behavioral activation approach to getting your life back *(A new harbinger self-help workbook)*. Oakland, CA: New Harbinger Publications.

American Psychiatric Association. (2013). *Diagnostic and statistical manual of mental disorders* (5th ed.). Washington, DC: Author.

Bedics, J. D., Atkins, D. C., Comtois, K. A., & Linehan, M. M. (2012a). Treatment differences in the therapeutic relationship and introject during a 2-year randomized controlled trial of dialectical behavior therapy versus nonbehavioral psychotherapy experts for borderline personality disorder. *Journal of Consulting and Clinical Psychology, 80*(1), 66–77.

Bedics, J. D., Atkins, D. C., Comtois, K. A., & Linehan, M. M. (2012b). Weekly therapist ratings of the therapeutic relationship and patient introject during the course of dialectical behavioral therapy for the treatment of borderline personality disorder. *Psychotherapy, 49*(2), 231–240.

Bedics, J. D., Atkins, D. C., Harned, M. S., & Linehan, M. M. (2015). The therapeutic alliance as a predictor of outcome in dialectical behavior therapy versus nonbehavioral psychotherapy by experts for borderline personality disorder. *Psychotherapy, 52*(1), 67–77.

Bordin, E. S. (1976). The generalizability of the psychoanalytic concept of the working alliance. *Psychotherapy, 16*, 252–260. Available from https://doi.org/10.1037/h0085885.

Brown, M. Z., Comtois, K. A., & Linehan, M. M. (2002). Reasons for suicide attempts and nonsucidal self-injury in women with borderline personality disorder. *Journal of Abnormal Psychology, 111*(1), 198–202.

Chapman, A. (2018). Phone coaching in dialectical behavior therapy *(Guilford DBT practice series)*. New York: Guilford Press.

Costa, P., & McCrae, R. (1992). *Revised NEO personality inventory and NEO five-factor inventory professional manual*. Odessa, FL: Psychological Assessment Resources.

Crits-Cristoph, P., Gibbons, M. B., & Mukherjee, D. (2013). Psychotherapy process-outcome research. In M. J. Lambert (Ed.), *Bergin and Garfield's handbook of psychotherapy behavior change* (6th ed., pp. 298–340). Hoboken, NJ: Wiley.

Crowell, S. E., Beauchaine, T. P., & Linehan, M. M. (2009). A biosocial developmental model of borderline personality: Elaborating and extending Linehan's theory. *Psychological Bulletin, 135*(3), 495–510.

Flückiger, C., Del Re, A. C., Wampold, B. E., & Horvath, A. O. (2018). The alliance in adult psychotherapy: A meta-analytic synthesis. *Psychotherapy, 55*(4), 316–340.

Gaston, L. (1991). Reliability and criterion-related validity of the California Psychotherapy Alliance Scales—patient version. *Psychological Assessment: A Journal of Consulting and Clinical Psychology, 3*(1), 68–74.

Greenson, R. R. (1965). The working alliance and the transference neuroses. *The Psychoanalytic Quarterly, 34*, 155–181.

Hirsh, J. B., Quilty, L. C., Bagby, R. M., & McMain, S. F. (2012). The relationship between agreeableness and the development of the working alliance in patients with borderline personality disorder. *Journal of Personality Disorders, 26*(4), 616–627.

Horvath, A. O., & Greenberg, L. S. (1989). Development and validation of the working alliance inventory. *Journal of Counseling Psychology, 36*, 223–233. Available from https://doi.org/10.1037/0022-0167.36.2.223.

Horvath, A. O., & Symonds, B. D. (1991). Relation between working alliance and outcome in psychotherapy: A meta-analysis. *Journal of Counseling Psychology, 38*, 139–149. Available from https://doi.org/10.1037/0022-0167.38.2.139.

Kiresuk, T. J., & Sherman, R. E. (1968). Goal attainment scaling: A general method for evaluating comprehensive community mental health programs. *Community Mental Health Journal, 4*, 443–453.

Linehan, M. (1993). Cognitive-behavioral treatment of borderline personality disorder *(Diagnosis and treatment of mental disorders)*. New York: Guilford Press.

Linehan, M. (2015). *DBT skills training handouts and worksheets* (2nd ed.). New York: Guilford Press.

Linehan, M. M., Comtois, K. A., & Ward-Ciesielski, E. F. (2012). Assessing and managing risk with suicidal individuals. *Cognitive and Behavioral Practice, 19*(2), 218–232. https://doi-org.ezproxy.callutheran.edu/10.1016/j.cbpra.2010.11.008.

Marmar, C. R., Horowitz, M. J., Weiss, D. S., & Marziali, E. (1986). The development of the therapeutic alliance rating system. In L. S. Green-berg, & W. M. Pinsof (Eds.), *The psychotherapeutic process: A research handbook* (pp. 367–390). New York: Guilford Press.

Shearin, E. N., & Linehan, M. M. (1992). Patient-therapist ratings and relationship to progress in dialectical behavior therapy for borderline personality disorder. *Behavior Therapy, 23*(4), 730–741.

Stanely, B., & Brown, G. K. (2012). Safety Planning Intervention: A brief intervention to mitigate suicide risk. *Cognitive and Behavioral Practice, 19*, 256–264.

Wampold, B. E., & Imel, Z. E. (2015). *The great psychotherapy debate – The evidence for what makes psychotherapy work*. New York: Routledge.

Zetzel, E. R. (1956). Current concepts of transference. *The International Journal of Psychoanalysis, 37*, 369–376.

CHAPTER

3

Mechanisms of change in dialectical behavior therapy

Alexander L. Chapman and Lynnaea Owens

Department of Psychology, Simon Fraser University, Vancouver, BC, Canada

Dr. Marsha Linehan and her clinical research group developed dialectical behavior therapy (DBT; Linehan, 1993a) through an iterative process aimed at improving the care of highly suicidal individuals. Linehan attempted to apply existing cognitive-behavioral oriented strategies to complex, highly suicidal clients and quickly discovered that the extant approach to cognitive behavior therapy (CBT) had some serious limitations. The notion that, to develop a life worth living, clients mainly had to change how they were thinking, modify their behavior, and learn coping skills, was too imbalance on the side of change to be effective. In addition, clients often felt misunderstood and perceived the heavy change focus of CBT as invalidating. As a result, they became emotionally dysregulated, had difficulty learning new ways of acting and coping, felt frustrated and demoralized, got angry with the therapist, and sometimes quit therapy. At some point in this process, Linehan discovered that many of her clients met the criteria for borderline personality disorder (BPD), characterized by interpersonal dysfunction, problems with impulse control, and emotional dysregulation that often arose in and hampered therapy. Through these trial-by-fire experiences, in combination with lessons learned during her own path to recovery from serious mental health concerns, Linehan began to realize that effective treatment needed to combine and synthesize acceptance of the client with efforts to help the client change and build a life worth living. DBT evolved into a comprehensive, cognitive-behaviorally oriented approach based on a dialectical world view promoting the synthesis of acceptance and change

DOI: https://doi.org/10.1016/B978-0-12-816384-9.00003-8

and a biosocial developmental theory of BPD (Crowell, Beauchaine, & Linehan, 2009; Linehan, 1993a) emphasizing the treatment of emotion dysregulation.

It would be fruitless to discuss mechanisms of change, or how and why a treatment works (Kazdin & Nock, 2003) unless the treatment has been shown to work. Twenty-six years after the first DBT manuals were published (Linehan, 1993a, 1993b), enough evidence has accumulated to consider DBT a well-established, efficacious treatment for BPD and related clinical problems. Findings of recent reviews have suggested that DBT has the strongest evidence among current treatments for BPD (Chapman, & Dixon-Gordon, in press; DeCou, Comtois, & Landes, 2019; Kliem, Kröger, & Kosfelder, 2010; Stoffers et al., 2012); thus we will only make a few key points here to open our discussion of possible mechanisms of change in DBT.

There are many forms of DBT-related treatment. Standard DBT (S-DBT) consists of the four primary treatment modes of individual therapy, group skills training, telephone consultation (often referred to as phone coaching), and the therapist consultation team. To date, there have been over 20 randomized controlled trials (RCTs) of S-DBT, nearly 20 RCTs examining various forms of DBT skills training, and many other randomized and nonrandomized trials examining adapted versions of DBT (for a regularly updated summary of the research on DBT, see https://behavioraltech.org/research/evidence/#RCT). Findings of studies examining S-DBT have suggested that this treatment has consistently outperformed treatment as usual (TAU) (e.g., Linehan, Armstrong, Suarez, Allmon, & Heard, 1991) and treatment provided by clinicians with expertise in personality disorder treatment (e.g., Linehan et al., 2006) in terms of the reduction of suicidal and related behaviors, severity of suicidal behavior, inpatient and hospital visits, among other outcomes. In some research, DBT also has often shown superior treatment retention (e.g., Linehan et al., 1991). In some cases, however, DBT has not demonstrated outcomes superior to alternative approaches, such as general psychiatric management (GPM: McMain et al., 2009) or transference-focused therapy (Clarkin, Levy, Lenzenweger, & Kernberg, 2007). These alternative treatments, provided by clinicians with expertise, are structured, manualized, emphasize the effective navigation of the therapy relationship, and include evidence-based approaches to assess and manage suicidal and self-injurious behaviors. It could be, therefore, that structured treatment, expertise in relevant domains (suicide, BPD), and evidence-based management of suicidal behavior are critical elements accounting for the effects of various treatments (including DBT) on outcomes among clients with BPD. The majority of the research on S-DBT has focused on individuals with BPD or related problems, such as suicidality and nonsuicidal self-injury. In this chapter, therefore, we will primarily focus on potential mechanisms of change in S-DBT as applied to these populations.

Mechanisms of change

Examination of mechanisms of change—how and why a treatment works—is an important part of the evolution of evidence-based treatments (Kazdin & Nock, 2003). Much of the extant research has focused on whether DBT works (efficacy), including studies conducted in controlled research settings, with clear inclusion and exclusion criteria and the monitoring of treatment fidelity. Other studies have examined effectiveness, or whether DBT works in real-world settings, in less controlled environments with a greater focus on external rather than internal validity. Now that findings have largely supported the efficacy and likely effectiveness of DBT, understanding how and why DBT works can help advance theory and inform effective clinical practice.

One way to understand mechanisms is to determine which *elements of treatment* comprise the most active or important ingredients. For example, in a multifaceted treatment for diabetes consisting of insulin treatment, dietary changes, and exercise, it would be important to know which of these components is responsible for the beneficial effects of the treatment package. This understanding would help to streamline the focus on those elements that are most critical, potentially making the treatment easier to disseminate and implement. Similarly, DBT is a multicomponent treatment, and understanding which components are necessary and/or sufficient to produce beneficial outcomes would provide guidance regarding which components to emphasize, particularly when resources are sparse. If all components of DBT are necessary for optimal outcomes, this would be a strong argument for increased resources, funding, and training to ensure that patients receive S-DBT (consisting of individual therapy, group skills training, telephone consultation, and the therapist consultation team). On the other hand, if certain elements of DBT are sufficient for optimal outcomes, such as group DBT skills training, the treatment may be easier to disseminate and implement.

A second way to illuminate mechanisms of change is to determine which *changes in the client* are responsible for the beneficial effects of the treatment. In the diabetes example, some key changes in the client might include modifications to blood sugar and hormone levels, which in turn could account for the beneficial effects of the treatment on the patient's diabetes symptoms. Knowing this, the clinician may focus on interventions that are most likely to change blood sugar and hormone levels. Diabetes is primarily an endocrine disorder, whereas BPD is often considered an emotion regulation disorder. In DBT, therefore, changes in behavioral, physiological, or neurological indications of emotion regulation may explain why the treatment reduces self-injury, suicidal behaviors, anger problems, and so forth. If this is the case, DBT modes and strategies known to produce these changes in emotion regulation might be emphasized.

One obstacle in research on mechanisms related to changes in the client is that it is not always clear which interventions or treatment components effect these changes. One excellent example of this challenge is found in the research comparing standard CBT to separate components of CBT for depression. Standard CBT for depression typically consists of a combination of activity scheduling (or the broader, more contemporary treatment package referred to as behavioral activation; Dimidjian et al., 2006), skills to identify automatic thoughts and maladaptive thinking patterns, cognitive schema-change methods, and so forth. In a landmark study, Jacobson et al. (1996) randomly assigned 150 patients to standard CBT, behavioral activation, or behavioral activation in addition to skills to identify automatic thoughts. Findings indicated no significant differences between conditions in terms of depressive symptom outcomes. Further, patients in both standard CBT and behavioral activation showed significant changes in negative thinking, and there were no significant differences between conditions. Baseline cognitive attribution style predicted outcomes in the behavioral activation but not full CBT condition. In psychosocial treatments, therefore, there seem to be many roads to Rome, and simply understanding the changes in the patient that are important for treatment outcomes (e.g., attribution style in CBT for depression; emotion regulation in DBT for BPD) does not necessarily clarify which interventions to emphasize. With these limitations in mind, we provide in the following a summary of the state of the research on DBT and then discuss treatment components and client changes that may serve as mechanisms of change in DBT, with an emphasis on the teaching and practicing of skills.

Theory

As the theoretical underpinnings of any treatment influence which interventions, skills, and client-related changes are emphasized, any discussion of potential mechanisms should take these theoretical foundations into consideration. Theory in DBT has several elements, including the DBT view on (1) the nature of reality, (2) the factors causing and maintaining human behavior, and (3) factors contributing to the development and maintenance of particular clinical problem areas, such as BPD (Chapman, & Dixon-Gordon, in press).

Dialectical philosophy and Zen practice influence the DBT perspective on the nature of reality. Within a dialectical framework, reality consists of polarities (e.g., thesis vs antithesis, right vs wrong, and positive vs negative charge) and continually changes as these polarities balance and synthesize. In DBT, the primary therapeutic polarity is that of acceptance and change. The therapist must (1) accept the client as they are *and* help them change and build a life worth living and (2) help the client learn to accept themselves *and* learn the skills needed to build a life worth living. Dialectical philosophy also holds that identity is relational, the reality is constantly changing, and that "truth" exists and can change.

Consistent with dialectical philosophy, Zen practice aims (although to suggest that Zen has goals is debatable) to help people experience the interconnected, holistic, and interdependent nature of the universe. People are both separate from and part of the fabric of the universe, just as a stitch has its own characteristics and is part of a broader tapestry. From a Zen perspective, suffering arises when we cling to particular states of being, as the universe is constantly changing.

Behavioral and emotion theory and science inform the DBT view of the causes of human behavior. The type of behavioral theory that is perhaps most consistent with DBT is *psychological behaviorism*, articulated by Staats (1975, 1996) and initially referred to as social behaviorism. This framework holds that through transactions of individual characteristics (e.g., biology, temperament, personality, and behavior) with the environment (e.g., rearing environment and socioeconomic context), individuals develop basic behavioral repertoires. These basic behavioral repertoires are characteristic response styles in particular contexts. For example, a client with a strongly emotional temperament whose emotional experiences were rejected or criticized, while emotion suppression was reinforced, might develop a basic behavioral repertoire consisting of emotional suppression and avoidance during interpersonal conflict. Thus when things get heated in an argument, the client would have a tendency to shut down emotionally, making it hard to connect with others and resolve conflict. Within this framework, basic behavioral repertoires are akin to the client's behavioral skills or capabilities within a particular situation. In DBT, as we discuss later, the aim is largely to address skill deficits and help clients learn to engage in new, effective behavior that helps them build a life worth living. DBT, therefore, is based on a *skill deficit model* and emphasizes learning and skill building.

At the level of factors causing and maintaining particular clinical problem areas or disorders, DBT is based on a *biosocial developmental framework*. Within this framework, trait impulsivity and emotion vulnerability constitute key, biologically based temperament features that increase an individual's risk of developing BPD in the context of an invalidating environment. Emotion vulnerability consists of emotional sensitivity (a low threshold for emotional responding), emotional reactivity (intense emotional responses), and a slow return to emotional baseline (delayed recovery from emotionally evocative events). Trait impulsivity is highly heritable and confers a unique vulnerability to the development of various childhood disorders, such as attention-deficit/hyperactivity disorder (ADHD) and oppositional defiant disorder. Within the biosocial developmental framework, trait impulsivity, in particular, makes the child vulnerable to developing serious emotion dysregulation in the context of adverse childhood environments. Emotion vulnerability transacts with the invalidating environment, as impulsive, emotional children are harder to raise, and invalidating caregiver responses (e.g., rejecting or criticizing the child for having or expressing emotions) can exacerbate emotion vulnerability. In addition, coercive behavioral processes can shape the development of emotion dysregulation. Such processes include the periodic reinforcement of intense emotional expression and the modeling of coercive behavioral control processes (e.g., threats, intimidation, and intense emotional expression) to modulate conflict. Over time the child develops worsening emotion dysregulation, is at risk of developing self-injury and other maladaptive coping strategies, and in turn, experiences worsening interpersonal, cognitive, and emotional functioning that coalesce into BPD in late adolescence (Beauchaine, Hinshaw, & Bridge, 2019; Chapman, 2019; Crowell et al., 2009).

Skills and skills training as the key ingredients of dialectical behavior therapy

One key implication of the theoretical foundations of DBT is that people with BPD and related complex mental health problems have not learned the skills needed to understand and manage emotions, effectively navigate relationships, and avoid acting on impulse. Broadly, the central role of emotion dysregulation in BPD suggests that learning to regulate emotions is a particularly important aspect of treatment. Many of the core behavioral problems related to BPD (e.g., self-injury) often occur in response to dysregulated emotional states and function to regulate emotions (Beblo et al., 2013; Chapman, Specht, & Cellucci, 2005; Dixon-Gordon, Chapman, Lovasz, & Walters, 2011; Linehan, 1993a). As such, DBT is a learning-oriented therapy that focuses on helping clients learn skills to regulate emotions. This occurs during structured skills training and as the opportunity arises (e.g., when a client experiences emotion dysregulation in session, such as intense anger toward the therapist and overwhelming sadness) during individual therapy sessions (see Chapman & Hope, 2020; for a description of how DBT targets emotion dysregulation in both contexts). Learning to regulate emotions and improve relationships, etc., requires consistent work and practice, and one of Linehan's major innovations in DBT was the packaging of emotion regulation and other strategies as skills that can be learned, practiced, reinforced, and generalized to all applicable situations. Therefore our emphasis in this chapter is on skills training as a potential mechanism of change, with a special emphasis on the role of improved emotion regulation skills as a particularly important potential mechanism.

Mechanisms related to treatment components: group skills training

Given the emphasis in DBT on skills deficits underlying the behavioral and emotional dysfunction observed among those with BPD, skills training is a reasonable place to start in terms of potentially essential treatment components. DBT skills training typically occurs in a weekly 1.5–2.5 hours group (with shorter groups more characteristic of adolescent or youth treatment) that is structured much like a class, with the beginning involving the review of the previous week's homework and the latter half of the group involving the teaching of new skills. The skills training group is not a process group, although clients are welcome to share personal details to the extent that these details are relevant to the skills being practiced or taught. There are also limits and rules regarding self-disclosure, with a primary limit being that clients are not to share specific details of dysfunctional behavior (e.g., details of methods of self-injury, suicide attempts, substance use, and disordered eating). A group leader and coleader work together to run each group, with the leader usually running the homework review and teaching portions of group and the coleader monitoring group process, elaborating on key concepts when needed, and providing validation and acceptance to balance the change-oriented stance of the leader.

Given the findings discussed previously suggesting that outcomes in DBT may be comparable to other structured, manualized treatments, it is reasonable to hypothesize that structure is one key element of skills training that may partially account for the effectiveness of DBT. Despite varying theoretical underpinnings, the psychosocial treatments that have shown promising evidence for the treatment of BPD are all structured to a certain extent. The structure and organization of a skills training group may provide complex, multiproblem clients suffering from emotion regulation problems with the opportunity to self-regulate, monitor, and manage difficult emotions arising during group, resist urges to talk or leave group when it is not appropriate to do so, and use interpersonal skills to effectively communicate their needs and wishes. We have run many groups in which clients struggled with overwhelming emotions prompted by group discussions or previous events that day. We often have coached these clients on ways to remain in group, avoid engaging in harmful behavior, stay focused, and contribute to discussions despite their distress. This type of practice in self- and emotion-regulation within a structured environment with key routines and rituals (often considered important "common factors" in psychotherapy; Wampold, 2015) may help clients build capacities that are needed in other settings. Everyday life contexts are not quite as structured, and while we all need to practice self- and emotion-regulation to get through most days, it is probably easier for clients to let their skills slide in their relatively less-structured, natural environments (e.g., when trying to get out of bed in the morning or attempting to resist urges to yell at their loved one during a conflict).

Group skills training also offers clients with the opportunity for more formalized practice of new skills. In DBT, there is a premium on "dragging out new behavior," or prompting the client to practice new skills and behavior. Indeed, for the purposes of adherence coding, each DBT session needs to include significant instances whereby the therapist prompts the client to engage in a new behavior. In this way, DBT is much more of an action-oriented than a talk therapy, and therapists encourage action in several ways throughout group. During skills training groups the leader usually leads a mindfulness practice at the beginning of the group, offering consistent, weekly practice in mindfulness skills. During the homework review portion a skilled leader will also help clients engage in brief practice of skills they are trying to learn or apply in challenging situations. One major aim of homework review is to provide clients with feedback and coaching on their use of skills in everyday situations; thus coaching, positive reinforcement, feedback, and practice in more effective applications of skills all may contribute to the replacement of problem behaviors with skills. In addition, during the teaching portion of group, skills trainers typically describe the new skill, demonstrate it, and then have clients engage in practice exercises. Finally, at the end of group, clients receive homework assignments to practice DBT skills throughout the week. Therefore through a combination of structured scaffolding and ad hoc skills practice opportunities, the skills training group offers clients the opportunity to actively engage with new skills. Notwithstanding, all of these potential key elements of skills training occur when the leaders conduct group effectively and adherently. DBT groups in various practice settings may vary in their adherence and effectiveness; thus certain key elements of skills training are likely to vary in the degree to which they account for the effects of treatment.

Various social or interpersonal aspects of group skills training may also serve as important elements or mechanisms of change. Theories of suicide emphasize the important role of social alienation and perceived burdensomeness in the generation of the desire to commit suicide (Joiner, 2005; Klonsky & May, 2015). DBT skills groups fostering social cohesion and connectedness may help reduce suicidal desire and risk. Although we would like to think that our brilliant teaching of skills carries much of the weight in treatment, anecdotally, clients often have suggested that the interpersonal aspects of group were most helpful. Important interpersonal elements likely include the opportunity to hear that others are struggling with similar issues, the direct experience of validation, support and encouragement from other group members, and a sense of belongingness in a group that shares a common goal of learning skills. Ad hoc peer modeling of effective skill use in challenging situations, pearls of wisdom gleaned from other clients, and prosocial interactions among group members, all likely contribute to the power of the interpersonal aspects of group to effect change. For this discussion, we are assuming that skills training is taught in a group context, although some clinicians teach DBT skills individually, and in that case, the beneficial interpersonal mechanisms of group would be less relevant and the relationship of the individual skills trainer with the client would be more paramount.

Evidence for skills training as a potential mechanism

It would be appealing to assume that skills training is a primary mechanism or component of DBT. Indeed, group skills training generally is easier to establish and maintain in resource-strapped systems, where caseloads are large and weekly individual therapy sessions would be considered a luxury. One of us has consulted with and trained clinicians in various large systems trying to implement DBT, and for the most part, the uptake of group skills training has far outpaced that of individual DBT. In some regions of the public health system in Canada, for example, policies dictate that there should be no waitlists for adult mental health services. As a result, case managers and clinicians have large caseloads, fairly strict limits on the number of sessions that they can have with each client, and are unable to fit in weekly individual therapy with more than a couple of clients at a time (if they are lucky). The suggestion that DBT skills training is the critical ingredient or mechanism of the treatment would be appealing to many mental health systems. Whether this is true, however, depends on the evidence on the effectiveness of DBT skills training alone and in comparison to other components of DBT.

To date, there have been nearly 20 published RCTs of various forms of DBT skills training, and this number grows regularly. We will briefly and broadly review the extant research (see also Valentine, Bankoff, Poulin, Reidler, & Pantalone, 2015 and Chapter 15 of this book; for a recent review) and then discuss more specific evidence for DBT skills training as an essential treatment component. The majority of RCTs examining DBT skills training have occurred outside of Marsha Linehan's research center (reducing concerns about allegiance effects), and over half of the studies have included an active control, such as an alternative type of group, self-study with diary cards or handouts, or medication. The other studies have included waitlist controls. Two of these trials have specifically selected clients with BPD, and the remainder included clients with a variety of other clinical problem areas, such as major depression, trauma and a history of childhood abuse, binge eating disorder, bulimia, attention-deficit/hyperactivity disorder, and bipolar disorder. In the majority of these trials, DBT skills training outperformed the control condition in terms of relevant clinical outcomes (e.g., depression, anxiety, general psychiatric symptoms, eating behaviors, ADHD symptoms, and emotion dysregulation; e.g., Soler et al., 2009; Valentine et al., 2015). In some cases, patients in DBT showed lower dropout rates than those in the control conditions (e.g., Safer, Robinson, & Jo, 2010). Although consultation team and phone coaching also are key components of any DBT program, the degree to which the DBT conditions included these components was either unclear (this was not mentioned) or inconsistent. Therefore, taken together, DBT skills training appears to be a promising treatment for lower severity problems that tend to fall within the quality of life domain (e.g., disordered eating, ADHD, depression, anxiety, and emotion dysregulation) and may be superior to waitlist for self-harming BPD patients (McMain, Gulmond, Barnhart, Habinski, & Streiner, 2017).

These findings suggest that DBT skills training (on its own or with other DBT components) may have significant and clinically relevant effects in its own right, but to consider DBT skills training to be a mechanism, evidence must show that DBT skills training (DBT-S) is a necessary and/or sufficient component of treatment. Linehan et al. (2015) published the first component analysis of DBT to answer this question. For this study, 99 women with BPD and at least two suicide attempts and/or nonsuicidal self-injury (NSSI) in the last 5 years, NSSI or a suicide attempt in the 8 weeks before screening, and at least one suicide attempt in the past year, were randomized to one of three treatment conditions. One condition consisted of standard DBT (S-DBT), including individual therapy, group DBT skills training, telephone consultation, and a therapist consultation team. Another condition (DBT-S) included group DBT skills training, as-needed, non-DBT case-management services, availability of case managers by phone between sessions, and a DBT therapist consultation team (case managers were not on this team). The third condition DBT individual therapy (DBT-I) involved individual DBT (with any mention or explicit teaching of DBT skills proscribed), an activity/psychoeducational group that met weekly (to control for group contact), and telephone consultation. A few key findings from this study are as follows:

- The S-DBT patients had a significantly lower treatment dropout rate compared with the DBT-I patients (24% vs 48%, respectively) and a lower (but not significantly) dropout rate compared with DBT-S patients (39%).
- There were no significant differences between conditions in terms of rates or frequency of suicidal behaviors.
- Among patients who engaged in NSSI during the treatment year, S-DBT and DBT-S patients reported a significantly lower frequency of NSSI compared with DBT-I patients.
- S-DBT and DBT-S patients showed greater improvements in depression and nonsignificantly greater improvements in anxiety during the treatment year, but DBT-I patients "caught up," showing greater improvements in both domains during the follow-up year.
- S-DBT patients had lower rates of emergency department and hospital visits for psychiatric reasons (but not for suicidal behavior) during the follow-up year.

Taken together, these findings suggest that skills training is likely an important but not necessarily sufficient component of DBT. S-DBT has an edge over skills training when it comes to patient retention (of note, findings from other recent research has suggested that S-DBT may have superior dropout rates compared with DBT skills alone; Lyng, Swales, Hastings, Millar, Duffy, & Booth, 2019) and has an advantage over DBT-I in terms of service utilization during follow-up. That said, when it comes to reductions in NSSI, the conditions that included skills training (S-DBT and DBT-S) appear to have the advantage over DBT-I. If a clinician is unable to offer S-DBT but has the option of offering DBT individual therapy or DBT skills group only to self-injuring patients, skills group may be most advantageous. It is important to remember, however, that the DBT-S condition involved frequent individual case management meetings, a DBT consultation team, the availability of case managers by phone for assistance, and the use of a structured crisis protocol to address suicidal behavior. These features are not always present in practice settings where clinicians offer DBT skills training only services. In our experience, such services typically consist of a DBT skills group and limited case management (e.g., monthly), due to high caseload demands.

Mechanisms related to changes in the client: increases in skilled behavior

One important change in the client that may underlie some of the effects of DBT more broadly, and skills training specifically, includes skills practice, or the practice of new, adaptive behaviors. As noted previously, in DBT, various forms of homework assignments (for a discussion of homework in DBT, see Lindenboim, Chapman, & Linehan, 2007) encourage clients to practice new behaviors in various contexts. Skills group homework follows a structured curriculum designed to help clients acquire and strengthen new skills in the areas of mindfulness, distress tolerance, emotion regulation, and interpersonal effectiveness. Homework assignments in individual therapy tend to occur as needed but often emphasize the use of DBT skills to help solve various problems. A client, for example, who has self-injured during the previous week, may leave the session having agreed to practice the emotion regulation PLEASE skills to reduce vulnerability to intense or overwhelming emotions, and to practice self-soothing as an alternative to self-injury. If the prompting event for self-injury included a conflict with the client's partner, the plan may also include interpersonal effectiveness skills to better navigate conflict, or various emotion regulation skills to regulate emotions during or in the aftermath of conflict. The client may practice these skills regularly in anticipation of relevant future events (e.g., another fight with the partner) or simply be ready to use them as needed. Indeed, the learning and practicing of new behaviors is a fundamental principle of DBT, and as such, skills practice itself may be a critical element underlying some of the beneficial effects of DBT.

Some research findings have supported the importance of skills practice as a potential client-based mechanism of change. In a study of participants with BPD who completed 1 year of DBT, increases in self-reported use of DBT skills (assessed across all four domains) predicted reductions in both self-injurious behaviors and risk of treatment drop-out (Barnicot, Gonzalez, McCabe, & Priebe, 2016). Similarly, reported skills use on DBT diary cards was associated with reduced BPD symptoms in one study with a primarily female sample (Stepp, Epler, Jahng, & Trull, 2008). In research comparing DBT to TAU or treatment by community experts, women with BPD who received DBT experienced greater reductions in self-injury and depression compared with women with BPD who received other treatments, and this difference was accounted for by self-reported increases in the use of adaptive skills (Neacsiu, Rizvi, & Linehan, 2010). Even for participants who do not receive S-DBT, increased adaptive skill use has important implications for outcomes. In a study comparing outcomes for participants with emotion dysregulation and depression or anxiety who received either DBT skills group or a supportive therapy group, increased use of adaptive skills accounted for greater improvements in anxiety and emotion dysregulation in the DBT condition (Neacsiu, Eberle, Kramer, Wiesmann, & Linehan, 2014).

Increased emotion regulation and mindfulness skills as mechanisms

Although an increase in skilled behavior generally may be a mechanism of change in DBT, there is some evidence that specific DBT skills influence therapeutic outcomes. Thus far, two domains of DBT skills have emerged as possibly related to important mechanisms of therapeutic change: emotion regulation and mindfulness. Although emotion regulation skills are addressed throughout treatment components of DBT (including in individual therapy and phone coaching), they are most clearly emphasized in the "emotion regulation skills" module of group skills training (Linehan, 2015). This module is the lengthiest of the four and targets the emotional reactivity and emotional dysregulation that are hallmark features of BPD. First, clients learn to understand emotions and to identify the components of emotional experiences, including physical sensations, cognitions, and behaviors (such as expressions, body posture, and action urges). This systematic breakdown of emotional experiences aims to increase a client's ability to identify their own emotions in the moment—a key first step in emotion regulation. This model also naturally progresses into exploration of how changing one aspect of an emotional response can impact other aspects of the system. For example, changing a physiological, cognitive, or behavioral component of the experience of anger may reduce the intensity of the emotional experience. Strategies to alter components of emotional experiences are included throughout the four skills modules. For example, the TIPP skills in the distress tolerance module are strategies for the client to reduce physiological arousal during intense emotional experiences in order to allow for clearer thinking and more effective skills use.

Increasing evidence suggests that emotion regulation skills are an important mechanism through which DBT produces change. DBT reduces self-reported difficulties in emotion regulation, and changes in emotion regulation have been found to account for the effects of DBT on behavior such as substance use (Axelrod, Perepletchikova, Holtzman, & Sinha, 2011). In laboratory research, participants who have completed DBT or components of DBT have demonstrated reduced reactivity to emotional stimuli (Dixon-Gordon, Chapman, & Turner, 2015; Goodman et al., 2014). In a study of suicidal college students with BPD in Taiwan, when compared to cognitive therapy, DBT skills training has produced greater increases in the reported use of acceptance-based emotion regulation strategies and greater decreases in reported use of emotion suppression (Lin et al., 2019).

The impacts of improved emotion regulation abilities have also been examined using neuroimaging techniques, revealing that DBT may produce changes in brain areas associated with experiencing and regulating emotions. For example, participants with BPD who completed 12-weeks of residential DBT experienced decreased activity in brain regions such as the supramarginal gyrus and the anterior cingulate (both regions associated with emotion regulation) when asked to reappraise emotional images (Schmitt, Winter, Niedtfeld, Herpertz, & Schmahl, 2016) or to distract from them (Winter et al., 2017). Another study of BPD (Schnell & Herpertz, 2007) examined the impacts of 12-weeks of inpatient DBT on reactivity to negative images. Compared to healthy controls who did not undergo treatment, participants who completed DBT showed reduced cingulate cortex activity in the anterior, temporal, and posterior regions. Patients who showed greater treatment response also showed reduced left amygdala reactivity when exposed to the negative images. Changes in amygdala activity following DBT were also found in research by Goodman et al. (2014). Participants with BPD who completed 12 months of standard comprehensive DBT showed decreased left amygdala response, which was associated with self-reported improvements in difficulties with emotion regulation. In contrast, untreated healthy controls did not show amygdala activity change. Finally, research by Niedtfeld et al. (2017) reveled that for participants with BPD, DBT has different impacts on amygdala response following pain when compared to TAU. Before treatment, BPD patients demonstrated reduced activity in the amygdala after experiencing physical pain. This relation suggested that pain was regulating emotional responses. Posttreatment, participants who completed DBT showed less amygdala deactivation after pain compared to participants in the TAU condition. As emotion regulation has been conceptualized as one negative reinforcer that contributes to reoccurring self-injury (Chapman, Gratz, & Brown, 2006), these findings indicate that DBT may reduce the link between self-injury and reduced emotional arousal.

Another potentially critical domain of skills that may serve as mechanisms of change in DBT is mindfulness. Mindfulness skills are considered foundational in DBT as being nonjudgmentally aware in the present moment is critical in order to effectively identify when to use a skill, select a skill to use, and put a skill into practice. It is perhaps unsurprising that clients report using mindfulness skills (and distress tolerance skills) the most across the course of DBT (Lindenboim, Comtois, & Linehan, 2007), and participating in DBT is associated with increases in mindfulness (Perroud, Nicastro, Jermann, & Huguelet, 2012). In a study comparing

DBT mindfulness skills training with GPM to GPM alone for patients with BPD, the time participants spent practicing mindfulness predicted improvements in mindfulness as well as reduced psychopathology and depression (Soler et al., 2012). Changes in attentional control and increased awareness may at least partially account for therapeutic impact of DBT and DBT skills training more specifically.

Conclusion and future directions

Theory underlying DBT conceptualizes BPD and other complex disorders as related to skills deficits broadly and emotion regulation deficits more specifically. Many of the interventions and core DBT strategies encourage the learning and practice of new behavior or skills, with the majority of this work occurring during structured weekly, group skills training sessions, but ad hoc practicing of skills, and new behavior occurring in individual therapy sessions or during phone coaching. As such, when it comes to mechanisms of change in DBT, it is reasonable to consider whether skills training could be an important treatment element accounting for outcomes in DBT, and whether client-related mechanisms include skills practice or improvement in particular skill domains, such as emotion regulation or mindfulness. Some evidence does suggest that skills training may be effective in its own right for various clinical problem areas, is a potentially necessary element of DBT, and may influence outcomes in several ways. Further, evidence suggests that skills practice could be an important client-related mechanism of change, and that DBT may result in changes in the emotion regulation system in particular (as evidenced by multimethod research, including self-reported outcomes and brain imaging). The findings on brain-related changes are consistent with the notion that skills practice is an important change mechanism, given that neural pathways take time and repetition to change. Indeed, cells that "fire together, wire together" (Shatz, 1992).

If skills training as a treatment component and skills practice as a client mechanism are essential to the effectiveness of DBT, further work might be done to enhance these components of the treatment. In terms of skills group, although a 2 hours weekly group in addition to between-session homework assignments seems like a significant commitment for complex clients who have enough difficulty simply making appointments, it might be worth considering whether a stronger dose of skills training would enhance the effects of DBT. A stronger dose does not necessarily need to involve more frequent groups, but perhaps the use of technology to insert ongoing skills training and encourage practice in everyday life. Several DBT apps have been developed to encourage practice. Perhaps additional work could be done to enhance the learning value of these applications, such as the development of programs that prompt repeated practice of various skills in increasingly challenging scenarios, remind clients to use skills when they are in particular situations, and so forth. Improving the effectiveness and automaticity of new behaviors requires frequent practice, and more could be done to enhance this feature of DBT.

Notwithstanding the importance of skills and skills training, several other features of DBT may contribute to its efficacy. Lynch, Chapman, Rosenthal, Kuo, and Linehan (2006) have described potential mechanisms associated with various DBT strategies, such as chain analysis, irreverence, dialectical strategies, and mindfulness. Given the similarity in findings between DBT and other structured treatments that use evidence-based protocols to address suicidal behavior, it could be that structure, expertise, and evidence-based suicide intervention are essential ingredients of DBT. With such a comprehensive treatment with so many moving parts, it is hard to know exactly which of these parts does what, whether the treatment would still work if some were removed and others were retained, and what changes in the client are essential targets. Further research will hopefully begin to completely answer these questions, ultimately helping to streamline and optimize the use of DBT to help clients continue to build lives worth living.

Acknowledgment

Work on this chapter was supported by a Michael Smith Foundation for Health Research Career Investigator Award and a Simon Fraser University FASS Dean's Research Grant.

References

Axelrod, S. R., Perepletchikova, F., Holtzman, K., & Sinha, R. (2011). Emotion regulation and substance use frequency in women with substance dependence and borderline personality disorder receiving dialectical behavior therapy. *The American Journal of Drug and Alcohol Abuse, 37*, 37–42.

Barnicot, K., Gonzalez, R., McCabe, R., & Priebe, S. (2016). Skills use and common treatment processes in dialectical behavior therapy for borderline personality disorder. *Journal of Behavior Therapy and Experimental Psychiatry, 52*, 147–156.

Beauchaine, T. P., Hinshaw, S. P., & Bridge, J. A. (2019). Nonsuicidal self-injury and suicidal behaviors in girls: The case for targeted prevention in preadolescence. *Clinical Psychological Science, 7*, 1–25.

Beblo, T., Fernando, S., Kamper, P., Griepenstroh, J., Aschenbrenner, S., Pastuszak, A., … Driessen, M. (2013). Increased attempts to suppress negative and positive emotions in borderline personality disorder. *Psychiatry Research, 210*, 505–509.

Chapman, A. L. (2019). Borderline personality disorder and emotion dysregulation. *Development and Psychopathology, 31*, 1143–1156.

Chapman, A. L., & Dixon-Gordon, K. L. (in press). *Dialectical Behavior Therapy* Washington, DC: American Psychological Association Books.

Chapman, A. L., Gratz, K. L., & Brown, M. Z. (2006). Solving the puzzle of deliberate self-harm: The experiential avoidance model. *Behaviour Research and Therapy, 44*, 371–394.

Chapman, A. L., & Hope, N. (2020). Dialectical behaviour therapy and treatment of emotion dysregulation. In T. Beauchaine, & S. Crowell (Eds.), *Oxford handbook of emotion dysregulation*. Oxford, UK: Oxford University Press.

Chapman, A. L., Specht, M. W., & Cellucci, T. (2005). Borderline personality disorder and deliberate self-harm: Does experiential avoidance play a role? *Suicide and Life-Threatening Behavior, 35*, 388–399.

Clarkin, J. F., Levy, K. N., Lenzenweger, M. F., & Kernberg, O. F. (2007). Evaluating three treatments for borderline personality disorder: A multiwave study. *The American Journal of Psychiatry, 164*, 922–928.

Crowell, S. E., Beauchaine, T. P., & Linehan, M. M. (2009). A biosocial developmental model of borderline personality: Elaborating and extending Linehan's theory. *Psychological Bulletin, 135*, 495–510.

DeCou, C. R., Comtois, K. A., & Landes, S. J. (2019). Dialectical behavior therapy is effective for the treatment of suicidal behavior: A meta-analysis. *Behavior Therapy, 50*, 60–72.

Dimidjian, S., Hollon, S. D., Dobson, K. S., Schmaling, K. B., Kohlenberg, R. J., Addis, M. E., & Gollan, J. K. (2006). Randomized trial of behavioral activation, cognitive therapy, and antidepressant medication in the acute treatment of adults with major depression. *Journal of Consulting and Clinical Psychology, 74*, 658–670.

Dixon-Gordon, K. L., Chapman, A. L., Lovasz, N., & Walters, K. N. (2011). Too upset to think: The interplay of borderline personality features, negative emotions, and social problem solving in the laboratory. *Personality Disorders: Theory, Research, and Treatment, 2*, 243–260.

Dixon-Gordon, K. L., Chapman, A. L., & Turner, B. J. (2015). A preliminary pilot study comparing dialectical behavior therapy emotion regulation skills with interpersonal effectiveness skills and a control group treatment. *Journal of Experimental Psychopathology, 6*, 369–388.

Goodman, M., Carpenter, D., Tang, C. Y., Goldstein, K. E., Avedon, J., Fernandez, N., ... Hazlett, E. A. (2014). Dialectical behavior therapy alters emotion regulation and amygdala activity in patients with borderline personality disorder. *Journal of Psychiatric Research, 57*, 108–116.

Jacobson, N. S., Dobson, K. S., Truax, P. A., Addis, M. E., Koerner, K., Gollan, J. K., Gortner, E., & Prince, S. E. (1996). A component analysis of cognitive-behavioral treatment for depression. *Journal of Consulting and Clinical Psychology, 64*, 295–304.

Joiner, T. E. (2005). *Why people die suicide*. Cambridge, MA: Harvard University Press.

Kazdin, A. E., & Nock, M. K. (2003). Delineating mechanisms of change in child and adolescent therapy: Methodological issues and research recommendations. *Journal of Child Psychology and Psychiatry, 44*, 1116–1129.

Kliem, S., Kröger, C., & Kosfelder, J. (2010). Dialectical behavior therapy for borderline personality disorder: A meta-analysis using mixed-effects modeling. *Journal of Consulting and Clinical Psychology, 78*, 936–951.

Klonsky, E. D., & May, A. M. (2015). The three-step theory (3ST): A new theory of suicide rooted in the "idea-to-action" framework. *International Journal of Cognitive Therapy, 8*, 114–129.

Lin, T. J., Ko, H. C., Wu, J. Y., Oei, T. P., Lane, H. Y., & Chen, C. H. (2019). The effectiveness of dialectical behavior therapy skills training group vs. cognitive therapy group on reducing depression and suicide attempts for borderline personality disorder in Taiwan. *Archives of Suicide Research, 23*, 82–99.

Lindenboim, N., Chapman, A. L., & Linehan, M. M. (2007). Borderline personality disorder. In N. Kazantzis, & L. L'Abate (Eds.), *Handbook of homework assignments in psychotherapy: Research, practice, prevention* (pp. 227–245). New York: Springer Science + Business Media.

Lindenboim, N., Comtois, K. A., & Linehan, M. M. (2007). Skills practice in dialectical behavior therapy for suicidal women meeting criteria for borderline personality disorder. *Cognitive and Behavioral Practice, 14*, 147–156.

Linehan, M. M. (1993a). *Cognitive-behavioral treatment of borderline personality disorder*. New York: Guildford Press.

Linehan, M. M. (1993b). *Skills training manual for treating borderline personality disorder*. New York: Guildford Press.

Linehan, M. M. (2015). *DBT skills training handouts and worksheets* (2nd ed.). New York: Guilford Press.

Linehan, M. M., Armstrong, H. E., Suarez, A., Allmon, D., & Heard, H. L. (1991). Cognitive-behavioral treatment of chronically parasuicidal borderline patients. *Archives of General Psychiatry, 48*, 1060–1064.

Linehan, M. M., Comtois, K. A., Murray, A. M., Brown, M. Z., Gallop, R. J., Heard, H. L., ... Lindenboim, N. (2006). Two-year randomized controlled trial and follow-up of dialectical behavior therapy vs therapy by experts for suicidal behaviors and borderline personality disorder. *Archives of General Psychiatry, 63*, 757–766.

Linehan, M. M., Korslund, K. E., Harned, M. A., Gallop, R. J., Lungu, A., Neacsiu, A. D., & Murray-Gregory, A. M. (2015). Dialectical behavior therapy for high suicide risk in individuals with borderline personality disorder: A randomized clinical trial and component analysis. *JAMA Psychiatry, 72*, 475–482.

Lynch, T. R., Chapman, A. L., Rosenthal, M. Z., Kuo, J. K., & Linehan, M. M. (2006). Mechanisms of change in dialectical behavior therapy: Theoretical and empirical observations. *Journal of Clinical Psychology, 62*, 459–480.

Lyng, S., Hastings, M., Duffy, D. J., & Booth, R. (2019). Standalone DBT skills training vs standard (i.e. all modes) DBT for BPD: A naturally occurring quasi-experiment in routine clinical practice. *Community Mental Health Journal*, 1–13.

McMain, S. F., Gulmond, T., Barnhart, R., Habinski, L., & Streiner, D. L. (2017). A randomized trial of brief dialectical behavior therapy skills training in suicidal patients suffering from borderline disorder. *Acta Psychiatrica Scandinavica, 135*, 138–148.

McMain, S. F., Links, P. S., Gnam, W. H., Guimond, T., Cardish, R. J., Korman, L., & Streiner, D. L. (2009). A randomized trial of dialectical behavior therapy versus general psychiatric management for borderline personality disorder. *The American Journal of Psychiatry, 166*, 1365–1374.

Neacsiu, A. D., Eberle, J. W., Kramer, R., Wiesmann, T., & Linehan, M. M. (2014). Dialectical behavior therapy for transdiagnostic emotion dysregulation: A pilot randomized controlled trial. *Behaviour Research and Therapy, 59*, 40–51.

Neacsiu, A. D., Rizvi, S. L., & Linehan, M. M. (2010). Dialectical behavior therapy skills use as a mediator and outcome of treatment for borderline personality disorder. *Behaviour Research and Therapy, 48*, 832–839.

Niedtfeld, I., Schmitt, R., Winter, D., Bohus, M., Schmahl, C., & Herpertz, S. C. (2017). Pain-mediated affect regulation is reduced after dialectical behavior therapy in borderline personality disorder: A longitudinal fMRI study. *Social Cognitive and Affective Neuroscience, 12*, 739–747.

Perroud, N., Nicastro, R., Jermann, F., & Huguelet, P. (2012). Mindfulness skills in borderline personality disorder patients during dialectical behavior therapy: Preliminary results. *International Journal of Psychiatry in Clinical Practice, 16*, 189–196.

Safer, D. L., Robinson, A. H., & Jo, B. (2010). Outcome from a randomized controlled trial of group therapy for binge eating disorder: Comparing dialectical behavior therapy adapted for binge eating to an active comparison group therapy. *Behavior Therapy, 41*, 106–120.

Schmitt, R., Winter, D., Niedtfeld, I., Herpertz, S. C., & Schmahl, C. (2016). Effects of psychotherapy on neuronal correlates of reappraisal in female patients with borderline personality disorder. *Biological Psychiatry: Cognitive Neuroscience and Neuroimaging, 1*, 548–557.

Schnell, K., & Herpertz, S. C. (2007). Effects of dialectic-behavioral-therapy on the neural correlates of affective hyperarousal in borderline personality disorder. *Journal of Psychiatric Research*, *41*, 837–847.

Shatz, C. J. (1992). The developing brain. *Scientific American*, *267*, 60–67.

Soler, J., Pascual, J. C., Tiana, T., Cebrià, A., Barrachina, J., Campins, M. J., ... Pérez, V. (2009). Dialectical behavior therapy skills training compared to standard group therapy in borderline personality disorder: a 3-month randomised controlled clinical trial. *Behaviour Research and Therapy*, *47*, 353–358.

Soler, J., Valdeperez, A., Feliu-Soler, A., Pascual, J. C., Portella, M. J., Martin-Blanco, A., ... Perez, V. (2012). Effects of the dialectical behavior therapy-mindfulness module on attention in patients with borderline personality disorder. *Behaviour Research and Therapy*, *50*, 150–157.

Staats, A. W. (1975). Social behaviorism. Oxford, England: Dorsey.

Staats, W. W. (1996). *Behavior and personality: Psychological behaviorism*. Springer Publishing Company.

Stepp, S. D., Epler, A. J., Jahng, S., & Trull, T. J. (2008). The effect of dialectical behavior therapy skills use on borderline personality disorder features. *Journal of Personality Disorders*, *22*, 549–563.

Stoffers, J. M., Volm, B. A., Rucker, G., Timmer, A., Huband, N., & Lieb, K. (2012). Psychological therapies for people with borderline personality disorder. *Cochrane Database of Systematic Reviews*, *15*, CD005652.

Valentine, S. E., Bankoff, S. M., Poulin, R. M., Reidler, E. B., & Pantalone, D. W. (2015). The use of dialectical behavior therapy skills training as a stand-alone treatment: A systematic review of the treatment outcome literature. *Journal of Clinical Psychology*, *71*, 1–20.

Wampold, B. E. (2015). How important are the common factors in psychotherapy? An update. *World Psychiatry*, *14*, 270–277.

Winter, D., Niedtfeld, I., Schmitt, R., Bohus, M., Schmahl, C., & Herpertz, S. C. (2017). Neural correlates of distraction in borderline personality disorder before and after dialectical behavior therapy. *European Archives of Psychiatry and Clinical Neuroscience*, *267*, 1–12.

Further reading

Burmeister, K., Höschel, K., von Auer, A. K., Reiske, S., Schweiger, U., Sipos, V., ... Bohus, M. (2014). Dialectical behavior therapy (DBT) – Developments and empirical evidence. *Psychiatrische Praxis*, *41*, 242–249.

CHAPTER

4

Accreditation, adherence, and training in dialectical behavior therapy: data review and practical applications

Erin M. Miga, Elizabeth R. LoTempio, Jared D. Michonski and Dorian A. Hunter

The Seattle Clinic LLC, Seattle, WA, United States

One of the chief strengths of dialectical behavior therapy is its deep body of research on its clinical efficacy, spanning the past 30 years. Further, the area of training and implementation of dialectical behavior therapy (DBT) has skyrocketed in both supply and demand over the past 10 years, in particular. Because of DBT's clinical efficacy, real-world effectiveness, and popularity amongst clinicians, it is imperative that we establish clarity of terminology that relates to the training and expertise of DBT providers and programs and identify areas of DBT training and monitoring that require more empirical investigation. This chapter will provide an overview of the extant data on DBT training modalities and adherence monitoring, as well as provide several pragmatic suggestions for incorporating adherence monitoring and supervision more readily into real-world clinical settings.

DBT training

Modes of training

Research that examines the effectiveness of different approaches to training in DBT is still in its infancy. Nonetheless, several modes of training do exist. These include instructor-led trainings, online or

The Handbook of Dialectical Behavior Therapy
DOI: https://doi.org/10.1016/B978-0-12-816384-9.00004-X

computer-based interactive trainings, self-study through reading DBT-treatment manuals, seminar and practicum trainings offered as part of one's graduate school training, and postgraduate supervision and consultation services. Regarding the last, although DBT training organizations such as Behavioral Tech (Behavioral Tech, n.d.; behavioraltech.org) and Treatment Implementation Collaborative (ticllc.org) offer supervision and/or consultation, to our knowledge no research has been published to-date which specifically examines the effectiveness of these services. Each of the other forms of training noted has received at least some attention in the research literature and are discussed later.

There are several different training companies that offer foundational and more advanced DBT trainings, including but not limited to Behavioral Tech, Treatment Implementation Collaborative, Portland DBT Institute (pdbti.org), and Practice Ground (practiceground.org). The most researched form of training to date has been the instructor-led DBT Intensive Training (DBT-IT); model developed by Behavioral Tech (see Landes & Linehan, 2012 for a discussion). The model has several important features. Because DBT is intended to be delivered within the supportive context of a consultation team, DBT-IT is most frequently oriented toward teams rather than individual practitioners. The instructor-led trainings occur in two 5-day training sessions, spaced 6 months apart. The 6-month spacing allows for a period of self-study and for an implementation period, as well as for consultation from the trainers. Prior to starting the training, participants are expected to have read the original DBT manual (Linehan, 1993a,b) and the updated skills manual (Linehan, 2015). The first week of training (Part I) aids participants in forming and functioning effectively as a DBT consultation team and covers the core DBT content areas, including theoretical background, skills training, targeting procedures, behavioral change and validation strategies, suicide assessment and risk management, and phone coaching. The second week (Part II) is focused on demonstrating and strengthening use of DBT strategies and on improving the functioning of consultation teams toward the end goal of DBT implementation (see Landes & Linehan, 2012 or behavioraltech.org, for elaboration).

For the remainder of this section, we will begin by reviewing outcomes for the DBT-IT approach to training, followed by research on other approaches to training, including online/web-based training, self-study, and the training that occurs within graduate school. Finally, we will offer an analysis of the current state of the empirical literature on DBT training and provide suggestions for future directions.

Outcomes for DBT intensive training

Clinician outcomes

Adoption of DBT modes. In several investigations of the DBT-IT approach, researchers administered self-report surveys to clinicians that had attended Behavioral Tech DBT-IT trainings, in the absence of any control group. Outcomes assessed in such studies included rate of adoption of all four modes of DBT (i.e., individual DBT therapy, skills groups, consultation teams, and phone coaching), confidence in the treatment, attitude toward clients meeting criteria for BPD, conceptual knowledge of DBT, and use of the treatment. Regarding adoption of DBT, DiGiorgio, Glass, and Arnkoff (2010) found that, of the 129 participants, those who attended a 10-day DBT-IT training ($n = 50$) were significantly more likely to adopt all four modes of treatment and, within a typical individual therapy session, were more likely to make use of diary card and homework worksheets and to review the target hierarchy than were participants who attended less intensive DBT trainings offered by Behavioral Tech ($n = 77$). Other studies that surveyed DBT teams that attended a 10-day DBT-IT training also reported relatively high rates of adoption of all four modes of the treatment [75% of 52 DBT teams that completed a follow-up survey 5–16 months following completion of the training (Navarro-Haro et al., 2019); 57% of 68 DBT programs, 2–15 years after completion of the United Kingdom's National Intensive Training (Swales, Taylor, & Hibbs, 2012)]. Reporting on the four modes individually, Ditty, Landes, Doyle, and Beidas (2015) found that adoption rates ranged from 87% for phone coaching to 99% for group skills training among 79 participants who completed a DBT-IT training at least 1 year prior to participating in their survey.

Attitudes toward DBT and BPD. Herschell, Lindhiem, Kogan, Celedonia, and Stein (2014) investigated attitudes toward client's diagnosed with BPD, confidence in DBT's effectiveness in helping those diagnosed with BPD, and use of DBT-specific intervention strategies in a sample of 64 clinicians from 10 community agencies that participated in a DBT implementation initiative. Outcome measures were assessed at different time points throughout the course of training, which included the 10-day DBT-IT training and an additional 2-day training, as well as access to phone consultation over the course of the training sequence. Results showed higher ratings on all outcome measures (attitude toward BPD, confidence in DBT's effectiveness, and use of DBT components) over from baseline assessment (prior to the initial 5-day training) to the fourth assessment period (22 months after the initial 5-day training and 8 months after completion of the full training). Additional findings emerged with respect to the interaction between baseline levels on the outcome measures and the rate of change: clinicians who initially reported the least favorable view of clients diagnosed with BPD showed greater increases, clinicians who initially had the least confidence in the treatment displayed higher gains, and clinicians who initially reported the lowest use of DBT components displayed the greatest increases in use.

Performance on tests of DBT knowledge. An additional outcome that has been studied in association with DBT training has been performance on a test of DBT knowledge. Hawkins and Sinha (1998) examined whether 109 clinicians from diverse backgrounds across 11 mental health programs can develop proficient conceptual knowledge of DBT, given its complexity. DBT Training consisted of 1–2-day workshops, on-site in-service training, recurring consultation, and the 10-day DBT-IT. Moreover, individual clinical sites organized study groups to discuss DBT readings. DBT knowledge exams were administered at two time points during the training process, and only a subsample (53 clinicians across 9 sites) of the larger sample participated in the second examination. Of note, the proportion of participants who had attended an intensive workshop (as well as their exposure to DBT training more generally) at the time of examination varied. Several relevant findings emerged with respect to the first knowledge exam. Performance on the exam correlated moderately with DBT training. Clinicians who attended a 5-day intensive workshop performed better than those who did not at the time of the first examination. However, it was unclear that the intensive training was uniquely responsible for the increased DBT knowledge over other forms of concurrent DBT training (e.g., reading, study groups, and consultation). Excluding participation in an intensive training, the strongest predictors of exam performance were reading, peer support/consultation, and participation in a study group. These factors (expert consultation, reading, and study group) also were the strongest predictors of exam performance at time 2, administered on average 7 months following the first. Finally, clinicians who attended the second 5-day intensive training performed significantly better in DBT knowledge than those who did not attend—however, once again, this finding was confounded by greater participation in training methods in general by those who attended the second intensive. Nonetheless, these results suggest that understanding of DBT theory can be attained by clinicians outside of the university, with diverse clinical backgrounds, working in diverse settings. This conclusion was bolstered by the fact that the upper quartile of performers on the second administration of the exam performed at a level equivalent to doctoral students taught by Marsha Linehan (79.9% vs 82.9%, respectively).

Client outcomes

Quasiexperimental studies. Only a few studies have attempted to examine client outcomes associated with clinician participation in DBT-IT trainings using quasiexperimental methods. Trupin, Stewart, Beach, and Boesky (2002) examined the effectiveness of DBT in a sample of incarcerated adolescent females who resided at one of two rehabilitative cottages where staff received training in DBT: (1) a mental health cottage ($n = 22$) or (2) a general population cottage ($n = 23$). Staff for both cottages received a minimum of 2 days of training in DBT; however, several staff from the mental health cottage participated in a DBT-IT training, while none of the staff from the general population received this training. Adolescents from the mental health cottage were observed to exhibit significant reductions in behavior problems (aggression, self-injury, and classroom disruptions) over the course of the 10 months of the study, while adolescents in the general population cottage exhibited no reductions. Although it is tempting to view such findings as indicating that the DBT-IT training is effective at producing positive client outcomes compared to a lower dose of training (cf. Landes & Linehan, 2012), some caution is warranted due to methodological limitations of the study. Namely, the adolescents differed significantly across the two cottages at baseline on important measures. Specifically, the mental health cottage had higher rates of mood disturbance, disruptive behavior and substance use disorders, self-injury ideation and behaviors, and thought disturbance. In addition, only four of the staff in the mental health cottage received the intensive training.

Pasieczny and Connor (2011) studied the effectiveness of DBT in an Australian sample of 90 clients meeting criteria for BPD who were seeking treatment from a community mental health service. They found that clients treated by four clinicians who attended a 10-day DBT-IT training displayed greater reduction in suicide attempts and NSSI behaviors over the course of 6 months of treatment compared to clients treated by 14 clinicians who attended a 4-day training. Nonsignificant differences were found for emergency department visits and psychiatric admissions, as well as for self-report measures of depression, suicidality, and anxiety.

Outcomes for self-study, computer-based, and short instructor–led trainings in DBT

Community mental health providers

A few additional studies examined the effectiveness of other modes of training, including online/computer-based trainings, self-study, and shorter instructor-led trainings. A number of such studies have been conducted by Dimeff and colleagues at the research arm of Behavioral Tech with community mental health providers (Dimeff et al., 2009; Dimeff et al., 2015; Dimeff, Woodcock, Harned, & Beadnell, 2011). Notably, these studies offer important methodological improvements over the studies reviewed above in that they employed an experimental design, with participants randomly assigned to respective treatment/control conditions. In addition, these studies have the benefit of testing the effectiveness of training that would be both more time- and cost-effective relative to longer, in-person trainings.

In the first of these studies, Dimeff et al. (2009) randomly assigned 150 clinicians who were naïve to DBT to one of three conditions providing training in DBT skills: (1) a 2-day instructor-led workshop, (2) a 20-hour interactive online training course, and (3) a self-study condition in which clinicians were given a copy of the original DBT Skills Training Manual (Linehan, 1993a,b) with a suggested reading guide. Outcome measures included self-report of satisfaction with the training, self-efficacy and motivation to teach DBT skills, the use of DBT skills in their practice at 90-day follow-up, as well as a knowledge test of DBT skills and a performance-based role play in applying DBT skills in a phone coaching scenario. Results showed that participants rated the two active training conditions as more satisfactory and as leading to greater self-efficacy at posttraining (but not at 90-day follow-up) than did those assigned to reading the treatment manual; no differences were found on these outcomes between the active training conditions, nor were any differences across the three conditions on self-reported use of DBT skills. All conditions improved in knowledge of the skills over time, with the online training condition showing greater improvement in knowledge than the other conditions, both at posttraining and 90-day follow-up. The instructor-led condition did not differ from the manual condition. Adherence and competence ratings of role play were conducted by a coding team of 2 DBT experts and a third primary coder trained to reliability. Ratings were derived using an original coding instrument developed by three DBT experts. On the role-play tasks, *all conditions improved* following the training both with respect to observational ratings of adherence and competence. At 90-day follow-up, on average participants, was rated as applying the skills at a minimal to moderate level of competency. Differences across conditions on role-play performance were not significant.

In their second study, Dimeff et al. (2011) specifically investigated training conditions for learning DBT distress tolerance skills, with 132 clinicians assigned to (1) an interactive computer-based training course, (2) a self-study condition in which clinicians received a copy of the crisis survival section of the original Skills Training Manual (Linehan, 1993a,b), or (3) a placebo online training course on caring for clients who meet criteria for BPD. Each condition took place in a structured learning environment that included time constrains and the presence of proctors. Outcomes assessed included self-reported satisfaction with the training, self-efficacy in ability to teach the distress tolerance skills, motivation to teach these skills and to learn more about DBT, the use of the skills in their practice at multiple follow-up time points, as well as a test of knowledge of and ability to apply the skills. Results indicated that the two treatment conditions both outperformed the placebo control condition on all outcomes, with the exception of motivation to learn and use DBT. Participants preferred the computer course over self-study, but no differences emerged between these conditions in skills knowledge (posttraining) or self-efficacy (both at posttraining and 15-week follow-up). At 15-month follow-up, those in the computer training condition exhibited greater knowledge of the skills than those in the self-study condition. In addition, clinicians in the computer training condition reported significantly greater use of the skills in their practice at all follow-up time points compared to the placebo condition, while differences were rarely significant between computer and self-study conditions and between the self-study and placebo conditions.

In the third of their studies, Dimeff et al. (2015) examined the effectiveness of different approaches for training 172 clinicians in two key DBT strategies of change and acceptance: behavioral chain analysis and validation. Participants were assigned to (1) a 2-day instructor-led workshop, (2) an interactive online training, or (3) self-study of a treatment manual covering the two topics. Participants were assessed posttraining and at 90-day follow-up for self-reported satisfaction in the training, self-efficacy in implementing the two DBT strategies, motivation to learn the strategies, and use of the strategies. In addition, participants were assessed on knowledge of these skills and, using role play, clinical proficiency in conducting a chain analysis while incorporating validation. Results indicated that the instructor-led training produced significantly higher ratings in satisfaction, self-efficacy, and motivation compared to the other training approaches. However, the online training was the most effective in increasing knowledge. In all conditions, participants' self-reported use of the strategies and observer-rated proficiency in demonstrating the strategies improved over time, but no differences were found across conditions. With respect to proficiency, on average, participants in each group achieved "moderate" proficiency, both at posttraining and at follow-up, in demonstrating the two strategies of chain analysis and validation as determined by ratings on a coding instrument derived from the relevant items on the gold standard, University of Washington Adherence Scale (DBT-ACS; Linehan & Korslund, 2003).

Graduate student trainees

A few studies have investigated approaches to training graduate students in DBT. Lungu, Gonzalez, and Linehan (2012) offered guidelines for doing so based on the training procedures employed in Dr. Linehan's training clinic at the University of Washington. Linehan advises that training compromises three components: (1) seminar coursework that covers behavioral theory and assessment, suicide assessment and intervention, and DBT-specific content; (2) a clinical practicum that includes treating multiple clients with individual DBT, coleading/leading skills training groups, reviewing tape of expert DBT clinicians and identifying DBT strategies, participation in a weekly consultation team, and weekly supervision; and (3) opportunities for teaching DBT in the mental health community. Surveying former students who had participated or current students who were participating in Linehan's clinical practicum, Lungu et al. (2012) found that students evaluated DBT training more favorably than other clinical trainings in preparing them to treat and conduct research with suicidal clients.

Rizvi, Hughes, Hittman, and Oliveira (2017) examined whether students in a training clinic, modeled after Linehan's training clinic, can achieve "good" outcomes in providing DBT. The trainees were doctoral students in their second year or higher of training who had completed a one semester course in the fundamentals of DBT and who were participating in a DBT clinical practicum for a duration of 1–2 years, which included weekly didactics in advanced DBT topics, weekly consultation team, and weekly supervision (from Dr. Rizvi). In addition, 10 out of the 15 student therapists also attended a 10-day DBT-IT training. Adult clients diagnosed with BPD ($n = 50$) participated in 6 months of DBT at the university-based training clinic and completed several measures of psychopathology. Although no control group was utilized, a benchmark approach was employed in which results were compared to those from an RCT of DBT (McMain et al., 2009). Rizvi et al. observed no suicides during the study and found significant reduction in both suicide attempts and NSSI and across all measures of psychopathology domains, as well as significant increases in skills use. More notably, effect sizes were equivalent to those found in McMain et al. (2009) with respect to all comparable measures (BPD symptoms severity, global psychopathology, and depression severity). Although no measures of therapist adherence or competence were measured to assure DBT was being faithfully and skillfully delivered in-session, the study at minimum suggests that graduate students in DBT can have positive outcomes in treatment. It is notable that such clinical progress was made within an abbreviated 6-month timeframe, as compared to the standard 1-year treatment course often delivered for adults in full model DBT.

With regard to method of training, this study is unable to speak to the relative impact of graduate school training versus DBT-IT.

In another study, Rizvi et al., (2016) investigated a particular approach to DBT supervision using a case study methodology. They were especially interested in how to train graduate students to adhere in delivering the treatment. The specific supervision method utilized was the "bug-in-the-eye" (BITE) approach. In contrast to the more familiar, "bug-in-the-ear" technique for live supervision, which provides real-time feedback through an auditory device placed in the trainee's ear, the BITE approach provides visual feedback on a computer screen. The supervisor provides real-time input by typing suggestions and/or feedback, which then appears on a computer screen in the therapy room, visible only to the student therapist.[1] A key advantage of the BITE approach, like other forms of live supervision, includes that the supervisor gets to make real-time observations and provide real-time coaching and evaluation, thus overcoming some of the limitations inherent to supervision that relies (1) solely on the verbal report of the supervisee or (2) on delayed review and discussion of video recorded sessions. In one previous study utilizing BITE for supervising eight psychiatry residents during a 1-year rotation in DBT (Carmel, Villatte, Rosenthal, Chalker, & Comtois, 2016), trainees assigned to BITE supervision obtained significantly higher scores on a DBT case conceptualization assignment than those assigned to supervision as usual. Moreover, the BITE condition trended toward higher scores on an exam measuring DBT knowledge.[2]

In the study by Rizvi et al. (2016) a third-year clinical psychology doctoral student provided 6 months of weekly individual DBT sessions to a female client that met criteria for BPD and who was concurrently participating in DBT skills group. The student was a novice therapist

1 In our own DBT practicum for doctoral psychology students, we use a variation of the BITE procedure that relies on texting such that the suggestions/feedback appear on a cell phone, visible only to student trainee. Sessions are observed live via a HIPAA compliant streaming software, Doxy. Anecdotally, we have found the BITE approach to result in a more active, behaviorally specific supervisory style, and trainees have largely welcomed the real-time feedback that can "shape" the session fluidly and dynamically. Of the five client-trainee dyads in our current 2018–19 cohort, no client has commented unfavorably about the phone-based in-vivo supervision. Supervisors have also taken steps to engage directly with the clients (and their families) as indicated, and this has enhanced client-supervisor rapport and facilitated continuity of care when a trainee is out of town and require a back-up therapist for coaching or treatment.

2 The lack of significance may have been due to the lower power of the study, which consisted of eight participants assigned to BITE supervision and four assigned to supervision as usual.

who had completed one graduate course in the fundamentals of DBT, attended a 2-week DBT intensive training, and completed treatment with one prior DBT case. DBT adherence was assessed using the DBT-ACS (Linehan & Korslund, 2003) by an independent rater, the same method of evaluating adherence used in most RCTs of DBT to date. Therapist adherence was assessed from sessions 8 to 21, and BITE supervision was implemented in sessions 12–17. Results revealed that the BITE approach to supervision was evaluated as acceptable to both the student therapist and the client, and both rated the therapy as more effective because of using BITE ("strongly agree" and "somewhat agree" for the therapist and client, respectively). In addition, neither the therapist nor the client rated the BITE approach as having a negative effect upon the therapeutic relationship. Regarding adherence, prior to implementing BITE, the therapist achieved adherence on only 1 out of the 4 sessions; whereas after implementing BITE, the therapist reached adherence on all but one of the 10 adherence assessments. In fact, after achieving adherence in session 14 (third BITE session), the therapist remained adherent for the remainder of the sessions, including the final four sessions (18–21), for which the BITE procedure was no longer used. While the generalizability of such findings is limited by the single subject design, such findings on the potential impact of live supervisory methods on adherence ratings offer promise for the effectiveness of real-time feedback in DBT supervision.

Summary of DBT training findings

A number of conclusions may be drawn from the small, albeit growing, literature on the effectiveness of different approaches to training in DBT. First, regarding the DBT-IT approach, this training model has produced moderate to high rates of adoption of all four modes of DBT (DiGiorgio et al., 2010; Ditty et al., 2015; Navarro-Haro et al., 2019; Swales et al., 2012) and has been found to improve the attitudes of clinicians toward clients who meet criteria for BPD (Herschell et al., 2014), to enhance clinician's confidence in the treatment (Herschell et al., 2014), and to increase use of DBT components in their practice (DiGiorgio et al., 2010; Herschell et al., 2014). Furthermore, there is some evidence that the DBT-IT approach has led to improved performance on tests of DBT knowledge (Hawkins & Sinha, 1998); however, this finding was confounded by other forms of training (e.g., self-study, reading groups, and consultation). Regarding client outcomes, preliminary findings suggested that clinician participation in DBT-IT training leads to better client outcomes than less intensive forms of training (Pasieczny & Connor, 2011). Further research is needed on the correlation between DBT-IT (and equivalent trainings) and clinician adherence and competence, especially given the cost and time investment in such trainings.

Dimeff et al. (2009, 2011, 2015) at Behavioral Tech isolated specific (non-DBT-IT) training approaches using RCT methodology to evaluate clinician outcomes for learning subsets of DBT strategies. They found that active forms of training (instructor-led and computer-based) were preferred over self-study, with some evidence that instructor-led training was preferred over computer training. However, all three forms of training (instructor-led, computer-based, and self-study) led to improvement in DBT knowledge, with online training tending to produce the greatest improvement. Similarly, each of these three training approaches led to improvement in clinicians' demonstration of teaching DBT skills in role-play tasks. Thus these studies offer little guidance regarding which approach to training is optimal. Moreover, participating in just one training was inadequate to produce highly skilled use of particular DBT strategies; performance ratings reached only "minimal" to "moderate" levels of DBT competence.

A third line of research reviewed involved training graduate students. In one study (Rizvi et al., 2017), graduate students receiving one course in DBT and DBT-IT were able to produce client outcomes equivalent to those reported in an RCT of DBT for BPD. *A limitation of this work was the absence of any assessment of the quality of DBT being delivered.* Furthermore, some evidence indicated that a particular form of supervision (BITE) may be especially useful in coaching up DBT trainees (Carmel et al., 2016; Rizvi et al., 2016).

Clarifying terminology: adherence, program fidelity, and certification

There are many terms used in the DBT community, and in the broader world of psychotherapy research that attempt to capture quality of the therapy being conducting including adherence, competence, fidelity, and certification. In this section, we will provide a broad overview of these concepts and summarize the relevant data on adherence and competence in the context of general evidence-based psychotherapy outcomes. Next, we will take steps to clarify these terms as they relate to DBT practice and training and highlight nascent research on the relationship between adherence and clinical outcomes in treatment more broadly, as well as in DBT specifically. Lastly, we discuss the process of certification in DBT.

Adherence in psychotherapy research

In the general psychotherapy literature, adherence is described as "the extent to which a therapist used interventions and approaches prescribed by the treatment manual and avoided the use of procedures proscribed by the manual" (Waltz, Addis, Koerner, & Jacobson, 1993, p. 620). Adherence is measured based on an individual session with a specific client and determines whether the therapist engaged in interventions and strategies that are consistent with the treatment manual in that session. Adherence is not an objective trait of the therapist but reflects whether the therapist has delivered the treatment during that session. High adherence has been linked to more successful patient outcomes in a number of treatments, including multisystemic therapy (Henggeler, Schoenwald, Borduin, Rowland, & Cunningham, 1998), assertive community treatment (Test & Stein, 1976; Test, 1992), and trauma-focused cognitive behavioral therapy (Cohen et al., 2016, as cited in McHugh & Barlow, 2012).

Adherence and outcomes in DBT

To date, there is limited data regarding adherence and outcomes in DBT specifically. In a recent review by Miga, Neacsiu, Lungu, Heard, and Dimeff (2019), out of a total of 31 distinct research trials (from 1993 to 2015) evaluating DBT for a range of problems, only 16 studies (~50%) reported the use of adherence monitoring of any kind. When comparing studies of comprehensive DBT that rated adherence of therapists ($n = 10$) to those that did not measure adherence ($n = 9$), there were no differences found in how DBT performed relative to the comparison treatment. There is some evidence, based on one study (Linehan et al.,1999), that adherence to DBT produces better outcomes in a sample of seven clients seeking treatment for BPD and substance-use dependence. This study found that patients ($n = 4$) with therapists that consistently demonstrated DBT adherence reported significantly better substance use outcomes compared to patients ($n = 3$) with therapists that did not achieve consistent DBT adherence.

Program fidelity

Program fidelity, on the other hand, refers to "the extent to which the various components of a given model are implemented" (Gaglia, 2019). Providing a treatment with program fidelity requires implementing specific treatment interventions with specific populations based on the research for that population. Broadly, lower fidelity has been linked to poorer program performance and reduced treatment effects compared to high-fidelity programs (Henggeler, Melton, Brondino, Scherer, &

Hanley, 1997; McHugo, Drake, Teague, & Xie, 1999). In DBT, program fidelity includes whether the modes of treatment (individual therapy, skills group, therapist consultation team, and availability of between-session phone coaching for skills generalization) are provided in a way consistent with the research for that client population. Are we delivering the modes of DBT in a manner consistent with what has been delivered in the research for this population? Or, simply, are we doing the evidence-based treatment? Given the variety of methods through which DBT can be delivered (i.e., standard DBT and DBT skills training only), this requires DBT providers to not only maintain an ongoing awareness of the evolving evidence-base but also clearly describe the modes of DBT being delivered in their practice to potential consumers.

Adherence monitoring in DBT

Formal DBT adherence, as endorsed by the treatment developer, is assessed by trained adherence coders using an empirically validated instrument (DBT-ACS) that has 66 items, 12 subscales, and a global adherence scale for the individual therapy and skills training modes of interventions in standard DBT. Each item is a behaviorally defined and operationalized DBT strategy linked to the adherence manual (Linehan & Korslund, 2003) and follows an "if–then" algorithm, which takes into account whether a particular strategy is necessary, and sufficient given the context of the treatment session and the necessary strategies outlined in the DBT-treatment manual. Clinicians are rated across 12 subscales, including but not limited to, structural strategies (how does one organize the session based on target hierarchy), problem assessment (defining the problem and clarifying goals), and problem-solving (didactics, solution generation, and dragging out new behavior). Acceptance-based subscales include validation strategies, and reciprocal communication strategies. Clinicians are also rated on exposure-based procedures, cognitive strategies, contingency management, irreverent strategies, and the use of dialectical strategies.

Scores range from 0 to 5.0, with an adherence threshold score of 4.0 and above indicating an adherent session. The process of adherence coding and adherence training is currently overseen by the University of Washington, where coders can receive training as well as resources to achieve interrater reliability with a gold standard. The DBT adherence measure has undergone several iterations (see Linehan, Armstrong, Suarez, Allmon, & Heard, 1991; Linehan, Lockard, Wagner, & Tutek, 1996) and was finalized in 2003 as the University of Washington Adherence Scale (DBT-ACS: Linehan & Korslund, 2003). Formal adherence ratings are typically utilized for several chief purposes:

(1) to assess % of adherent sessions in a research study evaluating DBT versus alternative treatment (2) for training new clinicians in DBT in the context of RCTs (3) to determine (along with other metrics) whether clinicians meet criteria for DBT-LBC certification (https://dbt-lbc.org).

A dialectical stance on adherence and training: merits and misunderstandings

Situational versus dispositional

Formal adherence ratings are derived by a calibrated DBT adherence coder reviewing a work sample (e.g., video) of an individual therapy session between a DBT provider and client, or DBT skills group. A coder generates a global adherence score (out of 5) utilizing a computer-generated algorithm that incorporates each subscore rating, across 12 subcategories of DBT (e.g. validation strategies, dialectical strategies, and problem-solving). Because adherence coding is conducted at the individual session (single event) level, *scores may and do naturally fluctuate across sessions and clients.* In addition, therapist can be below adherence on particular subscales while still being adherent in other subscales. While adherence assessment is *not dispositional* or an attribute that a single-person can acquire or obtain, it is best understood as a metric captured at a single point in time (i.e., one session). Such a metric offers valuable information about whether the DBT provider is "doing the treatment they claim to be delivering" at a single time point.

Synthesis

While adherence metrics offer us data on treatment delivery at one point in time, when collected over various time points, a consistent pattern of adherent scores offer us valuable information about the degree to which the provider is "sticking to the model" in delivering DBT. This information can then help consumers discern providers who are more likely to provide DBT "to model" versus those that do not/have not been formally assessed.

Judgments versus behaviorally specific

DBT clinicians are becoming more universally cognizant of concepts such as adherence and program fidelity, which affords both clear advantages and risks to clinicians and consumers. When reviewing posts on the DBT-Listserv (https://www.pdbti.org/dbt-l/), a popular mechanism by which clinicians exchange information and seek and provide referrals, the term "adherence" appears commonly misused amongst clinicians in several ways: (1) as an apparent proxy for the positive judgment "I like them" or "I respect them" or "well trained" and (2) as a label for a program that is comprehensive (i.e., delivers the 4 modes of DBT). It is harmful to clinical forums and consumers when labels are misused when marketing oneself or peers. Clinicians and programs are then (intentionally or unintentionally) misrepresented, consumers may be misled about the rigor of a clinicians DBT background and practice, and the meaning of "adherent" and "to fidelity" become diluted and confused. To be clear the DBT-Listserv has many valuable benefits to the community, and most clinicians and programs are accurate about use of such terms, and yet many clinicians are still using the terms loosely and inaccurately.

Synthesis

The tension between evaluative judgments versus behavioral self-descriptions can be synthesized through marketing that describes what is accurate, observable, and relevant to one's training background and current standing [e.g., intensively trained or foundational/core-clinical training (10 vs 5 days); DBT Certified Clinician, DBT Trainer for X organization] and avoid statements referring to "adherence" or "competence" without further clarity provided, as these terms often fail to accurately represent a provider or treatment program. We encourage clinicians and consumers to continue to consult online search engines included but not limited to behavioraltech.org and dbt-lbc.org who provide a "real-time" list of programs with Level 3 (intensive or foundational) training and certified providers and programs, respectively. A further consideration would be for the Listserv oversight body to provide clear parameters for posts; however, we recognize that it may be an additional burden on a largely volunteer-based DBT community.

Proprietary versus pragmatics

While formal adherence monitoring is a needed, core metric for evaluating clinical delivery in DBT, the DBT-ACS is proprietary and only accessible to a limited number of trained adherence coders internationally trained for the purpose of ongoing adherence monitoring via a research study or external funding. Formal adherence coding is an invaluable tool and has provided much needed feedback to both seasoned and novice DBT clinicians, over the past 25 years. Yet, demand for adherence coding far outweighs supply and is expensive and time-consuming to administer. Furthermore, adherence results do not automatically lead to increased "practice to improve" opportunities on team nor provide a clear *roadmap* by which to improve. We would argue that there is a dire need for other monitoring tools and practices to supplement the ACS that are more broadly used, accessible and feasible for the evaluator and clinician alike.

Synthesis

Increasing accountability to multimodal work samples (e.g., video demonstration and evaluation, monthly presentation on clinical team, internal CE training, case conceptualization work groups), in addition to a more flexible and clinically useful self or peer-administered adherence tool that providers and programs can readily administer.

Practical suggestions for ongoing assessment of adherence and competence

Given that the DBT-ACS is not broadly available for therapists and programs to use to assess their adherence and the lack of any available measure for the assessment of competence in DBT, it is useful to consider other options for monitoring whether therapists are administering DBT session that would be considered adherent. There is one measure known to us that has been specifically developed for this purpose and is freely available via the DBT therapist wiki (https://www.practiceground.org/dbt-therapist-wiki/): the DBT Therapist Rating and Feedback Form, developed by Fruzzetti (2010, 2011, 2012). The form includes 63 items that are each rated on a 6-point scale (1 = very effective, 2 = effective, 3 = mixed, 4 = ineffective, 5 = very ineffective, 6 = not needed and not delivered). This form attempts to capture both adherence (doing what is prescribed) and competence of delivering DBT. The form contains seven sections, namely, session structure, acceptance strategies, change strategies, dialectical strategies, in-session behavior management, mindfulness, and items for if a crisis emerges in the session or the session occurs in the middle of a client crisis. To our knowledge, there is no data evaluating the validity or reliability of this measure, although it has been used to measure adherence to DBT in at least one published study (Andreasson et al., 2016).

There are a variety of ways this measure has and can be used in real-world clinical settings. Koerner (2016) has recommended the use of this measure for supervision/consultation, to obtain a trainee self-assessment of average capabilities and skills to strengthen, at the start of consultation and/or paired with video review of one's performance. This measure could be a helpful way to structure team feedback of therapist behavior while reviewing video or audio recordings during team meetings: either determined by therapist's training needs or selecting an adherence-derived "topic of the week" that the team systematically rotates through with the aid of video samples or role play.

Alternatively, some teams use the tables from the original DBT text (Linehan, 1993a,b) and the levels of validation described in a later chapter (Linehan, 1997) to approximate the official adherence coding system and to provide feedback to therapists when formal coding is not available to the program. Linehan (1993a,b) includes 35 checklists of prescribed therapist behaviors (DBT strategies and interventions) and proscribed behaviors ("anti-DBT" therapist behaviors) in Chapters 7–15. It is likely not feasible to review every checklist for every session shared by a therapist, nor is it necessary (some checklists are only relevant for particular clinical situations, not every DBT session); however, focusing on 1–3 checklists, based on the therapist's consult need, while reviewing a session recording could help increase the specificity of feedback provided to the therapist and improve the adherence of team members, as well as deepen the training of new DBT therapists.

Developing validated and practical adherence and competence measures for real-world DBT programs is an important area for future development. We recognize that several DBT experts and researchers (Harned et al., Batcheler) are currently exploring ways to validate and disseminate a more feasible adherence tool. Above all, it is important for teams to find a system for *ongoing* assessment and feedback of all therapists on the team, even the most senior therapists, based on *actual work samples*, in order to avoid drift and to continue the work of sharpening therapist skills and competence in this complex treatment.

Options for certification in DBT

There are several advantages to certification in DBT, particularly the certification that requires skills to be demonstrated and evaluated objectively. Such certification encourages therapists to get training and supervision necessary to conduct treatments skillfully. It also provides consumers of DBT with an important data point to make informed choices about providers or programs. Further, it will likely serve to ensure quality in the dissemination of DBT going forward. While there has been some preliminary support for the use of positive DBT outcome data as an effective lobbying agent for increased insurance reimbursement (Koons, O'Rourke, Carter, & Erhardt, 2013), DBT certification may also play a key role in future lobbying with insurance companies.

At the time of this writing the authors were aware of two pathways to certification in DBT. One method of certification is through the Dialectical Behavior Therapy Linehan Board of Certification (DBT-Linehan Board of Certification, n.d.; see https://dbt-lbc.org/), a nonprofit organization founded by Dr. Marsha Linehan, the treatment developer. The other is through the Dialectical Behavior Therapy National Certification and Accreditation Association (DBTNCAA; https://www.evgci.com/), also a nonprofit organization. The DBT-LBC and DBTNCAA are not affiliated with one another. As a point of clarification, it is customary for organizations to provide a certificate of completion following participation in an online or in-person training, which often earns a provider continuing education credits. However, these are differentiated from certification in which the certificates provided by these training companies attest only to didactic training having been completed, while DBT certification (per DBT-LBC) also involves assessment of understanding of the intervention and demonstration of competence in treatment delivery and case conceptualization. It should be noted that two of the authors (Miga and Michonski) have been involved as volunteers in DBT-LBC certification efforts, and therefore we recognize that our involvement lends itself to potential bias.

The DBT-LBC certifies both individual providers and treatment programs. The process of becoming certified at the individual level through DBT-LBC involves a number of steps, which are costly, and may be burdensome for many clinicians. The first step is an online application that attests to a number of requirements, including having obtained a graduate degree from an accredited institution in a mental health-related field, a current independent and unrestricted license as a mental health practitioner, documentation of at least 40 hours of didactic training in DBT, evidence of clinical experience delivering DBT as shown by summarizing three completed Stage I DBT clients, current DBT consultation team participation, as well as a history of team participation of 1 year or longer. In addition, the applicant is required to attest to having read the main DBT text and DBT Skills Training Manual (Linehan, 1993a,b, 2015) and completed all of the homework assignments therein, as well as having taught or been a student in a group in each of the four modules of skills. Completion of mindfulness training and an ongoing mindfulness practice are both required. The DBT Consult Team Leader is required to submit a letter of recommendation on the applicant's behalf.

Once this initial application is approved, the applicant is authorized to sit for an exam based on the DBT-treatment manual; Cognitive-Behavioral Treatment of Borderline Personality Disorder (Linehan, 1993a,b); and Linehan's chapter, Validation and Psychotherapy (Linehan, 1997). The exam is offered at several times throughout the year at testing centers. Upon passing this exam the next step is to submit a detailed case conceptualization of a current DBT client. The conceptualization is required to be in a specific format and is scored by DBT experts using an objective measure. Once this portion is passed, the applicant is approved to submit three consecutive videos of the same client. Of the three tapes, at least one must meet criteria for adherence to DBT using the DBT-ACS (Linehan & Korslund, 2003). Once applicants have successfully passed each of these requirements, they are granted a time-limited credential. Maintenance of the credential requires again demonstrating competence. There are associated application fees throughout the process, an exam fee paid to the testing center, and an annual fee to maintain certification. Scholarships may be available. For more information, see: dbt-lbc.org.

Certification through the DBTNCAA is a less burdensome process. The applicant is required to document being a mental health practitioner with at least a Master's degree and have a current license in good standing with the licensing board and to not have been denied application or renewal of membership in any professional organization or have had professional privileges restricted in any way for malpractice within the past 5 years. The applicant must have completed at least 18 hours of DBT training, six of which are specific to Skills Training; 3 hours of suicide risk assessment and intervention. The applicant must attest to having read at least two books on the practice of DBT as a theoretical orientation, and at least two DBT skills training manuals, as well as the American Psychological Association (APA) policy on the Evidence Based Practice of Psychology (Levant & Hasan, 2008). The applicant must attest to having completed at least 500 therapy hours using DBT as a theoretical orientation and using clinical outcome evaluation procedures to monitor and adjust therapy in a way that is consistent with the APA policy on evidence-based practice. The certification is conferred by Therapy Evergreen Certification Institute (https://www.evgci.com/) and lasts for 2 years. There is a fee associated with the application.

Our team at The Seattle Clinic may serve as an example of a synthesis in the adoption of certification. One of the chief dialectics that we honor as a clinic is the ongoing tension between autonomy and professional and personal affiliation and connection. Each DBT clinician at The Seattle Clinic is an independent entity, maintaining his or her own practice while working collaboratively under the same shared mission and within a single DBT team. We have opted not to pursue program certification and have opted to require each nontrainee member to either be individually certified upon joining our team or to commit to pursuing individual certification (in order to uphold the high clinical standard that we strive to maintain).

Recommendations and future directions

Dialectical behavior therapy is a complex treatment to deliver and teach. We owe immense gratitude to the tireless community of clinicians and researchers that deliver and study the treatment and to the trainers and implementation scientists who teach the treatment and help clinicians deliver it with fidelity in a variety of settings. While DBT has demonstrated efficacy for treating a wide variety of problems, most notably suicidal and self-injurious behaviors (National Register for Evidence-based Programs & Practices, 2006), there are considerable gaps in the literature on how factors such as quantity and type of DBT training correlate with clinical outcomes. Much more research is needed on the interplay between therapist adherence, background training, and clinical outcomes. Further, we would argue that in many real-world settings, less effort and emphasis has been put into finding ways to incorporate ongoing training, monitoring, and real-time supervision into one's program. This is understandable due to time, monetary, and resource obstacles. In this chapter, we have suggested some pragmatic options for increasing monitoring in feasible ways that help clinicians achieve and maintain competence (pre/post self and supervisor administered DBT adherence rating forms, protected time on team to share work samples guided by feedback forms or checklists). These steps do indeed involve some forethought but are likely to be less burdensome than one might assume.

Lastly, we have clarified terms such as adherence and program fidelity, and raised concerns about the incorrect use of such terms. We encourage DBT providers to use care and specificity when marketing one's training and expertise, in order to present oneself and others with accuracy. DBT certification offers one clear "marker" of both background training and observable treatment delivery. For those not seeking certification as a goal, returning to identifying one's training experience is important when marketing. In taking more intentional and systematic steps when describing our own expertise at the individual and program level, we help our community of clients seeking DBT services become more empowered to make wise-minded choices for treatment.

References

Andreasson, K., Krogh, J., Wenneberg, C., Jessen, H. K., Krakauer, K., Gluud, C., ... Nordentoft, M. (2016). Effectiveness of dialectical behavior therapy versus collaborative assessment and management of suicidality treatment for reduction of self-harm in adults with borderline personality traits and disorder—A randomized observer-blinded clinical trial. *Depression and Anxiety*, *33*(6), 520–530.

Behavioral Tech. (n.d.). *DBT clinical resource directory*. Retrieved from <https://behavioraltech.org/resources/find-a-therapist/>.

Carmel, A., Villatte, J. L., Rosenthal, M. Z., Chalker, S., & Comtois, K. A. (2016). Applying technological approaches to clinical supervision in dialectical behavior therapy: A randomized feasibility trial of the bug-in-the-eye (BITE) model. *Cognitive and Behavioral Practice*, *23*(2), 221–229.

Cohen, J. A., Mannarino, A. P., & Deblinger, E. (2016). *Treating trauma and traumatic grief in children and adolescents*. Guilford Publications.

DBT-Linehan Board of Certification. (n.d). Retrieved from <https://dbt-lbc.org/>.

DiGiorgio, K. E., Glass, C. R., & Arnkoff, D. B. (2010). Therapists use of DBT: A survey study of clinical practice. *Cognitive and Behavioral Practice, 17*(2), 213–221.

Dimeff, L. A., Harned, M. S., Woodcock, E. A., Skutch, J. M., Koerner, K., & Linehan, M. M. (2015). Investigating bang for your training buck: A randomized controlled trial comparing three methods of training clinicians in two core strategies of dialectical behavior therapy. *Behavior Therapy, 46*(3), 283–295.

Dimeff, L. A., Koerner, K., Woodcock, E. A., Beadnell, B., Brown, M. Z., Skutch, J. M., & Harned, M. S. (2009). Which training method works best? A randomized controlled trial comparing three methods of training clinicians in dialectical behavior therapy skills. *Behaviour Research and Therapy, 47*(11), 921–930.

Dimeff, L. A., Woodcock, E. A., Harned, M. S., & Beadnell, B. (2011). Can dialectical behavior therapy be learned in highly structured learning environments? Results from a randomized controlled dissemination trial. *Behavior Therapy, 42*(2), 263–275.

Ditty, M. S., Landes, S. J., Doyle, A., & Beidas, R. S. (2015). It takes a village: A mixed method analysis of inner setting variables and dialectical behavior therapy implementation. *Administration and Policy in Mental Health and Mental Health Services Research, 42* (6), 672–681.

Fruzzetti, A. E. (2012). *DBT therapist rating and feedback form*. Unpublished.

Gaglia, A. (2019). Shaping therapists towards adherence: A how-to guide. In M. A. Swales (Ed.), *The Oxford handbook of dialectical behaviour therapy* (pp. 981–1002). Oxford University Press.

Hawkins, K. A., & Sinha, R. (1998). Can line clinicians master the conceptual complexities of dialectical behavior therapy? An evaluation of a State Department of Mental Health training program. *Journal of Psychiatric Research, 32*(6), 379–384.

Henggeler, S. W., Melton, G. B., Brondino, M. J., Scherer, D. G., & Hanley, J. H. (1997). Multisystemic therapy with violent and chronic juvenile offenders and their families: The role of treatment fidelity in successful dissemination. *Journal of Consulting and Clinical Psychology, 65*(5), 821–833.

Henggeler, S. W., Schoenwald, S. K., Borduin, C. M., Rowland, M. D., & Cunningham, P. B. (1998). *Multisystemic treatment of antisocial behavior in children and adolescents*. New York: Guilford Press.

Herschell, A. D., Lindhiem, O. J., Kogan, J. N., Celedonia, K. L., & Stein, B. D. (2014). Evaluation of an implementation initiative for embedding dialectical behavior therapy in community settings. *Evaluation and Program Planning, 43*(2), 55–63.

Koerner, K. (2016). *Evidence-based essentials of clinical supervision for the DBT supervisor*. <https://www.practiceground.org/koerner-dbt-supervision>.

Koons, C. R., O'Rourke, B., Carter, B., & Erhardt, E. B. (2013). Negotiating for improved reimbursement for dialectical behavior therapy: A successful project. *Cognitive and Behavioral Practice, 20*(3), 314–324.

Landes, S. J., & Linehan, M. M. (2012). Dissemination of dialectical behavior therapy: An intensive training model. In D. H. Barlow, & R. K. McHugh (Eds.), *Dissemination and implementation of evidence-based psychological interventions*. New York: Oxford University Press.

Levant, R. F., & Hasan, N. T. (2008). Evidence-based practice in psychology. *Professional Psychology: Research and Practice, 39*(6), 658.

Linehan, M. M. (1993a). *Cognitive-behavioral treatment of borderline personality disorder*. New York: Guilford Press.

Linehan, M. M. (1993b). *Skills training manual for treating borderline personality disorder*. New York: Guilford Press.

Linehan, M. M. (1997). Validation and psychotherapy. In A. C. Bohart, & L. S. Greenberg (Eds.), *Empathy reconsidered: New directions in psychotherapy* (pp. 353–392). Washington, DC, US: American Psychological Association.

Linehan, M. M. (2015). *DBT® skills training manual*. New York: Guilford Press.

Linehan, M. M., Armstrong, H. E., Suarez, A., Allmon, D., & Heard, H. L. (1991). Cognitive behavioral treatment of chronically suicidal borderline patients. *Archives of General Psychiatry, 48*, 1060–1064.

Linehan, M. M., & Korslund, K. E. (2003). *University of Washington Adherence Scale*. Unpublished manuscript, University of Washington, Seattle.

Linehan, M. M., Lockard, J. S., Wagner, A. W., & Tutek, D. (1996). *DBT expert rating scale*. Unpublished manuscript, University of Washington, Seattle, WA.

Linehan, M. M., Schmidt, H., III, Dimeff, L. A., Craft, J. C., Kanter, J., & Comtois, K. A. (1999). Dialectical behavior therapy for patients with borderline personality disorder and drug-dependence. *The American Journal on Addictions, 8*(4), 279–292.

Lungu, A., Gonzalez, M. R., & Linehan, M. M. (2012). Implementing a dialectical behavior therapy training program for graduate students. *The Behavior Therapist, 35*(1), 4–11.

McHugh, R. K., & Barlow, D. H. (Eds.), (2012). *Dissemination and implementation of evidence-based psychological interventions*. Oxford University Press.

McHugo, G. J., Drake, R. E., Teague, G. B., & Xie, H. (1999). Fidelity to assertive community treatment and client outcomes in the New Hampshire dual disorders study. *Psychiatric Services, 50*(6), 818–824.

McMain, S. F., Links, P. S., Gnam, W. H., Guimond, T., Cardish, R. J., Korman, L., & Streiner, D. L. (2009). A randomized trial of dialectical behavior therapy versus general psychiatric management for borderline personality disorder. *American Journal of Psychiatry, 166*, 1365–1374.

Miga, E. M., Neacsiu, A. D., Lungu, A., Heard, H. L., & Dimeff, L. A. (2019). Dialectical behaviour therapy from 1991-2015: What do we know about clinical efficacy and research quality? In M. A. Swales (Ed.), *The Oxford handbook of dialectical behaviour therapy* (pp. 415–465). Oxford University Press.

National Register for Evidence-based Programs and Practices. (2006). Retrieved from <nrepp.samsha.gov>.

Navarro-Haro, M. V., Harned, M. S., Korslund, K. E., DuBose, A., Chen, T., Ivanoff, A., & Linehan, M. M. (2019). Predictors of Adoption and Reach Following Dialectical Behavior Therapy Intensive Training™. *Community Mental Health Journal, 55*(1), 100–111.

Pasieczny, N., & Connor, J. (2011). The effectiveness of dialectical behaviour therapy in routine public mental health settings: An Australian controlled trial. *Behaviour Research and Therapy, 49*(1), 4–10.

Rizvi, S. L., Hughes, C. D., Hittman, A. D., & Oliveira, P. V. (2017). Can trainees effectively deliver dialectical behavior therapy for individuals with borderline personality disorder? Outcomes from a training clinic. *Journal of Clinical Psychology, 73*(12), 1599–1611.

Rizvi, S. L., Yu, J., Geisser, S., & Finnegan, D. (2016). The use of "bug-in-the-eye" live supervision for training in dialectical behavior therapy: A case study. *Clinical Case Studies, 15*(3), 243–258.

Swales, M. A., Taylor, B., & Hibbs, R. A. (2012). Implementing dialectical behaviour therapy: Programme survival in routine healthcare settings. *Journal of Mental Health, 21*, 548–555.

Test, M. A. (1992). Training in community living. *Handbook of Psychiatric Rehabilitation, 166*, 153–170.

Test, M. A., & Stein, L. I. (1976). Practical guidelines for the community treatment of markedly impaired patients. *Community Mental Health Journal, 12*(1), 72–82.

Trupin, E. W., Stewart, D. G., Beach, B., & Boesky, L. (2002). Effectiveness of dialectical behaviour therapy program for incarcerated female juvenile offenders. *Child and Adolescent Mental Health, 7*(3), 121–127.

Waltz, J., Addis, M. E., Koerner, K., & Jacobson, N. S. (1993). Testing the integrity of a psychotherapy protocol: Assessment of adherence and competence. *Journal of Consulting and Clinical Psychology, 61*(4), 620–630.

Further reading

Barber, J. P., Sharpless, B. A., Klostermann, S., & McCarthy, K. S. (2007). Assessing intervention competence and its relation to therapy outcome: A selected review derived from the outcome literature. *Professional Psychology: Research and Practice*, *38*(5), 493–500.

Koerner, K. (2013). What must you know and do to get good outcomes with DBT? *Behavior Therapy*, *44*(4), 568–579.

Webb, C. A., DeRubeis, R. J., & Barber, J. P. (2010). Therapist adherence/competence and treatment outcome: A meta-analytic review. *Journal of Consulting and Clinical Psychology*, *78*(2), 200–211.

Further reading

SECTION II

Clinical populations

CHAPTER

5

Efficacy of dialectical behavior therapy in the treatment of suicidal behavior

Christopher R. DeCou and Adam Carmel

Department of Psychiatry and Behavioral Sciences, University of Washington at Harborview Medical Center, Seattle, WA, United States

Borderline personality disorder (BPD) is a psychiatric disorder with a prevalence of approximately 1%–2% in the general population. (Lieb, Zanarini, Schmahl, Linehan, & Bohus, 2004; Trull, Jahng, Tomko, Wood, & Sher, 2010). Patients with BPD are associated with high utilization of psychiatric services, accounting for approximately 15% – 20% of psychiatric hospital and clinic admissions (Korzekwa, Dell, Links, Thabane, & Webb, 2008; Zimmerman, Chelminski, & Young, 2008), 10% – 15% of emergency room visits (Chaput & Lebel, 2007; Tomko, Trull, Wood, & Sher, 2014), 6% of primary care visits (Gross et al., 2002), 10%–22% of psychiatric outpatients, and 20% of psychiatric inpatients (Korzekwa et al., 2008; Torgersen, Kringlen, & Cramer, 2001). Thus BPD represents a disproportionate burden on psychiatric crisis services relative to the prevalence of BPD in the population.

BPD is marked by durable patterns of impulsivity and behavioral dyscontrol, including suicidal and self-injurious behaviors. Patients with BPD demonstrate high rates of chronic nonsuicidal self-injury (NSSI) and suicide attempts, consistent with these behaviors as a defined criterion of the disorder within DSM-5 (American Psychiatric Association, American Psychiatric Association, & DSM-5 Task Force, 2013; Pompili, Girardi, Ruberto, & Tatarelli, 2005). Rates of NSSI among individuals with BPD range from 69% to 80% (Clarkin, Widiger,

The Handbook of Dialectical Behavior Therapy
DOI: https://doi.org/10.1016/B978-0-12-816384-9.00005-1

Frances, Hurt, & Gilmore, 1983; Cowdry, Pickar, & Davies, 1985; Frances, Fyer, & Clarkin, 1986). The rate of death by suicide is 5%–10% among people with BPD, and twice that among people with BPD and a previous history of self-directed violence (Frances et al., 1986; Linehan, Rizvi, Welch, & Page, 2000; Stone, 1993). These high rates of fatal and nonfatal suicidal behavior among people with BPD contributes to disparate long-term outcomes for people with BPD and large burdens on healthcare systems. For example, within one large urban public health system in the United States, patients with BPD accounted for 29% of all patient death by suicide and 50% of all suicide attempts (Carmel, 2010).

Indeed, several studies have found that suicide risk in patients with personality disorders (PDs) is higher than those with other psychiatric disorders, suggesting the need for interventions that are responsive to the nature of PD symptoms as distinct from other patterns of mood and anxiety symptomatology. Among individuals who die by suicide, an estimate of 57% met criteria for a PD (McMain, 2007). Thus it is important for clinicians to incorporate evidence-based technologies of change and acceptance that promote effective resolution of suicidality in high risk clinical populations, such as those diagnosed with BPD.

Dialectical behavior therapy (DBT; described in the introductory chapter) conceptualizes suicidal behavior as a dysfunctional method of coping with life's problems. Suicidal behavior is both considered a faulty method of attempting to solve a problem and, therefore, is a problem in itself. The DBT therapist will implement the treatment by continuously seeking to help patients replace dysfunctional problem-solving strategies with functional and more adept problem-solving abilities in an effort to achieve their goals. Rather than emphasizing the treatment of suicidal behaviors, DBT places overall emphasis on the patient's ability to build a life worth living.

The goal of this chapter is to first define several subcategories of suicidal behavior and the DBT approach to conceptualization and treatment of suicidality in each domain. The chapter will then discuss the efficacy of DBT for reducing suicide-specific outcomes and other self-directed violence among patients with BPD.

Treating suicidal behaviors in dialectical behavior therapy

DBT is considered a standard of care in the treatment of chronically suicidal individuals with BPD. Chapter 15, A review of the empirical evidence for DBT skills training as a stand-alone intervention, of the DBT treatment manual includes principles and guidelines for responding to suicide risk (Linehan, 1993). Drawing from this content in its development, the Linehan Risk Assessment and Management Protocol

(LRAMP; formerly the University of Washington Risk Assessment and Management Protocol or the UWRAMP) is a suicide risk assessment and management protocol for therapists to utilize following clinical contact with a suicidal patient to guide in their clinical decision making [(Linehan, Comtois, & Ward-Ciesielski, 2012); available at http://depts.washington.edu/uwbrtc/wp-content/uploads/LSSN-LRAMP-v1.0.pdf]. The LRAMP serves as a crisis protocol that can assist the therapist in providing comprehensive clinical care of suicidal patients and provide a template for documentation of this care.

A critical pretreatment step in DBT is for the therapist to obtain a credible commitment from the patient to remain alive and discontinue suicidal means of coping. Obtaining this commitment (and strengthening the commitment over time) is the highest priority in treatment, given that if the patient dies, the treatment cannot work. Once a commitment is established, treatment proceeds with a hierarchy of behavioral targets, with reducing life-threatening behaviors as the highest priority (Linehan, 1993). The primary targets under the domain of life-threatening behavior are to decrease suicide crisis behaviors, then suicidal behaviors including attempts and NSSIs, then suicide communications and other ways of conveying suicidal intentions, and finally resolving other suicide-promoting emotions, expectancies, and beliefs. Notably, DBT emphasizes the reduction of overt behavior rather than the elimination of suicidal thoughts.

The DBT therapist approaches each of these subcategories of life-threatening behavior with an assessment-driven case conceptualization, identifying how each subcategory of suicidal behavior might have different functions for an individual patient. Each subcategory is defined below and includes clinical considerations for targeting the behavior using a DBT frame.

Suicide crisis behaviors

Suicide crisis behaviors are the patient's behaviors that activate their environment to respond as though they are at imminent risk for suicide. Examples of suicide crisis behaviors include communication of suicide intent, or planning and preparation, including obtaining lethal means (e.g., stockpiling medications and acquiring a firearm). Regardless of whether or not the therapist believes that risk is imminent, this subcategory of suicide-related behaviors is closely targeted. It is often the case that even when the therapist deems the patient's suicide risk as low, the suicide crisis behavior might mobilize the environment to respond in ways that are potentially problematic for the patient and the continuation of treatment, and warrant significant attention in order to reduce the behavior. For example, a patient announcing their plan to kill themselves might lead other providers to reactively recommend hospitalizations or emergency department (ED) visits that might be unhelpful for the patient and impede their engagement in outpatient DBT. Furthermore, there is limited empirical evidence as to the efficacy of inpatient psychiatric care and other hospital-based interventions as a primary response to suicidality, and some evidence that ED and inpatient care may have iatrogenic effects for some patients. A recent analysis by Coyle, Shaver, and Linehan (2018) found that the frequency of ED treatment mediated the association between DBT treatment condition and subsequent suicide attempts, such that DBT decreased the number of ED visits, which in turn manifested an overall decrease in suicide attempts later on.

Therapists responding to suicide crisis behaviors (and other subcategories of suicidal behavior) must always be on the side of life, versus on the side of death by suicide. This includes commitment of the therapist to insisting on patients overcoming suicidal thoughts and behavior even in the context of seemingly intractable problems. In the moment crisis management to resolve suicide crisis behaviors often involves reminding patients of prior commitments to taking suicide of the table and utilizing commitment strategies to increase recommit in the moment. Reminding the patient of their reasons for living and life-worth-living goals are often useful strategies, and similarly, the therapist will highlight the negative aspects of death by suicide such as a subsequent loss that family members will experience, fear of social disapproval, or self-involving self-disclosure of the effect that the patient's suicide will have on the therapist. This includes a calm, collaborative, and pragmatic style that emphasizes effectiveness in resolving immediate threats to remaining safe.

In the event that suicide risk is deemed to be low and the therapist conceptualizes the behavior as operant, the therapist will make every effort to increase the patient's awareness of the contingencies operating in this pattern and to work toward extinguish any reinforcing responses to suicide crisis behaviors within their environment. One published case report (Carmel, Templeton, Sorenson, & Logvinenko, 2018) on using the LRAMP and DBT crisis management strategies notes the role of the biosocial theory of BPD (Linehan, 1993) in conceptualizing suicide crisis behavior. This theory considers the transaction between emotional vulnerability and an invalidating environment where normative pain behavior is largely ignored yet escalated behavior is intermittently reinforced. Using this conceptualization, the DBT therapist strives to increase patients' insight and awareness of a potential pattern where suicide crisis behaviors are inadvertently reinforced and to increase commitment to changing this pattern. Recommended crisis management strategies include using dialectical strategies to magnify tension between two sides when a patient's urge to go to the hospital increases, such as highlighting both the hospitalization option which might be used to manage distress in their life, versus the newer and more challenging option of managing distress on an outpatient basis. In addition, the therapist can clarify the contingencies in a crisis scenario by describing the "if–then" relationship between suicidal behavior and consequences by highlighting how previous suicide attempts or hospitalizations were followed by intense shame, negative physical impact, and a disruption of progress on life goals related to work or relationships (Carmel et al., 2018).

Suicide attempts and nonsuicidal self-injury

Like suicide crisis behaviors, self-injurious behaviors are always targeted closely in DBT. A suicide attempt is a nonfatal self-directed potentially injurious behavior with any intent to die as a result of the behavior and may or may not result in injury (e.g., ingestion of a larger than prescribed dose of prescription medication). Suicide rehearsal involves acts or preparations toward making a suicide attempt, but before potential for harm has begun (e.g., stockpiling medications and researching how to make a ligature).

A prior history of attempted suicide is one of the strongest long-term predictors of death by suicide (Franklin et al., 2017). Further, there is evidence that NSSI is a potent predictor of subsequent suicidal behavior, particularly among young people (Klonsky, May, & Glenn, 2013). Thus DBT will prioritize the reduction of suicide attempts, and all other forms of self-injurious behavior (i.e., NSSI), given the risk associated with future suicide and the myriad consequences of habituation to physical and psychological pain from suicidal and NSSI over time. A therapist will respond to suicidal behaviors of their by patient by insisting that they (re) commit to abstaining from future suicidal and NSSI behaviors, and devoting the full resources of DBT in this goal. Linehan (1993) notes that in doing so, the DBT therapist is communicating compassion and care. For example, a therapist might state that conducting an assessment of a recent suicide attempt via completing a chain analysis is needed as part of the effort to get back on track and help the patient move toward their relevant life-worth-living goals. Without a chain analysis to understand the factors that led to a suicide attempt or an episode of NSSI, the therapist (and patient) is limited in their ability to reduce the likelihood of a future episode of NSSI or suicide attempt occurring.

Suicidal ideation and communications

As part of the process of blocking suicidogenic ways of coping and reinforcing adaptive efforts at coping with the problem at hand, DBT therapists aim to decrease the frequency and intensity of a patient's suicidal ideation and communications. This subcategory includes thinking about self-harm, experiencing strong urges to engage in self-harm, and engaging in fantasies and ruminative thinking about these behaviors. Consistent with the behavioral focus of DBT, these thoughts and beliefs are targeted within the context of potential behavioral sequelae, and considered relative to particular antecedents.

Suicidal communications involve the expression of these experiences to others, be it a family member, primary care physician, or a social media posting. Notably, the proliferation of suicidal communications via social media platforms has emerged as a critical frontier for suicide prevention research, and best practices are still evolving (Synnott, Ioannou, Coyne, & Hemingway, 2018). Suicidal communications might lack the urgency of suicide crisis behaviors and the subsequent response from others that the patient is at imminent risk, yet environmental responses are similarly problematic in many instances. For example, a patient commenting that they "wished they were dead" in one setting might prompt an urgent response similar to suicide crisis behaviors (e.g., calling 911) and another setting might include others responding minimally to what the patient is saying. This variability in others' responses may be complicated by long-standing patterns of suicidal communications and can potentially impede the responsiveness to genuine indicia of risk given repeated episodes of communications that did not result in suicidal behavior (Joiner, 2014).

DBT therapists might utilize a range of behavioral skills to help patients increase mindfulness of their suicide-related cognitions via observing and labeling thoughts, or applying cognitive modification strategies to highlight the consequences of suicidal communications (e.g., "when you've talk about wanting to die while in your doctors' office, it's led to them escorting you to the ED and unwanted hospitalization on more than one occasion"). Similarly, interpersonal effectiveness skills emphasize alternative ways for the patient to communicate distress and emotional pain in a manner that is more adaptive, and that appropriately balances the nature of the relationship, intensity of the situation, and the patient's specific goals for an interaction (Linehan, 1993). This is particularly important when it has been established through multiple chain analysis that expressing thoughts of suicide is an operant behavior with a communication function that elicits a particular response from one's environment.

Suicide-related expectancies and beliefs

DBT works to modify patients' assumptions and beliefs about the utility of coping via suicidal behavior. Noting the negatively reinforcing aspects of self-harm via cutting, for example, might involve the therapist reflecting to the patient the short-term effect of relief from anger, while also accounting for the long-term effect of increased shame (as well as other problems related to cutting, such as scarring or medical risk). It is perhaps more important for the DBT therapist to clarify the expectations about long-term coping via suicidal behaviors and to consider more adaptive methods of coping in the long run. Given that suicidal behavior is both considered a faulty method of solving a problem, and therefore a problem in itself, the therapist might challenge a patient's belief that their problems are actually solved when they continually overdose in response to marital conflict, for example, rather than adding problems and making things worse.

On the other hand, the DBT therapist might seek to validate what is valid in the patient's experience particularly with a change-focused approach of modifying ones thinking. For example, noticing that people engage in suicidal and self-harming behavior for reasons that make sense in the moment, even though their reasons may appear inaccurate, mistaken, or unhelpful upon reflection and after the emotional intensity of a suicidal crisis has decreased. Similarly, highlighting the ineffective nature of coping with interpersonal conflict via overdosing can be coupled with the therapist acknowledging the limited amount of coping skills in the patient's repertoire and understandable attempts on the part of the patient to try to alleviate their misery in response to a difficult relationship. This pragmatic approach reflects the core assumptions of DBT that everyone does the best they can with the skills they have, and needs to do more, better, and try harder to change painful and maladaptive patterns.

Suicide-related affect

Both self-harm behaviors as well as suicide-related thinking have the potential to offset intense, painful emotions (Chapman & Dixon-Gordon, 2007). Simply thinking about suicide, for certain individuals, has the effect of reducing emotional arousal. The overall goal here is to modify the patient's affective response both to suicidal behavior and to other related cognitions and reactions. In an effort to increase a patient's ability to tolerate negative affect, a therapist might block suicidal urges in the session and aim to increase emotional experiencing via exposure techniques. The therapist might test a hypothesis that suicidal thoughts function as a way to suppress painful emotions, in an effort to identify the controlling variables of the client's behavior.

Emotion regulation skills offer a range of strategies to promote the labeling and modulation of emotions (Linehan, 1993). DBT conceptualizes many problematic behaviors, including life-threatening behaviors, as having an emotion regulatory function; thus these skills provide ways to increase emotional experiencing rather than engaging in efforts to block or suppress them using a range of problem behaviors (e.g., cutting, substance use, or bingeing and purging).

The interventions and techniques described above highlight the range of strategies included in DBT for reducing the frequency of intensity of suicidal behaviors. In tandem with a focus on building a life worth living, these strategies offer clinicians a robust framework for managing their own distress in treating a patient with increased suicide risk. As a comprehensive treatment model, and as a repertoire of skills for acceptance and change, DBT is based upon a strong foundation of empirical research that can inform therapists' confidence in applying these strategies in their practice with DBT patients. Thus the DBT therapist utilizes different approaches in response to the problem behavior at hand (life-threatening or otherwise). If one approach does not lead to the client responding in the way the therapist intended, the therapist switches to another approach.

Evidence of dialectical behavior therapy efficacy for suicide-specific outcomes

Several studies have demonstrated that DBT is efficacious for reducing suicide risk behaviors, including attempted suicide, NSSI, and psychiatric crisis services to prevent suicide (DeCou, Comtois, & Landes, 2018), including among patients with BPD (Kliem, Kröger, & Kosfelder, 2010; Stoffers-Winterling et al., 2012). The efficacy of DBT to reduce suicidal ideation is less clear, as studies have suggested inconsistent treatment effects, in part due to limitations of the measurements used to assess suicidal ideation (DeCou et al., 2018). Understanding the effect sizes observed, time frames analyzed, and populations included in previous studies can aid practitioners in their consideration of DBT within treatment planning and decision making.

Self-directed violence

DBT prioritizes self-directed violence (i.e., suicide attempts, and NSSI) of any kind as a primary target of therapy. A large meta-analysis of randomized controlled trials (RCTs) from the Cochrane Collaboration found that DBT was efficacious for the reduction of self-directed violence (i.e., "parasuicidality") among patients with BPD ($d = -0.54$) (Stoffers-Winterling et al., 2012). Measuring self-directed violence as a single category may limit the extent to which interventions can be matched with particular patterns of behavior, as the broader suicide prevention literature has highlighted the imperativeness of considering both the overlap and distinctiveness of suicidal behavior and NSSI (Klonsky et al., 2013; Klonsky, May, & Saffer, 2016). Nonetheless, the radical behavioral approach of DBT that addresses self-directed violence within a single overarching category of self-injurious behavior as the highest priority behavioral target offers a reasonable approach to managing both the overlap and distinction among these categories. Specifically, DBT acknowledges the overlap in regard to risk of physical harm and escalation of self-directed violence over time via negative reinforcement and other contingencies and also includes fine-grained analysis of suicidal and nonsuicidal types of self-harm (i.e., chain analysis). Indeed, chain analysis can elucidate the particular drivers of NSSI and attempted suicide and thus can allow room for distinct intervention strategies within the broader goal of managing potentially life-threatening behavior (Linehan, 1993). Further, DBT conceptualizes the thoughts, behaviors and emotions associated with suicidal and NSSI behaviors within the context of (1) space and time, (2) the functional sequalae of behavior, and (3) acute stressors that preceded the behavior (Linehan, 1993). This in-depth approach to behavioral analysis and the related therapeutic sequence of collaboratively developing creative solutions and alternative contingencies surrounding the broad category of self-directed violence has been found to yield positive outcomes for patients with BPD and suicidality.

Several RCTs of Standard DBT (SDBT; i.e., all four modes) have demonstrated efficacy in the reduction of self-directed violence among patients with BPD. Linehan, Armstrong, Suarez, Allmon, and Heard (1991) RCT of DBT found that 64% of patients with BPD assigned to receive SDBT had any NSSI and/or attempted suicide (described as "parasuicide" at that time) during 12 months of follow-up, compared to 96% of those in the control condition. Further, among patients who had any medically treated self-directed violence, DBT patients tended to have lower medical severity of injuries from NSSI and/or attempted suicide (Linehan et al., 1991). Additional scholarship since this original study has replicated the efficacy of SDBT for reducing self-directed violence, as well as NSSI and attempted suicide as distinct types of injury within this broader category.

Nonsuicidal self-injury

Among studies of people with BPD who received SDBT, findings support the efficacy of DBT to reduce the odds of having any NSSI during the follow-up period. For example, Pasieczny and Connor (2011) found that SDBT was associated with reduced number of self-harm episodes during a 6-month treatment program. Specifically, this study found that DBT patients had on average 13 episodes of NSSI during the 6 months prior to DBT, and approximately 3 during the 6 months after beginning DBT. In contrast, patients in the treatment as usual (TAU) condition had approximately 19 episodes of self-harm prior to baseline and had 18 episodes on average during the treatment period (Pasieczny & Connor, 2011). This substantial reduction in the frequency of NSSI suggests that DBT yields both statistically and clinically significant benefits to patients with BPD.

Another trial of SDBT for patients with BPD found a significant treatment by time interaction, such that those assigned to DBT had fewer episodes of NSSI (i.e., "self-mutilating behavior") over the course of the 1-year treatment period (Verheul et al., 2003). Similar to findings from Linehan et al. (1991) and Pasieczny and Connor (2011), Verheul et al. (2003) found a significant difference in the number of DBT patients (i.e., 35%) who engaged in any NSSI compared to patients who received treatment-as-usual (i.e., 57%). These studies in combination with others (Kliem et al., 2010) suggest that DBT is efficacious for both reducing the odds of any NSSI during treatment, as well as the frequency of NSSI episodes/incidents over the course of treatment.

Attempted suicide

Previous scholarship has also indicated that DBT may be efficacious for the treatment of suicidal behavior among patients with BPD. However, given the relatively low base-rate of suicidal behavior relative to NSSI or other suicide-specific outcomes, it is difficult to achieve adequate statistical power to evaluate this outcome within the context of conventional RCT sample sizes (i.e., ≥ 100 patients). Despite this significant limitation, studies have indicated that participants assigned to DBT treatment conditions tend to have lower absolute incidents of attempted suicide, even though associated comparisons are underpowered for the purpose of making a robust statistical inference.

For example, Verheul et al. (2003) found that 7% ($n = 2$) of DBT patients attempted suicide compared to 26% ($n = 8$) of TAU patients. Similarly, Pasieczny and Connor (2011) found that DBT patients' number of suicide attempts reduced from an average of 1.63 attempts in the 6 months prior to DBT to 0.28 during the 6 months of DBT treatment. In contrast, TAU participants demonstrated a slight increase in average number of suicide attempts, from 1.66 attempts at baseline to 1.71 attempts during treatment. This study also observed additional reductions in frequency of suicide attempts for DBT patients who continued in treatment for an additional 6 months, such that number of attempts reduced to zero (Pasieczny & Connor, 2011). In both of these studies, statistical power was low, as the absolute number of suicide attempts and study participants was relatively low. Nonetheless, the direction of these findings are consistent with the studies described above that demonstrated an overall effect of DBT upon any self-directed violence and reflected the inherent challenge of detecting treatment effects relative to low base-rate outcomes, such as suicidal behavior.

Psychiatric crisis services

In addition to reducing the frequency and severity of self-directed violence, DBT has also been found to reduce the odds of psychiatric crisis services to prevent suicide, as well as the length of hospitalization among those who are admitted for inpatient psychiatric care (Linehan et al., 1991). This reduction in utilization of psychiatric crisis services is consistent with the treatment strategies noted above, including the use of phone consultation for DBT patients, and the focus on cultivating effective strategies for achieving specific goals. Indeed, patients' progress to resolving the situations and circumstances that drive suicidality may be thwarted by admission to inpatient psychiatric care that could insulate patients from opportunities to be effective and engage in DBT skills to mitigate crises directly (Coyle et al., 2018). Previous findings have demonstrated DBT as efficacious in reducing both ED and inpatient psychiatric admissions, both for suicide-specific concerns and any other psychiatric symptoms.

In an RCT that included women with past history of self-directed violence, and who were diagnosed with BPD, Linehan et al. (2006) found that DBT patients presented to the ED due to suicidality approximately half as often as patients receiving other community-based treatment by experts (15% vs 30% during treatment; 11% vs 18% during follow-up year). DBT patients were also less likely to present for ED treatment of any other psychiatric or substance use-related symptoms (43% vs 57% during treatment; 23% vs 29% during follow-up year), though to a lesser extent than was observed for suicide-specific ED care. In addition, DBT patients in this trial were less likely to be admitted to the hospital for suicide-specific concerns (10% vs 36% during treatment; 15% vs 18% during follow-up year) or any other psychiatric reason (20% vs 49% during treatment; 23% vs 29% during follow-up year) (Linehan et al., 2006). The pattern of attenuating treatment effects is notable with regard to psychiatric crisis services utilization during follow-up. This likely reflects the potency of the validation and phone consultation offered during a course of DBT and may suggest the need to consider effective options for developing long-term support in lieu of conventional models of crisis intervention via presentation for hospital-based care. Other studies have also noted positive effects of DBT with regard to inpatient psychiatric care (Linehan et al., 1991; Pasieczny & Connor, 2011), though some investigations have failed to detect an effect of DBT with regard to psychiatric crisis services utilization (Linehan et al., 1999).

Suicidal ideation

As noted previously, DBT emphasizes overt behavior as the primary target of therapeutic intervention. However, DBT also includes skills and strategies for mitigating negative thoughts, particularly as they relate to the initiation of problematic and therapy-interfering behaviors. Indeed, suicidal thoughts have been identified as an important outcome of psychotherapy for patients with suicidality, independent of the extent to which such thoughts occasion particular suicidal acts (Jobes & Joiner, 2019). Some evidence exists to suggest that DBT is efficacious for addressing thoughts of suicidality among patient populations that included a range of psychopathology. For example, a small study of adolescents diagnosed with bipolar affective disorder demonstrated a trend toward significance for DBT being efficacious to reduce the presence of any suicidal thoughts during 1 year of SDBT (Goldstein et al., 2015). Other studies have demonstrated nonsignificant effects with regard to suicidal ideation (Feigenbaum et al., 2012; Katz, Cox, Gunasekara, & Miller, 2004; Linehan et al., 2006). This could reflect limitations of the measurements employed for these studies, as well as the paucity of DBT trials overall that have utilized robust measures of suicidal ideation (e.g., the Scale for Suicide Ideation) (Beck, Brown, & Steer, 1997). Given the mixed literature with regard to this outcome, it is essential for clinicians to consider how to effectively manage and resolve suicidal thoughts to the extent this represents a primary concern for patients. Given the larger emphasis in DBT on behavioral interventions over cognitive interventions, clinicians may consider utilizing treatments that employ a broader range of cognitive restructuring techniques to reduce suicidal ideation specifically [Cognitive Therapy for Suicide Prevention (Brown et al., 2005)] following the completion of DBT.

Settings and adaptations

A recent meta-analysis found that DBT was effective across a wide variety of settings, patient populations, and via both the SDBT model and models that did not include all four modes of treatment (DeCou et al., 2018).

Although this chapter was focused primarily on SDBT for patients with BPD, it is important to note the flexibility and applicability of DBT skills and principles to a variety of presentations, including patients with BPD and concomitant substance use disorders (Linehan et al., 2002), and those receiving care via inpatient (Bohus et al., 2004) and outpatient settings (Linehan et al., 2006).

Conclusion

Taken together, the technologies of change and acceptance articulated within DBT offer durable and potent options for the management and treatment of self-directed violence, including NSSI, and suicidal thoughts and behavior. DBT also offers clinicians flexible options for balancing patients' needs for autonomy/efficacy and safety, as well as clear prescriptions as to the prioritization of self-directed violence within the context of other presenting concerns. Although evidence remains limited with regard to the efficacy of DBT to reduce suicidal ideation, there is clear evidence that DBT is efficacious for reducing the frequency and severity of self-directed violence among patients with BPD, as well as reducing the utilization of psychiatric crisis services. By adopting the techniques and principles of DBT, it is possible for DBT clinicians to support patients in understanding their experiences of NSSI and suicidal behavior as understandable and preventable responses to seemingly intolerable distress, within a rich ecology of behavior and achievable alternatives.

References

American Psychiatric Association, & American Psychiatric Association. DSM-5 Task Force. (2013). *Diagnostic and statistical manual of mental disorders: DSM-5.* (5th ed.). Retrieved from <http://dsm.psychiatryonline.org/book.aspx?bookid = 556>.

Beck, A. T., Brown, G. K., & Steer, R. A. (1997). Psychometric characteristics of the Scale for Suicide Ideation with psychiatric outpatients. *Behaviour Research and Therapy, 35*(11), 1039–1046. Available from https://doi.org/10.1016/S0005-7967(97)00073-9.

Bohus, M., Haaf, B., Simms, T., Limberger, M. F., Schmahl, C., Unckel, C., & Linehan, M. M. (2004). Effectiveness of inpatient dialectical behavioral therapy for borderline personality disorder: A controlled trial. *Behaviour Research and Therapy, 42*(5), 487–499. Available from https://doi.org/10.1016/S0005-7967(03)00174-8.

Brown, G. K., Ten Have, T., Henriques, G. R., Xie, S. X., Hollander, J. E., & Beck, A. T. (2005). Cognitive therapy for the prevention of suicide attempts: A randomized controlled trial. *Journal of the American Medical Association, 294*(5), 563–570.

Carmel, A. (2010). *Effectiveness of dialectical behavior therapy training in reducing clinical burnout in community behavioral health settings.* San Francisco Department of Public Health.

Carmel, A., Templeton, E., Sorenson, S. M., & Logvinenko, E. (2018). Using the Linehan risk assessment and management protocol with a chronically suicidal patient: A case report.

Cognitive and Behavioral Practice, 25(4), 449–459. Available from https://doi.org/10.1016/j.cbpra.2018.02.001.

Chapman, A. L., & Dixon-Gordon, K. L. (2007). Emotional antecedents and consequences of deliberate self-harm and suicide attempts. *Suicide and Life-Threatening Behavior, 37*(5), 543–552. Available from https://doi.org/10.1521/suli.2007.37.5.543.

Chaput, Y. J. A., & Lebel, M.-J. (2007). Demographic and clinical profiles of patients who make multiple visits to psychiatric emergency services. *Psychiatric Services (Washington, DC), 58*(3), 335–341. Available from https://doi.org/10.1176/ps.2007.58.3.335.

Clarkin, J. F., Widiger, T. A., Frances, A., Hurt, S. W., & Gilmore, M. (1983). Prototypic typology and the borderline personality disorder. *Journal of Abnormal Psychology, 92*(3), 263–275. Available from https://doi.org/10.1037/0021-843X.92.3.263.

Cowdry, R. W., Pickar, D., & Davies, R. (1985). Symptoms and EEG findings in the borderline syndrome. *International Journal of Psychiatry in Medicine, 15*(3), 1985–1986.

Coyle, T. N., Shaver, J. A., & Linehan, M. M. (2018). On the potential for iatrogenic effects of psychiatric crisis services: The example of dialectical behavior therapy for adult women with borderline personality disorder. *Journal of Consulting and Clinical Psychology, 86*(2), 116–124. Available from https://doi.org/10.1037/ccp0000275.

DeCou, C. R., Comtois, K. A., & Landes, S. J. (2018). Dialectical behavior therapy is effective for the treatment of suicidal behavior: A meta-analysis. *Behavior Therapy, 50*(1), 60–72. Available from https://doi.org/10.1016/j.beth.2018.03.009.

Feigenbaum, J. D., Fonagy, P., Pilling, S., Jones, A., Wildgoose, A., & Bebbington, P. E. (2012). A real-world study of the effectiveness of DBT in the UK National Health Service. *The British Journal of Clinical Psychology/the British Psychological Society, 51*(2), 121–141. Available from https://doi.org/10.1111/j.2044-8260.2011.02017.x.

Frances, A., Fyer, M., & Clarkin, J. (1986). Personality and suicide. *Annals of the New York Academy of Sciences, 487*, 281–293.

Franklin, J. C., Ribeiro, J. D., Fox, K. R., Bentley, K. H., Kleiman, E. M., Huang, X., & Nock, M. K. (2017). Risk factors for suicidal thoughts and behaviors: A meta-analysis of 50 years of research. *Psychological Bulletin, 143*(2), 187–232. Available from https://doi.org/10.1037/bul0000084.

Goldstein, T. R., Fersch-Podrat, R. K., Rivera, M., Axelson, D. A., Merranko, J., Yu, H., & Birmaher, B. (2015). Dialectical behavior therapy for adolescents with bipolar disorder: Results from a pilot randomized trial. *Journal of Child and Adolescent Psychopharmacology, 25*(2), 140–149. Available from https://doi.org/10.1089/cap.2013.0145.

Gross, R., Olfson, M., Gameroff, M., Shea, S., Feder, A., Fuentes, M., & Weissman, M. M. (2002). Borderline personality disorder in primary care. *Archives of Internal Medicine, 162*(1), 53–60.

Jobes, D. A., & Joiner, T. E. (2019). Reflections on suicidal ideation. *Crisis: The Journal of Crisis Intervention and Suicide Prevention, 40*(4), 227–230. Available from https://doi.org/10.1027/0227-5910/a000615.

Joiner, T. (2014). *The perversion of virtue: Understanding murder-suicide*. Oxford University Press.

Katz, L. Y., Cox, B. J., Gunasekara, S., & Miller, A. L. (2004). Feasibility of dialectical behavior therapy for suicidal adolescent inpatients. *Journal of the American Academy of Child & Adolescent Psychiatry, 43*(3), 276–282. Available from https://doi.org/10.1097/00004583-200403000-00008.

Kliem, S., Kröger, C., & Kosfelder, J. (2010). Dialectical behavior therapy for borderline personality disorder: A meta-analysis using mixed-effects modeling. *Journal of Consulting and Clinical Psychology, 78*(6), 936–951. Available from https://doi.org/10.1037/a0021015.

Klonsky, E. D., May, A. M., & Glenn, C. R. (2013). The relationship between nonsuicidal self-injury and attempted suicide: Converging evidence from four samples. *Journal of*

Abnormal Psychology, 122(1), 231–237. Available from https://doi.org/10.1037/a0030278.

Klonsky, E. D., May, A. M., & Saffer, B. Y. (2016). Suicide, suicide attempts, and suicidal ideation. *Annual Review of Clinical Psychology, 12*(1), 307–330. Available from https://doi.org/10.1146/annurev-clinpsy-021815-093204.

Korzekwa, M. I., Dell, P. F., Links, P. S., Thabane, L., & Webb, S. P. (2008). Estimating the prevalence of borderline personality disorder in psychiatric outpatients using a two-phase procedure. *Comprehensive Psychiatry, 49*(4), 380–386. Available from https://doi.org/10.1016/j.comppsych.2008.01.007.

Lieb, K., Zanarini, M. C., Schmahl, C., Linehan, M. M., & Bohus, M. (2004). Borderline personality disorder. *The Lancet, 364*(9432), 453–461. Available from https://doi.org/10.1016/S0140-6736(04)16770-6.

Linehan, M. (1993). *Cognitive-behavioral treatment of borderline personality disorder*. Guilford Press.

Linehan, M. M., Armstrong, H. E., Suarez, A., Allmon, D., & Heard, H. L. (1991). Cognitive-behavioral treatment of chronically parasuicidal borderline patients. *Archives of General Psychiatry, 48*(12), 1060–1064. Available from https://doi.org/10.1001/archpsyc.1991.01810360024003.

Linehan, M. M., Comtois, K. A., Murray, A. M., Brown, M. Z., Gallop, R. J., Heard, H. L., & Lindenboim, N. (2006). Two-year randomized controlled trial and follow-up of dialectical behavior therapy versus therapy by experts for suicidal behaviors and borderline personality disorder. *Archives of General Psychiatry, 63*, 757–766.

Linehan, M. M., Comtois, K. A., & Ward-Ciesielski, E. F. (2012). Assessing and managing risk with suicidal individuals. *Cognitive and Behavioral Practice, 19*(2), 218–232. Available from https://doi.org/10.1016/j.cbpra.2010.11.008.

Linehan, M. M., Dimeff, L. A., Reynolds, S. K., Comtois, K. A., Welch, S. S., Heagerty, P., & Kivlahan, D. R. (2002). Dialectical behavior therapy versus comprehensive validation therapy plus 12-step for the treatment of opioid dependent women meeting criteria for borderline personality disorder. *Drug and Alcohol Dependence, 67*(1), 13–26. Available from https://doi.org/10.1016/S0376-8716(02)00011-X.

Linehan, M. M., Schmidt, H., Dimeff, L. A., Craft, J. C., Kanter, J., & Comtois, K. A. (1999). Dialectical behavior therapy for patients with borderline personality disorder and drug-dependence. *American Journal on Addictions, 8*(4), 279–292. Available from https://doi.org/10.1080/105504999305686.

Linehan, M. M., Rizvi, S. L., Welch, S. S., Page, B. (2000). Psychiatric aspects of suicidal behaviour: Personality disorders. In K. Hawton & K. van Heeringen (Eds.), *The international handbook of suicide and attempted suicide* (pp. 147–178). https://doi.org/10.1002/9780470698976.ch10.

McMain, S. (2007). Effectiveness of psychosocial treatments on suicidality in personality disorders. *Canadian Journal of Psychiatry. Revue Canadienne de Psychiatrie, 52*(6).

Pasieczny, N., & Connor, J. (2011). The effectiveness of dialectical behaviour therapy in routine public mental health settings: An Australian controlled trial. *Behaviour Research and Therapy, 49*(1), 4–10. Available from https://doi.org/10.1016/j.brat.2010.09.006.

Pompili, M., Girardi, P., Ruberto, A., & Tatarelli, R. (2005). Suicide in borderline personality disorder: A meta-analysis. *Nordic Journal of Psychiatry, 59*(5), 319–324. Available from https://doi.org/10.1080/08039480500320025.

Stoffers-Winterling, J. M., Völlm, B. A., Rücker, G., Timmer, A., Huband, N., & Lieb, K. (2012). Psychological therapies for people with borderline personality disorder. *Cochrane Database of Systematic Reviews*. Available from https://doi.org/10.1002/14651858.CD005652.pub2.

Stone, M. H. (1993). Long-term outcome in personality disorders. *The British Journal of Psychiatry: The Journal of Mental Science, 162*, 299–313. Available from https://doi.org/10.1192/bjp.162.3.299.

Synnott, J., Ioannou, M., Coyne, A., & Hemingway, S. (2018). A content analysis of online suicide notes: Attempted suicide versus attempt resulting in suicide. *Suicide and Life-Threatening Behavior*, *48*(6), 767–778. Available from https://doi.org/10.1111/sltb.12398.

Tomko, R. L., Trull, T. J., Wood, P. K., & Sher, K. J. (2014). Characteristics of borderline personality disorder in a community sample: Comorbidity, treatment utilization, and general functioning. *Journal of Personality Disorders*, *28*(5), 734–750. Available from https://doi.org/10.1521/pedi_2012_26_093.

Torgersen, S., Kringlen, E., & Cramer, V. (2001). The prevalence of personality disorders in a community sample. *Archives of General Psychiatry*, *58*(6), 590–596.

Trull, T. J., Jahng, S., Tomko, R. L., Wood, P. K., & Sher, K. J. (2010). Revised NESARC personality disorder diagnoses: Gender, prevalence, and comorbidity with substance dependence disorders. *Journal of Personality Disorders*, *24*(4), 412–426. Available from https://doi.org/10.1521/pedi.2010.24.4.412.

Verheul, R., Bosch, L. M. C. V. D., Koeter, M. W. J., Ridder, M. A. J. D., Stijnen, T., & Brink, W. V. D. (2003). Dialectical behaviour therapy for women with borderline personality disorder: 12-month, randomised clinical trial in the Netherlands. *The British Journal of Psychiatry*, *182*(2), 135–140. Available from https://doi.org/10.1192/bjp.182.2.135.

Zimmerman, M., Chelminski, I., & Young, D. (2008). The frequency of personality disorders in psychiatric patients. *The Psychiatric Clinics of North America*, *31*(3), 405–420. Available from https://doi.org/10.1016/j.psc.2008.03.015, vi.

CHAPTER

6

Eating disorders

Autumn Askew, Erin Gallagher, Jesse Dzombak and Ann F. Haynos

University of Minnesota, Minneapolis, MN, United States

Over recent decades, substantial progress has been made in the identification of effective treatments for eating disorders. Citing the most notable examples, cognitive behavior therapy (CBT) has been found to produce symptom improvements for adults with bulimia nervosa (BN), binge-eating disorder (BED), and subthreshold eating disorders (Linardon, Wade, De la Piedad Garcia, & Brennan, 2017) and family-based therapy (FBT) has been demonstrated to be efficacious for adolescents and young adults with anorexia nervosa (AN) (Fisher, Skocic, Rutherford, & Hetrick, 2019). However, there remains much room for improvement in the treatment of eating disorder populations. Approximately 25%–50% of individuals receiving established eating disorder interventions discontinue treatment prematurely and, among completers, only 40%–50% achieve remission (Berkman et al., 2006; Grilo, Masheb, Wilson, Gueorguieva, & White, 2011; Wallier et al., 2009). In particular, individuals experiencing higher severity appear to receive the least benefit from standard treatments. For instance, longer illness duration, greater eating disorder symptoms, and higher rates of general and personality psychopathology have been associated with poorer outcomes from CBT for eating disorders (Fairburn et al., 2009; Johnson, Tobin, & Dennis, 1990; Wilfley et al., 2000). Further, for certain eating disorder populations, such as adult AN, no clearly efficacious treatments exist (Berkman et al., 2006). Therefore, there is a critical need to test novel treatment models for eating disorders.

In response to these issues concerning treatment, several research groups have begun to investigate other intervention approaches for eating disorders, including dialectical behavior therapy (DBT; Linehan, 1993).

The Handbook of Dialectical Behavior Therapy
DOI: https://doi.org/10.1016/B978-0-12-816384-9.00006-3

There are several reasons why DBT is an appealing treatment option for eating disorder populations. First, the high level of comorbidity between eating disorders and borderline personality disorder (BPD) (Martinussen et al., 2017; Shah & Zanarini, 2018), the diagnosis most commonly targeted by DBT, suggests a common etiology. There is mounting evidence to suggest that emotion dysregulation, the primary target of DBT, is a common mechanism underlying both BPD and eating disorders (Berking & Wupperman, 2012). Second, commitment to treatment is actively targeted in DBT (Linehan, 1993) and, therefore, DBT consistently has up to half as many dropouts as other treatments for severe, multiproblem clients (Feigenbaum, 2007). For this reason, DBT is well suited to address the high treatment attrition common to eating disorders (Berkman et al., 2006). Third, because individuals with eating disorders often present with multiple diagnoses and behavioral problems (Marucci et al., 2018), the treatment hierarchy employed in DBT can be advantageous for organizing intervention targets in a clear and consistent manner. Finally, treatment of eating disorders can be challenging for providers given the elevated medical and psychiatric acuity of this population (Wisniewski, Safer, Chen, Dimeff, & Koerner, 2007). Thus the availability of a consultation team within the DBT model is well suited to provide support and supervision to clinicians managing these difficult cases (Perseius, Kåver, Ekdahl, Asberg, & Samuelsson, 2007).

For these reasons, there is a growing interest in evaluating DBT for a range of eating disorder presentations. This chapter will review this literature on application of DBT to the treatment of eating disorders and identify gaps in this literature base warranting further research.

Review of studies

Dialectical behavior therapy for eating disorders comorbid with borderline personality disorder

Given the comorbidity between eating disorders and BPD, and the substantial literature base demonstrating the utility of DBT for treating individuals with BPD (Panos, Jackson, Hasan, & Panos, 2013), several groups have investigated DBT as a treatment option for individuals with co-occurring diagnoses of an eating disorder and BPD, or else significant personality pathology.

Case series. Several case series have examined applications of DBT for cooccurring eating disorders and personality psychopathology. Palmer et al. (2003) first investigated DBT for comorbid eating disorder and BPD in a small case series. These researchers evaluated the addition of DBT in an existing eating disorders service to manage complex and treatment-resistant patients [BN: $n = 5$; BED: $n = 1$; eating disorder not otherwise specified (EDNOS): $n = 1$], all of whom met BPD criteria. Patients received comprehensive DBT over 6–18 months. Further, a new module reflecting strategies for managing weight- and eating-related problems was implemented in the skills groups. Given the nature of the treatment setting, few outcome measures could be collected; however, treatment was associated with decreased public self-harm and inpatient hospitalization days. Following treatment, three patients no longer met eating disorder criteria and four had reduced in severity and met criteria for EDNOS.

A second case series (Chen, Matthews, Allen, Kuo, & Linehan, 2008) improved upon the prior study by adding standardized assessments to evaluate treatment effects. Participants with BPD and an eating disorder (BN: $n = 3$; BED: $n = 5$) received comprehensive DBT, with adaptations for an eating disorder population, including addition of eating- and body-related exercises in skills groups, alteration of diary cards to reflect eating-related goals, and weight monitoring in individual sessions. Treatment duration was also limited to 6 months. Following treatment, improvements were noted on suicide attempt, nonsuicidal self-injury, binge eating, global eating disorder symptoms, number of psychiatric diagnoses, and overall functioning. Half of the sample was abstinent from binge eating at posttreatment and 6-month follow-up and all were abstinent from purging by follow-up. Authors noted that the 6-month treatment length seemed insufficient, due to one posttreatment suicide attempt, several participants pursuing further treatment after the study, and participant feedback that treatment period was too short.

Finally, a third case series for multiproblem individuals with eating disorders was conducted by Federici and Wisniewski (2013). This trial examined a 6-month treatment that combined comprehensive DBT with standard CBT techniques in a day treatment or intensive outpatient setting. All participants had an eating disorder (AN: $n = 4$; EDNOS: $n = 3$) and characteristics of a personality disorder (BPD: $n = 6$). Participants were selected to participate in DBT due to not experiencing significant improvement in their symptoms from standard eating disorder treatments in the prior year. Most participants ($n = 6$) completed treatment and some ($n = 2$) requested a 3-month treatment extension. Following treatment, all individuals who were underweight experienced weight gain, most participants ($n = 5$) reported a reduction in restrictive eating and abstinence from suicidal and nonsuicidal self-injury, and all participants experienced a reduction or elimination of binge-eating and/or purging episodes.

Open trials. Several open trials have also examined DBT applications for comorbid eating disorders and BPD. The first was conducted with 24 females (AN: $n = 9$; BN: $n = 15$) on an inpatient unit specializing in treatment of BPD (Kröger et al., 2010). Treatment consisted of a 3-month DBT program adapted for an intensive setting, with other changes made to accommodate an eating disorder population, including placing restrictive and binge-eating behaviors at the top of the treatment hierarchy along with life-threatening behavior, using contingency management techniques to promote weight gain for those with AN, and adding a skills module targeting issues related to eating and weight. Individuals with AN experienced significant BMI gains from pretreatment to follow-up ($M = 16.71 - 18.45$ kg/m^2). Across the sample, improvements were noted for eating pathology, binge eating, and social functioning. However, several important variables (e.g., nonsuicidal self-injury and purging) were not assessed.

A second open trial was conducted to evaluate the impact of comorbid BPD diagnosis on the outcomes from a DBT-informed therapy for individuals with eating disorders (Ben-Porath, Wisniewski, & Warren, 2009). Individuals with mixed eating disorder diagnoses (AN: $n = 7$, BN: $n = 16$, EDNOS: $n = 15$), who either met criteria for BPD as detailed in the Diagnostic and Statistical Manual of Mental Disorders, fourth edition (DSM-IV; $n = 16$) or did not ($n = 24$), participated in a DBT-informed partial hospitalization program that provided twice weekly DBT skills groups, as well as additional groups focusing issues such as on motivation, commitment, goal setting, and chain analyses over an average of 10.5 weeks. Although treatment included telephone skills coaching and a consultation team, patients received minimal individual treatment, which consisted of 30 min/week to review diary cards and chain analyses and to address treatment-interfering behavior. Following treatment, all patients improved on eating pathology and mood. There was no difference in treatment response between those with or without a comorbid BPD diagnosis. However, a significant treatment by group interaction was noted for the putative mechanism of emotion regulation. Although the group with comorbid BPD reported poorer baseline emotion regulation, these abilities improved with treatment, while they remained static for those without a BPD diagnosis. This study provided further evidence suggesting the utility of employing DBT techniques in the treatment of eating disorders and also initial support for emotion dysregulation as a process of change in DBT for eating disorders and comorbid BPD.

Secondary analyses. An additional study utilized data previously collected for a trial comparing DBT to treatment by experts for individuals with BPD and conducted post hoc analyses to examine the effect of DBT on various psychiatric disorders, including eating disorders (Harned et al., 2008). In the full sample ($n = 101$), 15 met criteria for an eating disorder. Among these participants, DBT was associated with a remission rate of 64%, compared to 50% remission for those treated by experts. In addition, relapse rate for eating disorders following DBT was nearly half the rate following treatment by experts. However, these differences were not statistically significant, likely due to the small sample size.

Another secondary analysis was conducted on data from a trial of individuals with BPD ($n = 118$) enrolled in a DBT skills group to examine factors that predicted treatment dropout (Carmona et al., 2018). Results indicated that dropout was higher for individuals with eating disorders than any other comorbid diagnosis assessed. Specifically, 43% of the group with comorbid eating disorders did not complete treatment. These results highlight additional challenges in treating eating disorders in a DBT model that warrants further consideration, especially in the context of DBT skills group as the sole mode of intervention.

Summary. The feasibility and utility of applying DBT to the treatment of adults with an eating disorder and co-occurring BPD diagnosis or personality pathology has been examined using case series, open trial designs, and secondary analyses. These studies provide preliminary evidence that DBT may be associated with improvements in various eating disorder outcomes (e.g., binge eating, purging, and weight restoration), as well as improvements in traditional DBT behavioral targets (e.g., self-injurious behaviors). However, results should be interpreted somewhat cautiously. Four out of the seven studies were modified adaptions to address eating disorder symptoms. Modifications included blending procedures of CBT and DBT, use of a skills group only, addition of a weekly yoga class, and reduction of time spent on individual therapy. In addition, of the seven studies reviewed, none were coded for adherence to ensure DBT fidelity. Further, the case series and open trials have been limited by small samples and lack of a control group, and the secondary analyses have not been designed specifically to address treatment of cooccurring eating disorders. Finally, evidence is not available regarding whether this treatment approach would be appropriate for adolescents with comorbid BPD and eating disorders. More research, utilizing randomized, controlled designs and sampling different developmental periods, is necessary to reach definitive conclusions about the efficacy of DBT to treat individuals with BPD and an eating disorder.

Dialectical behavior therapy for mixed eating disorder samples

The majority of the DBT applications to eating disorder populations without an explicit BPD diagnosis have been conducted in mixed eating disorder samples, treating DBT as a transdiagnostic treatment. These applications have been varied, with some evaluating DBT as a stand-alone treatment, and others investigating it in combination with other therapeutic approaches. Further, some of these DBT applications have been conducted only in groups with binge-eating behavior, whereas others have targeted the full range of eating pathology.

Case series. One case series assessed the feasibility of DBT to treat adults with eating disorders (Klein, Skinner, & Hawley, 2012). This 17-session group-based DBT was administered in a community clinic to women meeting full- or subthreshold criteria for BN or BED ($n = 10$). Only 50% of the sample completed treatment. However, among completers, large effect size reductions were noted for binge-eating and global eating disorder symptoms. Despite high attrition, this study provided initial support for a modified group-based DBT in an adult binge-eating sample.

In addition, one case series examined an application of DBT in the treatment of adolescent females with AN ($n = 6$) or BN ($n = 6$) (Salbach-Andrae, Bohnekamp, Pfeiffer, & Miller, 2008). These researchers used the comprehensive DBT protocol for multiproblem adolescents (Miller, Rathus, Linehan, Wetzler, & Leigh, 2007) with two main adjustments for an eating disorder population: (1) extending treatment length to 25 weeks, due to the high relapse rates associated with eating disorders (Berends, Boonstra, & van Elburg, 2018) and (2) adding an eating disorder–specific skills module. Family members attended 8 of the 25 skills groups and individual sessions as needed. Only one participant with BN dropped out of treatment. For individuals with AN, BMI increased significantly from pre- to posttreatment ($M = 15.6–18.1$ kg/m^2) and five of the six no longer met criteria for an eating disorder, although one maintained an AN diagnosis. Results were less pronounced for BN. Of the five participants with BN completing treatment, three continued to meet criteria for BN, while two crossed over to an EDNOS diagnosis; however, all showed reductions in eating disorder symptoms. Binge eating, purging, restrictive eating, overall eating pathology, and general psychiatric severity significantly decreased across the sample, suggesting promise of this approach for adolescent eating disorders.

Open trials. Two open trials have investigated DBT combined with more standard eating disorder treatment for transdiagnostic samples. In the first, researchers evaluated the impact of a weekly DBT skills group paired with standard CBT in a sample of women with AN ($n = 43$) and BN ($n = 22$) in day treatment over an average of 3 weeks (Ben-Porath, Federici, Wisniewski, & Warren, 2014). The CBT-based components of this treatment program included goal setting, cognitive restructuring, food exposure, and meal planning. The attrition rate from this program was approximately 14%; however, data were not available for all completers due to administrative errors. Among participants for whom data were available, the program resulted in significant improvements in global eating disorder symptoms, binge eating, excessive exercise, purging, restrictive eating, and BMI. Significant, but small improvements were seen in emotion regulation abilities. Because the improvements in eating disorder symptoms were consistent with previous research on CBT in intensive settings (Dalle Grave, Calugi, Conti, Doll, & Fairburn, 2013), it is unclear whether symptom reduction could be attributed to the CBT or DBT components of treatment.

A second open trial was conducted among adolescents with eating disorders (AN: $n = 17$; BN: $n = 6$; EDNOS: $n = 28$) to evaluate DBT skills training paired with FBT to treat eating disorder symptoms transdiagnostically (Johnston, O'Gara, Koman, Baker, & Anderson, 2015). Treatment was conducted in an intensive outpatient program and involved separate DBT skills groups for adolescents and for their parents, multifamily group meals, and single-family FBT sessions over the course of 30 weeks. Thirty-six (71%) of the families completed treatment. Adolescents completing the treatment demonstrated significant increases in BMI and decreases in eating disorder symptoms. For those who participated in follow-up, weight gain and decreases in eating disorder symptoms continued 3, 6, and 12 months after treatment. Of those who completed the 12-month follow-up, 64% were classified as having a "good" outcome. However, because DBT and FBT components were combined, the active agents of change are unknown.

Randomized, controlled trials. Two randomized, controlled trials have compared DBT to other interventions for individuals with varied eating disorder diagnoses. Chen et al. (2017) conducted a treatment study aiming to improve outcomes for individuals with BN or BED ($n = 109$) who exhibited a weak response in early stages of a guided self-help version of CBT (CBTgsh; Fairburn, 1995). All participants first completed 4 weeks of CBTgsh and then were administered an eating disorder assessment to evaluate early treatment response. Participants with $\geq 65\%$ decrease in binge eating (and purging, as relevant) ($n = 42$) continued CBTgsh for up to 24 weeks, and those with a lesser response were randomized to receive 6 months of either an "enhanced" version of CBT (CBT-E; Fairburn, 2008; $n = 31$) or DBT ($n = 36$). Attrition rates were lowest in CBTgsh (26%), followed by DBT (31%) and CBT-E (45%) groups. All treatments demonstrated a significant reduction in binge eating, although this change occurred quicker for the CBTgsh group who showed the earliest improvement. At 6- and 12-month follow-up, both the CBTgsh and CBT-E group showed a gradual increase in binge-eating frequency from posttreatment, while the DBT group did not show this increase. DBT also demonstrated more improvement in purging at posttreatment compared to CBT-E. The CBTgsh group did not exhibit clinical levels of purging at randomization and remained asymptomatic posttreatment. Global eating disorder symptoms significantly decreased in all groups. This study is an example of a larger, randomized trial that highlights the promise of DBT as equivalent to other treatments for a mixed binge-eating sample.

In another randomized, controlled trial, researchers compared the use of a DBT adaptation to treatment as usual (TAU) for individuals with comorbid eating and substance use disorders (Courbasson, Nishikawa, & Dixon, 2011), due to the historical difficulty in treating these co-occurring problems (Kirkpatrick et al., 2019), and the initial success of DBT for substance use disorders (Dimeff, Rizvi, Brown, & Linehan, 2000; Linehan et al., 2002). DBT was administered in standard, multimodal format, with adaptations made to accommodate the population, most notably the addition of an extra skills module utilizing psychoeducation and CBT techniques to address eating disorder and substance use issues. Participants (AN: $n = 15$; BN: $n = 11$; BED: $n = 4$) were randomized to 1 year of treatment with either DBT ($n = 15$) or TAU ($n = 10$), which followed best practice guidelines for treatment of concurrent substance use and psychiatric disorders and consisted of weekly group therapy utilizing motivational interviewing, CBT, and relapse prevention techniques, with individual treatment as needed. The attrition results strongly favored DBT; the dropout rate was 20% for DBT and 80% for TAU. Due to the high attrition rate in the TAU condition, comparison analyses between the groups could not be conducted. However, DBT was associated with decreases in binge eating, general eating pathology, substance use, and depression. Large effect sizes were found for changes in eating and substance use (but not alcohol use) and these effects were maintained over the 6-month follow-up. DBT was associated with improvements in emotion regulation variables, and changes in emotion regulation were associated with improvements in substance use urges and emotional eating, lending support to emotion regulation as a process variable in this application of DBT.

An additional randomized, controlled trial compared two different DBT treatment approaches in a mixed eating disorders sample (Klein, Skinner, & Hawley, 2013). This study compared a 15-session group-based DBT program that included all functions of traditional DBT, to a self-monitoring condition using adapted DBT diary cards. The sample consisted of women with sub- or full-threshold BED or BN ($n = 36$) who experienced objective binge eating. Participants were randomized to either self-monitoring ($n = 12$) using diary cards with an additional 15-minute weekly individual check-in or a condensed, 15-session version of traditional DBT group treatment ($n = 8$) with added focus placed on eating mindfulness. Dropout rates were substantially higher for DBT group than for self-monitoring, which was attributed to the more time-intensive nature of this approach. Participants in both forms of treatment experienced decreases in binge eating with large effect sizes; however, decreases were significantly larger in the group-based DBT with an average of zero binge episodes following treatment. Further, group-based DBT experienced greater decreases in general eating disorder symptoms. The results of this study provide support for both self-monitoring and group-based DBT in samples with binge-eating behaviors. Although group-based DBT was demonstrated to be superior on most outcomes, the self-monitoring diary cards were significantly more effective at preventing dropout. These findings encourage consideration of a patient's clinical needs and time constraints when modifying DBT interventions.

Summary. These studies provide evidence for the feasibility and efficacy of DBT for adolescents and adults with mixed eating disorder diagnoses. However, this literature is highly mixed in terms of the populations targeted and the specific DBT applications evaluated. Of the seven studies reviewed, only one reported monitoring for therapy adherence by clinicians, and adherence ratings were not reported. Six out of the seven studies modified standard DBT protocol past an additional focus on disordered eating behaviors, which included modifying the length of treatment, focusing on skills group only, focusing on self-monitoring through diary cards, and blending treatment procedures with CBT and FBT. Further, there were no analyses available to discriminate whether DBT was more or less effective in any of the particular diagnostic groups. Therefore it is difficult to draw conclusions regarding the circumstances under which it would be most appropriate to implement DBT for eating disorders, as well as which adaptations may be most useful for these populations.

Dialectical behavior therapy for binge-eating disorder

Much of the research on DBT in eating disorders has focused on individuals with BED, and the majority has been conducted by a single academic group. In most studies evaluating DBT for BED (DBT-BED), a multimodal approach has not been used, but rather all DBT functions (skill acquisition, strengthening, and generalization, and increasing motivation) have been met within the delivery of DBT skills groups only (Wiser & Telch, 1999). Thus in addition to teaching and facilitating practice of new skills, group leaders instruct clients on how to conduct chain analyses on problematic behaviors and actively target treatment commitment. In an additional deviation from standard DBT, the interpersonal effectiveness module is removed in most studies of DBT-BED to accommodate a shorter time period. Trials of DBT-BED have typically used a 20-week treatment protocol, consisting of weekly 2-hour comprehensive DBT groups. The reduced treatment period from the typical DBT protocol reflects standard length of treatment for BED in other interventions (Wilson, Grilo, & Vitousek, 2007).

Case study and series. The first application of DBT-BED followed a series of women ($n = 11$) (Telch, Agras, & Linehan, 2000). Treatment retention was high, with no participant dropout and 91% of the sample attending at least 17 of the 20 group sessions. At the end of treatment, 82% ($n = 9$) of the subjects were abstinent from binge eating and no longer met BED criteria. At 6-month follow-up, 70% ($n = 7$) of the participants reported continued abstinence from binge eating and none met BED criteria. In addition, general eating pathology was significantly reduced and emotion regulation abilities regarding eating in response to emotional triggers was enhanced.

Several years later, a case study of DBT adapted for the treatment of an adolescent female with BED was published (Safer, Lock, & Couturier, 2007). Adaptations included family involvement in treatment, simplification of skills language, and use of adolescent appropriate skill examples. Treatment was delivered over 21 sessions using individual therapy (rather than skills group) to meet all functions of DBT. Thus individual sessions targeted treatment commitment and also provided for acquisition and strengthening of DBT skills. Following treatment, the adolescent had reduced binge eating from 22 to 4 days per month. At 3-month follow-up, she reported only one binge episode over the prior 3 months. Authors noted the importance of family involvement in this case. These cases provided initial evidence of the effectiveness of DBT adaptations for BED across developmental periods.

Randomized, controlled trials. Building off the promising case series results in adults, the same group (Telch, Agras, & Linehan, 2001) conducted a randomized, controlled trial comparing the comprehensive DBT skills group to a waitlist control for women with BED ($n = 44$) over the course of 20 weeks. At the end of treatment, significant differences favoring DBT were found for binge eating and general eating pathology. For instance, 89% of the DBT group was abstinent from binge eating versus 12.5% of the control group. However, at 6-month follow-up, DBT binge abstinence rates dropped to 56%. Further, changes in negative emotion and affect regulation were not detected, raising questions regarding whether treatment effects were due to nonspecific factors.

To address these concerns the same group conducted a second randomized, controlled trial, this time comparing DBT to an active treatment group with a BED population (Safer, Robinson, & Jo, 2010). The control condition used a client-centered approach to provide nonspecific components of therapy without addressing the hypothesized active treatment components of DBT (Safer & Hugo, 2006). Men and women diagnosed with BED ($n = 101$) were randomized to receive 20 weeks of DBT or control treatment. Overall, posttreatment and follow-up data were promising for DBT. Dropout rates were significantly lower in the DBT compared to control group (4% vs 33%). Abstinence rates were significantly higher for the DBT group (64%) at posttreatment than for the control group (36%). However, differences in abstinence rates were not significant at 12-month follow-up, at which point the DBT group showed 64% abstinence and the control group showed 56% abstinence from binge eating. The same trend was present for binge frequency; reduction in binge days was significantly greater for the DBT group at posttreatment but the 12-month follow-up showed no significant difference between the groups. Improvements on other eating pathology also favored DBT. However, contrary to expectations, the control group showed greater improvement in emotion regulation at follow-up.

Post hoc analyses were also conducted on these data examining (1) potential moderators of treatment response (Robinson & Safer, 2012) and (2) rapid response to treatment (Safer & Joyce, 2011). These analyses revealed that baseline diagnosis of avoidant personality disorder and earlier onset of dieting predicted better response to DBT over the control group (Robinson & Safer, 2012). DBT was associated with greater rapid response to treatment (56%) compared to the control group (26%) (Safer & Joyce, 2011). Results of these follow-up analyses further suggest the superiority of DBT over an active control group for BED in producing rapid treatment results and begin to indicate subgroups for which DBT would be best suited, although replication is required to solidify these findings.

A final randomized, controlled trial compared a group of waitlist controls ($n = 30$) to participants who received DBT in the form of guided self-help (DBTgsh; $n = 30$) (Masson, von Ranson, Wallace, & Safer, 2013), based on findings that CBT delivered in a guided self-help modality is as potent as CBT delivered through individual therapy sessions for BED (Wilson & Zandberg, 2012). Over 13 weeks, individuals who received DBTgsh were asked to attend one 45-minute orientation session and complete six biweekly 20-minute phone calls with an individual therapist to address any issues they encountered with implementing the treatment from the manual. Following treatment, the DBTgsh group demonstrated greater reductions in binge eating and improvements in quality of life and emotional regulation than the control group. However, the DBTgsh group also had higher dropout (30%) compared to the control group (10%). Only the DBTgsh group was reassessed 6 months posttreatment. At that time, participants reported a slight increase in binge eating from posttreatment. Although binge-eating frequency did not return to the baseline level, the authors noted that the reduction in binge eating was not as well maintained when treatment was delivered in this manner compared to prior studies utilizing a group therapy format.

Summary. The results from studies examining a DBT group adapted for BED suggest that this approach can lead to significant reductions in binge eating and other eating disorder symptoms. Each study reviewed contained modifications to standard DBT treatment, including use of guided self-help only, altering length of treatment, and addition of family sessions. There remains some concern that DBT may not outperform other treatments, even nonspecific treatment; however, one study demonstrated that DBT group seems to be associated with more rapid treatment response than nonspecific treatment. Though adherence to standard DBT treatment was not reported for any of these five studies, DBT-BED has been associated with very low attrition rates, suggesting high acceptability of this intervention. Of note, attrition rates are higher when the treatment is delivered in a guided self-help format (Masson et al., 2013). The mechanism of change in DBT for BED remains unclear; however, evidence from the two randomized, controlled trials suggest that emotion regulation may not be a process of change in DBT-BED. In addition, nearly all studies on DBT-BED have been conducted by the same research team; thus further replication by independent research groups is needed.

Dialectical behavior therapy for bulimia nervosa

Fewer studies have examined the application of DBT to treat BN specifically. However, a small handful of studies, most of which have been conducted by the same group of researchers that conducted the DBT trials in BED, demonstrate promise of DBT for BN.

Case study. The first investigation of DBT adapted for BN was a case report of treatment of an adult female with BN who had a 13-year history of binge eating and purging and had been unresponsive to treatment for 2 years (Safer, Telch, & Agras, 2001a). The intervention consisted of 20 individual DBT sessions, in which the functions of individual and skills group were combined. The patient showed a rapid decline in binge eating and purging and, by the fifth week of treatment, was abstinent from these behaviors. At 6-month follow-up the participant reported a total of two binge eating and purging episodes since treatment completion. The impressive results of this report provided initial support for investigating DBT for BN.

Open trial. One open pilot study has investigated a DBT adaptation in a sample of adolescents with BN ($n = 35$) (Murray et al., 2015). This study combined elements of FBT with DBT in a partial hospitalization setting and included individual, family, multifamily, and parent-only aspects over an average duration of 11 weeks. As in standard DBT for adolescents (Miller et al., 2007), diary card review and chain analysis of behaviors was conducted during individual therapy and DBT skills training occurred through the multifamily group. The parent-only groups taught parents the contingency management skills of FBT and these were implemented in family therapy sessions. At the end of treatment, participants demonstrated a significant reduction in binge eating and purging, as well as global eating pathology. However, emotional regulation did not improve significantly, again raising questions about the process of change in this application of DBT, as well as regarding whether changes could be attributed to FBT, as opposed to DBT, components of treatment.

Randomized, controlled trials. In the first randomized, controlled trial of DBT for BN (Safer, Telch, & Agras, 2001b), 31 women who experienced at least one binge/purge episode per week for the 3 months preceding treatment were randomized to 20 weeks of DBT ($n = 14$) or a waitlist ($n = 15$). Three participants did not complete the study due to dropout ($n = 1$) or investigator-initiated treatment withdrawal ($n = 2$). As in the adult case study (Safer et al., 2001a), all DBT functions were met through individual therapy. The DBT group had a 0% attrition rate and greater reductions in binge eating, purging, emotional eating, and negative affect compared to the control group. Following treatment, 29% ($n = 4$) of DBT participants were abstinent from binge eating and purging, and an additional 36% ($n = 5$) showed significantly reduced symptoms. In contrast, 80% of participants in the waitlist condition remained fully symptomatic. Authors note that although the abstinence rates in this trial were similar to those reported in CBT treatment trials for BN, the dropout rates were far lower than those previously reported (28%) (e.g., Agras, Walsh, Fairburn, Wilson, & Kraemer, 2000).

Although the results of this study (Safer et al., 2001b) were promising, the abstinence rates (29%; $n = 4$) were not as large as those reported in trials of DBT-BED (64%–89%; Safer et al., 2001a; Telch et al., 2001). In an effort to bolster the effects of DBT for BN, the research team added components of appetite awareness training (Craighead & Allen, 1995), an approach that targets enhancing awareness and responsiveness to internal hunger and satiety cues, to DBT in a subsequent trial (Hill, Craighead, & Safer, 2010). Participants who experienced at least one binge/purge episode per week for the 3 months preceding treatment ($n = 32$) were randomly assigned to appetite-focused DBT (DBT-AF; $n = 18$) or a 6-week waitlist control group ($n = 14$). The DBT-AF treatment consisted of 15 hours of individual treatment over a 12-week period in which appetite awareness skills were interwoven with DBT skills. DBT-AF was rated as highly acceptable, and after 6 weeks of treatment, participants receiving DBT-AF reported reduced binge eating, purging, and global eating pathology, as well as improved appetite awareness compared to the control group. At 6 weeks the DBT-AF and control groups did not differ on emotion regulation; however, at posttreatment significant improvement in emotion regulation was noted for those receiving DBT-AF. Following treatment, 27% ($n = 7$) of participants were abstinent from binge eating and purging, with an additional 15% ($n = 4$) abstinent from either binge eating or purging. These abstinence rates were nearly identical to those reported from prior work on DBT in disordered eating populations (Safer et al., 2001b) and CBT (Agras et al., 2000), but the authors note that they were detected after 12 weeks of treatment, as opposed to 20. Thus it is possible that DBT-AF might lead to more rapid improvements compared to more standard treatments.

Summary. Preliminary data suggest a modified adapted version of DBT to be associated with reductions in binge eating, purging, and general eating pathology among individuals with BN. Binge eating and purging abstinence rates following DBT are similar to those reported in trials of CBT for BN (Agras et al., 2000); however, DBT may have better treatment retention. A major limitation of the studies on DBT for BN is that each of these studies has presented an adaption of standard DBT leaving the reliability of findings in question. However, the modifications have led to intriguing avenues for future research. Addition of an appetite awareness focus may result in more rapid treatment results; however, no direct comparisons have been conducted between standard or eating disorder–adapted DBT and DBT-AF or any other active intervention. In addition, the combination of DBT and FBT has produced promising initial results for adolescents with BN; however, further information is needed to determine the degree to which outcomes are related to the DBT or FBT components. It is also important to note that treatment adherence to standard DBT was not reported for any of the studies reviewed for BN. Limited research has been done in this area and, as with DBT-BED, most has been conducted by one research group. Further investigation by a greater variety of researchers is needed to draw definitive conclusions about the efficacy of DBT for BN. In addition, as with BED, questions remain regarding whether emotion regulation is the mechanisms responsible for symptom change in DBT for BN.

Dialectical behavior therapy for anorexia nervosa

Similar to the literature on DBT for BN, there are few studies investigating DBT for AN specifically. Despite initial results from mixed eating disorder samples suggesting the promise of DBT for treating AN, several researchers have surmised that DBT may be a less appropriate treatment for AN, especially restricting subtype, because the rigid and emotionally constrained presentation that often accompanies AN stands in contrast to the behaviorally dysregulated, impulsive behavior that is often targeted in standard DBT (Hempel, Vanderbleek, & Lynch, 2018). As such, the majority of the research in AN has either investigated a version of DBT adapted for problems related to emotional and behavioral *over*control (rather than undercontrol), called radically open DBT (RO-DBT) (Lynch, Hempel, & Dunkley, 2015), or has examined DBT in combination with more standard AN treatments (e.g., FBT).

Case study and series. One case study evaluated traditional DBT combined with pharmacotherapy in the treatment of an adolescent female diagnosed with AN after a massive weight loss from a state of obesity (Wolter, Schneider, Pfeiffer, & Lehmkuhl, 2009). Treatment was associated with prevention of further weight loss and improvement in depressive symptoms.

Chen et al. (2014) conducted a pair of outpatient case series, one investigating standard, comprehensive DBT ($n = 6$) and a second investigating RO-DBT ($n = 9$) for adult women with full- or subthreshold AN. For the series investigating standard DBT, all but one participant (who transitioned to a higher level of care) completed treatment and, across the group, BMI demonstrated a moderate increase. In an effort to improve the BMI effect sizes, the research group then implemented RO-DBT for the next series of participants. While maintaining many of the same structural elements, RO-DBT deviates from standard DBT by targeting emotional loneliness, as opposed to emotional dysregulation, as the core therapeutic mechanism and focusing skills to alter behavioral patterns characteristic of overcontrol (e.g., emotional inhibition, rigidity, and avoidance), rather than those more relevant to undercontrol (Hempel et al., 2018). Following outpatient RO-DBT, all but one participant (who transitioned to a higher level of care) completed treatment. Participants demonstrated large, significant BMI improvements, which were maintained at 6- and 12-month follow-ups, and decreases in eating pathology.

Open trials. Following up from the promising case series of RO-DBT for AN, Lynch et al. (2013) conducted an open trial of inpatient treatment informed by RO-DBT for individuals with AN, restricting subtype ($n = 47$). RO-DBT was implemented across modalities (i.e., individual, group, and on-unit coaching) following acute nutritional rehabilitation and medical stabilization. Attrition rate was 28%, which is lower than that reported for outpatient CBT for AN (Fairburn et al., 2013) but higher than that reported for CBT-based inpatient treatment for AN (Dalle Grave et al., 2013). Following treatment, significant improvements were noted for BMI, eating disorder symptoms, distress, and quality of life. At the end of RO-DBT inpatient treatment, 21% of the sample met criteria for full AN remission and 41% for partial remission (Lynch et al., 2013), which is similar to CBT success rates (Dalle Grave et al., 2013).

Two additional open trials have examined the effects of combining of DBT and FBT approaches in the treatment of adolescents with AN. The first investigated the integration of DBT skills into an FBT-focused day treatment and intensive outpatient program for adolescents with AN, restricting type ($n = 11$) (Accurso, Astrachan-Fletcher, O'Brien, Mcclanahan, & Grange, 2017). Treatment consisted of 19 sessions; 4 of these focused explicitly on standard DBT skills (Linehan, 1993), including mindfulness, validation, distress tolerance, and emotion regulation.

Providers reported satisfaction with this treatment; however, they stated that they struggled to implement DBT skills in an FBT framework. Treatment was associated with improvements in adolescent BMI and caregiver-reported adolescent eating disorder symptoms. In the second open trial, adolescent females with full- or subthreshold AN ($n = 18$) participated in a 6-month DBT skills group as an adjunct to FBT (Peterson, Van Diest, Mara, & Matthews, 2019). In addition to participating in skills group, adolescents were encouraged to complete a diary card, which they discussed in individual FBT sessions. Two-thirds of the participants in this trial were retained and, among completers, small to medium effect sizes were noted for increases in weight and decreases in eating disorder and depressive symptoms, and large effect sizes were found for increases in DBT skill knowledge and use.

Randomized, controlled trials. Only one randomized, controlled trial has examined the impact of DBT on treatment of AN. In this study, adolescents with AN ($n = 50$) were assigned to receive treatment with either DBT (individual and group skills training) or CBT (Jaite et al., 2018). Although outcomes were reported for each treatment in this study, the primary aim was to examine predictors of patient and provider satisfaction across treatments; therefore direct statistical comparisons were not made between the two treatments. Both treatments involved 25 individual and group sessions. Parents took part in five of the individual and eight of the group sessions. Satisfaction did not differ between conditions and both treatments were associated with significant increases in BMI and decreases in eating disorder and general psychiatric symptoms. Overall, the effect sizes tended to be a bit lower in the DBT versus CBT condition.

Summary. Adaptations of DBT have been shown to hold promise for increasing weight and decreasing eating disorder and other psychiatric symptoms among individuals with AN. As is common in treatment of AN (Berkman et al., 2006), dropout rates tended to have been higher for these trials than many other DBT adaptations. There has been very little research evaluating traditional DBT for AN. Rather, much of the research in this area has centered on the application of RO-DBT for adults with AN and combinations of FBT and DBT for adolescents with AN. Although all of these studies demonstrate clinical improvement, because they have not directly compared DBT to more standard treatments for AN (e.g., CBT and FBT), there is not yet strong evidence that these DBT applications produce better outcomes. Further, it remains unclear whether adaptations of DBT (e.g., RO-DBT, FBT, and DBT combined) hold advantage over traditional DBT, as these approaches have never been directly compared. Finally, though four of five studies reviewed for AN-modified standard DBT, none of the studies reported adherence rates to treatment.

Conclusion and future directions

Summary of the research

A total of three case reports, eight case series, one secondary analysis, eight open trials, and nine randomized, controlled trials have been published on the use of DBT with eating disordered populations (Table 6.1). The majority of research has enrolled mixed diagnosis samples with or without comorbid BPD. Among the studies targeting a specific eating disorder diagnosis, most have focused on samples with BED. The cumulative results of this research highlight the feasibility and acceptability of DBT adaptations for a variety of eating disorder samples, including both adult and adolescent samples and those with and without a cooccurring diagnosis of BPD, and across a variety of treatment settings, including outpatient, intensive outpatient, partial hospitalization, and inpatient settings. Treatment with DBT has been shown to promote improvements in binge eating, purging, restrictive eating, low weight, and other eating and general psychiatric variables. Effect sizes for eating disorder–related outcomes mostly have been in the medium to large range, whereas effects of other psychiatric sequelae (e.g., depression and anxiety) have been more modest and mixed. The treatment effects to date are similar to those achieved by other psychotherapies for eating disorder populations; however, there is indication that DBT may enhance treatment retention, which is similar to findings from other groups treated with DBT (Feigenbaum, 2007).

Additional considerations and limitations

Study design. At this point the results of this literature ought to be regarded cautiously. Despite research on DBT for eating disorders increasing substantially in recent years, optimal study designs have not been widely utilized. Most studies have been limited by small samples. Few have used randomized, controlled designs, and among those that have, the control condition has generally been waitlist or a weaker therapeutic intervention. Although randomized, controlled trials are not the only valid intervention design, and effectiveness studies, such as many of those reported in this literature, provide useful information about real-world applications, data derived from studies with high internal validity are needed. Therefore first and foremost, future research directions should include larger samples and more stringent study designs.

Only one study (Chen et al., 2017) has directly compared DBT to any form of standard eating disorder treatment (i.e., CBT). Therefore other head-to-head comparisons of treatment effects between DBT and other active treatments (e.g., CBT, FBT, and interpersonal therapy) would

TABLE 6.1 Studies of dialectical behavior therapy (DBT)–based treatments for eating disorders.

Citation	Sample	Study design	Treatment duration	Significance	Effect size
DBT for eating disorders comorbid with BPD					
Palmer et al. (2003)	$n = 7$ (5 BN, 1 BED, 1 EDNOS; adult females)	Case series	24–72 weeks	–	Small (NSSI)
Chen et al. (2008)	$n = 8$ ED + BPD (3 BN, 5 BED; adults)	Case series	24 weeks	–	Large (binge eating, global eating disorder symptoms, and social functioning), medium to large (other psychiatric diagnoses), and small to medium (NSSI, suicidal behavior)
Federici and Wisniewski (2013)	$n = 7$ (4 AN, 3 EDNOS, adult females)	Case series	24 weeks	–	Large (BMI, restrictive eating, purging, and excessive exercise) and medium (binge eating, NSSI)
Kröger et al. (2010)	$n = 24$ (9 AN, 15 BN; adult females)	Open trial	12 weeks	Yes	Large (BMI, binge eating, and global functioning), medium to large (eating disorder symptoms), and small to medium (psychiatric symptoms)
Ben-Porath et al. (2009)	$n = 40$ (7 AN, 16 BN, 15 EDNOS adults)	Open trial	$M = 10.5$ weeks	Yes	Large (ED symptoms, depression, and anxiety), small to large (negative mood regulation)
Harned et al. (2008)	$n = 101$ BPD (15 comorbid ED + BPD; adults)	Secondary analysis	52 weeks	No	Small (remission) and medium (partial remission)
Carmona et al. (2018)	$n = 118$ BPD (37 comorbid ED + BPD; adults)	Secondary analysis	13 weeks	–	–

(*Continued*)

TABLE 6.1 (Continued)

Citation	Sample	Study design	Treatment duration	Significance	Effect size
DBT for mixed eating disorder samples					
Klein et al. (2012)	$n = 10$ (2 BN, 4 BED, 4 EDNOS; adult females)	Open trial	17 sessions	Yes	Large (binge eating, bulimic symptoms, drive for thinness, and body dissatisfaction)
Salbach-Andrae et al. (2008)	$n = 12$ (6 AN, 6 BN; adolescent females)	Case series	25 weeks	Yes	Large (BMI, binge eating, purging, bulimic symptoms, restrictive eating, and drive for thinness), medium (body dissatisfaction and psychiatric symptoms)
Ben-Porath et al. (2014)	$n = 65$ (22 AN, 43 BN; adult females)	Open trial	$M = 3$ weeks	Yes	Large (BMI), small to medium (ED symptoms), and small (emotion regulation abilities)
Johnston et al. (2015)	$n = 51$ (17 AN, 6 BN, 28 EDNOS; adolescent females)	Open trial	30 weeks	Yes	Medium to large (% ideal body weight, global eating disorder symptoms)
Chen et al. (2017)	$n = 109$ (31 BN, 78 BED; adult females)	RCT	28 weeks	Yes	Medium to large (global eating disorder symptoms), medium (binge-eating frequency and abstinence), small to medium (vomiting, global functioning), and small (BMI)
Courbasson et al. (2011)	$n = 21$ ED + SUD (10 AN, 8 BN, 3 BED; adult females)	RCT	52 weeks	Yes	Large (binge eating, bulimic symptoms, global eating disorder symptoms, and substance use symptoms), medium to large (depression), and small to large (negative mood regulation)
Klein et al. (2013)	$n = 36$ (10 BN, 19 BED, 7 EDNOS; adult females)	Open trial	15 sessions (16 weeks)	Yes	Large (binge eating and bulimic symptoms), medium to large (drive for thinness), and medium (purging and body dissatisfaction)

(Continued)

TABLE 6.1 (Continued)

Citation	Sample	Study design	Treatment duration	Significance	Effect size
DBT for BED					
Telch et al. (2000)	$n = 11$ BED (adult females)	Case series	20 weeks	Yes	Large (binge eating, body satisfaction, depression, anxiety, and positive affect), medium (negative mood regulation), and small (BMI, restraint, negative affect, self-esteem)
Safer et al. (2007)	$n = 1$ BED (adolescent female)	Case report	21 sessions	–	–
Telch et al. (2001)	$n = 44$ BED (adult females)	RCT	20 weeks	Yes	Large (binge eating, body dissatisfaction, and anxiety), small to medium (depression), and small (weight, restraint, negative mood regulation, and negative affect)
Safer et al. (2010)	$n = 101$ BED (adults)	RCT	20 weeks	Yes	Medium (restraint) and small (depression, anxiety, and negative affect)
Masson et al. (2013)	$n = 60$ BED (adults)	RCT	13 weeks	Yes	Medium to large (disorder-related quality of life and global eating disorder symptoms), medium (binge eating and emotion regulation abilities), and small to medium (restraint)
DBT for BN					
Safer et al. (2001a,b)	$n = 1$ BN (adult female)	Case report	20 sessions	–	–
Murray et al. (2015)	$n = 35$ BN (adolescent females)	Open trial	$M = 11$ weeks	Yes	Large (purging, restraint, and global eating disorder symptoms), medium (BMI), and small (binge eating)
Safer et al. (2001a,b)	$n = 31$ BN (adult females)	RCT	20 weeks	Yes	Large (BMI and binge eating), medium (purging, depression, anxiety, negative affect, and negative mood regulation)

(Continued)

TABLE 6.1 (Continued)

Citation	Sample	Study design	Treatment duration	Significance	Effect size
Hill et al. (2010)	$n = 32$ BN (adult females)	Open trial	12 weeks	Yes	Large (restraint and appetite awareness), medium (binge eating, purging, global eating disorder symptoms, depression, emotional eating, and negative mood regulation)
DBT for AN					
Wolter et al. (2009)	$n = 1$ AN (adolescent female)	Case report	Not specified	–	–
Chen et al. (2014)	Case series 1: $n = 6$ AN (adult females); case series 2: $n = 9$ (1 AN, 8 EDNOS; adult females)	Case series	Case series 1: $M = 29$ weeks; case series 2: $M = 13$ weeks	Yes	Case series 1 (standard DBT): medium (BMI); case series 2 (adapted DBT): large (BMI, other psychiatric disorders), small to medium (global eating disorder symptoms and global functioning)
Lynch et al. (2013)	$n = 47$ AN restricting subtype (adolescents and adults)	Open trial	$M = 22$ weeks	Yes	Large (BMI, eating disorder symptoms, psychological distress, and quality of life)
Accurso et al. (2017)	$n = 11$ (AN; adolescent females)	Open trial	19 sessions (15 weeks)	Yes	Large (BMI) and medium (caregiver-reported eating disorder symptomology)
Peterson et al. (2019)	$n = 18$ AN (adolescent females)	Open trial	24 weeks	Yes	Small to medium (% ideal body weight and global eating disorder symptoms) and large (DBT skill knowledge and use)
Jaite et al. (2018)	$n = 50$ (AN; adolescent females)	RCT	25 weeks	Yes	Medium (BMI and eating disorder symptoms) and small (psychiatric symptoms)

AN, Anorexia nervosa; *BED*, binge-eating disorder; *BN*, bulimia nervosa; *BPD*, borderline personality disorder; *ED*, eating disorder; *EDNOS*, eating disorder not otherwise specified; *NSSI*, non-suicidal self-injury; *SUD*, substance use disorder.

provide useful information, such as which treatment to offer as a first-line psychotherapy for particular eating disordered populations. However, perhaps even more useful data that could be gained by comparing active treatments would be information regarding moderators and mediators of DBT compared to other treatments (Kraemer, Wilson, Fairburn, & Agras, 2002). It is quite possible that DBT may best serve different subsets of the eating disorder population than more traditional eating disorder treatments. For instance, it has been suggested that DBT may be most appropriate for eating disordered individuals with greater symptom severity, higher rates of comorbidity, or a history of failing more traditional eating disorder treatment (Halmi, 2009). Unfortunately, because DBT has rarely been compared to other active treatments, this hypothesis remains untested. Further information regarding moderators and mediators of response to DBT versus other treatments would enhance the ability to effectively personalize eating disorder treatment according to the presenting characteristics or underlying functions of disordered eating.

Mechanisms of change. One curiosity in the literature on DBT for eating disorders is that regarding emotion regulation as a mechanism of change. While several studies report improvements in emotion regulation and related variables following DBT (Ben-Porath et al., 2009, 2014; Courbasson et al., 2011; Hill et al., 2010; Masson et al., 2013; Safer et al., 2001b; Telch et al., 2000), others have failed to detect improvements in emotion regulation or found superior improvement in emotion regulation from a nonspecific treatment (Murray et al., 2015; Safer et al., 2001a, b; Telch et al., 2001). These inconsistencies could reflect measurement issues (i.e., insensitive emotion regulation measurement devices), or they could suggest that DBT manipulates different mechanisms of change in certain eating disorder subsets compared to other clinical groups. Supporting the latter hypothesis, many of the effect sizes for emotion regulation changes that have been detected have been small (e.g., Ben-Porath et al., 2009, 2014; Courbasson et al., 2011). Information regarding mediators of any treatment is important as this allows researchers and clinicians to understand why and how an intervention is effective, to direct efforts toward enhancing active agents of treatment, and allowing greater flexibility in technique (Kraemer et al., 2002). Further, this information could provide context regarding whether the full DBT is needed, or whether particular components (e.g., mindfulness and motivational enhancement) may be sufficient for treating eating disorders.

Multiple adaptations. Another issue that arises in examining the literature on DBT applications for eating disorders is inconsistency in adaptation between trials. Of the 29 studies reported, 23 reported unique modifications and adaptions to DBT. Different adaptations have been made by various research groups, which include amending the DBT treatment hierarchy, removing skill modules, adjusting the format of treatment (i.e., group or individual treatment only), altering treatment length, and combining with other treatment approaches (e.g., CBT and FBT). In addition, several research groups have created additional skill modules to address concerns related to eating disorders (e.g., Wiser & Telch, 1999), and one group has created a new version of DBT, targeting novel processes, for specific eating disorder populations (Chen et al., 2014; Lynch et al., 2013). Although these adaptations have been made on sound theoretical bases, there has not been adequate coordination among researchers regarding which adaptations to apply in different contexts, leading to inconsistency in the literature, and potential danger of proliferating multiple DBT adaptations for eating disordered populations. Thus further coordination of efforts among researchers applying DBT to eating disorder populations is encouraged to enhance treatment consistency and comparability. Further, of the 29 studies reviewed, none reported ratings of standard DBT adherence to further verify the quality of the delivery of the treatment, though some did mention adherence was monitored through supervision and others reported adherence ratings as high for adapted forms of DBT.

Conclusion

Continued research is needed to investigate DBT for eating disorders. The data to date suggest promise for applications of DBT for such populations; however, more rigorous studies are needed. Further, it remains unclear which eating disorder groups, under what circumstances, may benefit from DBT, and which treatment mechanisms produce treatment effects. Further investigation of such questions is encouraged. However, there is growing evidence that DBT adaptations might aid in filling in gaps in the treatment for these serious and, at times, life-threatening, disorders.

References

Accurso, E. C., Astrachan-Fletcher, E., O'Brien, S., Mcclanahan, S. F., & Grange, D. L. (2017). Adaptation and implementation of family-based treatment enhanced with dialectical behavior therapy skills for anorexia nervosa in community-based specialist clinics. *Eating Disorders*, *26*, 149–163.

Agras, W. S., Walsh, T., Fairburn, C. G., Wilson, G. T., & Kraemer, H. C. (2000). A multicenter comparison of cognitive-behavioral therapy and interpersonal psychotherapy for bulimia nervosa. *Archives of General Psychiatry*, *57*, 459–466.

Ben-Porath, D. D., Federici, A., Wisniewski, L., & Warren, M. (2014). Dialectical behavior therapy: Does it bring about improvements in affect regulation in individuals with eating disorders? *Journal of Contemporary Psychotherapy*, *44*, 245–251.

Ben-Porath, D. D., Wisniewski, L., & Warren, M. (2009). Differential treatment response for eating disordered patients with and without a comorbid borderline personality diagnosis using a dialectical behavior therapy (DBT)-informed approach. *Eating Disorders, 17*, 225–241.

Berends, T., Boonstra, N., & van Elburg, A. (2018). Relapse in anorexia nervosa: A systematic review and meta-analysis. *Current Opinion in Psychiatry, 31*, 445–455.

Berking, M., & Wupperman, P. (2012). Emotion regulation and mental health. *Current Opinion in Psychiatry, 25*, 128–134.

Berkman, N., Bulik, C., Brownley, K., Lohr, K., Sedway, J., Rooks, A., & Gartlehner, G. (2006). Management of eating disorders. *Evidence Report Technology Assessment (Full Report), 135*, 1–166.

Carmona, C. F., Pascual, J. C., Elices, M., Navarro, H., Martin, A. B., & Soler, J. (2018). Factors predicting early dropout from dialectical behaviour therapy in individuals with borderline personality disorder. *Actas Espanolas de Psiquiatria, 46*, 226–233.

Chen, E. Y., Cacioppo, J., Fettich, K., Gallop, R., McCloskey, M. S., Olino, T., & Zeffiro, T. A. (2017). An adaptive randomized trial of dialectical behavior therapy and cognitive behavior therapy for binge-eating. *Psychological Medicine, 47*, 703–717.

Chen, E. Y., Matthews, L., Allen, C., Kuo, K. R., & Linehan, M. M. (2008). Dialectical behavior therapy for clients with binge-eating disorder or bulimia nervosa and borderline personality disorder. *International Journal of Eating Disorders, 41*, 505–512.

Chen, E. Y., Segal, K., Weissman, J., Zeffiro, T. A., Gallop, R., Linehan, M. M., ... Lynch, T. R. (2014). Adapting dialectical behavior therapy for outpatient adult anorexia nervosa—A pilot study. *International Journal of Eating Disorders, 48*, 123–132.

Courbasson, C., Nishikawa, Y., & Dixon, L. (2011). Outcome of dialectical behaviour therapy for concurrent eating and substance use disorders. *Clinical Psychology and Psychotherapy, 19*, 434–449.

Craighead, L. W., & Allen, H. N. (1995). Appetite awareness training: A cognitive behavioral intervention for binge eating. *Cognitive and Behavioral Practice, 2*, 249–270.

Dalle Grave, R., Calugi, S., Conti, M., Doll, H., & Fairburn, C. G. (2013). Inpatient cognitive behaviour therapy for anorexia nervosa: A randomized controlled trial. *Psychotherapy and Psychosomatics, 82*, 390–398.

Dimeff, L., Rizvi, S. L., Brown, M., & Linehan, M. M. (2000). Dialectical behavior therapy for substance abuse: A pilot application to methamphetamine-dependent women with borderline personality disorder. *Cognitive and Behavioral Practice, 7*, 457–468.

Fairburn, C. G. (1995). *Overcoming binge eating*. New York: Guilford Press.

Fairburn, C. G. (2008). *Cognitive behavior therapy and eating disorders*. New York: Guilford Press.

Fairburn, C., Cooper, Z., Doll, H., O'Connor, M., Bohn, K., Hawker, D., & Palmer, R. L. (2009). Transdiagnostic cognitive-behavioral therapy for patients with eating disorders: A two-site trial with 60-week follow-up. *American Journal of Psychiatry, 166*, 311–319.

Fairburn, C. G., Cooper, Z., Doll, H. A., O'Connor, M. E., Palmer, R. L., & Dalle Grave, R. (2013). Enhanced cognitive behaviour therapy for adults with anorexia nervosa: A UK–Italy study. *Behaviour Research and Therapy, 51*, R2–R8.

Federici, A., & Wisniewski, L. (2013). An intensive DBT program for patients with multidiagnostic eating disorder presentations: A case series analysis. *International Journal of Eating Disorders, 46*, 322–331.

Feigenbaum, J. (2007). Dialectical behavior therapy: An increasing evidence base. *Journal of Mental Health, 16*, 51–68.

Fisher, C. A., Skocic, S., Rutherford, K. A., & Hetrick, S. E. (2019). Family therapy approaches for anorexia nervosa. *Cochrane Database of Systematic Reviews, 5*, 1–214.

Grilo, C. M., Masheb, R. M., Wilson, G. T., Gueorguieva, R., & White, M. A. (2011). Cognitive-behavioral therapy, behavioral weight loss, and sequential treatment for obese patients with binge eating disorder: A randomized controlled trial. *Journal of Consulting and Clinical Psychology, 79*, 675–685.

Halmi, K. (2009). Salient components of a comprehensive service for eating disorders. *World Psychiatry, 8*, 150–155.

Harned, M. S., Chapman, A. L., Dexter-Mazza, E. T., Murray, A., Comtois, K. A., & Linehan, M. M. (2008). Treating co-occurring axis I disorders in recurrently suicidal women with borderline personality disorder: A 2-year randomized trial of dialectical behavior therapy versus community treatment by experts. *Journal of Consulting and Clinical Psychology, 76*, 1068–1075.

Hempel, R., Vanderbleek, E., & Lynch, T. R. (2018). Radically open DBT: Targeting emotional loneliness in anorexia nervosa. *Eating Disorders, 26*, 92–104.

Hill, D. M., Craighead, L. W., & Safer, D. L. (2010). Appetite-focused dialectical behavior therapy for the treatment of binge eating with purging: A preliminary trial. *International Journal of Eating Disorders, 44*, 249–261.

Jaite, C., Pfeiffer, A., Pfeiffer, E., Thurn, C., Bierbaum, T., Winter, S. M., ... Salbach, H. (2018). Subjective evaluation of outpatient treatment for adolescent patients with anorexia nervosa. *Eating and Weight Disorders*. Available from https://doi.org/10.1007/s40519-018-0620-0.

Johnston, J. A., O'Gara, J. S., Koman, S. L., Baker, C. W., & Anderson, D. A. (2015). A pilot study of Maudsley family therapy with group dialectical behavior therapy skills training in an intensive outpatient program for adolescent eating disorders. *Journal of Clinical Psychology, 71*, 527–543.

Johnson, C., Tobin, D., & Dennis, A. B. (1990). Differences in treatment outcome between borderline and nonborderline bulimics at one year follow-up. *International Journal of Eating Disorders, 9*, 617–628.

Kirkpatrick, R., Booij, L., Vance, A., Marshall, B., Kanellos-Sutton, M., Marchand, P., & Khalid-Khan, S. (2019). Eating disorders and substance use in adolescents: How substance users differ from nonsubstance users in an outpatient eating disorders treatment clinic. *International Journal of Eating Disorders, 52*, 175–182.

Klein, A. S., Skinner, J. B., & Hawley, K. M. (2012). Adapted group-based dialectical behaviour therapy for binge eating in a practicing clinic: Clinical outcomes and attrition. *European Eating Disorders Review, 20*, e148–e153.

Klein, A. S., Skinner, J. B., & Hawley, K. M. (2013). Targeting binge eating through components of dialectical behavior therapy: Preliminary outcomes for individually supported diary card self-monitoring versus group-based DBT. *Psychotherapy, 50*, 543.

Kraemer, H. C., Wilson, G. T., Fairburn, C. G., & Agras, W. S. (2002). Mediators and moderators of treatment effects in randomized clinical trials. *Archives of General Psychiatry, 59*, 877–883.

Kröger, C., Schweiger, U., Sipos, V., Kliem, S., Arnold, R., Schunert, T., & Reinecker, H. (2010). Dialectical behaviour therapy and an added cognitive behavioural treatment module for eating disorders in women with borderline personality disorder and anorexia nervosa or bulimia nervosa who failed to respond to previous treatments. An open trial with a 15-month follow-up. *Journal of Behavioral Therapy & Experimental Psychiatry, 41*, 381–388.

Linardon, J., Wade, T. D., De la Piedad Garcia, X., & Brennan, L. (2017). The efficacy of cognitive-behavioral therapy for eating disorders: A systematic review and meta-analysis. *Journal of Consulting and Clinical Psychology, 85*, 1080–1094.

Linehan, M. M. (1993). *Cognitive-behavioral treatment of borderline personality disorder*. New York: Guilford Press.

Linehan, M. M., Dimeff, L. A., Reynolds, S. K., Comtois, K. A., Welch, S. S., Heagerty, P., & Kivlahan, P. D. R. (2002). Dialectical behavior therapy versus comprehensive validation therapy plus 12-step for the treatment of opioid dependent women meeting criteria for borderline personality disorder. *Drug and Alcohol Dependence, 67*, 13–26.

Lynch, T. R., Gray, K. L., Hempel, R. J., Titley, M., Chen, E. Y., & O'Mahen, H. A. (2013). Radically open-dialectical behavior therapy for adult anorexia nervosa: Feasibility and outcomes from an inpatient program. *BMC Psychiatry, 13*, 293.

Lynch, T. R., Hempel, R. J., & Dunkley, C. (2015). Radically open-dialectical behavior therapy for disorders of over-control: Signaling matters. *American Journal of Psychotherapy, 69*, 141–162.

Martinussen, M., Friborg, O., Schmierer, P., Kaiser, S., Øvergård, K. T., Neunhoeffer, A., ... Rosenvinge, J. H. (2017). The comorbidity of personality disorders in eating disorders: A meta-analysis. *Eating and Weight Disorders, 22*, 201–209.

Marucci, S., Ragione, L. D., De Iaco, G., Mococci, T., Vicini, M., Guastamacchia, E., & Triggiani, V. (2018). Anorexia nervosa and comorbid psychopathology. *Endocrine, Metabolic & Immune Disorders Drug Targets, 18*, 316–324.

Masson, P. C., von Ranson, K. M., Wallace, L. M., & Safer, D. L. (2013). A randomized wait-list controlled pilot study of dialectical behaviour therapy guided self-help for binge eating disorder. *Behaviour Research and Therapy, 51*, 723–728.

Miller, A. L., Rathus, J. H., Linehan, M. M., Wetzler, S., & Leigh, E. (2007). Dialectical behavior therapy adapted for suicidal adolescents. *Journal of Practical Psychiatry and Behavioral Health, 56*, 1131–1152.

Murray, S. B., Anderson, L. K., Cusack, A., Nakamura, T., Rockwell, R., Griffiths, S., & Kaye, W. H. (2015). Integrating family-based treatment and dialectical behavior therapy for adolescent bulimia nervosa: Preliminary outcomes of an open pilot trial. *Eating Disorders, 23*, 336–344.

Palmer, R. L., Birchall, H., Damani, S., Gatward, N., McGrain, L., & Parker, L. (2003). A dialectical behavior therapy program for people with an eating disorder and borderline personality disorder—Description and outcome. *International Journal of Eating Disorders, 33*, 281–286.

Panos, P. T., Jackson, J. W., Hasan, O., & Panos, A. (2013). Meta-analysis and systematic review assessing the efficacy of dialectical behavior therapy (DBT). *Research on Social Work Practice, 24*, 213–223.

Perseius, K. I., Kåver, A., Ekdahl, S., Asberg, M., & Samuelsson, M. (2007). Stress and burnout in psychiatric professionals when starting to use dialectical behavioural therapy in the work with young self-harming women showing borderline personality symptoms. *Journal of Psychiatric and Mental Health Nursing, 14*, 635–643.

Peterson, C. M., Van Diest, A. M. K., Mara, C. A., & Matthews, A. (2019). Dialectical behavioral therapy skills group as an adjunct to family-based therapy in adolescents with restrictive eating disorders. *Eating Disorders*, 1–13. Available from https://doi.org/10.1080/10640266.2019.1568101.

Robinson, A. H., & Safer, D. L. (2012). Moderators of dialectical behavior therapy for binge eating disorder: Results from a randomized controlled trial. *International Journal of Eating Disorders, 45*, 597–602.

Safer, D. L., & Hugo, E. M. (2006). Designing a control group for a behavioral group therapy. *Behavior Therapy, 37*, 120–130.

Safer, D. L., & Joyce, E. E. (2011). Does rapid response to two group psychotherapies for binge eating disorder predict abstinence? *Behavior Research and Therapy, 49*, 339–345.

Safer, D. L., Lock, J., & Couturier, J. L. (2007). Dialectical behavior therapy modified for adolescent binge eating disorder: A case report. *Cognitive and Behavioral Practice, 14*, 157–167.

Safer, D. L., Robinson, A. H., & Jo, B. (2010). Outcome from a randomized controlled trial of group therapy for binge eating disorder: Comparing dialectical behavior therapy adapted for binge eating to an active comparison group therapy. *Behavior Therapy, 41*, 106–120.

Safer, D. L., Telch, C. S., & Agras, W. S. (2001a). Dialectical behavior therapy adapted for bulimia: A case report. *International Journal of Eating Disorders, 30*, 101–106.

Safer, D. L., Telch, C. S., & Agras, W. S. (2001b). Dialectical behavior therapy for bulimia nervosa. *American Journal of Psychiatry, 158*, 632–634.

Salbach-Andrae, H., Bohnekamp, I., Pfeiffer, E., & Miller, A. L. (2008). Dialectical behavior therapy of anorexia and bulimia nervosa among adolescents: A case series. *Cognitive and Behavioral Practice, 15*, 415–425.

Shah, R., & Zanarini, M. (2018). Comorbidity of borderline personality disorder: Current status and future directions. *Psychiatric Clinics of North America, 41*, 583–593.

Telch, C. F., Agras, W. S., & Linehan, M. M. (2000). Group dialectical behavior therapy for binge-eating disorder: A preliminary, uncontrolled trial. *Behavior Therapy, 31*, 569–582.

Telch, C. F., Agras, W. S., & Linehan, M. M. (2001). Dialectical behavior therapy for binge eating disorder. *Journal of Clinical and Consulting Psychology, 69*, 1061–1065.

Wallier, J., Vibert, S., Berthoz, S., Huas, C., Hubert, T., & Godart, N. (2009). Dropout from inpatient treatment for anorexia nervosa: Critical review of the literature. *International Journal of Eating Disorders, 42*, 636–637.

Wilfley, D. E., Friedman, M. A., Dounchis, J. Z., Stein, R. I., Welch, R. R., & Ball, S. A. (2000). Comorbid psychopathology in binge eating disorder: Relation to eating disorder severity at baseline and following treatment. *Journal of Consulting and Clinical Psychology, 68*, 641–649.

Wilson, G. T., Grilo, C. M., & Vitousek, K. M. (2007). Psychological treatment of eating disorders. *The American Psychologist, 62*, 199–216.

Wilson, G. T., & Zandberg, L. J. (2012). Cognitive–behavioral guided self-help for eating disorders: Effectiveness and scalability. *Clinical Psychology Review, 32*, 343–357.

Wiser, S., & Telch, C. F. (1999). Dialectical behavior therapy for binge eating. *Journal of Clinical Psychology, 55*, 755–768.

Wisniewski, L., Safer, D., Chen, E., Dimeff, L. A., & Koerner, K. (2007). *Dialectical behavior therapy and eating disorders. Dialectical behavior therapy in clinicalpractice: Applications across disorders and settings*, (pp. 174–221). New York, NY US: Guilford Press.

Wolter, H., Schneider, N., Pfeiffer, E., & Lehmkuhl, U. (2009). Diagnostic crossover from obesity to atypical anorexia nervosa – A case report. *Obesity Facts, 2*(1), 52–53. Available from https://doi.org/10.1159/000194641.

CHAPTER

7

Dialectical behavior therapy for individuals with substance use problems: theoretical adaptations and empirical evidence

Nicholas L. Salsman

School of Psychology, Xavier University, Cincinnati, OH, United States

Dialectical behavior therapy (DBT) for individuals with substance use disorders (SUDs) or more broadly, substance use problems, has amassed a significant amount of empirical support. This chapter reviews 8 randomized controlled trials (RCTs), 12 uncontrolled and quasiexperimental trials, as well as a variety of small N pilot and case studies that examine DBT with individuals with substance use problems, as well as DBT specifically targeting SUDs (i.e., DBT-SUD). Prior reviews of DBT for individuals with SUD have concluded that DBT is a leading treatment for individuals with SUD and borderline personality disorder (BPD) (Lee, Cameron, & Jenner, 2015; Substance Abuse and Mental Health Services Administration, 2014). This chapter will provide further details about the varied research studies and developments of DBT for individuals with substance use problems.

What is dialectical behavior therapy-substance use disorder

Linehan described DBT as she developed it in her original treatment manuals (Linehan, 1993a, 1993b) and specifically addressed applications

DOI: https://doi.org/10.1016/B978-0-12-816384-9.00007-5

for individuals with SUDs in her revised skills training manuals (Linehan, 2015a, 2015b). DBT was developed as an outpatient treatment for individuals with BPD, and particularly those with chronically suicidal behavior whose problems were conceptualized as resulting from pervasive emotion dysregulation. Standard or comprehensive DBT is a yearlong outpatient treatment that involves four modes of treatment: weekly individual therapy, weekly skills training typically delivered in group format, weekly therapist consultation team, and as needed telephone coaching. In individual therapy, therapists use a hierarchy of targets (i.e., decreasing life-threatening behaviors, decreasing therapy-interfering behaviors, decreasing quality-of-life-interfering behaviors, and increasing the capability to use skills) to determine the focus of sessions. Individual therapists use tools, including a diary card to monitor important variables, chain analysis to assess and understand problem behaviors, and solution analysis to help prevent further repetitions of the problem behaviors. In skills training, clients learn the four skill sets of mindfulness, interpersonal effectiveness, emotion regulation, and distress tolerance.

Subsequent to the original conception of DBT, Linehan created a slight adaptation of DBT to specifically target SUDs (DBT-SUD; Linehan & Dimeff, 1997). DBT-SUD was developed in the context of a study funded by the National Institute on Drug Abuse (Linehan et al., 1999) and was focused on helping individuals whose struggles with pervasive emotion dysregulation included substance use problems. DBT-SUD practitioners strive to treat substance use problems and other mental health problems simultaneously. DBT-SUD included all of the standard modes and strategies of comprehensive DBT but added additional skills and points of emphasis to help therapists and clients conceptualize and treat SUDs.

In DBT-SUD, Linehan (2015a) added seven new skills in the distress tolerance section for when addiction is a crisis. Collectively, these are known as the DCBA skills based on the first initial of each of the seven skills. *Dialectical abstinence* focuses on helping individuals synthesize a pure abstinence approach with a harm reduction approach. *Clear mind* is a skill where individuals use wisdom to navigate a middle path between the pulls and the dangers of both addict mind (i.e., a life centered on addiction) and clean mind (i.e., believing one is immune to addiction). *Community reinforcement* teaches individuals to alter their environments so that they shape abstinence behaviors. *Burning bridges* further focuses on altering the environment by making access to substances more difficult. *Building new bridges* involves teaching people to use images and smells to compete with drug cravings. *Alternate rebellion* is designed to help people find less destructive ways to rebel, other than substance use. Finally, *adaptive denial* is a skill where people use their thoughts to compel themselves to be abstinent. With these additional skills, DBT-SUD focuses on empowering the client to utilize skillful behaviors to regulate their emotions (as well as their physiology, actions, cognition, and environment) and thereby decrease the motivation to use substances.

There are a number of points of emphasis in DBT-SUD, which are intended to help providers increase their effectiveness with individuals with SUD. While the target hierarchy remains the same as in comprehensive DBT, DBT-SUD includes an emphasis on abstinence from the drug of choice as the top quality of life target with a focus on the *Path to Clear Mind* described by McMain, Sayrs, Dimeff, and Linehan (2007). DBT-SUD therapists are called to recognize that by the nature of the SUD, there is high potential that individuals with these disorders will have problems with attending sessions regularly and attaching to therapists, often referred to as butterfly attachment (Linehan, 1993a, 1993b). These therapy-interfering behaviors are targeted with added emphasis on the use of attachment strategies and contingency management. Further, there is also an emphasis for clinicians to utilize the DBT case management strategies to help manage the chaos that is often comorbid with SUD. As a part of DBT-SUD, it is recommended that clients use empirically supported replacement medications. The therapist and client team also use toxicology screening to monitor substance use and overcome the potential for incorrect self-reports. These points of emphasis help DBT providers structure the treatment by anticipating some of the therapy- and quality-of-life-interfering behaviors that are common among individuals with SUD.

A review of the literature resulted in finding eight published RCTs involving DBT for individuals with substance use problems, summarized in Table 7.1. Among the eight RCTs, five examined comprehensive DBT, while three involved modified DBT. Notably, among the five RCTs of comprehensive DBT, all were with women only and four were with individuals who had a comorbid diagnosis of BPD. A review of the RCTs that examine comprehensive DBT is presented first, followed by those studies that examine modifications to DBT.

Randomized controlled trials of dialectical behavior therapy for individuals with substance use problems

Randomized controlled trials of comprehensive dialectical behavior therapy

Two seminal RCTs conducted in Marsha Linehan's lab established the roots of experimental research on DBT-SUD. The first trial was

TABLE 7.1 Randomized controlled trials of dialectical behavior therapy (DBT) for individuals with substance use problems.

RCT publication or dissertation	Sample descriptors	Treatments	DBT modes	DBT training and/or adherence	Primary findings
RCTs of comprehensive DBT					
Linehan et al. (1999) Publication	*n* = 28 women in the United States BPD and SUD Age: between 18 and 45 Mean age: 30.4	DBT (*n* = 12) and TAU (*n* = 15)	One year of comprehensive DBT-SUD with weekly individual therapy, weekly skills training group (including addiction skills), weekly therapist consultation team, and as needed telephone consultation. Plus, transitional *maintenance replacement* medication pharmacotherapy protocol for individuals with stimulant or opiate dependence	The treatment developer was a therapist and member of the consultation team and supervised the other therapists. Adherence was monitored and inconsistent. Analyses indicated that clients whose therapists were adherent had better *outcomes*	Individuals in DBT had less treatment dropout than those in TAU (i.e., 36% vs 73%). Individuals in the DBT condition had significantly greater reductions in positive drug screens measured through urinalysis and interviews and had *significantly greater* increases in global and social adjustment compared to individuals in the TAU condition. Notably, analyses of therapist adherence to the DBT model found that clients of therapists who were consistently adherent had significantly better outcomes on urinalyses than therapists who were not consistently adherent

Linehan et al. (2002) Publication	$n = 23$ women in the United States BPD and opiate dependence Age: between 18 and 45 Mean age: 36.1	DBT ($n = 11$) and CVT + 12S ($n = 12$)	One year of comprehensive DBT-SUD with weekly individual therapy, weekly skills training group (including addiction skills), weekly therapist consultation team, and as needed telephone consultation. Plus LAAM opiate agonist therapy	Clinicians had a minimum of 8 months of training and weekly supervision to monitor adherence	Individuals in CVT + 12S had lower dropout than DBT (i.e., 0% vs 36%). Individuals in both treatment conditions had significant reductions in opiate use as measured by urinalysis. However, those in the DBT condition had significantly greater reductions in the last 4 months of treatment than those in CVT + 12S, who actually had increases in positive urinalysis. Individuals in both conditions had significant reductions in psychopathology. In addition, those in the DBT condition had lower discrepancies between their urinalysis and self-report than individuals in the CVT + 12S
van den Bosch et al. (2002), Verheul et al. (2003), van den Bosch et al. (2005) Publications	$n = 58$ women in The Netherlands BPD and 53% had substance abuse Age: between 18 and 70 Mean age: 34.9	DBT ($n = 27$) and TAU ($n = 31$)	One year of comprehensive DBT with weekly individual therapy, weekly skills training group, weekly therapist consultation team, and as needed telephone consultation	Clinicians had training and supervision in DBT. Clinicians in the study had a median adherence rating of 3.8, where a 4.0 indicates full adherence to the model	DBT had lower dropout rates than TAU during treatment (i.e., 37% vs 77%). Individuals in DBT had significantly greater reductions in symptoms of BPD, self-injury, impulsive actions, and self-reported use of alcohol than TAU. DBT was not found to produce significantly greater reductions in other substance abuse measures than TAU, however

(*Continued*)

TABLE 7.1 (Continued)

RCT publication or dissertation	Sample descriptors	Treatments	DBT modes	DBT training and/or adherence	Primary findings
Linehan et al. (2006), Harned et al. (2008) Publications	$n = 101$ women in the United States BPD, at least two suicide attempts or self-injuries and one in the last 8 weeks. 73.3% had a lifetime SUD and 29.7% had a current SUD Age: between 18 and 45 Mean age: 29.3	DBT ($n = 52$) and CTBE ($n = 49$)	One year of comprehensive DBT with weekly individual therapy, weekly skills training group, weekly therapist consultation team, and as needed telephone consultation	Clinicians had a 45-h DBT seminar and supervised practice. Clinicians had to have at least six of eight practice sessions rated as adherent to be hired. Adherence was monitored during the trial. Clinicians in the study had a mean adherence rating of 4.0, where a 4.0 indicates full adherence to the model	Individuals in the DBT had significantly lower dropout (i.e., 19.2% vs 42.9%), greater reductions in suicide attempts, lower hospitalizations for suicidal ideation, lower medical risk of self-injurious acts, and fewer psychiatric hospitalizations and ED visits. Individuals in the DBT condition were more likely to have full remission of their substance dependence disorder, have more time in partial remission, have less time meeting full substance dependence disorder criteria, and have more self-reported days abstinent from drug and alcohol than individuals in CTBE. There were no significant differences between individuals in DBT and CTBE in reductions of major depressive disorder, anxiety disorders, and ED

Courbasson et al. (2012) Publication	$n = 25$ women in Canada SUD and ED Age: 18 and older Mean age: 32.5	DBT ($n = 15$) and TAU ($n = 10$)	One year of comprehensive DBT-SUD with weekly individual therapy, weekly skills training group (including addiction skills), weekly therapist consultation team, and as needed telephone consultation	Clinicians had training in DBT and were supervised weekly by an experienced DBT clinician	DBT had lower dropout rates than TAU during treatment (i.e., 20% vs 80%). No other between-group comparisons were conducted due to the small amount of data collected from individuals in TAU. Individuals in DBT had significant improvements in the severity of substance use, number of binge eating episodes, measures of ED behaviors and attitudes, depression, and mood regulation
RCTs of modified DBT					
Whiteside (2011) Dissertation	$n = 145$ men and women in the United States Depressed and/or anxious heavy drinking college students. Age: 17–26 Mean age: 18.9	DBT-BASICS ($n = 43$), BASICS ($n = 49$), and RCC ($n = 53$)	One 60-min individual session using standard BASICS interventions, plus identification and reinforcement of existing skills and teaching the DBT skills of mindfulness, opposite action, and mindfulness of current emotions	Therapists were trained in DBT skills by the author and had weekly individual and group supervision	Individuals in DBT-BASICS had significantly lower alcohol-related problems at 3-month follow-up than individuals in the BASICS or RCC conditions. Individuals in DBT-BASICS had significantly greater improvements on coping drinking, anxiety, depression, and difficulties with emotion regulations than those in RCC

(Continued)

TABLE 7.1 (Continued)

RCT publication or dissertation	Sample descriptors	Treatments	DBT modes	DBT training and/or adherence	Primary findings
Wilks et al. (2017) Publication	$n = 59$ men and women in the United States Suicidal ideation in the past month, heavy episodic drinking, and high emotion dysregulation. Mean Age: 38.0	iDBT-ST ($n = 31$) and 8-week waitlist followed by iDBT-ST ($n = 28$)	Eight weekly, online skills sessions involving 30–50 min of content, including video, teaching points, interactive and guided practice, and homework assignment. Individuals were prompted to practice the skills via texts and/or emails	The authors developed iDBT-ST utilizing Linehan's (2014) DBT skills training as a model and another computerized version of DBT for emotion regulation (Lungu, 2015)	Seven individuals (22.6%) dropped out of iDBT versus four (13.8%) in the waitlist condition, although nearly two-thirds of individuals in the study did not fully complete the treatment. Overall, participants in both conditions had significant improvements on outcomes, including suicidal ideation, alcohol use, and difficulties in emotion regulation over the 4 months they were assessed in the study. Individuals in the iDBT-ST reduced their alcohol consumption significantly quicker than those in the control condition

Nyamathi et al. (2017) Publication	$n = 130$ women in the United States Homeless parolees or probationers. Mostly Black and Latina. Age: between 18 and 65 Mean Age: 38.8	DBT-CM ($n = 65$) and HP ($n = 65$)	Twelve weeks of treatment with six once per week group skills training sessions (including addiction skills) and six once per week individual sessions	The program director monitored providers' management of sessions, preparation of content, clarity, and environment	Individuals in both conditions had high retention, with 89.0% of individuals in DBT-CM having complete attendance (defined as attending 75% or more of sessions) and 84.0% of individuals in HP having complete attendance. Overall dropout rates were 9.9% of the DBT-CM and 12.3% in HP. Results indicated that individuals in the DBT-CM were significantly more likely to become abstinent from drugs and alcohol during the treatment and had significantly greater likelihood of abstinence from both drug and alcohol use than those in the HP program through the follow-up period

BASICS, Brief Alcohol Screening and Intervention for College Students; *BPD*, borderline personality disorder; *CTBE*, community treatment by experts; *DBT-CM*, DBT-corrections modified; *HP*, health promotion; *iDBT-ST*, Internet-delivered DBT skills training intervention; *RCC*, Relaxation Control Condition; *RCT*, randomized controlled trials; *SUD*, substance use disorders; *TAU*, treatment as usual.

published by Linehan et al. (1999). A total of 28 women with diagnoses of BPD and substance dependence were randomly assigned to either 1 year of comprehensive DBT or treatment as usual (TAU). Substance use diagnoses included 74% of the sample with multiple substance dependence, 58% with a cocaine use disorder, and 52% with alcohol dependence. Among participants reporting primary substances used, the substances of choice were cocaine ($n = 8$), opiates ($n = 6$), marijuana ($n = 4$), methamphetamine ($n = 3$), hallucinogens ($n = 1$), and both methamphetamine and cocaine ($n = 1$). Individuals in DBT had less treatment dropout than those in TAU (i.e., 36% vs 73%). Over the treatment year and follow-up period of 4 months, individuals in the DBT condition had significantly greater reductions in positive drug screens measured through urinalysis and interviews and had significantly greater increases in global and social adjustment compared to individuals in the TAU condition. In addition, DBT therapists were rated on the degree to which they adhered to the model on a rigorous adherence measure developed in Linehan's lab. Notably, analyses of therapist adherence to the DBT model found that clients of therapists who consistently had sessions rated as adherent had significantly better outcomes on urinalyses than therapists who did not have sessions consistently rated as adherent. This finding suggests that the number of sessions rated as adherent to the DBT model may be an important factor in improving substance use outcomes in comprehensive DBT.

The second trial of DBT-SUD conducted by Linehan et al. (2002) examined 23 women with BPD and opiate dependence who were randomly assigned to either 1 year of treatment in comprehensive DBT-SUD or comprehensive validation therapy with a 12-step program (CVT + 12S). All participants also received the opiate agonist LAAM throughout the year of treatment. CVT + 12S had lower dropout than DBT (i.e., 0% vs 36%), which highlights the potential importance of validation with regards to treatment retention. Individuals in both treatment conditions had significant reductions in opiate use as measured by urinalysis from baseline to the end of the treatment year. However, those in the DBT condition had significantly greater reductions in the last 4 months of active treatment than those in CVT + 12S, who actually had increases in positive urinalysis. At the single urinalysis completed at the 16-month follow-up, there were no significant differences between conditions with individuals from both conditions showing low levels of positive urinalysis. Individuals in both conditions had significant reductions in psychopathology. In addition, those in the DBT condition had lower discrepancies between their urinalysis and self-report than individuals in the CVT + 12S. Although DBT therapists had session adherence rated, this variable was not explored in association with outcomes in this study.

van den Bosch, Verheul, Schippers, and van den Brink (2002) and Verheul et al. (2003) describe the first study of DBT for individuals with SUD conducted outside of Linehan's lab. The authors designed this study, conducted in The Netherlands, to examine if comprehensive DBT can successfully be implemented in a population of women with BPD where some engage in substance abuse and some do not. Among the sample of 58, 53% had substance abuse as defined by scoring 5 or higher on the European version of the Addiction Severity Index (ASI; Kokkevi & Hartgers, 1995). Among the 31 participants crossing the threshold of the ASI, 64% reported polysubstance abuse, 64% reported sedative medication abuse, 50% reported alcohol abuse, 30% reported cannabis abuse, 17% reported cocaine abuse, 13% reported methadone abuse, and 9% reported heroin abuse. Participants were randomly assigned to either 1 year of DBT or TAU. Session-rated adherence for DBT therapists was a median of 3.8, where 4.0 indicates full adherence to the model. DBT therapists utilized comprehensive DBT with all four modes of treatment; however, unlike RCTs conducted in Linehan's lab, there were no modifications for the treatment of substance abuse. Verheul et al. (2003) report that 16 participants with addictive problems were assigned to each condition. There were no differences in session attendance for individuals with and without substance use problems. DBT was also not found to produce significantly greater reductions on substance use measured by the ASI.

van den Bosch, Koeter, Stijnen, Verheul, and van den Brink (2005) described analyses of follow-up data collected 6 months after treatment ended from this RCT. In this analysis, substance use outcomes were presented based on assessment via the BPD Severity Index (Arntz et al., 2003), a semistructured interview, which included questions on three categories of self-damaging impulsivity via substance use: alcohol, soft drugs, and hard drugs. In the follow-up time period, individuals in the DBT condition reported significantly lower levels of self-injury, impulsive behaviors, and alcohol use than individuals in the TAU condition. There were no differences between the conditions for other substance abuse measures.

Another RCT that included a mixture of individuals with and without SUDs was conducted by Linehan et al. (2006). In this RCT, 101 women with BPD and at least 2 suicide attempts or self-injuries in the last 5 years and at least 1 in the previous 8 weeks were randomly assigned to either DBT or community treatment by experts (CTBE). The sample was assessed for SUDs using the Structured Clinical Interview for DSM-IV (SCID, First, Spitzer, Gibbons, & Williams, 1995) at pretreatment and 73.3% had a lifetime SUD diagnosis and 29.7% had a current SUD diagnosis at the beginning of treatment (i.e., 23% in the DBT condition and 37% in CTBE). CTBE was developed to control for therapist expertise/training and clinical experience, therapist sex, allegiance to the treatment provided, availability of clinical supervision, institutional prestige, assistance finding a therapist, and availability of affordable and sufficient treatment hours. Session-rated adherence for DBT therapists was a mean of 4.0, where 4.0 indicates full adherence to the model. Critical to this review, Harned et al. (2008) conducted secondary analyses on reductions in cooccurring diagnoses among individuals in this RCT. They utilized data gathered with the Longitudinal Interval Follow-up Evaluation (Keller et al., 1987), which involved interviewers assigning weekly psychological status ratings (PSR) for SUD with options of 1 = none, 2 = moderate, and 3 = severe. Remission criteria from DSM-IV-TR (American Psychiatric Association, 2000) were used such that early partial remission was defined as PSR = 2 for at least 4 consecutive weeks and early full remission was defined as PSR = 1 for at least 4 consecutive weeks. They found that individuals in the DBT condition were more likely to have full remission of their substance dependence disorder, have more time in partial remission, have less time meeting full substance dependence disorder criteria, and have more self-reported days abstinent from drug and alcohol than individuals in CTBE.

Courbasson, Nishikawa, and Dixon (2012) conducted an RCT of a modified comprehensive DBT with 25 women diagnosed with both SUD and an ED using the SCID. The participants were randomly assigned to either 1 year of comprehensive DBT or TAU and only 21 participants actually initiated treatment. The primary substance used in problematic ways was cocaine (i.e., 70% in TAU and 64% in DBT), and the secondary problematic substance was benzodiazepines in TAU (i.e., 50%) and alcohol in DBT (i.e., 58%). The authors modified comprehensive DBT-SUD by adding, "a psychoeducational and cognitive behavioral focus on ED, SUD and their interrelationships" (p. 439). DBT session-rated adherence was not reported. Due to significant attrition in the TAU group, the researchers ended recruitment early resulting in a small sample size in the TAU group preventing meaningful between-groups analyses. Individuals in the DBT condition did, however, report significant improvement pre- to posttreatment and through 3- and 6-month follow-up in the severity of substance use measured by the ASI (although not for alcohol use).

Several RCTs have examined comprehensive DBT with samples that contain significant proportions of individuals with SUD, although they did not test outcomes related to substance use (therefore these studies are not included in Table 7.1). Some examples of these RCTs include a study conducted by Pistorello, Fruzzetti, MacLane, Gallop, and Iverson (2012) of 7–12 months of comprehensive DBT for college students where the total sample included 36.5% of individuals with SUD. Feigenbaum et al. (2012) also conducted an RCT of 1 year of comprehensive DBT versus TAU for individuals with BPD, antisocial personality disorder, histrionic personality disorder, and/or narcissistic personality disorder where the total sample included 46.3% meeting criteria for a substance abuse diagnosis. Lastly, Goodman et al. (2016) conducted an RCT of 6 months of comprehensive DBT versus TAU among 91 male and female (33.0% women) veterans at high risk for suicide with 51.6% of the sample meeting criteria for BPD. The total sample included 67.0% of individuals with substance abuse. Overall, the findings in these RCTs indicated that individuals diagnosed with SUDs among a variety of comorbid conditions can be effectively treated in trials of comprehensive DBT that do not specifically recruit for individuals with SUDs.

Summary of randomized controlled trials of comprehensive dialectical behavior therapy

Overall, results are encouraging for comprehensive DBT in the treatment of SUD. Of the RCTs reported, two published studies explicitly targeted only individuals with SUDs and had statistical comparisons between DBT and a control group (i.e., Linehan et al., 1999, 2002). Of these, one RCT comparing DBT to TAU showed comprehensive DBT to be effective in treating clients with BPD and a variety of comorbid SUDs over the treatment year and 4-month follow-up (Linehan et al., 1999). The single published RCT that explicitly targeted SUD with a rigorous control group (i.e., CVT + 12S) focused on opioid dependence only and showed DBT to be superior in reducing opioid use in the last 4 months of treatment (Linehan et al., 2002). Two RCTs did not explicitly target individuals with SUDs but included samples with high proportions of individuals with SUDs with success (i.e., Harned et al., 2008; Linehan et al., 2006; van den Bosch et al., 2002, 2005). Very little evidence suggests that individuals treated with DBT have worse outcomes than individuals in control treatments on SUD or other outcomes. Nonetheless, comparison across studies is complicated by variability in measurement of outcomes and with regard to which outcomes are significantly different between conditions.

Randomized controlled trials of modified dialectical behavior therapy

Several RCTs did not directly test comprehensive DBT-SUD but instead examined modified versions of DBT for individuals with substance use problems. Modifications from comprehensive DBT-SUD can lead to treatments that are less time and cost intensive. Several studies have highlighted the importance of skills training contributing to the effectiveness of DBT (Linehan et al., 2015; McMain, Guimond, Barnhart, Habinski, & Streiner, 2017). The RCTs covered here focus on innovative methods of delivering skills, outside of the context of comprehensive DBT, to individuals with substance use problems.

Whiteside (2011) conducted an RCT of a brief motivational intervention incorporating DBT skills for college students with heavy drinking behavior and depression and/or anxiety. Participants were 145 men and women who were randomly assigned to a 60-minute individual session of either a Brief Alcohol Screening and Intervention for College Students (BASICS), DBT skills enhanced BASICS (DBT-BASICS), or a Relaxation Control Condition (RCC). In the DBT-BASICS condition, individuals were given feedback about their coping and taught the DBT skills of mindfulness and two skills from the emotion regulation skills: opposite action and mindfulness of current emotion. Individuals in DBT-BASICS had significantly lower alcohol-related problems at 3-month follow-up than individuals in the BASICS or RCC conditions. Individuals in DBT-BASICS had significantly greater improvements on coping drinking, anxiety, depression, and difficulties with emotion regulations than those in RCC.

Wilks et al. (2017) conducted a pilot RCT examining the efficacy of an Internet-delivered DBT skills training intervention (iDBT-ST) for individuals who engage in heavy episodic drinking, suicidal ideation in the past month, and high emotion dysregulation. The authors analyzed data from 59 men and women recruited from the internet who were randomly assigned to receive either iDBT-ST immediately or after spending 8 weeks on a waitlist. The authors developed iDBT-ST utilizing Linehan's (2015a, 2015b) DBT skills training as a model and another computerized version of DBT for emotion regulation (Lungu, 2015). Individuals were taught mindfulness skills for 2 weeks, 2 weeks on the DCBA skills, 3 weeks of emotion regulation skills, and 1 week on distress tolerance skills. The eight online skills sessions involved 30–50 minutes of content, including video, teaching points, interactive and guided practice, and homework assignment. Individuals were prompted to practice the skills via texts and/or emails. Dropout was defined as not completing online sessions for 3 weeks in a row. Seven individuals (22.6%) dropped out of iDBT versus four (13.8%) in the waitlist condition, although nearly two-thirds of individuals in the study did not fully complete the treatment. Technical difficulties with accessibility were cited as one of the biggest contributors to dropout and noncompletion. Overall, participants in both conditions had significant improvements on outcomes, including suicidal ideation, alcohol use, and difficulties in emotion regulation over the 4 months they were assessed in the study. Individuals in the iDBT-ST reduced their alcohol consumption significantly quicker than those in the control condition.

Nyamathi et al. (2017) conducted an RCT of a DBT-corrections modified (DBT-CM) program among 130 homeless women parolees/

probationers to help them abstain from drugs and alcohol. Participants were randomly assigned to receive either DBT-CM or a health promotion (HP) program. DBT-CM was developed as a 12-week program involving 6 weeks with one group session per week and 6 weeks with a 45–50 minute individual session per week. Individuals in DBT-CM were taught some of the DCBA skills in the sessions. In the individual sessions the clinicians utilized DBT techniques, including structuring the session's agenda using a diary card and treatment targets, using chain analysis for target behaviors, and utilizing solution analysis. Individuals in both conditions had high retention, with 89.0% of individuals in DBT-CM having complete attendance (defined as attending 75% or more of sessions) and 84.0% of individuals in HP having complete attendance. Overall dropout rates were 9.9% of the DBT-CM and 12.3% in HP. Results indicated that individuals in the DBT-CM were significantly more likely to become abstinent from drugs and alcohol during the treatment and had significantly greater likelihood of abstinence from both drug and alcohol use than those in the HP program through the follow-up period.

Two RCTs have examined modified DBT with samples of individuals with a high degree of SUDs but did not include analyses of substance use variables (therefore these studies are not included in Table 7.1). Linehan et al. (2015) conducted a component analysis that compared individuals randomly assigned to comprehensive DBT, DBT individual therapy plus activities group, or DBT skills training plus case management. Among the 99 participants, 69.7% met criteria for a lifetime SUD and 37.4% met criteria for a current SUD. Individuals in all conditions had improvements in suicide attempts and ideation, use of crisis services, and reasons for living. Individuals in the conditions that included skills training had greater improvements in self-injury and depression, and they also had a significant reduction in anxiety over the treatment year. Those in comprehensive DBT were less likely to drop out and use crisis services than those in individual DBT. Neacsiu et al. (2014) conducted an RCT to examine an application of 16 weeks of DBT skills training (DBT-ST) for transdiagnostic emotion dysregulation. Among the 44 participants, 50% met criteria for a lifetime SUD and 6.8% met criteria for current SUD. The main outcomes reported include that those in DBT-ST had significantly greater reductions in emotion dysregulation and anxiety and greater increases in skill use than those in the activities group.

Summary of randomized controlled trials of modified dialectical behavior therapy

The RCTs of modified DBT have examined three applications of DBT that show promise and are in need of further study. Outcomes from each of the three studies indicate that each version of modified DBT shows evidence of improving substance use variables relative to the control condition. Also of note is that these studies had elements of increased diversity (e.g., sex, race, and individuals recruited via the internet) in their samples compared to trials of comprehensive DBT.

Uncontrolled trials and quasiexperimental trials of dialectical behavior therapy for individuals with substance use problems

An advantage of RCTs, as reviewed earlier, is that the studies are well controlled and demonstrate through experimentation the efficacy of a treatment. Conversely, a disadvantage is that because of the high degree of control and internal validity, there can be questions remaining regarding external validity. In other words, RCTs do not provide indications of whether the treatment is effective in naturalistic settings in the real world. The RCTs reviewed here have some limitations regarding external validity and effectiveness. For example, most of the RCTs have taken place in Western cultures with mostly Caucasian samples, most of the RCTs directly studying substance use as a primary outcome have only included women, and all RCTs reviewed have examined individuals over the age of 18. Limitations such as these have begun to be addressed through uncontrolled trials (i.e., where DBT is studied without a comparison group) and quasiexperimental research (i.e., where outcomes from DBT are compared to those from a control condition, but participants are not randomly assigned to the condition) that address the effectiveness of DBT for individuals with substance use problems, often in naturalistic settings.

A review of the literature indicated 12 uncontrolled or quasiexperimental trials of DBT for individuals with substance use problems, summarized in Table 7.2. Among the 12 studies, 6 examined comprehensive DBT and 6 examined modified DBT. The trials that examine comprehensive DBT are presented first in chronological order.

Uncontrolled and quasiexperimental trials of comprehensive dialectical behavior therapy

In one of the first published uncontrolled trials examining comprehensive DBT for individuals with substance use problems, Axelrod, Perepletchikova, Holtzman, and Sinha (2011) analyzed data from 27 women with BPD and one or more DSM-IV substance dependence diagnoses. The participants had an average of 1.7 substance dependence diagnoses with 88% meeting DSM-IV criteria for alcohol dependence, 44% for cocaine, 25% for opiates, and 6% for marijuana. Participants

TABLE 7.2 Uncontrolled trials and quasiexperimental trials of dialectical behavior therapy (DBT) for individuals with substance use problems.

Publication	Sample descriptors	Design	DBT modes	DBT training and/or adherence	Primary findings
Trials of comprehensive DBT					
Axelrod et al. (2011)	$n = 27$ women BPD and substance dependence Age: between 27 and 51 Mean age: 38.0	Uncontrolled, pre–post, within-subjects design	Twenty weeks of comprehensive DBT-SUD Weekly individual therapy, weekly 90-min skills training group, weekly therapist consultation team, and as needed telephone coaching	Therapists were monitored for adherence (but not in a systematic way) and supervised by a trainer who was trained by Linehan	Participants had significant reductions in substance use and that improvements in emotion regulation explained a significant amount of the variance in the reductions in substance use, while improvements in depression did not
Beckstead et al. (2015)	$n = 229$ adolescent boys and girls from 39 Native American tribes SUD Age: 12–18 Mean age: 16	Uncontrolled, pre–post, within-subjects design in the context of a residential treatment (mean of 120 days of treatment) program for American Indian/Alaska Native youth	Comprehensive residential (mean length = 120 days) adolescent DBT-SUD Individual therapy, skills training group (including addiction skills), therapist consultation team, and as needed counselor aide skills coaching available daily. Plus, milieu schedule with school, alcoholic anonymous groups, health education, and recreational therapy. Plus, weekly sweat lodge, smudging, and talking circle ceremonies	Therapists completed a 2-week DBT intensive training plus twice yearly on-site training and monthly consultation	Of the, 229 adolescents who completed assessments, 96% of adolescents met clinically significant change criteria for "recovered" or "improved" on the Youth Outcome Questionnaire-Self-Report version, a measure of adolescent distress, based on the standards established by Jacobson and Truax (1991). In addition, the participants' scores on the measure showed overall significant pre-to-post reductions with a large effect size ($d = 1.315$)

(*Continued*)

TABLE 7.2 (Continued)

Publication	Sample descriptors	Design	DBT modes	DBT training and/or adherence	Primary findings
McCay et al. (2015)	$n = 139$ male and female youths in Canada High problem drinking scores Age: 16–24 Mean age: 21.0	Quasiexperimental design for street-involved youths in the context of drop-in, shelter, and transitional housing services. DBT ($n = 60$), waitlist ($n = 29$), and dropout ($n = 50$)	Twelve weeks of comprehensive adolescent DBT with weekly individual therapy, weekly skills training group, weekly therapist consultation team, and crisis planning + 24 h crisis support line	Agency staff were trained through 32 h of online training, eight sessions/webinars by a DBT expert, and reading the manuals by Linehan (1993b) and Miller et al. (2007). In addition, a random sample of 5% of recorded sessions was rated on the DBT-specific integrity checklists created by the authors. The sessions that were coded achieved a greater than 90% rating of treatment integrity	There were no significant changes within any of the groups, pre to post for either group on a measure of alcoholism, which was the only substance use measure. Nonetheless, those in the DBT group had significant improvements pre to post on a measure of overall symptoms, depression, anxiety, hopelessness, resilience, self-esteem, and social connectedness. Individuals in the waitlist control did not have statistically significant improvement on any of these measures. Analyses indicated that the improvements among those in the DBT group were maintained at 4 and 10 weeks after the intervention

Abdelkarim et al. (2017)	$n = 40$ men and women (77.5% women) in Egypt BPD and SUD Age: 18–40 Mean age: 25.2	Quasiexperimental nonrandomized trial comparing individuals in comprehensive DBT ($n = 20$) and TAU ($n = 20$)	One year of comprehensive DBT-SUD with weekly individual therapy, weekly skills training group (including addiction skills), weekly therapist consultation team, and as needed telephone consultation	Therapists completed a 2-week DBT intensive training	Individuals in DBT abstained from alcohol and other drugs for longer duration than individuals in TAU and had significantly lower doses of drugs used. Those in DBT also had significantly greater improvements on suicide attempts, self-injury, rates of hospital admission, emergency room visits, and emotion regulation than individuals in TAU. In addition, these improvements were maintained for the posttreatment follow-up of 4 months
Navarro-Haro et al. (2018)	$n = 118$ women in Spain BPD and ED Excluded individuals with substance dependence; however, 57.5% had substance use. Age: 18 and over Mean age: 27.4	Quasiexperimental nonrandomized, naturalistic trial comparing individuals assigned to DBT ($n = 71$) or TAUCBT ($n = 47$). Treatments were delivered in outpatient and/or day hospital	Six months of comprehensive DBT with weekly individual therapy, weekly skills training group (including addiction skills), weekly therapist consultation team, and as needed telephone consultation. Those in the day hospital also had problem-solving training, weekend planning, and normalization of habits	DBT therapists had 40 h of DBT seminars and supervision from a DBT expert. Their video-recorded sessions were monitored for effective use of strategies and therapists were given feedback	The women in DBT had significantly greater improvements on dysfunctional behaviors (including substance abuse), nonsuicidal self-injury, depression, global functioning, and cognitive reappraisal than did women in TAUCBT

(*Continued*)

TABLE 7.2 (Continued)

Publication	Sample descriptors	Design	DBT modes	DBT training and/or adherence	Primary findings
Rabinovitz and Nagar (2018)	$n = 30$ adolescent girls in Israel Alcohol and cannabis dependent Age: between 14 and 18 Mean age: 16.7	Quasiexperimental nonrandomized trial comparing individuals at pretreatment ($n = 12$), following four months of treatment ($n = 11$), and following 12 months of treatment ($n = 7$)	Twelve months of DBT + therapeutic community: long-term residential treatment that incorporates a 12-step, motivational enhancement, cognitive behavioral, and psychiatric care with DBT. DBT included: weekly individual therapy, weekly skills training group (including addiction skills), weekly therapist consultation team, and between-session coaching	Therapists structured the DBT program based on Linehan's manuals. Progress was monitored in consultation team	They found that those who completed 12 months of DBT had lower attentional bias and higher response inhibition during drug craving induction, than those who had less treatment
Trials of modified DBT					
Azizi et al. (2010)	$n = 39$ men in Iran Opioid dependence Age: between 20 and 45 Mean age: 26.7 No personality disorder, major	Quasiexperimental DBT group therapy ($n = 13$), cognitive group therapy ($n = 13$), and Naltrexone only control ($n = 13$) All participants took Naltrexone	Ten 90-min DBT group sessions covering mindfulness and emotion regulation. Naltrexone replacement medication	The DBT group was modeled after Linehan's (1993a, 1993b) manuals	Treatment compliance was significantly higher for both DBT and cognitive therapy than the control group. At the end of treatment, the relapse rate of the three groups was significantly different with DBT at 23% performing significantly

	depressive disorder, bipolar disorder, schizophrenia				better than both cognitive therapy at 31% and Naltrexone only at 67%. DBT was more effective at improving distress tolerance and emotion regulation than both groups. Both DBT and cognitive therapy outperformed the control group with regards to improvements in amount of drug abuse, anxiety, depression, somatic symptoms, health improvement, social functioning, and social dysfunction
Rizvi et al. (2011)	$n = 22$ men and women (81.8% women) in the United States BPD and SUD Age: 18 and over Mean age: 33.9	Uncontrolled, pre–post, within-subjects design to examine the DBT Coach app focused on coaching opposite action	DBT Coach + comprehensive DBT with weekly individual therapy, weekly skills training group (including addiction skills), weekly therapist consultation team, and as needed telephone consultation	DBT was provided in one of three standard, comprehensive DBT programs	On average, participants used the app 14.9 times and rated it as having high helpfulness and usability. Within each session of using the app, individuals had significant reductions in substance use urges and emotion intensity. During the period when using the app, participants also reported significant improvements in distress, depression, and ability to identify and use opposite action

(*Continued*)

TABLE 7.2 (Continued)

Publication	Sample descriptors	Design	DBT modes	DBT training and/or adherence	Primary findings
Ramezanzadeh et al. (2014), Ramazanzadeh et al. (2016)	$n = 24$ adolescent girls in Iran. High risk for emotion dysregulation and substance use Age: between 14 and 18 Mean age: 15.3	Quasiexperimental pre- and posttest with waitlist control group ($n = 12$) and DBT emotion regulation skills group ($n = 12$)	Eight 80-min group DBT sessions focusing on the emotion regulation skills	Cited Linehan's treatment manuals as informing the treatment	Individuals in the DBT group had improvements in substance use risk profile, adaptive emotional schemas, maladaptive emotional schemas, use of adaptive emotion regulation strategies, maladaptive emotion regulation strategies, and executive functioning
Sahranavard and Miri (2018)	$n = 30$ women in Iran Drug abuse and high depression Age: between 25 and 40 Mean age: 34.1	Quasiexperimental pre- and posttest design with participants assigned to DBT ($n = 10$), CBT ($n = 10$), or control ($n = 10$)	Eight 90-min DBT group sessions covering mindfulness, interpersonal effectiveness, emotion regulation, and distress tolerance	Therapists had "specialized expertise" in DBT	Mean depression scores significantly reduced for both individuals in the CBT group and DBT group over the course of time in the treatment, but did not reduce for those in the control condition
Maffei et al. (2018)	$n = 244$ men and women in Italy Alcohol use disorder Age: between 21 and 71	Uncontrolled, pre–post, within-subjects design in the context of admission to an alcohol dependence treatment unit	Three months of 180-min DBT skills training group sessions. For the first month, there were five sessions per week, and for the second and third months, there were two sessions per week. The	Skills training leaders completed 90 h of intensive training. Videos of skills training sessions were watched and supervised weekly by an expert DBT therapist trained by Linehan	Among 157 treatment completers, 73.2% were abstinent from alcohol and improvements in alcohol use were independent of severity of alcohol addiction at the beginning of treatment.

	Mean age: 47.1		addiction skills were taught. Therapists met for a weekly consultation team		Those who completed treatment also showed improved emotion regulation and emotion regulation partially mediated substance use outcomes
Cavicchioli, et al. (2019)	$n = 171$ men and women in Italy Alcohol use disorder Age: between 25 and 75 Mean age: 47.9	Quasiexperimental design with participants in DBT skills training outpatient only ($n = 171$) or DBT delivered in a mix of inpatient and outpatient ($n = 244$)—the sample used in Maffei et al. (2018)	Three months of 180-min DBT skills training group sessions. For the first month, there were five sessions per week, and for the second and third months, there were two sessions per week. The addiction skills were taught. Therapists met for a weekly consultation team	Skills training leaders completed 90 h of intensive training. Videos of skills training sessions were watched and supervised weekly by an expert DBT therapist trained by Linehan	Weekly urinalysis showed that individuals in the DBT skills training outpatient had better abstinence maintenance than those involved in both inpatient and outpatient. In addition, individuals in DBT-ST-OP had lower rates of attrition, higher treatment attendance, and better gains in emotion regulation. Further analyses supported a model where improvements in emotion regulation fully mediated improvements in abstinence maintenance

BPD, Borderline personality disorder; *CBT*, cognitive behavioral therapy; *DBT-ST-OP*, DBT skills training only outpatient program; *SUD*, substance use disorders; *TAU*, treatment as usual.

were enrolled in 20 weeks of comprehensive DBT, which was supervised by a DBT expert, but not systematically monitored for adherence. They found that participants had significant reductions in substance use from pre- to postintervention and those improvements in emotion regulation explained a significant amount of the variance in the reductions in substance use, while improvements in depression did not.

Beckstead, Lambert, DuBose, and Linehan (2015) conducted an uncontrolled pilot study to examine if DBT incorporated into a substance use residential treatment for American Indian/Alaska Native adolescents diagnosed with SUD would produce significant pre–post changes. The highest proportion of adolescents (i.e. 77%) had cannabis and alcohol SUD and 9% had amphetamine SUD, 5% had opiate SUD, 5% had cocaine SUD, 3% had inhalant SUD, and 1% had hallucinogenic SUD. The authors developed the DBT program to integrate the adolescents' cultural, traditional, and spiritual practices. There was no systematic measurement of session-based adherence reported. Participants stayed in the residential program for an average of 120 days. Of the 229 adolescents who completed assessments, 96% of adolescents met clinically significant change criteria for "recovered" or "improved" on the outcome questionnaire measuring adolescent distress, based on the standards established by Jacobson and Truax (1991). In addition, the participants' scores on the measure showed overall significant pre-to-post reductions with a large effect size ($d = 1.32$). However, no substance-related outcomes were assessed. Nonetheless, these findings suggest that comprehensive DBT can successfully be blended with and used within American Indian/Alaska Native practices when working with adolescents who meet diagnostic criteria for SUD.

McCay et al. (2015) conducted a quasiexperimental study to examine 12 weeks of comprehensive DBT for street-involved youths (aged 16–24) in the context of drop-in, shelter, and transitional housing services provided by two Canadian agencies. The authors examined data from 139 youths with scores on a measure of alcoholism being on average in the range of being a problem drinker. They compared those who received the DBT intervention to youths on a waitlist. The authors shortened comprehensive adolescent DBT described by Miller, Rathus, and Linehan (2007) from 16 to 12 weeks. A random sample of 5% of recorded sessions was rated on the DBT-specific integrity checklist created by the authors, and the coded sessions achieved a greater than 90% rating of treatment integrity. There were no significant changes within any of the groups, pre to post for either group on a measure of alcoholism, which was the only substance use measure. Nonetheless, those in the DBT group had significant improvements pre to post on a measure of overall symptoms, depression, anxiety, hopelessness, resilience, self-esteem, and social connectedness. Individuals in the waitlist control group did not have statistically significant improvement on any of these measures. Analyses indicated that the improvements among those in the DBT group were maintained at 4 and 10 weeks after the intervention.

Abdelkarim, Molokhia, Rady, and Ivanoff (2017) conducted a nonrandomized trial of 1 year of DBT versus TAU with 40 women and men with BPD and SUD in Egypt. There was no systematic analysis of adherence data. Individuals in DBT had higher retention rates than those in TAU. Individuals in DBT abstained from alcohol and other drugs for longer duration than individuals in TAU and had significantly lower doses of drugs used. Those in DBT also had significantly greater improvements on suicide attempts, self-injury, and rates of hospital admission, emergency room visits, and emotion regulation than individuals in TAU. In addition, these improvements were maintained for the posttreatment follow-up of 4 months.

Navarro-Haro et al. (2018) conducted a naturalistic study examining 118 women diagnosed with BPD and one or more ED who were treated in a day hospital and/or outpatient treatment facility in Spain. Although individuals with substance dependence were excluded from this pilot study, 57.5% of the sample engaged in substance use and the researchers analyzed outcome data on substance abuse as a dysfunctional behavior, related to BPD, and used to regulate emotions. The women in the study were assigned to treatment by either therapists who trained to deliver 6 months of comprehensive DBT or therapists who delivered 6 months of TAU cognitive behavioral therapy (TAUCBT). DBT therapists' video-recorded sessions were monitored for use of DBT strategies, and therapists were given feedback, although there was no systematic analysis of adherence data. The women in DBT had significantly greater improvements on dysfunctional behaviors (including substance abuse), nonsuicidal self-injury, depression, global functioning, and cognitive reappraisal than did women in TAUCBT.

Rabinovitz and Nagar (2018) conducted a quasiexperimental study with 30 female adolescents in Israel with alcohol and cannabis dependence in a long-term residential treatment targeting abstinence from drugs. The treatment center incorporated both the usual therapeutic community with comprehensive DBT. There was no systematic analysis of adherence data. The authors compared individuals who were at the pretreatment phase, those who had completed 4 months of treatment, and those who had completed 12 months of treatment. They found that those who completed 12 months of DBT had lower attentional bias and higher response inhibition during drug craving induction than those who had less treatment.

Summary of uncontrolled and quasiexperimental trials of comprehensive dialectical behavior therapy

The uncontrolled and quasiexperimental trials of comprehensive DBT generally support the effectiveness of DBT applied in naturalistic settings. In multiple studies, individuals in DBT showed significant improvements on substance use outcomes. Further, DBT tended to be associated with improvements on other outcomes, including suicidal behavior, self-injury, symptoms, and emergency service use. In addition, these trials provide evidence that DBT can be effective with diverse populations with substance use problems, including Native American adolescents; street-involved Canadian youths, men, and women in Egypt; women in Spain with ED and BPD; and female adolescents in Israel.

Uncontrolled and quasiexperimental trials of modified dialectical behavior therapy

Six uncontrolled and quasiexperimental trials have examined modifications to standard, comprehensive DBT. Consistent with the modified treatments conducted in experimental designs described previously, the studies described later review adaptations to comprehensive DBT based on the need for flexible approaches to diverse individuals with substance use problems.

First, Azizi, Borjali, and Golzari (2010) conducted a quasiexperimental trial where 39 men in Iran diagnosed with opioid dependence were randomly assigned to three conditions, and all were given Naltrexone replacement medication. The two experimental treatments were 10 sessions of either DBT group or cognitive therapy group, and the third condition was a Naltrexone only control. Individuals in the DBT group were taught the emotion regulation and mindfulness skills. Treatment compliance was significantly higher in both experimental groups than the control group. At the end of treatment, the relapse rates of the three groups were significantly different, with DBT at 23% performing significantly better than both cognitive therapy at 31% and Naltrexone only at 67%. DBT was more effective at improving distress tolerance and emotion regulation than both other groups. Individuals in DBT and cognitive therapy had greater reductions than those in the control group in amount of drug abuse, anxiety, depression, somatic symptoms, health improvement, social functioning, and social dysfunction.

Second, Rizvi et al. (2011) conducted a quasiexperimental study of the DBT Coach app for 22 individuals (81.8% women) with BPD and SUD receiving comprehensive DBT. Substance dependence diagnosis was based on clinicians' report, while participants self-reported 72%

having nicotine problems, 18% with marijuana, 13.5% with methamphetamine and/or painkillers, and 9% with alcohol. Participants had to have participated in DBT for at least 2 months and have been taught the skill of opposite action. The DBT Coach app focused on coaching opposite action in particular. Participants were oriented to the app and instructed to use it over the next 10–14 days, with a mean of 12.9 days. On average, participants used the app 14.9 times and rated it as having high helpfulness and usability. Within each session of using the app, individuals had significant reductions in substance use urges and emotion intensity. During the period when using the app, participants also reported significant improvements in distress, depression, and ability to identify and use opposite action. This suggests that the use of the DBT Coach app may help enhance the treatment of individuals with BPD and SUD in DBT, although well-controlled experimental research is needed. Notably, both this study and the RCT by Whiteside (2011) focused on utilization of the specific DBT skill of opposite action to target substance use problems. Further exploration of how this skill may be helpful for individuals with substance use problems may also be warranted.

Third, Ramezanzadeh, Moradi, and Mohammadkhani (2014) and Ramazanzadeh, Alireza, and Shahram (2016) describe pre- and posttest analyses of 24 adolescent females in Iran with emotion dysregulation and substance use difficulties. The adolescents either were assigned to a waitlist control group or an 8-week DBT skills training group covering the emotion regulation skills. Individuals in the DBT group had significant improvements in substance use risk profile, adaptive emotional schemas, and maladaptive emotional schemas (Ramazanzadeh et al., 2016), as well as use of adaptive emotion regulation strategies, maladaptive emotion regulation strategies, and executive functioning (Ramezanzadeh et al., 2014).

Fourth, Sahranavard and Miri (2018) conducted a quasiexperimental study comparing modified DBT, CBT, and a control condition for 30 Iranian women with substance addiction and symptoms of depression treated in an addiction treatment center. The modified DBT intervention involved eight sessions that were 90 minutes each. Mean depression scores significantly reduced for both individuals in the CBT group and DBT group over the course of time in the treatment but did not significantly reduce for those in the control condition.

Fifth, Maffei, Cavicchioli, Movalli, Cavallaro, and Fossati (2018) conducted an open trial of an implementation in Italy of 3 months of DBT skills training, including the DCBA skills for individuals with alcohol dependence treated in both inpatient and outpatient settings. Among the study sample of 244 individuals over the age of 21 (38.9% women), 44.7% met criteria for a personality disorder and 157 completed treatment. Among treatment completers, 73.2% were abstinent from alcohol and improvements in alcohol use were independent of severity of alcohol addiction at the beginning of treatment. Those who completed treatment also showed improved emotion regulation and emotion regulation partially mediated substance use outcomes. This demonstrated that this treatment shows promise for individuals with alcohol dependence.

Sixth, Cavicchioli et al. (2019) conducted a quasiexperimental study in Italy examining a 3-month DBT skills training only outpatient program (DBT-ST-OP) compared with the same intervention delivered in a combination of inpatient and outpatient settings. The sample included 171 men and women (60.8% men) with alcohol use disorder who participated only in an outpatient program and compared these individuals to the sample of 244 women and men from the Maffei et al. (2018) study who participated in a combination of inpatient and outpatient treatment. Weekly urinalysis showed that individuals in the DBT-ST-OP had better abstinence maintenance than those involved in both inpatient and outpatient. In addition, individuals in DBT-ST-OP had lower rates of attrition, higher treatment attendance, and better gains in emotion regulation. Further analyses supported a model where improvements in emotion regulation fully mediated improvements in abstinence maintenance. Taken together with the findings of Axelrod et al. (2011) where improvements in emotion regulation explained a significant amount of the variance in the reductions in substance use, and Maffei et al. (2018) where improvements in emotion regulation partially mediated substance use outcomes, these findings suggest that improving difficulties with emotion regulation may be a mechanism leading to improvements in substance use outcomes among individuals treated with DBT skills.

Summary of uncontrolled and quasiexperimental trials of modified dialectical behavior therapy

The uncontrolled and quasiexperimental research trials have helped to provide additional data about the effectiveness of DBT for individuals with substance use problems. For example, a number of these trials have included both men and women and generally have shown that DBT is effective when men and women are included together. Further, a number of uncontrolled and quasiexperimental trials have examined individuals under the age of 18, and several have taken place outside of Western cultures and with non-Caucasian samples. These studies suggest that DBT may be effective for individuals in varied cultures. Further, modifications of DBT, such as those using abbreviated skills training, also may be effective for treating substance use problems.

Small N pilot studies and case studies involving dialectical behavior therapy for individuals with substance use

Small N pilot studies allow for examination of new and unique applications of DBT, which may be prime for further study. Dimeff, Rizvi, Brown, and Linehan (2000) assessed three women with BPD who were dependent on methamphetamine and found that two treatment completers were abstinent from drugs through the second half of treatment. Schultz Fischer (2007) completed a dissertation using four cases in which she examined a modified version of DBT to successfully treat women with methamphetamine abuse or dependence and features of BPD. A small N study conducted by Cooperman, Rizvi, Hughes, and Williams (2019) examined DBT skills training for relapse prevention with seven individuals with opioid and tobacco dependence in methadone treatment. At follow-up assessment compared to baseline, participants had smoked significantly fewer cigarettes and had not used drugs.

Case studies allow for in-depth exploration of how DBT may work with an individual with unique circumstances. Wagner, Miller, Greene, and Winiarski (2004) described the development of and presented a successful case study of 1 year of comprehensive DBT for an individual with SUD, BPD, and HIV/AIDS. Dietz and Dunn (2014) described a successful application, by a graduate student under supervision, of 9 months of individual DBT skills training combined with Motivational Enhancement Therapy and Relapse Prevention with a 28-year-old woman with synthetic cannabis use disorder. Barrett, Tolle, and Salsman (2017) described a successful application of 6 months of individual DBT skills training, by a graduate student under supervision, with a 57-year-old African-American woman with persistent complex bereavement disorder, persistent depressive disorder, and alcohol and cannabis abuse. Owens, Nason, and Yeater (2018) described 16 months of comprehensive DBT, by a graduate student under supervision, with a man with BPD, alcohol use disorder, and cannabis use disorder who was treated and had improvements in substance use, suicidal ideation, self-harm, and skill use. The three case studies where DBT was delivered by a graduate student, taken together with the RCT by Linehan et al. (2006), where the majority of DBT was delivered trainees, provide strong evidence that trainees can deliver effective DBT for individuals with SUDs.

Conclusion

DBT-SUD's efficaciousness has been supported in five well-controlled efficacy studies in three independent labs in the United

States, The Netherlands, and Canada. Further, three RCTs have shown how modifications of DBT can be effective for individuals with substance use problems. Six uncontrolled and quasiexperimental trials of comprehensive DBT have demonstrated evidence of the effectiveness of the treatment and extended its relevance to populations, including adolescents and individuals from non-Western cultures. An additional six uncontrolled and quasiexperimental trials have demonstrated that modifications of DBT, particularly those using skills training outside of the context of comprehensive DBT, can be effective with individuals with substance use problems.

Criteria for evaluating empirically supported treatments have been developed and debated by a variety of authors. Chambless et al. (1998) proposed that a treatment is well established when it meets criteria, including having at least two independent, controlled, and well-designed studies of the manualized study demonstrating superiority to a comparison treatment. The evidence of DBT for individuals with SUD appears to cross this threshold. Subsequently, Tolin, McKay, Forman, Klonsky, and Thombs (2015) have argued that the criteria should be updated to more thoroughly address the quality of the research studies, the strength of findings, the relevance of findings to the functioning of individuals and to diverse individuals, and identification of principles of change. This chapter has provided information relevant to the recommended revised criteria, including the identification of three studies that indicate that among individuals with substance use problems changes in emotion regulation may be an empirically supported principle of change (Axelrod et al., 2011; Cavicchioli et al., 2019; Maffei et al., 2018).

Limitations and future directions for dialectical behavior therapy with individuals with substance use problems

Nonetheless, there are a number of limitations to the research literature examining DBT for individuals with substance use problems. The efficacy research represented by the RCTs of comprehensive DBT is limited by the populations studied. All of the RCTs are with adult women and four of five RCTs include only individuals with BPD. Some of the uncontrolled and quasiexperimental studies address these limitations, but further experimental evidence is needed on the efficacy of DBT for men, adolescents, and individuals who do not have BPD.

Another set of limitations of the research is that cross-study comparison is complicated by factors related to variability among the studies. Many of the studies vary with regards to types of outcome measurement, change in outcomes, and DBT adherence monitoring. Synthesis of this research literature will require careful attention to these factors.

Further, the RCTs examine a mixture of types of SUDs with regards to the substances used and degree of the disorder (i.e., dependence vs abuse). Future research may examine if DBT is differentially effective for individuals with different SUDs. In addition, a variety of comorbid problems other than BPD that have been studied include EDs (Navarro-Haro et al., 2018; Courbasson et al., 2012), depression (Sahranavard & Miri, 2018; Whiteside, 2011), and youths at high risk for future problems (Beckstead et al., 2015; McCay et al., 2015; Ramazanzadeh et al., 2016; Ramezanzadeh et al., 2014). Future research may address if comorbid problems impact outcomes. While these factors of variability may limit the comparability of studies, they are also strengths in terms of increasing the generalizability of findings to diverse people.

References

Abdelkarim, A., Molokhia, T., Rady, A., & Ivanoff, A. (2017). DBT for co-morbid borderline personality disorder and substance use disorder without drug replacement in Egyptian outpatient settings: A non-randomized trial. *European Psychiatry*, *41*, S260–S261.

Arntz, A., Van den Hoorn, M., Cornelis, J., Verheul, R., Van den Bosch, W., & De Bie, A. (2003). Reliability and validity of the borderline personality disorder severity index. *Journal of Personality Disorders*, *17*, 45–59.

American Psychiatric Association, Diagnostic and statistical manual of mental disorders: DSM-IV-TR, 2000, Washington, DC.

Axelrod, S. R., Perepletchikova, F., Holtzman, K., & Sinha, R. (2011). Emotion regulation and substance use frequency in women with substance dependence and borderline personality disorder receiving dialectical behavior therapy. *American Journal of Drug and Alcohol Abuse*, *37*(1), 37–42.

Azizi, A., Borjali, A., & Golzari, M. (2010). The effectiveness of emotion regulation training and cognitive therapy on the emotional and addictional problems of substance abusers. *Iranian Journal of Psychiatry*, *5*(2), 60.

Barrett, J. J., Tolle, K. A., & Salsman, N. L. (2017). Dialectical behavior therapy skills training for persistent complex bereavement disorder. *Clinical Case Studies*, *16*, 388–400.

Beckstead, D. J., Lambert, M. J., DuBose, A. P., & Linehan, M. (2015). Dialectical behavior therapy with American Indian/Alaska Native adolescents diagnosed with substance use disorders: Combining an evidence based treatment with cultural, traditional, and spiritual beliefs. *Addictive Behaviors*, *51*, 84–87.

Cavicchioli, M., Movalli, M., Ramella, P., Vassena, G., Prudenziati, F., & Maffei, C. (2019). Feasibility of dialectical behavior therapy skills training as an outpatient program in treating alcohol use disorder: The role of difficulties with emotion regulation and experiential avoidance. *Addiction Research & Theory*. Available from https://doi.org/10.1080/16066359.2019.1590558.

Chambless, D. L., Baker, M. J., Baucom, D. H., Beutler, L. E., Calhoun, K. S., Crits-Christoph, P., ... Woody, S. (1998). Update on empirically validated therapies. II. *The Clinical Psychologist*, *51*(1), 3–16.

Cooperman, N. A., Rizvi, S. L., Hughes, C. D., & Williams, J. M. (2019). Field test of dialectical behavior therapy skills training-based intervention for smoking cessation and opioid relapse prevention in methadone treatment. *Journal of Dual Diagnosis*, *15*, 67–73.

Courbasson, C., Nishikawa, Y., & Dixon, L. (2012). Outcome of dialectical behavior therapy for concurrent eating and substance use disorders. *Clinical Psychology & Psychotherapy, 19*(5), 434–449.

Dietz, A. R., & Dunn, M. E. (2014). The use of motivational interviewing in conjunction with adapted dialectical behavior therapy to treat synthetic cannabis use disorder. *Clinical Case Studies, 13*, 455–471. Available from https://doi.org/10.1177/1534650114521496.

Dimeff, L., Rizvi, S. L., Brown, M., & Linehan, M. M. (2000). Dialectical behavior therapy for substance abuse: A pilot application to methamphetamine-dependent women with borderline personality disorder. *Cognitive and Behavioral Practice, 7*, 457–468.

Feigenbaum, J. D., Fonagy, P., Pilling, S., Jones, A., Wildgoose, A., & Bebbington, P. E. (2012). A real-world study of the effectiveness of DBT in the UK National Health Service. *British Journal of Clinical Psychology, 51*, 121–141.

First, M. B., Spitzer, R. L., Gibbons, M., & Williams, J. B. W. (1995). *Structured clinical interview for axis I DSM-IV disorders-patient edition (SCID-I/P)*. New York: Biometrics Research Department, New York State Psychiatric Institute.

Goodman, M., Banthin, D., Blair, N. J., Mascitelli, K. A., Wilsnack, J., Chen, J., … New, A. S. (2016). A randomized trial of dialectical behavior therapy in high-risk suicidal veterans. *Journal of Clinical Psychiatry, 77*, e1591–e1600.

Harned, M. S., Chapman, A. L., Dexter-Mazza, E. T., Murray, A., Comtois, K. A., & Linehan, M. M. (2008). Treating co-occurring axis I disorders in recurrently suicidal women with borderline personality disorder: A 2-year randomized trial of dialectical therapy versus community treatment by experts. *Journal of Consulting and Clinical Psychology, 76*(6), 1068–1075.

Jacobson, N. S., & Truax, P. (1991). Clinical significance: A statistical approach to defining meaningful change in psychotherapy research. *Journal of Consulting and Clinical Psychology, 59*, 12–19.

Keller, M. B., Lavori, P. W., Friedman, B., Nielsen, E., Endicott, J., McDonald-Scott, P., & Andreasen, N. C. (1987). The longitudinal interval follow-up evaluation: A comprehensive method for assessing outcome in prospective longitudinal studies. *Archives of General Psychiatry, 44*, 540–548.

Kokkevi, A., & Hartgers, C. (1995). EuropASI: European adaptation of a multidimensional assessment instrument for drug and alcohol dependence. *European Addiction Research, 1*, 208–210.

Lee, N. K., Cameron, J., & Jenner, L. (2015). A systematic review of interventions for co-occurring substance use and borderline personality disorders. *Drug and Alcohol Review, 34*, 663–672.

Linehan, M. M. (1993a). *Cognitive-behavioral treatment of borderline personality disorder*. New York: Guilford Press.

Linehan, M. M. (1993b). *Skills training manual for treating borderline personality disorder*. New York: Guilford Press.

Linehan, M. M. (2015a). *DBT skills training manual* (2nd ed.). New York: Guilford Press.

Linehan, M. M. (2015b). *DBT skills training handouts and worksheets* (2nd ed.). New York: Guilford Press.

Linehan, M. M., Comtois, K. A., Murray, A. M., Brown, M. Z., Gallop, R. J., Heard, H. L., …… Lindenboim, N. (2006). Two-year randomized trial and follow-up of dialectical behavior therapy vs. therapy by experts for suicidal behaviors and borderline personality disorder. *Archives of General Psychiatry, 63*(7), 757–766.

Linehan, M. M., & Dimeff, L. A. (1997). *Dialectical behavior therapy manual of treatment interventions for drug abusers with borderline personality disorder*. Seattle, WA: University of Washington.

Linehan, M. M., Dimeff, L. A., Reynolds, S. K., Comtois, K. A., Welch, S. S., Heagerty, P., & Kivlahan, D. R. (2002). Dialectical behavior therapy versus comprehensive validation therapy plus 12-step for the treatment of opioid dependent women meeting criteria for borderline personality disorder. *Drug and Alcohol Dependence, 67*, 13–26.

Linehan, M. M., Korslund, K. E., Harned, M. S., Gallop, R. J., Lungu, A., Neacsiu, A. D., ... Murray-Gregory, A. M. (2015). Dialectical behavior therapy for high suicide risk in borderline personality disorder: A component analysis. *JAMA Psychiatry, 75*, 475–482. Available from https://doi.org/10.1001/jamapsychiatry.2014.3039.

Linehan, M. M., Schmidt, H., Dimeff, L. A., Craft, J. C., Kanter, J., & Comtois, K. A. (1999). Dialectical behavior therapy for patients with borderline personality disorder and drug dependence. *The American Journal on Addictions, 8*, 279–292.

Lungu, A. (2015). Computerized trans-diagnostic dialectical behavior therapy skills training for emotion dysregulation (Unpublished doctoral dissertation). Seattle, WA: University of Washington.

Maffei, C., Cavicchioli, M., Movalli, M., Cavallaro, R., & Fossati, A. (2018). Dialectical behavior therapy skills training in alcohol dependence treatment: Findings based on an open trial. *Substance Use and Misuse, 53*, 2368–2385.

McCay, E., Carter, C., Aiello, A., Quesnel, S., Langley, J., Hwang, S., ... Karabanow, J. (2015). Dialectical behavior therapy as a catalyst for change in street-involved youth: A mixed method study. *Children and Youth Services Review, 58*, 187–199.

McMain, S. F., Guimond, T., Barnhart, R., Habinski, L., & Streiner, D. L. (2017). A randomized trial of brief dialectical behavior therapy skills training in suicidal patients suffering from borderline disorder. *Acta Psychiatrica Scandinavica, 135*, 138–148.

McMain, S., Sayrs, J. H., Dimeff, L. A., & Linehan, M. M. (2007). Dialectical behavior therapy for individuals with borderline personality disorder and substance dependence. In L. Dimeff, & K. Koerner (Eds.), *Dialectical behavior therapy in clinical practice* (pp. 145–173). New York: Guilford Press.

Miller, A. L., Rathus, J. H., & Linehan, M. M. (2007). *Dialectical behavior therapy with suicidal adolescents*. New York: Guilford Press.

Navarro-Haro, M. V., Botella, C., Guillen, V., Moliner, R., Marco, H., Jorquera, M., ... Garcia-Palacios, A. (2018). Dialectical behavior therapy in the treatment of borderline personality disorder and eating disorders comorbidity: A pilot study in a naturalistic setting. *Cognitive Therapy & Research, 42*, 636–649.

Neacsiu, A. D., Eberle, J. W., Kramer, R., Wiesmann, T., & Linehan, M. M. (2014). Dialectical behavior therapy skills for transdiagnostic emotion dysregulation: A pilot randomized controlled trial. *Behaviour Research and Therapy, 59*, 40–51.

Nyamathi, A. M., Shin, S. S., Smeltzer, J., Salem, B. E., Yadav, K., Ekstrand, M. L., ... Faucette, M. (2017). Achieving drug and alcohol abstinence among recently incarcerated homeless women: A randomized controlled trial comparing dialectical behavioral therapy-case management with a health promotion program. *Nursing Research, 66*, 432–441.

Owens, M. D., Nason, E., & Yeater, E. (2018). Dialectical behavior therapy for multiple treatment targets: A case study of a male with comorbid personality and substance use disorders. *International Journal of Mental Health Addiction, 16*, 436–450.

Pistorello, J., Fruzzetti, A. E., MacLane, C., Gallop, R., & Iverson, K. M. (2012). Dialectical behavior therapy applied to college students: A randomized clinical trial. *Journal of Consulting and Clinical Psychology, 80*, 982–994.

Rabinovitz, S., & Nagar, M. (2018). The effects of craving on implicit cognitive mechanisms involved in risk behavior: Can dialectical behavior therapy in therapeutic communities make a difference? A pilot study. *Journal of Therapeutic Communities, 39*, 83–92.

Ramazanzadeh, F., Alireza, M., & Shahram, M. (2016). Effectiveness training emotion regulation skills in emotional schema and substance use profile of adolescents at risk. *Journal of Psychology, 19*, 380–393.

Ramezanzadeh, F., Moradi, A., & Mohammadkhani, S. (2014). Effectiveness training emotion regulation skills in executive function and emotion regulation strategies of adolescents at risk. *Journal of Cognitive Psychology, 2*(2), 37–45.

Rizvi, S. L., Dimeff, L. A., Skutch, J., Carroll, D., & Linehan, M. M. (2011). A pilot study of the DBT coach: An interactive mobile phone application for individuals with borderline personality disorder and substance use disorder. *Behavior Therapy, 42*, 589–600.

Sahranavard, S., & Miri, M. R. (2018). A comparative study of the effectiveness of group-based cognitive behavioral therapy and dialectical behavior therapy in reducing depressive symptoms in Iranian women substance abusers. *Psicologia: Reflexao e Critica, 31*, 15.

Schultz Fischer, J. R. (2007). Treatment of co-morbid methamphetamine substance abuse and borderline personality disorder features using modified dialectical behavior therapy (Unpublished doctoral dissertation). Kalamazoo, MI: Western Michigan University.

Substance Abuse and Mental Health Services Administration. (2014). An introduction to co-occurring borderline personality disorder and substance use disorders. *In Brief, 8*(3), 1–8.

Tolin, D. F., McKay, D., Forman, E. M., Klonsky, E. D., & Thombs, B. D. (2015). Empirically supported treatment: Recommendations for a new model. *Clinical Psychology Science and Practice, 22*, 317–338.

van den Bosch, L. M., Koeter, M. W., Stijnen, T., Verheul, R., & van den Brink, W. (2005). Sustained efficacy of dialectical behaviour therapy for borderline personality disorder. *Behaviour Research and Therapy, 43*, 1231–1241.

van den Bosch, L. M., Verheul, R., Schippers, G. M., & van den Brink, W. (2002). Dialectical behavior therapy of borderline patients with and without substance use problems: Implementation and long-term effects. *Addictive Behaviors, 27*(6), 911–923.

Verheul, R., van den Bosch, L. M., Koeter, M. W. J., De Ridder, M. A. J., Stijnen, T., & van den Brink, W. (2003). Dialectical behavior therapy for women with borderline personality disorder: 12-month, randomized clinical trial in The Netherlands. *British Journal of Psychiatry, 182*, 135–140.

Wagner, E. E., Miller, A. L., Greene, L. I., & Winiarski, M. G. (2004). Dialectical behavior therapy for substance abusers adapted for persons living with HIV/AIDS with substance use diagnoses and borderline personality disorder. *Cognitive and Behavioral Practice, 11*(2), 202–212.

Whiteside, U. (2011). A brief motivational intervention incorporating DBT skills for depressed and anxious young drinkers (Ph.D. dissertation). Seattle, WA: University of Washington.

Wilks, C., Lungu, A., Ang, S. Y., Matsumiya, B., Yin, Q., & Linehan, M. M. (2017). A randomized controlled trial of an Internet delivered dialectical behavior therapy skills training for suicidal and heavy episodic drinkers. *Journal of Affective Disorders, 232*, 219–228.

Further reading

Linehan, M. M., Lynch, T. R., Harned, M. S., Korslund, K. E., & Rosenthal, Z. M. (2009). Preliminary outcomes of a randomized controlled trial of DBT vs. drug counseling for opiate-dependent BPD men and women. In: *Paper presented at the 43rd annual ABCT convention*. New York.

CHAPTER

8

Dialectical behavior therapy for adolescents: a review of the research

Jill H. Rathus[1], Michele S. Berk[2], Alec L. Miller[3] and Rebekah Halpert[4]

[1]Department of Psychology, Long Island University-Post, Brookville, NY, United States, [2]Department of Psychiatry and Behavioral Sciences, Division of Child and Adolescent Psychiatry, Stanford University, Stanford, CA, United States, [3]Cognitive and Behavioral Consultants, White Plains, NY, United States, [4]Department of Psychiatry, New York Presbyterian-Columbia University Medical Center, NY, United States

Introduction

Suicide among adolescents has increased significantly in the last decade and was the second leading cause of death in this group in the year 2017 (Centers for Disease Control and Prevention, 2018; Curtin, Warner & Hedegaard, 2016). For every completed suicide, there are significantly more suicide attempts and even greater instances of nonsuicidal self-injury (NSSI; Asarnow et al., 2011; Cox et al., 2012; Mościcki, 2001). Moreover, NSSI itself is a significant predictor of suicide attempts, and NSSI beginning in early adolescence (13–16 years) increases these odds (Muehlenkamp, Xhunga, & Brausch, 2018; Wilkinson, Kelvin, Roberts, Dubicka, & Goodyer, 2011).

Dialectical behavior therapy (DBT), originally developed to treat chronically suicidal adult women, has been established as an empirically supported treatment for suicidal adolescents with complex, multidiagnostic presentations [DBT for adolescents (DBT-A); e.g., McCauley

The Handbook of Dialectical Behavior Therapy
DOI: https://doi.org/10.1016/B978-0-12-816384-9.00008-7

et al., 2018; Mehlum et al., 2014; Miller, Rathus, & Linehan, 2007; Rathus & Miller, 2002]. This chapter will begin with a brief overview of DBT, a rationale for its adaptation to an adolescent population (DBT-A), and a description of modifications included in DBT-A. A review of the research on DBT-A will follow. The chapter will conclude by identifying areas of future research.

Dialectical behavior therapy

DBT was developed by Linehan (1993) to treat suicidal adult women, many of whom met criteria for borderline personality disorder (BPD), a condition characterized by severe emotional, interpersonal, behavioral, and self-dysregulation. Individuals with BPD struggle to take balanced action to regulate their emotions and often resort to impulsive, unhelpful behaviors that have been reinforced by their environments and by reductions in painful emotions. DBT combines cognitive-behavior therapy (CBT) strategies with Zen principles to foster an adaptive approach to managing difficult emotions and behaviors; underlying all elements of the treatment is the core dialectic of working toward acceptance and change. At present, 27 randomized controlled trials (RCTs) support the efficacy of comprehensive DBT in reducing suicidal behaviors, BPD features, or emotion dysregulation in individuals with BPD or chronic suicidality (e.g., Koons et al., 2001; Linehan et al., 2006; Linehan, Armstrong, Suarez, Allmon, & Heard, 1991).

DBT's biosocial model for conceptualizing BPD identifies the transaction between a biologically based emotional vulnerability and an invalidating environment. Emotional vulnerability is defined by high sensitivity to emotional stimuli, high reactivity or intensity of responses, and a slow return to emotional baseline. An invalidating environment can include any environment that involves a lack of fit between the child and his or her environment, including "ordinary" families with an exquisitely sensitive child, abusive or "chaotic" families, and "perfect" families that discourage displays of vulnerability and negative emotion. Invalidating environments ignore or punish the negative emotional reactions of the child and oversimplify the ease of solving problems without offering relevant strategies to teach emotion regulation or distress tolerance. Children in such environments can become classically conditioned to respond with shame to their own emotions; at the same time, they also learn that alarmed family members will at times respond to extreme displays of distress, such as suicide attempts or threats, and thus a pattern of escalation becomes intermittently reinforced. DBT thus seeks to target this vacillation between self-invalidation and emotional escalation (Linehan, 1993). It is important to note that for adolescents, many sources of invalidation can occur other than caregivers, including staff in school environments and sports or other activities, peers, broader society or community, and social media, which has become immersive and pervasive for the most recent generation of our youth.

DBT is a comprehensive, multifaceted treatment that serves five functions: to improve client motivation, enhance client capabilities, assure generalization beyond the therapy room, structure the environment to support effective behaviors, and enhance therapist capabilities. Its four standard outpatient modes—individual therapy, group skills training, phone consultation, and therapist consultation meetings—are designed to achieve these five functions, although inpatient and other settings might offer variations in modes to address these functions. The DBT group skills training component itself is divided into four modules, designed to address the different areas of dysregulation in the patient with chronic suicidality or borderline personality features: Distress Tolerance (for behavioral dysregulation), Emotion Regulation (for emotion dysregulation), Mindfulness (for self and cognitive dysregulation), and Interpersonal Effectiveness (for interpersonal dysregulation). DBT also contains a hierarchy of treatment targets that organize the treatment and the session structure. Following a pretreatment and commitment stage, primary treatment targets in stage one of treatment (which addresses attaining safety and behavioral control) include reducing life-threatening behaviors, decreasing therapy-interfering behaviors, decreasing quality-of-life-interfering behaviors, and increasing behavioral skills. Secondary treatment targets include addressing the dialectical dilemmas, or behavioral extremes used to attempt to regulate overwhelming negative emotions, that are present in BPD individuals.

Dialectical behavior therapy for adolescents

DBT was adapted for an adolescent population by Rathus and Miller (Miller et al., 1997; Rathus & Miller, 2002) in their efforts to develop an effective treatment for multiproblem adolescents with suicidality and self-harm behaviors. DBT-A accounts for developmental and environmental considerations—including cognitive and emotional capacities, school attendance, and dependence on family/caregivers—that are present when working with adolescents (Miller et al., 2007). Comprehensive DBT-A therefore involves several modifications to the original DBT modes and skills modules, including multifamily skills training groups involving both the adolescent and primary caregiver(s), phone coaching for teens as well as family members, family and/or parenting sessions as needed, additional skills, and more teen-friendly skills handouts (Miller et al., 2007; Rathus & Miller, 2015). Rathus and Miller (Miller et al., 2007; Rathus & Miller, 2000, 2015) also defined three additional dialectical dilemmas and associated secondary treatment targets that are often present in teen–parent interactions: (1) excessive leniency versus authoritarian control; (2) normalizing pathological behaviors versus pathologizing normative behaviors; and (3) forcing autonomy versus fostering dependence. These three patterns are addressed in DBT-A's Walking the Middle Path, a DBT-A skills module that helps foster more balanced interactions between caregivers and teens by teaching dialectics, validation, and standard behavior modification principles and skills. Other modifications include additional skills such as the THINK skill, an interpersonal effectiveness skill that teaches teens and parents perspective taking to ultimately help them with validation and dialectics; Parent–Teen Shared Pleasant Activities, an additional emotion regulation skill to increase positive emotions in the short term while enhancing family cohesion; and additions to already-existing DBT skills, including the supplemental handouts on eating habits and sleep hygiene for the PLEASE emotion regulation skill (Rathus & Miller, 2015).

Empirical support for dialectical behavior therapy for adolescents

As shown in Tables 8.1 and 8.2, numerous open trials and quasiexperimental studies, as well as three RCTs (see Table 8.1), support DBT-A as a treatment for multiple target behaviors among multiproblem, suicidal or self-harming adolescents. In these tables, we include research that included self-harm as an outcome. At present, DBT is the only treatment to demonstrate efficacy for reducing self-harm among adolescents that has been replicated across two independently conducted and adequately powered RCTs (McCauley et al., 2018; Mehlum et al., 2014). In addition, at least 10 nonrandomized trials have been conducted on DBT for adolescents across a variety of treatment settings and diagnoses that include self-harm outcomes (see Table 8.2). In the remainder of this chapter, we will review extant research on DBT with adolescents and provide suggestions for future research directions.

Randomized controlled trials of dialectical behavior therapy for adolescents

Mehlum et al. (2014) conducted an RCT in Norway of 77 adolescents comparing outpatient DBT-A to enhanced usual care (EUC), which involved 19 weeks of either psychodynamic therapy or CBT, plus psychopharmacological treatment ("enhanced" indicated the study

TABLE 8.1 Randomized controlled trials of dialectical behavior therapy (DBT) with adolescents with self-harm behaviors[a].

	N	Age range/gender/race and Ethnicity	Treatment length	Study conditions	Formal adherence ratings? (Y/N)	Timing of outcome assessments	Outcome measure	Significance	Effect size
1. McCauley et al. (2018)	173	12–18 Female: 95% Caucasian: 56% Hispanic: 27% African-American: 7% Asian: 6%	6 months	Standard DBT for adolescents versus individual and group supportive therapy	Y				
Primary									
Suicide attempts						6 months	SASII	$P < .05$	NNT = 8.46
						12 months	SASII	ns	
NSSI						6 months	SASII	$P < .05$	NNT = 5.92
						12 months	SASII	ns	
Total self-harm						6 months	SASII	$P < .05$	NNT = 5.78
						12 months	SASII	ns	
Suicidal ideation						6 months	SIQ-Jr.	$P < .03$	$d = 0.34$
						12 months	SIQ-Jr.	ns	
2. Mehlum et al. (2014) and Mehlum et al. (2016)	77	12–18 Female: 88% Norwegian ethnicity: 85%	19 weeks	Standard DBT for adolescents versus enhanced usual care	Y				

(*Continued*)

TABLE 8.1 (Continued)

	N	Age range/gender/race and Ethnicity	Treatment length	Study conditions	Formal adherence ratings? (Y/N)	Timing of outcome assessments	Outcome measure	Significance	Effect size
Primary									
Self-harm						19 weeks	Lifetime Parasuicide Count	$P < .02$	
Suicidal ideation						19 weeks	SIQ-Jr.	$P < .01$	$d = 0.16$
Self-harm						1-year follow-up	Lifetime Parasuicide Count	$P < .05$	
Suicidal ideation						1-year follow-up	SIQ-Jr.	ns	
Secondary									
Hopelessness						19 weeks	Beck Hopelessness Scale	$P < .07$	0.22
Depression						19 weeks	Short Mood and Feelings Questionnaire	ns	0.41
						19 weeks	Montgomery–Asberg Depression Rating Scale	$P < .02$	0.24
Borderline symptoms						19 weeks	Borderline Symptom List	$P < .05$	0.25
Hopelessness						1 year	Beck Hopelessness Scale	ns	
Depression						1 year	Short Mood and Feelings Questionnaire	ns	
						1 year	Montgomery–Asberg Depression Rating Scale	ns	

Borderline symptoms						1 year	Borderline Symptom List	ns	
3. Goldstein et al. (2014)	20	12–18 Female: 75% Caucasian: 80% African-American: 13% Mixed race: 13%	1 year	Standard DBT for adolescents modified for youth with bipolar disorders versus standard of care psychotherapy	Y				
Primary									
Suicide attempts						1 year (posttreatment)	LIFE Self-Injurious/ Suicidal Behavior Scale	ns	
NSSI episodes						1 year (posttreatment)	LIFE Self-Injurious/ Suicidal Behavior Scale	ns	
Suicidal ideation						1 year (posttreatment)	SIQ-Jr.	ns	
Depression						1 year (posttreatment)	KSADS Depression Rating Scale	$P < 0.05$	$d = 0.98$
Mania						1 year (posttreatment)	KSADS Mania Rating Scale	ns	
Emotion dysregulation						1 year (posttreatment)	Children's Affective Lability Scale	ns	

[a]*Fields left blank indicate that the information was not provided in the published article.*

KSADS, Kiddie Schedule for Affective Disorders and Schizophrenia; *LIFE*, Longitudinal Interval Follow-Up Evaluation; *NNT*, number needed to treat; *NSSI*, nonsuicidal self-injury; *SASII*, suicide attempt and self-injury interview; *SIQ-Jr.*, Suicidal Ideation Questionnaire Junior.

TABLE 8.2 Nonrandomized trials of dialectical behavior therapy (DBT) with adolescents with self-harm behaviors[a].

	N	Age range/gender/race and ethnicity	Treatment length	Study conditions and design	Formal adherence ratings? (Y/N)	Timing of outcome assessments	Outcome measure	Significance	Effect size
1. Rathus and Miller (2002)	111	12–18 Female: 93% in DBT condition Hispanic: 68% African-American 17% Caucasian 8%	12 weeks	Standard DBT for adolescents ($n = 29$) and treatment as usual ($n = 82$) Quasiexperimental trial, patients with (1) a suicide attempt within the past 4 months or current SI and (2) traits of BPD were assigned to DBT; teens with either (1) or (2) were assigned to TAU	N	12 weeks (posttreatment)			
Primary									
Between-group differences									
No. of inpatient hospitalizations							Clinical records	$P < .04$	
No. of suicide attempts							Clinical records	ns	
Treatment completion							Clinical records	$P < .04$	
Within-group differences (DBT only)									
Suicidal ideation							Harkavy–Asnis Suicide Survey	$P < .03$	
Psychopathology							SCL-90 Global Severity Index	$P < .02$	
							SCL-90 Positive Symptom Distress Index	$P < .006$	
							SCL-90 Anxiety Scale	$P < .05$	

							SCL-90 Depression Scale	$P < .004$	
							SCL-90 Interpersonal Sensitivity Scale	$P < .02$	
							SCL-90 Obsessive Compulsive Scale	$P < .006$	
Borderline personality disorder symptoms							LPI Total Score	$P < .009$	
							LPI Confusion About Self Scale	$P < .007$	
							LPI Impulsivity Scale	$P < .005$	
							LPI Emotion Dysregulation Scale	$P < .006$	
							LPI Interpersonal Difficulties Scale	$P < .05$	
2. Berk et al. (2019)	22	12–17 Female: 92% Hispanic: 63% Caucasian: 17%	6 months	Standard DBT for adolescents Open trial, adolescents treated in a county, outpatient mental health clinic	N	6 months (posttreatment)			
Primary									
No. of suicide attempts							Structured clinical interview	$P < .05$	
No. of NSSI behaviors							Structured clinical interview	$P < .01$	
Suicidal ideation							SIQ-Jr.	$P < .01$	
ER visits							Structured clinical interview	ns	
Hospitalizations							Structured clinical interview	ns	

(Continued)

TABLE 8.2 (Continued)

	N	Age range/ gender/race and ethnicity	Treatment length	Study conditions and design	Formal adherence ratings? (Y/N)	Timing of outcome assessments	Outcome measure	Significance	Effect size
Secondary									
Emotion dysregulation							DERS	$P < .01$	
Depression							BDI	$P < .01$	
Reasons for living							RFL-A	$P < .01$	
Global psychopathology							CBCL, Total Problems Score	$P < .01$	
							YSR, Total Problems Score	$P < .01$	
Borderline traits							SCID-II, Borderline Scale	$P < .01$	
3. Woodberry and Popenoe (2008)	46	13–18 Female: 89% Caucasian: 96%	15 weeks	Standard DBT for adolescents Open trial, adolescents treated in a community, outpatient mental health clinic	N	15 weeks (posttreatment)			
Primary									
Suicidal and self-harm ideation							One item "wanting to hurt self" from the TSCC	$d = 0.62$, $P = .004$	
							One item "wanting to kill self" from the TSCC	$d = .73$, $P = .001$	
							Parent report on one CBCL item "deliberately harms	$P < .06$	$d = 0.46$

							self or attempts suicide" Parent report on one CBCL item "talks about killing self"	 ns	
Secondary									
Depression							Reynolds Adolescent Depression Scale	$P < .001$	
PTSD symptoms							TSCC Dissociation Scale	$P < .002$	
							TSCC PTSD Scale	ns	
4. Katz et al. (2004)	62	14–17 Female: 84% Caucasian: 72.6% First Nations populations: 19% Hispanic: 1.6% Asian/Pacific Islander: 5%	2 weeks	2-week modified inpatient version of standard adolescent DBT versus TAU (psychodynamically oriented unit) Nonrandomized, youth inpatient admission assigned to one of two units based on bed availability	N	2 weeks (posttreatment) and 1-year follow-up			
Primary									
Self-harm behaviors						1 year	Lifetime Parasuicide Count	No significant between-group differences, both groups significantly decreased at follow-up	DBT: $d = 0.63$ TAU: $d = 0.73$

(Continued)

TABLE 8.2 (Continued)

	N	Age range/gender/race and ethnicity	Treatment length	Study conditions and design	Formal adherence ratings? (Y/N)	Timing of outcome assessments	Outcome measure	Significance	Effect size
Suicidal ideation						Posttreatment	SIQ-Jr.	No significant between-group differences, both groups significantly decreased at follow-up	
						1 year	SIQ-Jr.	No significant between-group differences, both groups significantly decreased at follow-up	DBT: $d = 2.12$ TAU: $d = 1.36$
Depression						Posttreatment	BDI-13	No significant between-group differences, both groups significantly decreased at follow-up	
						1 year	BDI-13	No significant between-group differences, both groups significantly decreased at follow-up	DBT: $d = 1.67$ TAU: $d = 1.05$

Hopelessness						Posttreatment	Kazdin Hopelessness Scale for Children	No significant between-group differences, both groups significantly decreased at follow-up	
						1 year	Kazdin Hopelessness Scale for Children	No significant between-group differences, both groups significantly decreased at follow-up	DBT: $d = 0.73$ TAU: $d = 0.33$
5. Fleischhaker et al. (2011)	12	13–19 Female: 100%	16–24 weeks	Standard DBT for adolescents Open trial	N				
Primary									
Borderline personality disorder traits						1-year follow-up	Structured Clinical Interview for DSM-IV, Axis II, German version (SKID-II)	$P < .003$	$d = 0.78$
NSSI behavior						Posttreatment	Lifetime Parasuicide Count	$P < .02$	$d = 0.89$
						1-year follow-up (as compared to the month before starting treatment)	Lifetime Parasuicide Count	$P < .02$	$d = 0.92$
Global functioning						1 year	GAF Scale	$P < .01$	$d = -1.91$
						1 year	CGI Scale	$P < .007$	$d = 3.40$
Quality of life						1 year	Inventory of Life Quality in Children and Adolescents	$P < .004$	$d = 2.84$

(Continued)

TABLE 8.2 (Continued)

	N	Age range/gender/race and ethnicity	Treatment length	Study conditions and design	Formal adherence ratings? (Y/N)	Timing of outcome assessments	Outcome measure	Significance	Effect size
Psychopathology						1 year	SCL-90 R, Global Severity Index	$P < .008$	$d = 1.30$
							SCL-90 R, Positive Symptom Total Index	$P < .02$	d +1.08
Depression						1 year	Depression Inventory for Children and Adolescents	$P < .02$	d +1.51
6. James et al. (2008)	16	15–18 Female: 100%	1 year	Standard DBT for adolescents in a community clinic Open trial	N				
Primary									
Deliberate self-harm						Follow-up conducted at a mean of 268 days since end of treatment	Clinical Interview	$P < .001$	
Depression						Follow-up conducted at a mean of 268 days since end of treatment	BDI	$P < .001$	
Hopelessness						Follow-up conducted at a mean of 268 days since end of treatment	BHS	$P < .001$	
Global functioning						Follow-up conducted at a mean of 268 days since end of treatment	GAF	$P < .001$	
Borderline traits						Follow-up conducted at a mean of 268 days since end of treatment	SCID-II	$P < .001$	

7. James et al. (2011)	25	13–17 Female: 88%	1 year	Standard DBT adapted for youth in the "Looked After Care" system in the United Kingdom (similar to "ward of the court," or involvement with Child Protective Services or Foster Care system in the United States) Open trial	N	End of treatment			
Primary									
Self-harm						End of treatment	Clinical Interview	$P < .001$	
Depression						End of treatment	BDI	$P < .002$	
Hopelessness						End of treatment	BHS	$P < .002$	
Global functioning						End of treatment	GAF	$P < .001$	
8. McDonell et al. (2010)	106	12–17 Female: 58%	12 months	Youth on a long-term inpatient psychiatric unit assigned to one of three forms of DBT depending on clinical judgment (milieu DBT only; DBT skills training group only or milieu + skills group + individual DBT) Used historical data from youth previously hospitalized at the same facility who received TAU Quasiexperimental design	N				
Primary									
NSSI behaviors						12 months Pre/posttreatment for DBT group	Medical Record Review	$P < .001$	
						12 months Comparison to historical control group among youths with a history of three or more episodes of NSSI during their stay	Medical Record Review	$P < .05$	

(Continued)

TABLE 8.2 (Continued)

	N	Age range/gender/race and ethnicity	Treatment length	Study conditions and design	Formal adherence ratings? (Y/N)	Timing of outcome assessments	Outcome measure	Significance	Effect size
Global functioning						12 months Pre/posttreatment for DBT group	Clinician rating of Child Global Assessment Scale	$P < .001$	
No. of psychiatric medication prescribed						12 months Pre/posttreatment for DBT group	Medical Record Review	$P < .001$	
Episodes of locked seclusion						12 months Pre/posttreatment for DBT group	Medical Record Review	ns	
9. Goldstein et al. (2007)	10	12–18 Female: 80% Caucasian: 60% Mixed race: 30% African-American: 10%	12 months	Standard DBT for adolescents adapted for youth with Bipolar Disorders Open trial	N				
Primary									
Suicidal ideation						Pre/posttreatment	Modified Scale for Suicidal Ideation	$P < .04$	$d = 1.2$
NSSI behaviors						Pre/posttreatment	KSADS Depression Rating Scale	ns	
Depression						Pre/posttreatment	KSADS Depression Rating Scale	$P < .04$	$d = 0.9$

Mania						Pre/posttreatment	KSADS Mania Rating Scale	ns	
No. of psychotropic medications prescribed						Pre/posttreatment	Chart review	ns	
Interpersonal functioning						Pre/posttreatment	Matson Evaluation of Social Skills with Youngsters	ns	
Emotion dysregulation						Pre/posttreatment	Children's Affective Lability Scale	$P = .02$	$d = 0.3$
10. Tebbett-Mock et al. (2019)	801	12–17 Female: 66% Caucasian: 41% Hispanic: 14% Multiracial: 20% African-American: 20% Asian: 9%	Mean length of hospital stay was 8 days	Chart review comparing 425 adolescents who received DBT on an inpatient unit to a historical control group of 376 adolescents who were on the unit before DBT was implemented	N				
Primary									
Suicide attempts						Data extracted from medical records of hospital stay	Data extracted from medical records of hospital stay	$P < .01$	$r = 0.10$
Self-injury						Data extracted from medical records of hospital stay	Data extracted from medical records of hospital stay	$P < .04$	$r = 0.07$
Aggression patient to patient						Data extracted from medical records of hospital stay	Data extracted from medical records of hospital stay	ns	$r = 0.03$

(Continued)

TABLE 8.2 (Continued)

	N	Age range/gender/race and ethnicity	Treatment length	Study conditions and design	Formal adherence ratings? (Y/N)	Timing of outcome assessments	Outcome measure	Significance	Effect size
Aggression patient to staff						Data extracted from medical records of hospital stay	Data extracted from medical records of hospital stay	ns	$r = 0.01$
Constant observation hours						Data extracted from medical records of hospital stay	Data extracted from medical records of hospital stay	$P < .01$ for SI, ns for SI and aggression	$r = 0.09$ (SI); $r = 0.06$ (SI); $r = 0.04$ (aggression)
Restraints						Data extracted from medical records of hospital stay	Data extracted from medical records of hospital stay	$P < .01$	$r = 0.09$
Seclusions						Data extracted from medical records of hospital stay	Data extracted from medical records of hospital stay	ns	$r = 0.04$
Reductions in days hospitalized						Data extracted from medical records of hospital stay	Data extracted from medical records of hospital stay	$P < .01$	$r = 0.10$
Readmissions						Data extracted from medical records of hospital stay	Data extracted from medical records of hospital stay	ns	$r = 0.06$

[a]*Fields left blank indicate that the information was not provided in the published article.*

BDI, Beck Depression Inventory II; *CBCL*, Child Behavior Checklist; *CGI*, Clinical Global Impression; *DERS*, Difficulties in Emotion Dysregulation Scale; *GAF*, Global Assessment of Functioning; *LPI*, Life problems inventory; *NSSI*, nonsuicidal self-injury; *RFL-A*, Reasons for Living Scale for Adolescents; *SCID-II*, Structured Clinical Interview for DSM-IV, Axis II; *SI*, self-injury; *SIQ-Jr.*, Suicidal Ideation Questionnaire Junior; *TAU*, treatment as usual; *TSCC*, Trauma Symptom Checklist for Children; *YSR*, Youth Self-Report; *KSADS*, Kiddie Schedule for Affective Disorders and Schizophrenia; *BHS*, Beck Hopelessness Scale; *PTSD*, post traumatic stress disorder.

requirement for (1) control group therapists to administer on average at least one weekly treatment session per client, (2) control group therapists to be trained in the Linehan (2016) risk assessment and management protocol, and (3) that the research team alerted EUC therapists (as well as DBT therapists) if the teens were endorsing suicidality during their periodic research evaluations). Study participants had at least three borderline features along with repetitive self-harm. Attrition and use of emergency services was generally low in both conditions. DBT therapists followed the Rathus and Miller (2015) protocol, including the Walking the Middle Path module; parents attended skills training with teens, and therapists offered as-needed family sessions. Therapists were trained to adherence as measured by the DBT Adherence Scale (Linehan & Korslund, 2003). DBT-A was found to be superior to EUC in reducing the frequency of self-harm, severity of suicidal ideation, and interviewer-rated depressive symptoms (but not self-reported depressive symptoms) and BPD symptoms. Moreover, the DBT-A group evidenced large effect sizes across pre/posttreatment outcomes as compared to the control group (Mehlum et al., 2014). A 1-year follow-up (Mehlum et al., 2016) showed that statistically significant differences between the two groups on instances of self-harm were maintained. Reductions in depression, hopelessness, suicidal ideation, and borderline symptoms continued as well, though these were not significant compared with EUC at the follow-up period, mainly due to continued improvements in the EUC group and maintenance of gains in the DBT-A group during this time. In addition, DBT participants utilized outpatient therapy less than control participants at 1-year follow-up, and this trend approached significance. More recently, Mehlum et al.'s (2019) 3-year follow-up to their 2014 study showed that those who received DBT-A continued to evidence statistically significant reductions in self-harm compared with EUC. Furthermore, neither group showed symptom relapse for suicide ideation, hopelessness, and depressive and borderline symptoms, though there were no significant between-group differences on these variables. The study also found that much of the effect (70.8%) of DBT-A on long-term self-harm outcomes was mediated by a reduction in feelings of hopelessness during the trial treatment phase. Finally, DBT-A participants who received 3 months of follow-up treatment following the trial phase experienced additional symptom improvement (Mehlum et al., 2019). Mehlum et al.'s follow-up studies suggest that DBT-A works more quickly than treatment as usual (TAU) in reducing hopelessness, depression, and suicidal ideation; maintains its gains; can be bolstered by booster treatment; and is superior in reducing self-harm. The robust findings for self-harm even at 3 years posttreatment indicate the lasting impact of DBT-A on treating self-harm in adolescents.

McCauley et al.'s (2018) recently completed large-scale, multisite RCT, the Collaborative Adolescent Research on Emotion and Suicide, compared the effects of DBT-A to individual and group supportive therapy (IGST) on adolescent suicide attempts, NSSI, and overall self-harm. Participants were 173 high-risk adolescents aged 12–18 and had at least three lifetime self-harm episodes, including one in the 12 weeks before the study's screening, at least one lifetime suicide attempt, and three or more borderline features. The DBT-A condition followed Linehan's (2015a, 2015b) skills manual for skills training but followed Miller et al (2007) regarding inclusion of caregivers in skills training and offering as-needed family sessions. Adherence, as measured by the DBT Adherence Scale (DBT group) and the IGST/client-centered therapy adherence scale (IGST group), was strong for both groups. The authors found significant decreases in suicide attempts, NSSI, total self-harm behaviors (suicide attempts and NSSI combined), and suicidal ideation compared to the comparison group; these findings remained significant at 6-month but not 12-month follow-up, due to continued IGST improvements (McCauley et al., 2018). Secondary analyses revealed that the percentage of DBT-A adolescents with no self-harm behavior remained significantly greater than that for IGST adolescents even at 12 months (51.2% and 32.2% for the DBT and IGST groups, respectively). In addition, those in the DBT-A group attended significantly more individual and group sessions and had significantly higher rates of treatment completion. This RCT was the first of its kind to demonstrate that DBT-A is effective in reducing suicide attempts, and these effects are made further robust by the fact that DBT was compared to another manualized treatment. Given the weakening of treatment gains at the 12-month mark, it also supports the need for additional research examining longer term approaches that involves continuous risk management (McCauley et al., 2018).

Goldstein et al.'s (2015) RCT adapted Linehan's (1993) and Rathus and Miller's (Miller & Rathus, 2007; Rathus & Miller, 2002) DBT protocol for teens with bipolar disorder. Twenty adolescents with bipolar disorder were randomized to either DBT or TAU, with treatment lasting 1 year. Skills training and individual sessions alternated weekly for 1 year. The DBT condition included all components of DBT, except "groups" consisted of individual family units (rather than the multifamily skills group format) as well as additional modifications for the target population, including psychoeducation about bipolar disorder. Study therapists were trained by the authors, and sessions were videotaped and rated by study supervisors. The authors found that though adolescents in the DBT condition had more severe ratings of manic symptoms and parent-rated emotional dysregulation at baseline, they showed significant improvements in depression, were more likely to show improvement in suicidal ideation, and attended significantly more treatment sessions than TAU participants. A large effect size for the DBT group was present for the number of weeks of euthymic mood, and the DBT group had pre–post decreases in manic symptoms and emotion dysregulation (Goldstein et al., 2015).

Dialectical behavior therapy with preteens/children

Perepletchikova et al. (2017) conducted an RCT of DBT for children (DBT-C) with a diagnosis of disruptive mood dysregulation disorder (DMDD). Forty three children, aged 7–12 years, were randomly assigned to 32 weeks of either DBT-C or TAU. DBT-C included all four components of standard DBT, including individual therapy, skills training, telephone coaching, and therapist consultation meetings. Parent training was also provided. Sessions were held one time per week, for 90 minutes and were divided into child, parent training and family skills training components. Study therapists demonstrated adherence to the DBT model as rated using the DBT Adherence Rating Scale. Children, who received DBT-C attended a higher average number of therapy sessions, had higher rates of treatment completion (100%) and showed greater reduction in symptoms of DMDD and global functioning at treatment completion and 3-month follow-up than those who received TAU.

Nonrandomized studies of dialectical behavior therapy for adolescents

In the first outcome study of DBT-A, a quasiexperimental safety and feasibility trial, 111 adolescents were admitted to a large academic medical center outpatient program for depression and suicidality (Rathus & Miller, 2002). The authors compared DBT-A ($n = 29$), comprised 12 weeks of twice-weekly individual therapy and multifamily skills training, as well as telephone coaching, to TAU ($n = 82$), which included 12 weeks of twice-weekly supportive-psychodynamic psychotherapy and weekly family therapy. The sample consisted of inner-city adolescents who mostly (91.91%) identified as nonwhite ethnic minorities and most met criteria for a depressive disorder. Adolescents in this study were assigned to DBT-A if they endorsed a suicide attempt within the last 4 months *and* had either a diagnosis of BPD or three borderline personality features; participants with only one or neither of these criteria were assigned to TAU. DBT-A participants at pretreatment showed a significantly greater number of prior inpatient hospitalizations as well as diagnoses of depressive, substance use, BPD, and total number of Axis I diagnoses, than TAU participants. The two groups did not significantly differ at pretreatment on history of suicidal behavior, including past suicide attempts, NSSI, and time in years since one's first instance of suicidal ideation or attempt; however, the DBT group did show a nonsignificant trend toward greater current suicidal ideation and was significantly more depressed. The lack of difference in the two group's prior suicidal behavior was likely due to their all entering a specialty depression and suicide program. Participants as a whole had an average of 1.5 (SD = 2.1) prior suicide attempts reported a mean of 1.8 years (SD = 2.23) since their first suicide attempt, and 32% of the total sample reported prior NSSI. Study therapists included doctoral-level clinical psychologists and predoctoral interns all intensively trained in DBT. Therapists followed a formally modified DBT skills training protocol (Miller et al., 1997), and skills training and individual DBT therapy sessions were video- and audiotaped, respectively, to enhance adherence. Therapists also participated in weekly DBT consultation teams, and predoctoral therapists were provided with weekly supervision by highly trained DBT therapists. The study found that despite greater symptom severity in the DBT group prior to the intervention phase, DBT-A participants evidenced significantly greater treatment completion rates, with 62% of DBT participants completing treatment versus 40% of TAU participants. The study also demonstrated significantly lower rates of hospitalization during the study period for DBT participants than those receiving TAU, with 13% of those in TAU hospitalized during the course of treatment versus no DBT-A admissions. Those in the DBT-A group also evidenced significant reductions from pre- to posttreatment in suicidal ideation as well as borderline personality symptoms. Significant reductions in anxiety, depression, interpersonal sensitivity, and obsessive compulsive symptoms were also observed in the DBT-A group. There were no significant between-group differences on the reported number of suicide attempts during treatment, with 7.3% of the total sample attempting suicide during the study; however, although the total number of attempters in the sample was too low to obtain significance, the number of attempters in the DBT-A group ($n = 1$) was lower than those in the TAU group ($n = 7$). Taken together, the study's results were notable given the higher symptom severity of those in the DBT-A condition and offered positive outcomes for safety and feasibility and promising preliminary outcomes for DBT's effectiveness in addressing the symptoms of a multiproblem, high-risk adolescent population.

Subsequent quasiexperimental and open trials have replicated Rathus and Miller's adaptation in outpatient settings and have also extended it to other treatment settings. The studies outlined in this section illustrate promising findings for self-harming, multidiagnostic adolescents in academic hospital outpatient, community, inpatient, residential, and forensic settings. For the sake of clarity, the term "DBT-A" will be used to refer to studies that used our adolescent DBT protocol, while studies that used other adaptations of Linehan's DBT will be described accordingly.

Fleischhaker et al.'s (2011) open pilot trial, including a 1-year follow-up, adapted Rathus and Miller's (2002) DBT-A for an outpatient, German-speaking population seeking treatment at an academic medical center. Adolescent females ($n = 12$) aged 13–19 received 16–24 weeks of DBT-A, including phone coaching, all five skills modules, and weekly individual therapy (1 hour) and skills group (2 hours), and were measured pre- and posttreatment. The study reported significant reductions in NSSI at the conclusion of treatment compared with pretreatment. Though instances of NSSI had increased somewhat at 1-year follow-up, significant reductions from pretreatment to 1-year follow-up remained. In addition, there were significant reductions in the number of BPD criteria from pretreatment to 1-year follow-up. Improvements in overall functioning were significant from pretreatment to 1-year follow-up, as were improvements in quality of life and symptom reduction. Finally, the treatment had a 75% retention rate.

James, Taylor, Winmill, and Alfoadari (2008)'s open trial examined the effect of an adapted DBT protocol in reducing deliberate self-harm, depression, and hopelessness and improving functioning in a community sample of 16 female adolescents. Participants, aged 15–18 years, all with a recent history (i.e., within the last 6 months) of severe and persistent self-harm behavior, received weekly individual DBT therapy (1 hour) and skills group (1.5 hours) as well as phone coaching; adolescent skills groups included Linehan's four original skills training modules (no information on a therapist consultation team was included). Participants experienced significant postintervention reductions in depression, hopelessness, and frequency of deliberate self-harm (as reported in clinical interview), as well as gains in overall functioning that were maintained at 8-month follow-up (James et al., 2008). The authors subsequently tested their DBT adaptation in a community sample of self-harming adolescents in the foster care system ($n = 25$); while this open trial found a significant reduction in reports of depression, hopelessness, and self-harm, as well as a significant increase in global functioning among those who completed treatment, 35% of the sample failed to engage in treatment in the first place (James, Winmill, Anderson, & Alfoadari, 2011; see James, et al., 2008, for a description of the treatment package and measures).

Woodberry and Popenoe (2008), in a community-based open trial ($n = 46$), used both adolescent and parent ratings to measure the efficacy of a 15-week DBT-A intervention on symptoms of self-harm urges and behavior, suicide ideation, and suicide attempts. Adolescents aged 13–18, who were from various SES backgrounds and had a history of suicide attempts, self-injury, and/or emotional or interpersonal dysregulation in the previous 3–6 months, were included in the study, along with at least one caregiver per participant. Level of training in DBT varied among the study therapists, ranging from intensive training to chapter-by-chapter review of Linehan's (1993) primary text for DBT. The authors found that adolescent self-reports of self-harm urges (wanting to hurt self) and suicidal ideation (wanting to kill self) decreased significantly from pre- to posttreatment but not their reports of self-harm or suicide attempts. Parent reports indicated a marginally significant drop in teen self-harm behaviors and suicide attempts but not in suicidal ideation, indicating that parents may not be fully aware of teen's internal experiences of urges and ideation, nor accurate in their knowledge of teen's self-harm. Parents also evidenced significant decreases in parental depression, though parents who reported higher depression scores in the initial phase of treatment were more likely to drop out of the study. In addition, significant improvements were seen in several domains of internalizing and externalizing symptoms on both parent and adolescent self-reports (Woodberry & Popenoe, 2008).This study illustrated the generalizability of DBT-A to a naturalistic, community-based setting, in which the patient population is more heterogeneous than in research settings and in which clinicians are not highly trained in evidence-based treatment and do not regularly conduct formal adherence ratings. In addition, it was the first DBT-A study of suicidal adolescents to collect parent reports of adolescent and parental improvement, thereby providing an additional source of information for adolescent treatment outcomes. Parent findings also highlight the needs of parents of high-risk adolescents and illustrate potential benefits to parents (beyond those to youth) of integrating them into DBT-A treatment.

In a more recent community-based study, Berk, Starace, Black, and Avina (2019) conducted an open trial of comprehensive DBT-A among disadvantaged, ethnic minority clients aged 12–17 ($n = 22$). Adolescents enrolled in the study, which included 6 months of comprehensive DBT-A as per the protocol developed by Miller and Rathus (Miller et al., 2007; Rathus & Miller, 2002), were at high risk for suicide, as evidenced by having had at least one suicide attempt or NSSI within the past 4 months and by meeting at least three BPD criteria. All DBT therapists participated in a 2-day DBT training, given by a DBT expert trained by Linehan, prior to administering the treatment, and they received ongoing support and supervision during case consultation meetings and weekly supervision. No formal adherence measures were conducted but supervisors did listen to audio recordings of individual sessions and provide feedback. The study found significant decreases from pre- to posttreatment in suicide attempts, NSSI, and suicidal ideation. Significant decreases in related factors, such as emotion dysregulation, depression, impulsivity, BPD symptoms, and post traumatic stress disorder symptoms, as well as psychopathology and substance use, were also noted. Youth also reported significant improvement in family expressiveness and high rates of treatment acceptability. The previous three community-based studies provide encouraging findings regarding the feasibility of implementing DBT-A in environments where successful implementation of evidence-based treatments has been difficult (Shafran et al., 2009).

An increasing number of studies have examined the use of adolescent DBT in inpatient and forensic settings. Katz, Cox, Gunasekara, and Miller (2004)'s quasiexperimental study explored the efficacy of short-term DBT-A in reducing suicide ideation, hopelessness, and depression among adolescents ($n = 62$) aged 14–17 in an acute psychiatric inpatient setting. Participants, who were all admitted due to recent suicide attempt or serious suicide ideation, were assigned to a unit that provided either a 2-week version of DBT-A or a psychodynamically oriented TAU condition; assignment depended largely on bed availability. The 2-week DBT-A treatment was modified for an inpatient setting and included daily skills training sessions, twice-weekly individual therapy, and participation in a DBT-oriented milieu with DBT-trained nursing staff (to achieve the function of skills generalization in lieu of phone coaching). The treatment also included DBT consultation team meetings for therapists and program evaluation by a DBT consultant; no other adherence measures were taken. Both groups received adjunctive treatments (e.g., pharmacotherapy, family or crisis intervention) as needed, and groups did not differ on demographic characteristics or clinician expertise. The DBT-A group showed significantly fewer behavioral incidents (defined here by the number of completed incident reports by unit staff concerning events such as violence toward self or others) on the unit than the TAU group, and it had a 100% treatment retention rate, significantly higher than the TAU group. Both groups showed significant improvements from admission to discharge on measures of depression, hopelessness, and suicide ideation, as well as number of parasuicidal (i.e., NSSI) behaviors, and no between-group differences were present for these variables; in addition, though within-group gains were maintained after discharge, no significant differences between groups were found on the abovementioned variables, at a 1-year follow-up. Yet the DBT-A group contained larger effect sizes than the TAU group on hopelessness, suicide ideation, and depression, and thus the authors proposed that a future study with a larger sample size may yield significant between-group differences.

Tebbett-Mock, Saito, McGee, Woloszyn, and Venuti (2019)'s recent retrospective analysis of a large sample of adolescent inpatient data supports the above authors' recommendation for a larger sample size and yielded promising findings on several outcomes. In this study the authors compared the hospital charts of adolescents ($n = 425$) who received DBT-A on an acute psychiatric unit to a historical control group ($n = 376$) treated on the unit before the introduction of DBT (i.e., TAU). Adolescents 12–17 years of age were admitted because of imminent danger to themselves or others and endorsed a range of diagnoses, most commonly a mood or psychotic disorder. Treatment providers, comprised multidisciplinary team members, were all intensively trained through Behavioral Tech (behavioraltech.org), and the intervention was adapted for an acute inpatient unit with consultation of a Behavioral Tech DBT trainer. The DBT-A intervention was adapted for a shortened length of stay (i.e., 8–11 days for this sample) and included 9 DBT-A skills groups and three individual therapy session per week, one to two family/collateral sessions weekly, weekly consultation team, and DBT milieu treatment, including skills coaching, a token economy along with chain and solution analyses for "egregious behavior," and readily available therapeutic tools such as DBT-A handouts and coping skills boxes. The study found that patients receiving DBT-A had significantly fewer suicide attempts and self-injury, incidences of restraints, constant observation (CO) hours for self-injury, and days hospitalized compared with TAU patients. Moreover, a cost analysis showed that $251,609 less was spent on staff CO hours for the DBT-A group compared with the TAU group, illustrating the potential cost-effectiveness of DBT-A compared with standard inpatient treatment. The previous two studies highlight the benefits of this treatment even in significantly shortened form; Tebbett-Mock et al.'s study additionally lends support for the more global benefit of DBT on the health-care system.

Teens in longer term inpatient care also appear to benefit from DBT. Sunseri's (2004) study of children and adolescents aged 12–18 in a residential treatment facility ($n = 68$) in which the average length of stay is 18 months, compared the time periods before and after the implementation of DBT. Therapists were intensively trained by Linehan et al. Individual therapy was offered on a weekly basis, with some new clients receiving more frequent sessions. Skills group was offered twice weekly for 90 minutes each; the DBT skills in this program were modified only for preadolescents; for teens, the skills were administered exactly how they appeared in Linehan's manual for adults. Skills coaching was also offered and therapists met weekly for team consultation. Based on program records, the authors found that compared with residents treated prior to the implementation of DBT, residents treated with DBT demonstrated a significant reduction in premature terminations due to suicidal behavior (and subsequent acute hospitalization), number of days spent in inpatient hospitalization, and duration of physical restraints and seclusions (Sunseri, 2004).

In another examination of DBT on long-term units, McDonell et al. (2010) compared the hospital records of adolescents receiving DBT on a long-term psychiatric inpatient unit ($n = 106$) with historical control participants (i.e., who received treatment prior to the introduction of DBT to the unit) ($n = 104$). Three variations of DBT treatment—"milieu DBT;" milieu DBT plus DBT skills group; or milieu, group, and individual DBT (full DBT)—were offered to treatment group participants based on clinical characteristics (e.g., diagnosis or self-harm history) rather than randomization. Milieu DBT included chain analyses and DBT skills taught individually. Clinicians were all DBT-trained, and data were analyzed for DBT patients as a whole, including all three variations. Statistically significant improvements in overall functioning, as well as significant reductions in the number of psychiatric medication and NSSI, were observed within the DBT group from admission to discharge. In addition, DBT patients evidenced significantly lower rates of NSSI over 12 months of hospitalization compared with historical controls. Unfortunately, historical control group data on the measurement of overall functioning and number of psychiatric medications were not available to the study's authors. Though these results from acute and long-term stay inpatient units are promising and can be studied quasiexperimentally using data from historical records prior to implementing DBT, additional studies of DBT in long-term settings, along with the presence of concurrent and even randomized control groups, when possible, would yield more robust findings of DBT's effectiveness in this context.

Finally, there is some support for the use of DBT in an adolescent forensic population. Trupin, Stewart, Beach, and Boesky (2002)'s quasiexperimental study of incarcerated female juvenile offenders ($n = 60$) implemented an adapted DBT intervention on two prison units—one general population cottage (GPC) unit and one mental health cottage (MHC) unit—and compared the results to a TAU unit as well as to historical records of an additional 30 non-DBT offenders. The adapted DBT treatment modified behavioral targets in individual sessions to reflect the forensic setting, provided support to trained staff in implementation to mimic DBT's therapist consultation team, added a fifth "self-management skills" module to the original four DBT skills training modules, and offered formal skills groups one to two times weekly as well as skills coaching in the milieu. The study showed mixed results for the effectiveness of the modified DBT treatment in reducing suicidality and other behavior problems among residents of the two treatment units as compared to the nontreatment condition. However, the study did show a significant reduction in staff's punitive behavior on the MHC unit (characterized by a focus on punishment, isolation, restriction, and failure to reward adaptive behavior), where staff members received significantly more hours of training in DBT (80 vs 16) than those on the GPC unit. Though the variability in staff training in DBT, consistency of treatment implementation, significant baseline differences, and a discrepancy in the scope of the data obtained for the treatment and comparison units made it difficult to draw comparisons between the treatment and comparison units, the study did suggest that intensive training, motivated staff, and residents on a dedicated mental health unit can contribute to success in DBT in a forensic setting.

DBT-A has shown success in treating adolescents with other diagnoses as well, including anorexia, bulimia, binge eating disorder (BED), bipolar disorder, and oppositional defiant disorder (ODD) (e.g., Goldstein, Axelson, Birmaher, & Brent, 2007; Nelson-Gray et al., 2006; Safer, Couturier, & Lock, 2007; Salbach-Andrae, Bohnekamp, Pfeiffer, Lehmkuhl, & Miller, 2008). An open trial of a 25-week modified DBT-A program that included most standard DBT-A components (though it included families in skills training groups for only eight sessions) plus a sixth skills module called "dealing with food and body image" evidenced significant reductions in eating disordered behavior among adolescents with anorexia and bulimia ($n = 12$) (Salbach-Andrae et al., 2008). For adolescents with BED an open pilot trial found that a modified DBT protocol, adapted for teens from an adult protocol for DBT for BED and including age-appropriate changes such as multifamily skills groups, produced reduction in BED symptoms (Safer et al., 2007). Finally, Pennell, Webb, Agar, Federici, and Couturier (2019) conducted a retrospective analysis of hospital records for 24 adolescents in a day hospital program for eating disorders. The treatment program utilized a modified DBT approach that included elements of family-based therapy. The authors found that patients' weight and percentage of ideal body weight was significantly greater at discharge than at admission. In addition, according to information contained in discharge summaries, binge–purge status upon discharge was either reduced or completely absent. Readmission rates were low, with only five adolescents requiring readmission over the 2-year study period (Pennell et al., 2019).

In addition, Nelson-Gray et al.'s (2006) open trial examined the efficacy of a skills-only DBT-A treatment for children and adolescents with ODD. The 16-session manualized DBT-ST intervention was comprised all standard DBT skills and included modifications to duration (16 weeks instead of 24) as well as changes to make the skill presentations more age-appropriate, including the use of simpler language and making the group more activity-based than didactic. Results of their study showed significant improvements from pre- to posttreatment on ODD symptoms, interpersonal strength, depressive symptoms, and internalizing behaviors.

Future directions and conclusions

In recent years, the study of adolescent DBT has broadened significantly, extending across multiple treatment settings, diagnoses, and community and cultural characteristics. Based on the completion of two large, RCTs with adherence ratings from two different research groups, we can now conclude that DBT is a well-established, empirically supported treatment for self-harm behavior in high-risk adolescents. Recently, other adaptations of adolescent DBT have taken into account cultural differences to enhance DBT's applicability among various cultural minorities, including suicidal Latinas and Native Americans with substance use disorders (Beckstead et al., 2015; German et al., 2015). In addition, studies of specific components of adolescent DBT, such as skills-only treatment, are emerging (e.g., Nelson-Gray et al., 2006). The breadth of DBT-A research is thus large and growing.

The two RCTs that support DBT as an evidence-based treatment for decreasing self-harm in adolescents constitute a significant step forward in the field of adolescent suicide prevention. However, there is still considerable room for improvement in outcomes for suicidal youth treated with DBT. In Mehlum et al.'s study, the mean number of self-harm episodes in the DBT condition at posttreatment and 1-year follow-up was 9.0 and 5.5, respectively, suggesting that a number of participants continued to engage in repeated self-harm. Similarly, in McCauley et al.'s study, at 6 months, 53.5% of youth in the DBT condition had at least one self-harm during treatment and 49.8% had at least one self-harm between 6- and 12-month follow-up. Hence, treatment with standard DBT alone may not result in complete remission of self-harm behaviors, including suicide, among some youth. Research identifying new ways to further increase the effectiveness of DBT is an urgent priority in reducing risk of death by suicide in adolescents.

While DBT-A is emerging as a treatment with strong empirical support, several gaps remain. Several studies of adolescent DBT included the authors' independent modifications; consistent implementation of a standardized adolescent DBT protocol, along with consistent and rigorous measures to code for adherence across all DBT-A studies (i.e., for open trials, quasiexperimental, and for DBT-A for other clinical populations), would significantly improve empirical support for this vital treatment for adolescent suicidality, self-harm, and other problems. Additional RCT's are also needed to examine applications of DBT-A to populations other than suicidal and self-harming youth. Additional research should also examine adolescent populations with important and common comorbidities, such as self-harm features along with trauma, and the impact of newer evidence-based applications of DBT, such as DBT-PE (e.g., Harned, Wilks, Schmidt, & Coyle, 2018).

Future research could examine specific elements of DBT-A through component analyses. No published studies have yet examined the independent contributions (i.e., the incremental validity) of adding caregivers to skills training, or of family therapy sessions in DBT-A, and it is not clear which modes contribute to which outcomes. Moreover, no study to date has directly compared adolescent DBT with multifamily group format to other conditions, such as skills training for teens only with no caregivers present, or including caregivers in a separate, parallel skills group format, despite clinical variation along these lines in real-world settings. In addition, research into the optional parenting mode and its impact would be useful. Berk, Rathus, Kessler, Clarke, & Chick (under review) have piloted an intervention for parents of suicidal teens based on the Middle Path module. Providing an 8-to 10-week manualized treatment (consisting of Middle Path skills plus biosocial theory, mindfulness, and safety monitoring) for parents only, whose adolescent children were engaging in self-harm, Berk et al. found significant reductions in parental depression and caregiver strain. Moreover, they found a significant pre–post reduction in self-harm among the participants' adolescent children, despite the fact that they were not included in the intervention. A randomized trial with this parent-only intervention is thus warranted.

Given the relative intensity of outpatient DBT-A with its multiple modes and numerous skills modules, determining the optimal length of DBT for adolescents is an important research direction. Gillespie, Joyce, Flynn, and Corcoran (2019) recently conducted a quasiexperimental treatment length metric trial comparing 16 weeks (84 adolescents plus caregivers) with 24 weeks (68 adolescents plus caregivers) of DBT-A in Ireland using the Rathus and Miller model. Adolescents in both conditions experienced reductions in self-harm, suicidal ideation, and depression, and adolescents in each condition reached equivalent reductions (25%) in self-harm. Notably, parents in both conditions experienced significant and equivalent reductions in caregiver burden, grief, and stress. In comparing the two treatment lengths, the 24-week participants experienced significantly greater reductions in depression and suicidal ideation than the 16-week participants, but had a higher drop-out rate: 29.4% versus 15.5%. Such considerations are important in light of cost and resource availability, and a randomized comparison of treatment length would be a useful next step. However, given that this research was conducted in a naturalistic clinical setting that has implemented DBT-A, this study also represents an important step in effectiveness research, a natural progression following the publication of the Mehlum et al. and McCauley et al. RCTs.

Future research could also examine the acceptability and efficacy of the skills developed specifically for adolescents and caregivers in DBT-A. Rathus, Campbell, Miller, & Smith (2015) found that both teens and parents found the new Walking the Middle Path module highly acceptable and helpful for improving family interactions and assigned the highest ratings for favorability to the Middle Path skills of

Validation and Positive Reinforcement. The promising roles of DBT-A's caregiver-involved modalities and the Walking the Middle Path module thus merit more research attention, including examining impacts of caregiver change on teen outcomes and further examining the impact of DBT-A on caregiver outcomes. As adolescent suicide and self-injury remains a critically important public health challenge, and DBT-A has proven an efficacious treatment for this group, further refining our ability to best apply the treatment to those who need it promises to be a worthy goal.

References

Asarnow, J. R., Porta, G., Spirito, A., Emslie, G., Clarke, G., Wagner, K. D., ... Brent, D. A. (2011). Suicide attempts and nonsuicidal self-injury in the treatment of resistant depression in adolescents: Findings from the TORDIA study. *Journal of the American Academy of Child and Adolescent Psychiatry*, *50*(8), 772–781.

Beckstead, D. J., Lambert, M. J., DuBose, A. P., & Linehan, M. M. (2015). Dialectical behavior therapy with American Indian/Alaska Native adolescents diagnosed with substance use disorders: Combining an evidence-based treatment with cultural, traditional, and spiritual beliefs. *Addictive Behaviors*, *51*, 81–87.

Berk, M, Rathus, J., Kessler, M., Clarke, S., Chick, C., Shen, H., & Llewellyn T., Pilot test of a DBT-based parenting intervention for parents of youth with recent self-harm, *Cognitive Behavioral Practice*. (under review).

Berk, M. S., Starace, N. K., Black, V. P., & Avina, C. (2019). Implementation of dialectical behavior therapy with suicidal and self-harming adolescents in a community clinic. *Archives of Suicide Research*, 1–20.

Centers for Disease Control and Prevention. (2018). Ten leading causes of death and injury. In *Web-based Injury Statistics Query and Reporting System (WISQARS)*. Available from <https://www.cdc.gov/injury/wisqars/leadingcauses.html> Accessed 28.07.19.

Cox, L. J., Stanley, B. H., Melhem, N. M., Oquendo, M. A., Birmaher, B., Burke, A., ... Brent, D. A. (2012). A longitudinal study of nonsuicidal self-injury in offspring at high risk for mood disorder. *The Journal of Clinical Psychiatry*, *73*(6), 821–828.

Curtin, S. C., Warner, M., & Hedegaard, H. (2016). Increase in suicide in the United States, 1999-2014. PubMed.gov. *NCHS Data Brief*, *241*, 1–8.

Fleischhaker, C., Böhme, R., Sixt, B., Brück, C., Schneider, C., & Schulz, E. (2011). Dialectical behavioral therapy for adolescents (DBT-A): A clinical trial for patients with suicidal and self-injurious behavior and borderline symptoms with a one-year follow-up. *Child and Adolescent Psychiatry and Mental Health*, *5*(1), 3.

German, M., Smith, H. L., Rivera-Morales, C., Gonzalez, G., Haliczer, L. A., Haaz, C., & Miller, A. L. (2015). Dialectical behavior therapy for suicidal latina adolescents: Supplemental dialectical corollaries and treatment targets. *American Journal of Psychotherapy*, *69*(2), 179–197.

Gillespie, C., Joyce, M., Flynn, D., & Corcoran, P. (2019). Dialectical behaviour therapy for adolescents: A comparison of 16-week and 24-week programmes delivered in a public community setting. *Child and Adolescent Mental Health*. Available from https://doi.org/10.1111/camh.12325.

Goldstein, T. R., Axelson, D. A., Birmaher, B., & Brent, D. A. (2007). Dialectical behavior therapy for adolescents with bipolar disorder: A 1-year open trial. *Journal of the American Academy of Child & Adolescent Psychiatry*, *46*(7), 820–830.

Goldstein, T. R., Fersch-Podrat, R. K., Rivera, M., Axelson, D. A., Merranko, J., Yu, H., ... Birmaher, B. (2015). Dialectical behavior therapy for adolescents with bipolar disorder: Results from a pilot randomized trial. *Journal of Child and Adolescent Psychopharmacology, 25*(2), 140–149.

Goldstein, T., Fersch-Podrat, R. K., Rivera, M., Axelson, D. A., Merranko, J., Haifeng, Y., & Birmaher, B. (2015). DBT for adolescents with bipolar disorder: Results from a pilot randomized trial. *Journal of Child and Adolescent Psychopharmacology, 25*(2), 140–149.

Harned, M. S., Wilks, C. R., Schmidt, S. C., & Coyle, T. N. (2018). Improving functional outcomes in borderline personality disorder by changing PTSD severity and post-traumatic cognitions. *Behaviour Research and Therapy, 103*, 53–61.

James, A. C., Taylor, A., Winmill, L., & Alfoadari, K. (2008). A preliminary community study of dialectical behaviour therapy (DBT) with adolescent females demonstrating persistent, deliberate self-harm (DSH). *Child and Adolescent Mental Health, 13*(3), 148–152.

James, A. C., Winmill, L., Anderson, C., & Alfoadari, K. (2011). A preliminary study of an extension of a community dialectic behaviour therapy (DBT) programme to adolescents in the looked after care system. *Child and Adolescent Mental Health, 16*(1), 9–13.

Katz, L. Y., Cox, B. J., Gunasekara, S., & Miller, A. L. (2004). Feasibility of dialectical behavior therapy for suicidal adolescent inpatients. *Journal of the American Academy of Child & Adolescent Psychiatry, 43*(3), 276–282.

Koons, C. R., Robins, C. J., Tweed, J. L., Lynch, T. R., Gonzalez, A. M., Morse, J. Q., ... Bastian, L. A. (2001). Efficacy of dialectical behavior therapy in women veterans with borderline personality disorder. *Behavior Therapy, 32*(2), 371–390.

Linehan, M. M. (1993). *Cognitive-behavioral treatment of borderline personality disorder*. New York: Guilford Press.

Linehan, M. L. (2015a). *DBT skills training manual*. New York: Guilford Press.

Linehan, M. L. (2015b). *DBT skills training handouts and worksheets*. New York: Guilford Press.

Linehan, M. M. (2016). *Linehan risk assessment and management protocol (LRAMP)*. Retrieved from <http://depts.washington.edu/uwbrtc/wp-content/uploads/LSSN-LRAMP-v1.0.pdf>.

Linehan, M. M., Armstrong, H. E., Suarez, A., Allmon, D., & Heard, H. L. (1991). Cognitive-behavioral treatment of chronically parasuicidal borderline patients. *Archives of General Psychiatry, 48*(12), 1060–1064.

Linehan, M. M., Comtois, K. A., Murray, A. M., Brown, M. Z., Gallop, R. J., Heard, H. L., ... Lindenboim, N. (2006). Two-year randomized controlled trial and follow-up of dialectical behavior therapy versus therapy by experts for suicidal behaviors and borderline personality disorder. *Archives of General Psychiatry, 63*(7), 757–766.

Linehan, M. M., & Korslund, K. (2003). *Dialectical behavior therapy adherence manual* (Unpublished manual). Seattle: University of Washington.

McCauley, E., Berk, M. S., Asarnow, J. R., Adrian, M., Cohen, J., Korslund, K., ... Linehan, M. (2018). Efficacy of dialectical behavior therapy for adolescents at high risk for suicide: A randomized clinical trial. *JAMA Psychiatry*. Available from https://doi.org/10.1001/jamapsychiatry.2018.1109.

McDonell, M. G., Tarantino, J., Dubose, A. P., Matestic, P., Steinmetz, K., Galbreath, H., & McClellan, J. M. (2010). A pilot evaluation of dialectical behavioural therapy in adolescent long-term inpatient care. *Child and Adolescent Mental Health, 15*(4), 193–196.

Mehlum, L., Ramberg, M., Tormoen, A. J., Haga, E., Diep, L. M., Stanley, B. H., ... Groholt, B. (2016). Dialectical behavior therapy compared with enhanced usual care for adolescents with repeated suicidal and self-harming behavior: Outcomes over a one-year follow-up. *Journal of the American Academy of Child and Adolescent Psychiatry, 55*, 295–300.

Mehlum, L., Ramleth, R. K., Tørmoen, A. J., Haga, E., Diep, L. M., Stanley, B. H., ... Grøholt, B. (2019). Long term effectiveness of dialectical behavior therapy versus enhanced usual care for adolescents with self-harming and suicidal behavior. *Journal of Child Psychology and Psychiatry*. Available from https://doi.org/10.1111/jcpp.13077.

Mehlum, L., Tørmoen, A. J., Ramberg, M., Haga, E., Diep, L. M., Laberg, S., ... Grøholt, B. (2014). Dialectical behavior therapy for adolescents with repeated suicidal and self-harming behavior: A randomized trial. *Journal of the American Academy of Child & Adolescent Psychiatry*, *53*(10), 1082–1091.

Miller, A. L., Rathus, J. H., Linehan, M. M., Wetzler, S., & Leigh, E. (1997). Dialectical behavior therapy adapted for suicidal adolescents. *Journal of Psychiatric Practice*, *3*(2), 78.

Miller, A. L., Rathus, J. H., & Linehan, M. M. (2007). *Dialectical behavior therapy with suicidal adolescents*. New York: Guilford Press.

Mościcki, E. K. (2001). Epidemiology of completed and attempted suicide: Toward a framework for prevention. *Clinical Neuroscience Research*, *1*(5), 310–323.

Muehlenkamp, J. J., Xhunga, N., & Brausch, A. M. (2018). Self-injury age of onset: A risk factor for NSSI severity and suicidal behavior. *Archives of Suicide Research*. Available from https://doi.org/10.1080/13811118.2018.1486252.

Nelson-Gray, R. O., Keane, S. P., Hurst, R. M., Mitchell, J. T., Warburton, J. B., Chok, J. T., & Cobb, A. R. (2006). A modified DBT skills training program for oppositional defiant adolescents: Promising preliminary findings. *Behaviour Research and Therapy*, *44*(12), 1811–1820.

Pennell, A., Webb, C., Agar, P., Federici, A., & Couturier, J. (2019). Implementation of dialectical behavior therapy in a day hospital setting for adolescents with eating disorders. *Journal of the Canadian Academy of Child and Adolescent Psychiatry*, *28*(1), 21.

Perepletchikova, F., et al. (2017). RCT of DBT for preadolescent children with disruptive mood dysregulation disorder: Feasibility and outcomes. *Journal of the Academy of Child and Adolescent Psychiatry*, *56*(10), 832–840.

Rathus, J. H., & Miller, A. L. (2000). DBT for adolescents: Dialectical dilemmas and secondary treatment targets. *Cognitive and Behavioral Practice*, *7*(4), 425–434.

Rathus, J. H., & Miller, A. L. (2002). Dialectical behavior therapy adapted for suicidal adolescents. *Suicide and Life-Threatening Behavior*, *32*(2), 146–157.

Rathus, J. H., & Miller, A. L. (2015). *DBT skills manual for adolescents*. New York: Guilford Press.

Rathus, J. H., Campbell, B., Miller, A., & Smith, H. (2015). Treatment acceptability study of walking the middle path, a new DBT skills module for adolescents and their families. *American Journal of Psychotherapy*, *69*(2), 163–178.

Safer, D. L., Couturier, J. L., & Lock, J. (2007). Dialectical behavior therapy modified for adolescent binge eating disorder: A case report. *Cognitive and Behavioral Practice*, *14*(2), 157–167.

Salbach-Andrae, H., Bohnekamp, I., Pfeiffer, E., Lehmkuhl, U., & Miller, A. L. (2008). Dialectical behavior therapy of anorexia and bulimia nervosa among adolescents: A case series. *Cognitive and Behavioral Practice*, *15*(4), 415–425.

Shafran, R., Clark, D. M., Fairburn, C. G., Arntz, A., Barlow, D. H., Ehlers, A., ... Wilson, G. T. (2009). Mind the gap: Improving the dissemination of CBT. *Behaviour Research and Therapy*, *47*(11), 902–909. Available from https://doi.org/10.1016/j.brat.2009.07.003.

Sunseri, P. A. (2004). Preliminary outcomes on the use of dialectical behavior therapy to reduce hospitalization among adolescents in residential care. *Residential Treatment for Children & Youth*, *21*(4), 59–76.

Tebbett-Mock, A. A., Saito, E., McGee, M., Woloszyn, P., & Venuti, M. (2019). Efficacy of dialectical behavior therapy versus treatment as usual for acute-care inpatient adolescents. *Journal of the American Academy of Child & Adolescent Psychiatry*, *59*, 149–156.

Trupin, E. W., Stewart, D. G., Beach, B., & Boesky, L. (2002). Effectiveness of a dialectical behaviour therapy program for incarcerated female juvenile offenders. *Child and Adolescent Mental Health*, *7*(3), 121–127.

Wilkinson, P., Kelvin, R., Roberts, C., Dubicka, B., & Goodyer, I. (2011). Clinical and psychosocial predictors of suicide attempts and nonsuicidal self-injury in the Adolescent Depression Antidepressants and Psychotherapy Trial (ADAPT). *American Journal of Psychiatry*, *168*(5), 495–501.

Woodberry, K. A., & Popenoe, E. J. (2008). Implementing dialectical behavior therapy with adolescents and their families in a community outpatient clinic. *Cognitive and Behavioral Practice*, *15*(3), 277–286.

CHAPTER

9

Clinical illustration of the dialectical behavior therapy for preadolescent children: addressing primary targets

Francheska Perepletchikova
Weill Cornell Medicine, White Plains, NY, United States

Prepubertal children with severe irritability and temper outbursts have been often diagnosed with pediatric bipolar disorder and treated with mood stabilizers (Moreno et al., 2007). Recently, there was significant controversy in the field regarding whether severe nonepisodic irritability was a developmental presentation of mania. Children with classic bipolar illness are different than children with chronic irritability in terms of neurobiological correlates, family loading for mania, response to lithium, and the longitudinal course of illness (Dickstein, Brazel, Goldberg, & Hunt, 2009; Leibenluft, 2011; Roy et al., 2013). The distinctive pattern of symptoms in children with chronic irritability led to a new diagnostic category, disruptive mood dysregulation disorder (DMDD), in the *Diagnostic and Statistical Manual of Mental Disorders* (5th ed.) [American Psychiatric Association (APA), 2013].

DMDD is characterized by severe and recurrent verbal and/or behavioral outbursts that are grossly out of proportion to the situation, inconsistent with a child's developmental level, and occur at least three times per week for 1 year or more (APA, 2013). Between outbursts, children have to display a persistently irritable or angry mood. Prevalence rates of DMDD are estimated to be 1%, with up to 26% in clinical population (Baweja, Mayes, Hamed, & Waxmonsky, 2016). Impulsivity and chronic irritability of the kind exhibited in DMDD

The Handbook of Dialectical Behavior Therapy
DOI: https://doi.org/10.1016/B978-0-12-816384-9.00009-9

are associated with poor functioning and severe impairment in affected children, as well as with negative outcomes in adulthood (Althoff, Verhulst, Retlew, Hudziak, & Van der Ende, 2010). Indeed, research shows that children with the emotional dysregulation characteristic of DMDD are significantly impaired in their functioning at home, school, and with peers, where they exhibit anxiety and depression, impulsive–aggressive behavior, negative affect, and cognitive problems (Althoff et al., 2010; Roy et al., 2013). The emotional dysregulation and irritability symptoms seen in DMDD are also associated with adult personality disorders, substance abuse, and mood disorders (Althoff et al., 2010). These behaviors are also a significant predictor of suicidality in adulthood (Stringaris, 2011).

Emotion regulation, defined as a modulation of the experience and expression of emotions based on internal or external demands, appears to be a core deficit in DMDD (APA, 2013). Aberrant activation in brain regions involved in emotion processing is associated with symptoms common to DMDD (Brotman et al., 2010; Deveny et al., 2013). Despite urgent need, there were no empirically established treatments for DMDD (Tourian, 2015). Emotion regulation deficits and the clinical characteristics of DMDD suggest that interventions such as DBT (Linehan et al., 2006) may be relevant to this disorder.

Dialectical behavior therapy for preadolescent children (DBT-C) has been developed to treat DMDD. The results of a randomized clinical trial of DBT-C for DMDD (Perepletchikova et al., 2017) indicated feasibility and efficacy of DBT-C. Participants in DBT-C attended 89% of sessions, while participants in treatment-as-usual (TAU) attended 48.6%. Drop-out rate in TAU was 36.4%, as compared to none in DBT-C. Parents and children in DBT-C expressed significantly higher treatment satisfaction than those in TAU. Treatment response was assessed using the *Clinical Global Impression Scale* (CGI; Guy, 1976), rated by independent blinded clinical psychologists. On CGI, 90% of children in DBT-C responded to the intervention as compared to 45.5% in TAU, despite three times as many subjects in TAU as in DBT-C receiving additional psychopharmacological treatment. Differences between groups were shown for both mood symptoms and behavior outbursts. Observed changes were also clinically significant and maintained at 3-month follow-up, with 95.2% response rate for DBT-C as compared to 45.5% for TAU.

DBT-C retains the theoretical model, principles, and therapeutic strategies of the adult DBT model and includes most of its skills training curriculum and corresponding didactics. The model has been detailed elsewhere (Perepletchikova & Goodman, 2014; Perepletchikova et al., 2011; Perepletchikova, 2019). The main objectives of this chapter are to (1) provide a composite case example to illustrate application of the DBT-C model to primary treatment targets and (2) demonstrate treatment delivery via session transcripts.

Treatment targets

DBT-C aims to reduce the risk of the child developing psychopathology in the future, while ameliorating the current presenting issues by altering the transaction between the child and the environment. DBT-C stipulates that there are three main mechanisms of change: parental self-regulation, validation, and reinforced practice. The main message throughout the treatment is that the child's behavior is *irrelevant* until parents are able to establish an environment conducive to change. Thus the main goals of the treatment are to (1) teach parents how to create a validating and change-ready environment; (2) empower parents to become coaches for their child so as to promote adaptive responding during treatment and after therapy is completed; and (3) teach parents and their children effective coping and problem-solving skills.

As is evident from the above-stated goals, DBT-C is a family-oriented approach, where parental involvement, participation, and commitment to treatment are required, while a child's commitment is preferred. In DBT-C, parental emotion regulation and ability to create an environment conducive to change are prioritized. As the family is treated as a unit, the hierarchy of treatment targets was greatly extended for DBT-C as compared to DBT for adults and adolescents. In the original model the treatment target hierarchy consists of four main categories: life-threatening behaviors, therapy-interfering behaviors, quality-of-life interfering behaviors, and skills training. DBT-C hierarchy for primary targets includes three main categories, divided into 10 subcategories (detailed below). While in the adult DBT model, the hierarchy is primarily meant for therapists to guide treatment, in DBT-C parents are instructed to use in and outside of sessions. The following composite case example will help exemplify the assessment and treatment paradigms used in DBT-C and illustrate each of the primary targets and how they are addressed in treatment. The composite example represents a typical case treated with DBT-C, in terms of the child's symptom severity, family functioning, and course of treatment.

Case illustration

Matthew is a 10-year-old Caucasian male who lives with his biological parents, a 13-year-old brother, and a 5-year-old sister. Matthew was referred for services after an inpatient hospitalization for his first suicide attempt.

Child emotional and behavioral difficulties

At the time of the initial evaluation, the child and his parents indicated the following:

1. Suicidality

   Suicidality is defined as deliberately hurting oneself with an intent to die. Matthew had voiced suicidal ideation (SI) since age 8. He had said to his parents that he wished he had never been born, that his family would be better off without him, that he wanted to die, and that life was too difficult. SI occurred at least twice per month. Three months prior to the suicide attempt, SI was exacerbated to several times per week. The increase in SI was associated with an increase in problems with peers at school. Matthew attempted suicide 2 months after the school year started and stated that he was being bullied. The child had attempted to choke himself with his hands in a school bathroom. There were marks left on his neck and the child reported that he had an intent to die.
2. Non-suicidal self injury (NSSI)

   NSSI is defined as deliberately hurting oneself without an intent to die. Matthew had been engaging in NSSI since age 9, which involved primarily scratching his hands with nails or pieces of glass. The frequency of NSSI increased from about twice per month to almost daily 2 months prior to his suicide attempt. At that time, Matthew also started to use knives to cut his arm. The worst incident of NSSI occurred within a month before the suicide attempt, when he cut his hand with a piece of glass, drawing blood and requiring stitches. This alerted parents to the child engaging in NSSI. At the time of treatment, NSSI occurred once per week and NSSI urges occurred several times per week, following confrontations with family members or peers.
3. Physical aggression

   Physical aggression is defined as acts directed toward a person with an intent to cause physical pain or damage (e.g., if an object is thrown in a direction of a person and misses, this act is counted as physical aggression). Parents indicated that Matthew had daily physically aggressive behaviors since age 5. He was in outpatient treatment since age 6, at which time he was diagnosed with oppositional defiant disorder. The frequency of physically aggressive behaviors slightly decreased as he grew older from multiple times per day to four times per week. However, the severity of such behaviors increased. Matthew used to spit or throw soft objects (e.g., pillows) when younger and started to punch and kick as he grew older. Matthew's mother, older brother, and babysitters were the primary targets for physical aggression. The worst episode involved pushing his brother, where the brother lost balance, fell, and broke his arm. Matthew tended to be quite upset at himself and remorseful after aggressive episodes. Matthew had been receiving psychiatric management since age 8. At the time of the initial assessment, Matthew was taking Focalin 5 mg twice daily and Geodon 20 mg twice daily.

4. Verbal aggression

Verbal aggression is defined as verbal (e.g., swearing, threatening, and name calling) or nonverbal aggression (e.g., yelling and growling) that lasts for at least 1 minute or more. Matthew's parents indicated that he had been verbally aggressive since age 3 and that the severity of his verbal aggression intensified with age. At the time of the evaluation, Matthew had multiple daily verbally aggressive behaviors, including screaming, yelling, swearing, threatening (e.g., "I will punch you!"), name calling (You are fat and ugly!), and derogatory verbalizations (You are the worst mother in the world!). Episodes of verbal aggression would last up to 45 minutes. The worst episode involved 2.5 hours of a verbal temper tantrum during an argument about school attendance.

5. Talking back

Talking back is defined as verbal and nonverbal aggression that is less than 1 minute in duration. Parents indicate multiple daily talking back behaviors (e.g., name calling, swearing, and sassy comments).

6. Destructive behaviors

Destructive behaviors are defined as aggression against property. Parents reported that Matthew rarely engaged in severe property destruction, and would usually just rip papers, throw a book across a room or push pillows off a bed. Such incidents occurred once per week on average. The worst incident of destructive behavior happened when Matthew pushed his mother's laptop off the table and broke it.

7. Angry/irritable mood

Between temper outbursts, Matthew displayed behaviors that would indicate an angry/irritable mood, including snappy comments, irritable replies to requests, mumbling under his breath, brushing against people when walking by, stomping away, angry posturing (with arms crossed), rolling eyes, sucking teeth, tightening lips, squinting eyes, sighing impatiently, moaning, groaning, growling, and frequent complaining. Parents reported that Matthew would often wake up in an irritable mood and seemed ready to snap throughout the day.

8. Associated problems

   Matthew and his parents reported that the child had significant interpersonal problems. He had difficulties forming and maintaining friendships; did not have close friends; was infrequently invited to birthday parties or play dates; was rejected by peers at school and in the neighborhood; and had conflicts with parents, siblings, teachers, and babysitters. It was also noted that Matthew had had issues that are frequently associated with emotional sensitivity, such as rapidly shifting attention, an extreme thinking style (e.g., black and white thinking), a tendency to ruminate, low tolerance for delayed gratification, transitions and change, low self-esteem, being easily bored, a need for constant stimulation, and impulsive behaviors (e.g., acting before thinking, and lying). Yet, when emotionally stable, Matthew would be very empathic toward his siblings and other children, was caring toward parents and grandparents, loved animals, and was very creative.

Diagnostic impressions

Primary diagnosis—disruptive mood dysregulation disorder

Matthew displayed behaviors and mood patterns consistent with a diagnosis of DMDD. He had almost daily physical and verbal outbursts that were not commensurate with the situation and his developmental age. Further, in between outbursts, he displayed daily angry/irritable mood. Problems with his mood and associated disruptive behaviors occurred in multiple settings. Most of the problems happened at home with parents and babysitters; however, teachers also reported irritability and oppositional behaviors at school with adults and disagreements with peers. Moreover, his suicide attempt occurred on school grounds. Temper outbursts frequently happened in public, such as when shopping, going to movies, and day trips with family and grandparents.

Provisional diagnoses—anxiety other specified and attention deficit hyperactivity disorder other type

Children with emotional sensitivity often display symptoms of generalized, social or separation anxiety, depressed mood, hyperactivity, and difficulty with sustained attention. However, such problem may not be clinically distinct but rather represent different manifestations of emotional dysregulation. Indeed, emotional dysregulation is often seen as a transdiagnostic factor and an underlying mechanism to be targeted with interventions. When working with children, a parsimonious model of the diagnostic impression is advised to avoid overpathologizing.

If comorbid conditions do not predate problems with emotional regulation, have low severity or primarily fit "other-specified" and "not-specified" categories, only diagnoses that best describe the clinical picture are advised. Additional diagnoses are given if conditions persist after emotion regulation has been improved.

Matthew exhibited excessive worry upon separation from parents, fear of being negatively evaluated by peers, marked self-consciousness, a fear of the dark, and repeated complaints of physical symptoms not accounted for by a medical condition (e.g., stomach aches, headaches, and muscle tension). However, these symptoms did not meet full criteria for any specific anxiety disorders in regards to the number of symptoms, duration, and severity. Matthew also avoided activities that required sustained attention (primarily for boring or school-related tasks), had difficulty with listening and following instructions, tended to interrupt and fidget. Symptoms of inattention or hyperactivity-impulsivity did not meet full criteria for either subtype of ADHD.

Parental emotional and behavioral difficulties

In DBT-C the parents' emotion regulation and ability to validate and create a change-ready environment are prioritized. Thus parental functioning is closely assessed and monitored throughout treatment. At the beginning of treatment, Matthew' parents exhibited the following responses that interfered with effective parenting:

1. Modeling of dysfunctional behaviors
   Matthew parents' capacity to tolerate his escalations had been overextended, and parents felt overwhelmed by his needs. They frequently engaged in verbal fights with Matthew and with each other. Further, they would often threaten Matthew with sending him away to boarding school or residential care.
2. Difficulty with having to champion behavior change
   Through the negative transaction, Matthew and his parents felt hurt, with each party waiting for the change in the other to repair the relationship. At the beginning of treatment, parents expressed feelings of resentment toward Matthew, indicated that he was depriving them from enjoying life, and that most of the family had to revolve around Matthew, trying to prevent his outbursts. Parents were assuming that changes would be primarily driven by Matthew learning self-control. They did not fully appreciate their contribution to problems.
3. Difficulty with letting go of attachment to the outcome and "shoulds"

Matthew's parents had very specific, and mostly unrealistic, expectations about their children and themselves. In DBT-C these expectations are called "shoulds." "Shoulds" are defined as assumptions that people treat as facts. Matthew's parents believed that he should have been able to follow directions right away, be polite, complete homework, and cooperate with siblings without much shaping or reinforcement for such behaviors.

4. Low tolerance of escalation and resultant accommodation

Matthew's parents had significant difficulty with ignoring his dysfunctional behaviors. Parents alternated between punishment and heavy accommodation. Parents indicated that the entire family has been "walking on eggshells" around Matthew for years. This included driving him to school instead of him taking a school bus, not asking him to do chores or homework, giving in to his demands to avoid escalations and public humiliations, and failing to consistently monitor his personal hygiene (e.g., Matthew resisted brushing teeth and showering).

5. Excessive and inappropriate use of punishment

As noted, Matthew's parents often alternated between accommodating Matthew and resorting to forceful means to obtain his compliance, such as screaming, yelling, and threatening. They also used excessive and inappropriate punishment, including grounding Matthew for extended periods of time (e.g., no computer for a week) and using punishment for verbal outbursts and talking back (these behaviors are best addressed with planned ignoring). In addition, most of the time the use of punishment was mood-dependent and inconsistent. Thus parents were mostly retaliating instead of using punishment strategically to suppress unwanted behaviors.

6. Use of shaming, criticism, and judgments

Matthew's parents frequently resorted to shaming (e.g., "You are acting like a baby! Shame on you! Just stop it!"), criticizing and scolding (e.g., "No wonder you got a bad grade, you did not study enough. What's the use to cry now?!"), judgments (e.g., "What you are doing is ridiculous!"), comparing (e.g., "Why can't you be more like your brother?!"), blaming (You totally asked for it!), and telling the child what he "should" think, feel, or do (e.g., "You shouldn't be angry. There is nothing to feel angry about!").

7. Low reliance on reinforcement

Given that most of the behaviors that parents wanted Matthew to do were "shoulds," parents rarely used reinforcement and shaping of desired behaviors. Instead, they were passively waiting for these behaviors to spontaneously occur. Only significant progress was praised, while daily positive behaviors were not acknowledged.

When the parents first started DBT-C, they had difficulty understanding the value of reinforcement. They thought of reinforcement as bribing the child for what he "should" be doing anyway.

8. Difficulty with self-care

   Matthew's parents were exhausted by Mathew's physical and verbal aggression, noncompliance, and argumentativeness. Yet, they rarely took care of their own needs to reduce vulnerabilities. Matthew's mother stated that she often felt guilty for spending any time and resources on herself instead of her children. Matthew's father indicated that he had to work long hours to support his family and would rarely find time to relax.

9. Parental discord

   Difficulties with the children had also negatively affected the relationship between parents. Matthew's temper tantrums would, as his father said, "Suck up all the oxygen in the home." Parents would frequently disagree on how to handle his negative behaviors, what caused them, and who was to blame for their occurrence. All these problems left little time and energy for their relationship, while increasing their vulnerability to stress. Parents would end up in screaming matches with each other. They tried to keep their disagreement away from the children as much as possible, but it was hard to contain their anger and frustration with the situation.

Treatment structure

The child and his family were treated with DBT-C in weekly 90 minute sessions, roughly divided between individual counseling with the child (30 minutes), a parent training component (20 minutes), and skills training with the child and parents (40 minutes). For the first 6 weeks, parents were seen in treatment without their child in order to prepare them to support Matthew's progress. During this period, the child was seen only twice to commit to safety, develop a safety plan, and teach the child several distress-tolerance skills that were included in the plan; while parents were (1) trained in select emotion regulation skills; (2) provided with psychoeducation about factors that can interfere with their child's functioning and factors that negatively affect effective parenting; (3) presented with the behavior change model; (4) instructed on validation; and (5) provided with the introduction to behaviorism and taught essential behavior modification strategies (e.g., reinforcement, planned ignoring). Whenever possible, grandparents, babysitters, and siblings were invited to participate in treatment.

Treatment target hierarchy

In order to address the needs of this family as a unit, the DBT-C treatment targets hierarchy, with corresponding interventions, was as follows:

1. Decrease the risk of psychopathology in adolescence and adulthood
   a. Decrease life-threatening behaviors of a child
      This target includes (1) suicidal acts; (2) NSSI; (3) suicidal communications and ideations; (4) suicide-related expectations and beliefs; and (5) suicide-related affect. Using a diary card, Matthew and parents monitored his life-threatening behaviors on a daily basis. The child was reinforced via a point system for using coping skills instead of NSSI. Environmental interventions, problem-solving, and teaching the child interpersonal effectiveness techniques were used to address problems at school and with being bullied by peers.
   b. Decrease therapy destroying behaviors (TDBs) of a child
      In DBT-C, TDBs refer to child's responses that prevent the therapist and/or the parents from safely implementing the needed strategies. These usually include behaviors that severely threaten the safety of the child, other people or property. Examples of *in-session* TDBs include physical aggression toward a therapist and/or parent(s), and destruction of property. Examples of *out-of-session* TDBs include choking a sibling, running into traffic, and breaking furniture. At the beginning of the treatment, Matthew lacked motivation for change and did not engage in therapy. He was initially aggressive toward his mother during sessions. These behaviors were dangerous and were immediately suppressed by parents by putting the child in time out, or the session had to be stopped with the child (whenever possible the session would continue with just the parents). Further, preventive measures were implemented, including developing a strong therapist–child relationship, creating a validating environment and reinforcing treatment engagement (e.g., praise, tangible rewards).
   c. Decrease therapy interfering behaviors of parents and the therapist
      In order for the child's treatment progress to be promoted and maintained, parental engagement is key. To achieve long-lasting results, parents have to be ready to support their child's progress by modeling skills, providing validation and reinforcement, consistently practicing techniques with their child, and developing a positive child–parent relationship. Thus missing sessions, frequent rescheduling, noncollaborative behaviors, failing to follow agreed-upon treatment plans, etc. are treated as parent therapy interfering

behaviors (TIBs). Matthew's parents had initially attended sessions consistently. However, Matthew's father started to miss sessions after the first month of treatment, and this behavior had to be addressed. If the father was unable to attend in person, he was asked to call in during the parent and skill training sections of sessions. Further, parents had difficulty with consistently monitoring and helping the child with recording behaviors on his diary card and conducting daily practice of skills. These behaviors were addressed by providing psychoeducation, motivational enhancement, reinforcement, and helping parents understand functions of their own behaviors.

d. Improve parental emotion regulation

The child's self-regulation cannot be expected in a dysregulated environment. Indeed, in the DBT-C model the child's behavior is seen as irrelevant until the environment is stabilized. Without a stable and validating environment to support and promote progress, any improvements in children's behavior tend to be isolated and sporadic. Parents have to learn to replace mood-dependent behaviors (e.g., punishing child's swearing) with target-relevant responding (e.g., ignoring swearing to preclude reinforcement with attention, followed by processing a situation with reinforced rehearsal of adaptive behaviors after the incident).

Matthew's parents had significant difficulty with maintaining self-control and tolerating escalations. Without learning and practicing emotion regulation techniques, parents cannot consistently model effective coping and problem-solving, ignore maladaptive responses, validate their child's suffering, and reinforcing desirable behaviors. To address these needs, Matthew's parents were trained in several coping skills ahead of starting therapy with the child and continued to receive training during the remainder of the treatment.

Throughout therapy, parental emotion regulation was treated as a higher priority over the child's emotion regulation. In DBT-C, whether an incident had been effectively resolved is evaluated primarily by the response of the environment. If a parent was responding to a stressful event in an effective way (e.g., stayed calm, modeled use of skills, validated and ignored as needed), while a child had a 2-hour temper outburst, the situation is seen as effectively resolved. In this case the environment was no longer transacting with the child in a dysfunctional way, and the child will eventually have to adapt his behaviors to the new way that the parents are responding. If applied consistently, effective parenting over time may result in the creation of a validating and change-ready environment, and the resulting transaction may improve the child's emotion regulation and behavioral control.

e. Teach effective parenting techniques

Frequently the negative transaction between the child and the parents leads to severe disruption in the child–environment system. When parents are stressed, they tend to resort to screaming and yelling at a child, as well as using excessive, prolonged or physical punishment. Yet, to achieve the desired changes, parents have to learn to rely primarily on validation, reinforcement, ignoring, and natural consequences, and to use punishment only sparingly and strategically.

Matthew's parents had relied on punishment and accommodation for most of the child's life. The situation worsened in recent years when Matthew's behavioral problems escalated. However, increase in the use of maladaptive parenting further intensified the problems with the child's emotional dysregulation and dysfunctional behaviors. It cannot be realistically expected that the child will be able to stop this vicious circle without teaching parents how to create an environment that can support such change. In DBT-C, parents are seen in treatment for about 6 weeks by themselves (prior to engaging a child in therapy) to learn behavior modification and validation techniques and to start learning and using emotion regulation techniques. Matthew's parents were taught how to replace a critical and judgmental stance with validation, reinforcement, and shaping of appropriate behaviors, while ignoring of maladaptive behaviors. Further, parents tended to accommodate their child in an effort to prevent outbursts. Such practice was addressed by helping parents set and maintain appropriate limits. Parental ability to create and maintain an environment conducive to change was closely monitored and refined throughout therapy.

2. Target parent–child relationship

a. Improve parent–child relationship

A positive parent–child relationship has multiple functions: (1) it models a relationship that is built on acceptance, trust, reinforcement, shared interests, and mutual respect that helps instill in the child the sense of self-love, safety, and belonging; (2) it increases the child's desire to spend time with parents, which provides parents with more opportunities to model adaptive coping, prompt effective responding, and provide validation and reinforcement; (3) it increases the child's motivation to behave in ways that would please parents, make them proud, and to earn rewards, instead of attempting to inflict pain and misery; and (4) it helps build pathways in the child's developing brain associated with adaptive behaviors.

The relationship between Matthew and his parents was strained over the years of negative transaction. His parents had to change the way they were relating to their child *before* they could have expected any meaningful changes in Matthew's behavior. Close attention had been paid to increasing Matthew's interest to spend time with his parents. Parents were instructed to focus on doing activities with their child that he found enjoyable (e.g., playing video games, constructing machines) to build reciprocity.

3. Target the child's presenting problems

a. Decrease risky, unsafe, and aggressive behaviors of a child

The risky or unsafe behaviors category includes any behaviors that threaten the safety of the child, other people or property and, therefore, cannot be ignored. This category usually includes physical aggression and destructive behaviors that are not dangerous enough to be TDB. These behaviors are mild to moderate in severity, as they are not likely to cause significant damage to the child, other people or property, or severely disrupt a treatment process.

Matthew has exhibited aggressive behaviors toward his mother and older brother multiple times per week. DBT-C teaches parents how to use appropriate punishment techniques (e.g., reprimands, time out, chores, and removal of privileges) to suppress physical aggression. Although DBT-C heavily relies on validation, reinforcement, and planned ignoring, punishment is still used but only when a short-term outcome (e.g., ensuring child's or other people's safety) is prioritized over long-term gains (e.g., modeling skillful conflict resolution instead of using force). Further, punishment is combined with reinforcement of positive opposite behaviors (e.g., using coping skills instead of punching).

b. Decrease quality-of-life interfering issues

The quality-of-life interfering problems category refers to the child's and environmental issues that negatively affect the child's functioning. Matthew's quality-of-life interfering issues included (1) anxiety and attention difficulties; (2) verbal aggression and talking back; (3) severe interpersonal difficulties with parents, babysitters and peers; (4) issues with delayed gratification and impulse control; and (5) school problems (e.g., difficulty with completing homework). To address these issues, Matthew was instructed in effective problem solving, self-regulation and social skills, taught cognitive restructuring, engaged in behavioral analyses, and provided with exposures. Reinforcement and shaping programs were developed to promote adaptive behaviors at home and at school.

c. Provide skills training

Physical and verbal aggression, temper outbursts, suicidality, and NSSI are frequently the result of children being overwhelmed by the intensity of their emotional responses, and the lack of adaptive coping skills. DBT-C is a skills-building approach that focuses on teaching children and their families effective emotion regulation and problem-solving techniques. The treatment requires that the skills training curriculum is completed by children as well as their parents. Matthew's mother was the identified parent to come in every week to learn skills and other techniques, with a goal of communicating what she learned to other caregivers (e.g., father, grandparents, and babysitters). Matthew's father participated by coming in person as frequently as his work schedule allowed, and attending sessions by phone when in-person participation was not possible.

Matthew and his parents received training in five modules: didactics on emotions, mindfulness, distress tolerance, emotion regulation, and interpersonal effectiveness. Parents were also asked to practice skills with their child in hypothetical situations via role-plays (practice "in pretend mode") several times per day. Failure to do this was treated as parents' TIB. Daily reinforced practice of skills "in pretend mode" is seen as one of the main mechanisms of change, as it helps establish adaptive behaviors through multiple repetitions. Skills use "in real mode" in actual problematic situation and skills practice "in pretend mode" were monitored via the diary card. During individual sessions, Matthew learned how to apply learned skills to everyday problems.

d. Decrease therapy interfering behaviors of a child

DBT-C is very tolerant of children's problematic behaviors that occur in sessions (except for physical aggression or destructive behaviors). Matthews's verbal aggression, threats, cursing, screaming, devaluing treatment as a waste of time, and other distracting behaviors during treatment sessions were ignored and targeted by reinforcement for engagement in sessions and shaping programs. Further, his maladaptive behaviors during sessions were treated as informative of parent–child interactions and target-relevant, as they allowed the therapist to model skills use, planned ignoring and problem-solving, and to further refine parental ability to use their emotion regulation techniques and effective parenting skills.

Illustrative transcripts

The following three transcripts represent actual examples of the therapeutic process. These dialogues were chosen to provide illustrations of the application of DBT strategies and procedures for pediatric population for parent training and individual therapy with the child. The illustrations are preceded by session goals and include specifications of the utilized DBT strategies.

Parent training component: evaluation of parental readiness for treatment

Main goals: (1) psychoeducation on the importance of parental participation; (2) assessment of parental readiness to engage in treatment; and (3) initiating emotion regulation skills training with parents.

In DBT-C the initial evaluation is divided into two parts: (1) assessment of the child's symptoms with parents only and (2) assessment of the symptoms with the child. This is done for two reasons: (1) given the developmental and cognitive level, children may not be the best reporters of the issues, and having information from their parents helps to guide the evaluation process with the child, and (2) parental readiness to engage in treatment has to be assessed before the child is invited for an evaluation. As has been noted, DBT-C necessitates parental participation to provide a foundation for change. Thus orienting parents to the level of the required commitment is critical to increase chances of the needed engagement. During the evaluation, parents are given a brief overview of the model to help them understand their role in their child's therapy, and are asked for a commitment to treatment if their child qualifies for DBT-C. The following exemplifies the assessment of parental readiness.

Therapist: So far, from the information you have provided, it looks like Matthew may indeed fit the profile of a child who can benefit from DBT-C. Now, before I conduct further assessments with Matthew, I need to know whether you are willing to participate in treatment given the requirements.

Father: What about Matthew's willingness?

Therapist: Of course, the best way to start therapy is when the child and his parents are both ready, willing and committed. However, parental readiness is the most important part of the equation. The child is usually not quite ready emotionally, developmentally or cognitively to fully appreciate what it means to be in therapy and to take a full advantage of the material I will be teaching. Thus, your awareness of what is involved and your participation are key.

Father: Yes, you mentioned on the phone, when we were making an appointment, that this is a family therapy and that parents are required to participate. But I think we are prepared for this. Matt was in treatment before and we met with prior therapists every month or so to discuss his progress. Is this what you mean?

(The therapist shakes her head).

Therapist: That's why we needed to talk about the process. DBT-C is different from a more common approach where a child is the identified patient and is seen on a weekly basis, while parents come in once in a while. DBT-C is usually recommended when there is a very serious disruption in the child's functioning, including severe emotional instability, high level of aggression, suicidality and self-harm. To better help the child with such severe problems, the entire family has to be engaged. In DBT-C, the family as a unit is the identified patient, and parental ability to create an environment conducive to change is absolutely critical. So, although addressing Matthew's issues is our priority and I will do a lot of work with him, you, as his parents, will be in the spotlight. I will be asking a lot of you in terms of engagement, participation, commitment, learning, and practicing; much more than I would ask of Matthew. Indeed, during the first month or even two I will not meet with Matthew as much as I will meet with you. **[orientation to treatment and parental role in therapy]**

Father: Really?! Why is that?

Therapist: The initial work with parents is necessary to prepare the foundation on which we can promote the child's change. The work with parents is also necessary to increase the chances that the child will not lose the therapeutic gains soon after treatment ends. I will be preparing you to assume my role as counselors for your child and my goal is to have you ready to be in this role for as long as your child may need your help. Matthew will always be emotionally sensitive, and even though he will hopefully learn and use skills to be in a better control of his reactions, he may require your assistance with regulation and problem-solving long after I am no longer working with your family. Also, as I already noted, Matthew may be too young to take full advantage of the material that I will be giving him. However, you can definitely understand all of what I have to offer and can keep teaching him as he grows and develops. **[orientation to treatment and parental role in therapy]**

Mother: Well, it does make sense. But this also means that at least in the next month or even more, Matt will not be learning much and will not get better?

Therapist: Yes, you are right. Chances are that Matthew will not get better in the next month or so. However, we cannot expect to be able to build a solid house of change without first preparing a solid foundation. **[use of a metaphor]** Also, when I start working with Matthew, it's very likely that things initially will get worse before they get better. We will be disrupting a dynamic in the family. Although, I presume, nobody is happy about the current situation, everyone is accustomed to the way things are and knows what to expect from each other. Therapy will disrupt this dynamic and, thus, things almost invariably will get worse at the beginning. You need to be ready to withstand the pressure, as otherwise there is a high chance that we will exacerbate Matthew's problems even more.

Mother: What do you mean?

Therapist: I'm glad, Melanie and Greg, that you are asking for clarifications. **[reinforcement]** I hope you will keep this up throughout therapy. It is very important that we are on the same page and that everything is clear. So I will use a technique called planned ignoring as an example. At some point, I will be asking you not to pay attention to behaviors that you don't like, such as his screaming, throwing temper tantrums, and giving you sassy replies, while attending to his positive behaviors. If the child is used to getting parental attention for his verbal aggression, such as parents yelling back or even telling him calmly to stop, and now parents ignore, most often, the child's behavior escalates. He will be like, "what's happening!" and will try to get parents to respond to him by screaming even longer or using swear words. If parents brace themselves and this time ignore the child for 20 minutes, but eventually give in because they are not prepared to withstand escalation, what do you think ends up happening? **[activating a new behavior – eliciting an active response]**

Mother: I guess, we made it worse.

Therapist: Precisely! **[reinforcement]** You just reinforced escalation and the next time, the child is likely to start a temper outburst at an escalated level.

Mother: Well, I am not sure we can totally ignore his yelling. He can go for an hour and you are telling us that he may go for two hours when we start to ignore!

Therapist: Yes, Melanie, it will be very difficult to ignore escalation! Absolutely! It's hard for parents to maintain composure while sustaining, what can only be called, a verbal abuse from their own child! **[validating level 5 – in terms of current events]** That is why I will not be asking you to implement any strategies until you are ready to follow through. And by being ready, I mean strengthening your own emotion regulation muscles. Indeed, throughout the first phase of treatment, when I am only working with you, I will also be teaching you skills. If you practice them, you will be in a much better shape to withstand the unwanted behaviors.

Father: I see. So what do we do now about his screaming in the meantime?

Therapist: Business as usual. Matthew had these issues for years. Several more weeks will not make much difference. Do what you have been doing so far and concentrate on yourself, learning the material and practicing skills. I will be teaching you a skill or two per session on top of other material and will assign you daily practice. And I will teach you one skill today. And you will have homework to do before our next meeting.

Father: Hmm. Already?

Therapist: Not too eager to start, I see (therapist smile) **[irreverence]** (The father smiles and shakes his head).

Father: I just did not expect that I will be the one learning the skills.

Therapist: Yes, Greg, this is not something that parents usually expect when they come in for an evaluation of their child. **[validation level 5 – in terms of current events]** Actually a lot of what I will be saying may at first seem counterintuitive, unusual or at least not mainstream. For example, I will be asking you not to stop your child when he is swearing at you.

Father: Hmmm. Yes, this is not quite mainstream, as you put it, but I think I am starting to catch up with the system. This is about ignoring, right?

Therapist: Awesome! You got it! **[reinforcement]** When he swears at you, he may want you to react. When you tell him to stop or scream at him, you gave him that reaction and reinforced this behavior. There is much more to planned ignoring that we will discuss in the future. But I am very happy to hear how fast you are catching up with the system! **[reinforcement]**

(Parents smile).

Therapist: There are other messages that I will be giving you that may seem 'not mainstream.' For example, our main stance during the treatment will be - your child's behavior is *irrelevant* until you change the way you respond to your child.

Father: Well, all right. This one is harder to swallow, but I get the gist from what you said so far.

(The mother nods. The therapist smiles and gives parents thumbs-up). **[reinforcement]**

Therapist: Hey, you guys are fast! **[reinforcement]** What about this one? We are going to do what we know can lead to changes and we will not expect any changes from the child.

(Parents look confused).

Father: Hmmm. Then what's the point? I was not that happy with what you said before, but this one in particular does not sit right with me!

Therapist: I like your candor, Greg! You are actually making me happier and happier as we speak. **[reinforcement]** It looks like I can rely on you to tell me as it is, instead of giving me a lip-service. There is a good chance that you will be confused or unhappy with my recommendations during treatment, and not just once or twice. I need you to tell me about it, so we can discuss and problem-solve.

(Parents nod).

Therapist: Now, about your question. Having specific expectations about when and how changes will happen and what exactly they will look like will most definitely lead us to being disappointed, as reality almost never exactly matches the pictures we paint in our mind. We call such expectations "shoulds." "Shoulds" can lead us to feel frustrated, hopeless and give up soon after we start if we don't see the changes we want when we want them. A watched pot never boils, so to speak. **[use of metaphors]** And, most importantly, being attached to our 'shoulds" increases risk of us forcing changes to happen, and this makes the situation even worse.

Father: I see.

Therapist: Moreover, this treatment is quite complex and has many parts to it. I can only give you one or two pieces of the puzzle at a time. Until you have enough puzzle pieces to see the full picture it may be hard to keep up **[use of metaphors]** I will be asking you to plough through, follow my recommendations, and so to speak, "act as if" you fully understand the model before you actually get there.

Mother: Wow! That's quite a list!

Therapist: You are right; it's quite demanding! **[validation level 5]** And at the same time, we know that all this hard work can help you and your child. **[modeling dialectical thinking]** In fact, you will be my main tools. Yes, you heard correctly (smiles). Parents are my main tools of change. I am only going to see your child for an hour or so per week. The rest of the time, he is with you. I can only instruct. You will implement.

(Parents nod).

Father: Well, I think it's a lot but it does make sense.

Therapist: It is a lot and that is why I want you to consider this seriously. So what do you think, do you want to do this?

Mother: **I think we can do what is required. We are at the end of the rope, and we are scared for Matthew!**

Father: Yes, we tried medications and other treatments, nothing worked so far. So we are willing to do what it takes.

Therapist: Even if it means that you will have to do things that are counterintuitive and may make things much worse initially, and will require a lot of learning and practicing skills yourself?! **[devil's advocate - strengthening commitment]**

Father: I think it will not hurt to improve our own self-control.

Therapist: Hey, I thought that you were not that eager to learn the skills just yet! (therapist smiles) **[unorthodox irreverence – use of humor]**

(Parents smile).

Therapist: So is this a yes?!

Mother: Yes, sure.

Father: Yes, it feels like I am signing a contract or something.

Therapist: You will most definitely sign a contract when we start treatment and I explain the model in greater detail. We will have an official commitment and orientation session. Right now I was just assessing whether you are *willing* to do the program given the specific aspects of the treatment. Now, let see if you can *do* this program given your schedules. You will have to be here every week for an hour and a half. Can you both do that?

Father: Well, I work full time and as far as I understand you want both of us to be here.

Therapist: That would be best, but I fully understand that this may not be always possible. I do need one parent to be here consistently. So, who will be the designated parent?

Mother: I will.

Therapist: So, Greg, I hope you can be here as often as possible and when you can't, you will be able to call in for the parent part and the skills training part. Would this be possible?

Father: Yes, I can do that. May be I can do a late lunch on that day.

Therapist: Perfect! I also anticipate that there will be days when you cannot call in. For the sessions that Greg misses, I will be asking you, Melanie, to reiterate to Greg what was communicated during the session and to practice learned techniques.

(Parents nod).

Therapist: And I will be checking your knowledge, Greg, the next time I see you.

Father: I don't doubt that!

(Everybody smiles).

(At the end of the session, the therapist teaches parents a distress-tolerance skill of paced breathing and assigns them to practice it everyday. She briefly orients them to a diary card and asks them to use it to monitor their daily skills practice.)

Individual therapy with the child

Main goals of the session: (1) behavior analysis; (2) application of learned DBT-C skills; (3) problem-solving: (4) behavior activation; and (5) modeling, coaching, and shaping parental responses.

Matthew was refusing to come to this session. Hed threw a temper tantrum in the car on the way to the clinic. The child was screaming in the waiting room saying that he will not go into the therapist's office. The therapist just motioned for parents to follow her, not noticing nor speaking to the child. **[ignoring the child's TIB]** Parents walk with the therapist, discussing the upcoming weekend plans. Within a couple of minutes, the child joins them but continued to scream. The therapist gestures to the parents to continue to ignore.

Child: I hate this! This is stupid! Therapy is stupid! Why do you make me come here?! It's not fair! You are ruining my life!

(Therapist invites parents to sit down, looks only at them, appears relax and calm, and gestures to parents to continue breathing in and out, maintain composure and continue with ignoring). **[ignoring the child's TIB] [activating behavior - parents' coping skills use and ignoring]**

Therapist: So, how was your week?

Mother: Actually, not too bad. (gives therapist a diary card). Only three major temper tantrums. Mostly verbal stuff but he did punch his brother. Not hard. But he did a lot of skills practices too. He was quite keen on getting that hamster, so it helped.

Therapist: Wonderful! Did he get the hamster?

Mother: Yes. And this is the problem. He did not want to come in today because he wanted to stay home and play with it.

(The child quiets down for a moment).

Therapist: Thank you, Matthew, for calming down! **[reinforcement] [modeling attending to positive behavior during planned ignoring]**

(Therapist gestures to parents to also praise the child). **[activating behavior]**

Father: Thank you, Matt!

Mother: Yes, good job!

(Therapist gives parents thumb-up. The child starts screaming and yelling again. Therapist immediately diverts her attention back to parents, gesturing to them to keep breathing, using their half-smile skill and ignoring the child. Therapist looks back at the diary card).

Therapist: So, you are telling me that Matthew may be so upset right now because he had to come here instead of playing with his hamster. **[validation level 2 – reflecting]** Wow! You know I would totally feel the same if I had a pet, especially if I just got it! No wonder! **[validation level 5]**

(The child stops screaming but stands with his back to the therapist with his arms crossed).

Therapist: Thank you, Matthew for calming down! **[reinforcement]**

(The child sighs impatiently. The therapist looks at the diary card).

Therapist: Look at this! Practice of skills every day! Great job, Matthew! Great job, parents! (gives both parents a high five) **[reinforcement]** I also see that Matthew used his paced breathing skill twice, and tense and release one time. That is wonderful! **[reinforcement]**... No suicidal thoughts. No urges for self-harm. Now, I see seven verbal outbursts and only one aggressive behavior. Matt, this is definitely a great improvement! Remember I told you that you will get one extra prize if you have five or less aggressive behaviors? And you had only one this week! Great job! You earned it! **[shaping]**. Now I want you to also get a bonus prize next time. Remember what can get you a bonus prize?

Child: No hitting

Therapist: Yes! So today I want to discuss what happened that day, so we can figure out what to do instead **[initiates agenda setting]**

Child: None of your business! I do not want to talk about it!

(The child stomps his feet and clutches his fists. The therapist assumes an even more relaxed pose, breathes in and out, and, calmly smiling at parents, gestures for them to continue the conversation). **[modeling skills use]**

Mother: Matt got upset because Jeff won a game he played with Matt. So Matt punched Jeff in the chest.

Therapist: Wow! That is a big deal! I know how much Matt hates loosing in games! **[validation level 5]**

(The child quiets down and looks at the therapist. The therapist immediately turns to the child and smiles warmly). **[nonverbal reinforcement]**

Therapist: I was just saying to your parents that it is very upsetting when you really working hard to win in a game and you end up losing! I would feel angry too! **[validation level 5]** Gosh! What do you think, parents? **[activating behavior - validation from parents]**

Father: Well, I don't think that punching is a good idea and...

(The child throws his skills training binder off the table and stomps out of the office. The therapist and parents continue to sit calmly. During initial evaluation, the therapist assessed possible risks during the therapeutic process. Specifically, the therapist inquired whether the child tended to run out of the treatment room. Parents indicated that the child indeed used to run out of the office with the previous therapist, but always stayed in the vicinity of the office).

Therapist: The good thing is that we can safely continue to ignore. First of all, I would like to say great job with ignoring and using your skills! **[reinforcement]** It was very hard! **[validating level 5]**

(Parents nod. Father looks down, frowning).

Therapist: Greg, you seem angry. **[validation level 3 – mindreading of unstated emotions]** Is this because of Matthew or of what you said?

Father: I am losing my marbles with Matt! But you are right, I should have known better. I think you would call what I said "invalidation."

Therapist: Oh wow, Greg! You know what just happened? You turned your attention away from your child's problem behavior and to the effectiveness of your own response! This is the moment when therapy starts in earnest! I am so proud of you and of myself! (pats herself on the shoulder) **[reinforcement] [modeling of self-reinforcement]**

(The father smiles)

Father: Should I pat myself on the back?

Therapist: Absolutely! Now, you indeed invalidated Matthew's response. However, I want you to acknowledge that you invalidated the invalid. Punching indeed is not the most effective way of dealing with disappointments. So what you said was an accurate corrective feedback. **[validation level 5]** The reaction from Matthew was probably triggered because you did not first validate the valid – his feelings of being hurt. Remember our discussion – acceptance and validation are our foundation for eliciting change. Without them, we will not get far.

(The father nods, smiles and appear more relaxed)

Therapist: I am glad we are on the same page now! You know what will be a cherry on the top for me? If you identify the unrealistic expectation that you just stated. **[activating behavior – catching "shoulds"]**

(The father appears puzzled).

Mother: I think she means that you said that you *should* have known better.

(The therapist smiles and claps her hands) **[nonverbal reinforcement]**

(The child opens the door, comes into the room, sits down and stares at the ceiling, pouting).

Therapist: Thank you so much for coming back, Matthew! **[reinforcement]** I know that this is not easy to have to spend time with me - a really mean lady who screams and yells at kids and throws binders at them **[unorthodox irreverence – use of humor].**

(The child smiles).

Therapist: Hey, I really want to know about your hamster! What's his name?

Child: JoJo

Therapist: Do you have a picture?

(The therapist, parents and the child engage in looking at pictures and discussing the pet)

Therapist: Matthew, you know what you just did? You let go of your anger and started to participate in session! Great job! (gives the child high five) **[reinforcement]**

Father: Yes, Matt, you did really well!

(The therapist gives a thumbs-up to the parent for praising the child) **[reinforcement]**

Therapist: What do you think? (looks at the child) How well did you do with getting unstuck from your anger and disappointment? **[activating behavior - self-reinforcement]**

Child: I don't know. It was fine.

Therapist: Just fine?! Yes, it took you a couple of minutes before you were able to let it go. But you did it! You came back and started to participate in session! You deserve a pat on the back! Go ahead, pat yourself on the back **[activating behavior – self-reinforcement]**

(The child smiles and pats himself on the back).

Therapist: You look just like your dad, when he patted himself on the back two minutes ago.

(Everybody laughs).

Therapist: So great job getting unstuck, returning to the room and participating. Do you think there is a skill that you could have used to stay in session? Do you remember the skill you learned last time? **[lemonade out of lemons]**

Child: Half-smile?

Therapist: Yes! Half-smile and willing hands. Great job remembering! **[reinforcement]** Let's all practice it now. Now, everyone, do your half-smile and willing hands. **[activating behavior – skills practice]**

(The therapist practices half-smile and willing hands with the family) **[modeling skills]**

Therapist: Great job participating, Matthew! **[reinforcement]** Did you feel relaxed inside when you were doing half-smile? (child nods). What about parents? (parents nod) **[assessing adequate implementation of a skill]** Awesome job everyone! **[reinforcement]** What do you think, Matthew, can you use this skill the next time when you feel angry? (child shrugs shoulders) Well, listen, you definitely don't need to practice skills. Who cares about skills and learning to be in control?! Who cares about earning points and great toys and stuff we can get for them?! And the fluffy, snuggly pets we can buy... Who cares, right?! (smiles) **[unorthodox irreverence]**

(The child smiles)

Therapist: So, what do you say, can you practice this skill a lot with mom and dad, so it will be easier to use it the next time you feel upset? **[eliciting commitment]**

(The child shrugs shoulders again)

Therapist: Hey, I thought you said that you wanted to get JoJo that big spinner, so he can run in it and have fun! **[enhancing motivation]** How many points do you need to get it?

(The mother takes point chart out of the binder)

Mother: He has 50 points left after buying the hamster, the cage, and other stuff, so he needs about 50 more. It's about $10.

Therapist: Wow! You earned a lot of points if you could afford a hamster and a cage, a water bottle, and bedding! **[reinforcement]** And only 50 more to get a spinner! Do you realize that you only need to do 12 practices to get 50 points?! And how long does each practice last?

Child: Couple of minutes.

Therapist: Yeah! You can earn 50 points by the end of the day, if you want to! But you probably don't really want to... **[irreverence – use of humorous response]**

Child: Mom, can we practice on the ride back?

Mother: Sure!

Therapist: That's the spirit! **[reinforcement]**

(The child and parents smile)

Therapist: Now, let's do a mindfulness practice. I don't know about you, guys, but I definitely need to get my head cleared and ready for the rest of the session. **[activating behavior – practice of skill]** Matthew, what would you like to do for mindfulness today?

Child: Eat candy.

Therapist: Of course, why did I even ask?! (rolls her eyes humorously) **[irreverence]**

(Everyone smiles)

Therapist: Well, yes, we are going to eat a candy. (looks at the family with a mischievous smile). You, guys, are now mindfulness pros, so I want to kick this up a notch. Today we are going to do a mindfulness *and* willingness exercise. We are going to do a "bean boozled challenge." I have these special jelly beans. You never know if you get a regular flavor like peach or coconut, or a not so regular flavor like dog food or stinky socks or vomit.

(Parents grimace in disgust, the child smiles).

Child: I know those. They are really gross!

Therapist: Yeah! Quite unpleasant. The mindfulness part is the same as usual – we will attend to the taste, the texture and the smell of the candy, catch our mind running away and gently bringing it back to the candy. The willingness part is experiencing the candy fully if you get an irregular flavor instead of spitting it out. (parents cringe) Yes, I know. It can be quite hard. You know what will help? Our favorite skill – half smile and willing hands. It will help us relax and not add fuel to the fire by tensing our body and face in disgust. Just keep relaxing. So, we are going to assume our half-smile and willing hands position as soon as we put a jelly bean in our mouths, just in case. Any questions? Okay. (distributes candy) Ready? No past, no future, just this one moment.

(The therapist and the family do the mindfulness exercise. The child starts moving and making sounds and commenting on the flavor of the jelly bean he got. The therapist continues to engage in the practice without paying attention to the child) **[modeling effective skills use]**

Therapist: So how was it? What did you notice?

Mother: Oh, it was quite an experience. I think I got something that tasted like spoiled milk.

Therapist: Oh yes. Moldy cheese.

Mother: I kept doing the relaxing skill and you know, it definitely helped to get through this.

Therapist: Aha, happy to hear that! **[reinforcement]** Did you catch your mind running away?

Mother: Not really. I was very focused.

Therapist: Our mind runs away no matter how focused we are. It's just that the more focused that we are, the harder it is to notice our mind running away. Who noticed their mind running away?

Dad: I had a normal flavor – it tasted sweet and pleasant and reminded me of cotton candy. So my mind went to the county fair, where we ate cotton candy.

Therapist: Great catch! **[reinforcement]** Did you bring your mind back?

Father: Yes.

Therapist: Great! **[reinforcement]** What about you, Matthew?

Child: I had toothpaste. But I like it, so it was good.

Therapist: Did you catch your mind running away?

Child: I thought about a cavity I have and that I have to go to the dentist.

Therapist: Awesome job catching your mind! **[reinforcement]** Did you bring it back?

Child: Yes.

Therapist: I betcha! You are a pro! High five! (gives the child a high five) **[reinforcement]**. Now mindfully describe your experience with eating candy.

Child: It was sweet, it tasted like toothpaste, it tasted like mint, I liked it.

Therapist: Wow! Your description was all facts! Nice job! **[reinforcement]**. Now let's go back to our diary card. We are a bit back and forth today. And it is what it is. **[modeling acceptance]** We can let the parents go for now, so we can finish Matthew's part of the session.

(Parents leave. Therapist looks at the diary card)

Therapist: I am very happy about the skills you used and all the practice that you did! **[reinforcement].** So, I just want to talk about the situation with your brother.

Child: Can we play a game?

Therapist: We can definitely play a game for our wind-down at the end of the session if you keep participating. Any game that you want! And, by the way, I got a new version of Spot It... **[motivational enhancement]** So, tell me what happened? **[initiating mini chain analysis]**

Child: I don't know.

Therapist: Well, as far as I remember Jeff and you were playing some sort of a game and Jeff won.

Child: Yeah. But who cares! He always wins! I hate this!

Therapist: So, let me get it straight – your brother won a game and you had a thought "I hate this" **[identification of thought]**

(Child looks down and nods).

Therapist: I understand. What did you feel?

(The child tenses up and makes fists)

Therapist: And that made you feel....?

Child: Like I was stupid!

Therapist: Aha. Another thought – "I am stupid" **[identification of thought]** So how did that thought make you feel?

Child: Like mad.

Therapist: Yes, of course! Anger. And what does anger usually tell us to do?

Child: Punch and kick.

Therapist: And that's what happened, right?

(The child nods)

Therapist. Yes, anger never tells us to hug somebody, right? So, it makes perfect sense that you would have an action urge to punch your brother. **[validation level 5]** Now, what happened next?

Child: Mom told me to go to time out, but I did not go, and she took my iPad.

Therapist: Yeah, that must have hurt! **[validation level 3]** Did you like the way this situation ended?

(The child shakes head).

Therapist: So, it looks like you were not happy with the outcome, right? **[validation level 2 – reflecting]** Let's think together, what else you could have done that would have given you a different outcome? **[eliciting solution generation]**

(The child rolls his eyes).

Child: I know, I know.... Use your skills and stuff...

Therapist: Hey, you don't have to. I just thought that you were not happy about your iPad being taken away...

Child: Ignore?

Therapist: Aha! We are thinking very similarly. Ignoring works best when someone bothers you and is trying to get a reaction out of you. **[solution evaluation]** Your brother was not trying to bother you, he just happened to win a game. I think accepting the situation, paced breathing, half-smile and willing hands, could have worked. Do you think this would have helped? **[solution evaluation]**

Child: May be.

Therapist: Well, it depends on how upset you are. We can always back it up with another skill, something even stronger.

(Child nods).

Therapist: What could that be? Any thoughts?

Child: What about ice? It hurts but I did it once and it helped.

Therapist: Perfect! You grab an ice cube and hold it in your hand until you can think straight again.

Child: Aha.

Therapist: Oh, wonderful! Did you think about using skills when your brother won that game?

Child: Yes, but I didn't want to.

Therapist: I am very happy that you thought about using a skill in such a difficult situation! **[reinforcement].** For next time, remember that it's hard to *want* to use skills in the moment. We usually just want to do what our feelings tell us to do. What may help us is getting a motivation from another "want." You have many "wants" – you want to learn how to be in control, you want to keep yourself and other people safe, you want to improve relationships with your mom and dad and your brother, you want to get more stuff for your hamster. See?! That is quite a list! Keeping these "wants" in mind may help. And these "wants" may still not be enough in the heat of the moment unless you practice, practice, practice when there are no problems! When a problem comes your way, it's too late to practice. You need to be ready.

(The child nods).

Therapist: Now, what would happen if you were to let go and use your skills?

Child: I would get points.

Therapist: For sure! What else?

Child: I would not get in trouble.

Therapist: Yeap! And your parents would be...?

Child: Happy.

Therapist: Of course and this would help with your goal of improving your relationship with them. What about your brother?

Child: He would not be mad.

Therapist: And that would help...?

Child: Get along with him.

Therapist: And how are you going to feel about yourself being able to be the boss of yourself?

Child: Pat myself on the back (smiles)

Therapist: That's right! (gives the child high five **[reinforcement]**) Let's practice right now. I will be your brother and I just won the game and you are going to... **[activation of behavior – skills rehearsal]**

Child: Get ice.

Therapist: Let's role-play both – paced breathing and then getting ice.

(The therapist and the child role-play the use of skills).

Therapist: Wonderful job! Now, do you think you can do this next time? **[eliciting commitment]**

(The child nods).

Therapist: And why would you want to do this? It will be hard! **[strengthening commitment - devils' advocate]**

Child: To keep me from getting in trouble.

(The therapist nods and gives the child thumbs-up) **[reinforcement]**

Therapist: What may stand in the way of using skills? **[troubleshooting]**

Child: I will forget.

Therapist: Yep, that may happen. What can you do to help yourself not forget? Practice...(gestures to the child to finish the sentence that is often said by the therapist during sessions).

Child:.....practice, practice... (smiles)

Therapist: So, when your parents tell you "we have a couple of minutes, let's do a practice" you will say...?

Child: Okay (smiles)

Therapist: Are you sure? (child nods) Deal? (child nods) Shake hands kind of a deal? (child nods) **[eliciting commitment]**

(The therapist and the child shake hands)

Therapist: So that means that when I see you next week, you will have at least two checks per day for "skills practice" on your diary card, right? (child nods) **[generalizing skills]** Wonderful, you did sooo well today! You are getting a participation prize, for sure! **[reinforcement].** Now let's play a game, like I promised. And if I win this game and you get upset, you are going to use... **[coping ahead]**

Child: Paced breathing (smiles).

(The therapist and the child play a game for a wind-down at the end of the session).

Summary

This chapter illustrates clinical application of the DBT-C model. DBT-C postulates that the main mechanisms of change include parental emotion regulation, creation of a validating environment, and daily reinforced practice of skills. Indeed, DBT-C, as opposed to original model DBT, can directly target the invalidating environment. An ability to alter maladaptive transactions between the patient and family during the formative years is an undoubtable advantage of working with children. Using this advantage to the fullest may be key in making the treatment work. The provided example represents the typical therapeutic process and highlights the emphasis on parental participation to address maladaptive family dynamics, support children's participation in therapy, model adaptive behaviors, and reinforce progress. Further research is needed to evaluate the mechanisms of change and the extent to which changes in the environment affect changes in the child's functioning.

References

Althoff, R. R., Verhulst, F. C., Retlew, D. C., Hudziak, J. J., & Van der Ende, J. (2010). Adult outcomes of childhood dysregulation: A 14-year follow-up study. *Journal of the American Academy of Child and Adolescent Psychiatry*, *49*(11), 1105–1116.

American Psychiatric Association (APA). (2013). *Diagnostic and statistical manual of mental disorders* (5th ed.). Washington, DC: Author.

Baweja, R., Mayes, S. D., Hamed, U., & Waxmonsky, J. G. (2016). Disruptive mood dysregulation disorder: Current insights. *Neuropsychiatric Disease and Treatment*, *12*, 2115–2124.

Brotman, M. A., Rich, B. A., Guyer, A. E., Lunsford, J. R., Horsey, S. E., ... Liebenluft, E. (2010). Amygdala activation during emotion processing of neural faces in children with severe mood dysregulation versus ADHD or bipolar disorder. *American Journal of Psychiatry, 167*(1), 61–69.

Deveny, C. M., Connolly, M. E., Haring, C. T., Bones, B. L., Reynolds, R. C., Kim, P., ... Liebenluft, E. (2013). Neural mechanism of frustration in chronically irritable children. *American Journal of Psychiatry, 170*(10), 1186–1194.

Dickstein, D. P., Brazel, A. C., Goldberg, L. D., & Hunt, J. I. (2009). Affect regulation in pediatric bipolar disorder. *Child and Adolescent Psychiatric Clinics of North America, 18*(2), 405–420.

Guy, W. (1976). The clinical global impression scale. In *ECDEU assessment manual for psychopharmacology-revised* (pp. 218–222). Rockville, MD: US Dept. of Health, Education and Welfare, ADAMHA, NIMH Psychopharmacology Research Branch.

Liebenluft, E. (2011). Severe mood dysregulation, irritability, and the diagnostic boundaries of bipolar disorder in youths. *American Journal of Psychiatry, 168*(2), 129–142.

Linehan, M. M., Comtois, K. A., Murray, A. M., Brown, M. Z., Gallop, R. J., Heard, H. L., ... Lindenboim, N. (2006). Two-year randomized controlled trial and follow-up of dialectical behavior therapy vs therapy by experts for suicidal and borderline personality disorder. *Archives of General Psychiatry, 63*(7), 757–766.

Moreno, C., Laje, G., Blanco, C., Jiang, H., Schmidt, A. B., & Olfson, M. (2007). National trends in the outpatient diagnosis and treatment of bipolar disorder in youth. *Archives of General Psychiatry, 64*(9), 1032–1039.

Perepletchikova, F. (2019). Dialectical behavior therapy for pre-adolescent children. In M. Swales (Ed.), *The Oxford handbook of dialectical behaviour therapy* (pp. 691–718). UK: Oxford University Press.

Perepletchikova, F., Axelrod, S., Kaufman, J., Rounsaville, B. J., Douglas-Palumberi, H., & Miller, A. (2011). Adapting dialectical behavior therapy for children: Towards a new research agenda for paediatric suicidal and non-suicidal self-injurious behaviors. *Child and Adolescent Mental Health, 16*(2), 116–121.

Perepletchikova, F., & Goodman, G. (2014). Two approaches to treating pre-adolescent children with severe emotional and behavioral problems: Dialectical behavior therapy adapted for children and mentalization-based child therapy. *Journal of Psychotherapy Integration, 24*(4), 298–312.

Perepletchikova, F., Nathanson, D., Axelrod, S. R., Merrill, C., Walker, A., Grossman, M., ... Walkup, J. (2017). Dialectical behavior therapy for pre-adolescent children with disruptive mood dysregulation disorder: Feasibility and primary outcomes. *Journal of the American Academy of Child and Adolescent Psychiatry, 56*, 832–840.

Roy, A. K., Klein, R. G., Angelosante, A., Bar-Heim, Y., Liebenluft, E., Hulvershorn, L., ... Spindel, C. (2013). Clinical features of young children referred for impairing temper outbursts. *Journal of Child and Adolescent Psychopharmacology, 25*(9), 588–596.

Stringaris, A. (2011). Irritability in children and adolescents: A challenge for DSM-5. *European Child & Adolescent Psychiatry, 20*(2), 61–66.

Tourian, L. (2015). Treatment options for the cardinal symptoms of disruptive mood dysregulation disorder. *Journal of the Canadian Academy of Child and Adolescent Psychiatry, 24*(1), 41–54.

SECTION III

Specific settings and populations

CHAPTER

10

Research of dialectical behavior therapy in schools

Alec L. Miller[1], *Nora Gerardi*[1], *James J. Mazza*[2] *and Elizabeth Dexter-Mazza*[2]

[1]Cognitive & Behavioral Consultants, White Plains, NY, United States, [2]Mazza Consulting, Seattle, Washington, United States

Introduction

Mental health disorders among youth in the United States

Mental health and psychological problems are among the most prevalent health issues for school-aged youth (Erskine et al., 2015; Flynn, Joyce, Weihrauch, & Corcoran, 2018). There is an abundance of research that points to high rates of mental health problems among youth. In the United States, approximately 1 in 5 school-age children has a mental health disorder, with 7.4%, 7.1%, and 3.2% of youth aged 3–17 years have a behavior, anxiety, and depression diagnosis, respectively (Ghandour et al., 2019; Merikangas et al., 2010). Among those with a mental health problem, approximately one-third are estimated to have more than one disorder (Waddell, Shepherd, Schwartz, & Barican, 2014). Alarmingly, the rates of mental health disorders have increased over the past several years; among children 6–17 years old, the rates of diagnoses of anxiety and depression increased from 5.4% in 2003 to 8% in 2007 to 8.4% in 2011–12 (Bitsko et al., 2018).

Suicidal behaviors are among the most troubling behaviors associated with mental health disorders in youth. Between 2001 and 2017 the total suicide rate in the United States increased by 31% from 10.7 to 14.0 suicides per 100,000 persons (The Centers for Disease Control and Prevention, 2019). This increase in suicide is true for children and

The Handbook of Dialectical Behavior Therapy
DOI: https://doi.org/10.1016/B978-0-12-816384-9.00010-5

teenagers aged 10–19, for whom suicide is the second leading cause of death (Murphy, Xu, Kochanek, & Arias, 2018). The number of suicide attempts is far greater than deaths by suicide, with estimates of 7.4% of school-aged youth actually attempting suicide one or more times (Kann et al., 2018). In addition to completed and attempted suicides, research points to a high prevalence of suicidal ideation; nearly 20% of high school students seriously considering suicide and 13.6% of all school-aged youth making a plan about how they would attempt suicide in the past year (Kann et al., 2018; Perou et al., 2013). Nonsuicidal self-injury (NSSI) is on the spectrum of suicidal behaviors and is defined as direct destruction of one's body tissue without suicidal intent (Klonsky, 2007). Nearly one out of four adolescents in community studies reports engaging in NSSI behaviors such as cutting, burning, and punching oneself (Miller & Smith, 2008). Other estimates suggest a 12-month prevalence estimate of 7.3% for NSSI among adolescents in the United States (Muehlenkamp, Claes, Havertape, & Plener, 2012; Taliaferro, Muehlenkamp, Borowsky, McMorris, & Kugler, 2012).

Impact of mental health disorders among youth

A number of long-term negative consequences are indicated for children with mental health disorders, including poor psychosocial functioning and difficulties in a variety of settings including within their own families at home, in school, and in the larger community (Kessler et al., 2001; Perou et al., 2013). Academically, school-aged youth with mental health disorders are at risk for low academic achievement, high scholastic anxiety, increased school suspensions, a decreased ability or desire to complete homework, and difficulty with concentrating in class (Försterling & Binser, 2002; Humensky et al., 2010; Rushton, Forcier, & Schectman, 2002). These difficulties also impair social functioning, as school-aged youth with mental health problems engage in more aggressive behaviors and have poorer peer relationships (Blackorby & Cameto, 2004). The impact of mental health disorders can persist after school-aged years. For example, mental health problems may inhibit advanced educational attainment, as only 32% of students with a serious mental illness continue onto postsecondary education (United States Government Accountability Office, 2008). Further, early mental health problems can lead to damaging economic and financial implications, including adult psychiatric problems, unwanted pregnancies, criminal convictions, and the persistence of personality traits that are not conducive to success in the labor market (United States Government Accountability Office, 2008). Given the immediate and long-standing impacts of mental health disorders, early intervention is critical in order to reduce such functional impairments.

Mental health services in schools

In spite of high, and growing, rates of mental health problems among youth, less than half of children in need of mental health services actually receive help (Merikangas et al., 2010). Research points to many factors that get in the way of mental healthcare for those in need, including high cost and insufficient insurance coverage, limited options and long waits, and social stigma (Andrade et al., 2014; Mojtabai et al., 2011). As such, schools present a unique service delivery opportunity; that is, school-based mental health intervention can be easily accessible, of high quality (e.g., delivery of evidence-based interventions), and free of cost. Further, children and adolescents are 21 times more likely to visit schools for their mental healthcare than a community-based service (Juszczak, Melinkovich, & Kaplan, 2003).

Mental health staff working within school settings is poised with opportunity for specialized training and service delivery. Given the access to students and the unique ability to provide multitiered models of mental and behavioral health support (e.g., universal, targeted and intensive), children and adolescents' mental health needs can and should be treated within the school setting (National Association of School Psychologists (NASP), 2014, 2015).

Development of dialectical behavior therapy in schools

Beginning in 1995, Miller and Rathus adopted and then adapted Linehan's dialectical behavior therapy (DBT) for suicidal multiproblem adolescents. They published their pilot data followed by their treatment manuals (Miller, Rathus, & Linehan, 2007; Rathus & Miller, 2002, 2015). During this time period, two separate research groups conducted and published the results of two randomized controlled trials of DBT with suicidal multiproblem adolescents making DBT the first evidence-based treatment for suicidal teens (McCauley et al., 2018; Mehlum et al., 2014). While DBT for adolescents began as a treatment for suicidal and self-harming youth, it has evolved into a more transdiagnostic treatment for adolescents presenting with a range of emotional and behavioral problems (Miller et al., 2007; Ritschel, Miller, & Taylor, 2013).

Given the efficacy and effectiveness of DBT with outpatient youth, school psychologists from one NY State public school approached one of the treatment developers (ALM) and requested assistance in trying to adopt comprehensive DBT into a school setting. They wanted assistance with not only their suicidal and self-injurious students but also those with varying degrees of emotion regulation problems that led to detentions, suspensions, and psychiatric inpatient hospitalizations, emergency room visits, and even out of district placements for some students. Following a 4-day training and biweekly consultation from expert DBT therapists for a minimum of 2 years, the school personnel began implementing comprehensive school–based DBT (CSB-DBT) with positive outcomes (see in the "Comprehensive school–based dialectical behavior therapy in schools: outcomes data" section; Mason, Catucci, Lusk, & Johnson, 2011). These preliminary outcomes inspired the school personnel involved who then reported feeling less "burned out" by their jobs. Other schools in the county heard about this one school's experience and began to express an interest in receiving training to implement CSB-DBT in their school districts as well. CSB-DBT has five modes: (1) weekly individual DBT counseling, (2) weekly skills group/class for typically 30 weeks, (3) skills coaching for the student by a DBT-trained personnel as needed during school hours, (4) weekly DBT provider consultation team meeting, comprised all those trained and providing direct service to students (which may include building administrators if they're having face-to-face contact/disciplinary meetings with students), and (5) parent skills review (monthly)/or family meetings as needed. Implementation of all five modes of CSB-DBT to fidelity can take up to 2–4 years.

To date, we have trained over 50 school districts in the application of CSB-DBT. Pilot studies from several schools suggest promising outcomes that are presented later in this chapter. Anecdotal reports from staff members applying the treatment are also very encouraging. Of course, to verify the effectiveness of DBT in schools, more research is required. A natural outgrowth of this work has been the notion of starting DBT further "upstream," that is, starting to teach DBT skills to students in schools with primary prevention in mind and not wait until the student is exhibiting significant social, emotional, or behavioral problems to intervene. Simultaneously, NY State has a new law enacted in 2018 requiring schools to provide students with some degree of mental health education. The DBT curriculum is one obvious choice given the breadth and depth of skills being taught, including mindfulness, distress tolerance, emotion regulation, and interpersonal effectiveness skills that map on so well to the needs of many of our students. Furthermore, the NY State Education Department Mental Health Education Literacy in Schools guidelines (2018) recommend schools to consider DBT as a Tier 3 intervention. We believe it is equally useful to consider DBT as a Tier 1 and Tier 2 intervention. Hence, came the birth of DBT skills in schools: skills training for emotional problem solving for adolescents (DBT STEPS-A) (Mazza, Dexter-Mazza, Miller, Rathus, & Murphy, 2016). DBT STEPS-A is intended for general education and health teachers to teach DBT skills to students. The DBT STEPS-A manual was adapted from Rathus and Miller's (2015) DBT skills manual for adolescents and written for nonclinical personnel to be able to teach 30 lesson plans in 42-minute class periods. Research data evaluating DBT STEPS-A is also promising and presented later in this chapter.

Research examining dialectical behavior therapy in schools

There are two different types of DBT in schools: (1) CSB-DBT for youth exhibiting a range of social, emotional, behavioral, and psychological problems and (2) DBT STEPS-A, considered a Tier 1 universal application of DBT skills. Next, we start with reviewing the research on CSB-DBT and then turn to a review of the data on DBT STEPS-A.

Feasibility of comprehensive school–based dialectical behavior therapy

To our knowledge, CSB-DBT has been implemented in schools for over 17 years (Miller, Graling, & Dadd, 2019). Cognitive & Behavioral Consultants (CBC), a private group practice and training center in White Plains and Manhattan, NY, provides training and consultation to school districts implementing DBT. During the 2018–19 school year, CBC consulted to 32 school districts in the tristate area implementing CSB-DBT in their schools. Within these districts, 51 DBT teams provided services to both students mandated for special education services as well as nonmandated students. Members of school-based DBT teams included school counselors, school psychologists, social workers, and interns. One-hundred fifty-three DBT skills groups were ran across elementary, middle, and high school levels. Approximately 60% of school DBT teams used the adolescent DBT skills manual (Rathus & Miller, 2015) and 12% used the DBT STEPS-A manual (Mazza et al., 2016). Approximately two-thirds of CSB-DBT intervention delivery occurred through integration into existing social–emotional support programs.

A survey from the 2016 to 2017 academic school year among DBT consultees also provided insight as to the implementation process (Graling & Miller, 2017). The sample consisted of 34 consultees who were part of a school-based DBT team. One-hundred-percent of respondents stated that they are running weekly DBT consultation teams. The majority of respondents (88.2%) reported that their teams implemented a DBT skills group for students. In terms of the other modes of treatments, individual DBT and skills coaching were implemented by 76.5% and 44.1%, respectively.

Comprehensive school–based dialectical behavior therapy in schools: Outcomes data

In 2007 Miller et al. began consulting with schools in Westchester County, NY, to develop and implement CSB-DBT programs. Preliminary results from an open trial of 12 high school students showed that those students participating in CSB-DBT had reduced disciplinary referrals to the assistant principal, absenteeism in class, and detentions and suspensions (Mason et al., 2011). Further, the data demonstrated anecdotal reductions in depression, anxiety, and nonsuicidal self-injurious behaviors. These initial findings demonstrated not only the feasibility of implementing CSB-DBT but also the effectiveness of the intervention on behavioral and emotional outcomes for school-aged youth.

Since 2007 CSB-DBT has been implemented in many school districts in different parts of the country, which has also examined outcomes related to its implementation. In another high school in Westchester County, NY, adolescents who participated in a CSB-DBT program demonstrated significant reductions in depression and social stress [as measured by the Behavioral Assessment System for Children—second edition (BASC-2) (Dadd, 2016) and Reynolds & Kamphaus, 2004]. Dadd (2016) also reported student improvement in their use of adaptive coping skills (e.g., mindfulness skills) as well as increased abilities to tolerate distressing situations. The following year, Dadd (2016) implemented CSB-DBT within a high school in Fairfield County, CT. The data again pointed toward student improvements (Table 10.1).

In a third public high school, located in Portland, OR, Hanson (2016) provided CSB-DBT services to 56 at-risk high school students (e.g., students with histories of NSSI, suicide attempts, and suicidal ideation). Students who participated in the CSB-DBT program showed significant improvement in grade point average from pre- to postintervention and remarkably significant reductions in anxiety, depression, social stress, and anger control as measured by the BASC-2 (Hanson, 2016). Prior to CSB-DBT implementation, Hanson (2016) reported that, on average, there were two student placements to local day treatment programs per year. In the 9 years since implementing the CSB-DBT program, there has only been one placement. Even more notable are the rates of students' suicides; before implementing CSB-DBT, there were multiple student suicides (1–2) per year over many years (Hanson, 2016). Since implementing CSB-DBT, over the past 9 years, there have been no student suicides. Data was also collected in the same school for the 2018–19 year (Hanson, 2019) using the BASC-3 (Reynolds & Kamphaus, 2015), which is reported in Table 10.2.

TABLE 10.1 Percent change in outcomes from the Ways of Coping Checklist (WCC) and Difficulties in Emotion Regulation Scale (DERS) among high school students participating in comprehensive school–based dialectical behavior therapy in Fairfield County, CT.

	Time	Percent change	Notes
1. Dadd (2016)			
WCC	Pre–post one academic year		
Skills use		+71	Students reported an increase in adaptive skills use
General dysfunctional coping		−57	Students reported a decrease in dysfunctional coping strategies
Blaming others		−86	Students reported a decrease in blaming others for their problems
DERS	Pre–post one academic year	−50	Students reported a decrease in their emotion dysregulation

Taken together, these studies demonstrate promising results for CSB-DBT implementation. It is important to note, though, that they are small open trials. Randomized controlled trials are needed to further empirically assess and demonstrate the efficacy and effectiveness of CSB-DBT.

Staff outcomes related to comprehensive school–based dialectical behavior therapy implementation: reducing burnout

In addition to student outcomes, many districts have looked at the effects of CSB-DBT implementation on staff burnout ratings. Schwartz et al. (2017) provide a summary of staff burnout over time. Data was collected using the Copenhagen Burnout Inventory (Kristensen, Borritz, Villadsen, & Christensen, 2005) among a sample of 22 school psychologists (31.8%), special education teachers (9.1%), teaching assistants (9.1%), and behavioral analysts (4.5%) in four middle/high schools. Data was collected before the initial CSB-DBT training and after one academic year of implementing CSB-DBT. The data indicated no significant reduction in burnout pre- and post-year one of implementation; one explanation for these nonsignificant findings is that burnout may increase initially as school staff adjust

TABLE 10.2 Student outcomes on the Behavioral Assessment System for Children—third edition (BASC-3) among high school students participating in comprehensive school–based dialectical behavior therapy during the 2018–19 academic year in Portland, OR.

	Time	Average *t*-score change (BASC-3 self-report)*	Average *t*-score change (BASC-3 parent-report)*
1. Hanson (2019)			
BASC-3	Pre–post one academic year		
Emotional Symptoms Index		−13.9	−5.2
Internalizing problems		−11.6	–
Anxiety		−9.0	−7.2
Depression		−16.3	−3.2
Somatization		−6.5	−4.2
Sense of inadequacy		−10.0	–
Emotional self-control		–	+5.4
Locus of control		−6.8	–
Social stress		−9.8	–
Withdrawal		–	−3.8
Overall personal adjustment		+8.8	–
Interpersonal relations		+5.0	–
Attitude to teachers		+3.1	–
Self-esteem		+12.3	–
Self-reliance		+8.1	–

* Changes in *t*-scores of 3.5–4.0 and greater are generally significant.

to learning and implementing a new comprehensive treatment while also managing all of their other professional responsibilities (Schwartz et al., 2017). Researchers hypothesized that burnout is likely to decrease significantly over time as school staff becomes more confident and competent in CSB-DBT, as well as effect larger change among students and the school (Schwartz et al., 2017). Despite a lack of decrease in burnout, school staff did report positive changes in the work they are doing with students after CSB-DBT training; for example, on a Likert scale from 0 to 6 (6 indicating "strongly agree"), the mean agreement score with the item, "being part of implementing CSB-DBT at your school has improved the quality of your professional work," was 4.71 ($SD = 1.42$; Schwartz et al., 2017). A limitation to this study was the small sample size of school-based staff. Taken together, CSB-DBT may not initially reduce staff burnout, though staff does indicate that being part of the DBT implementation process may increase the quality of their professional work.

Universal application of dialectical behavior therapy skills in schools

The work cited previously highlights that CSB-DBT is a feasible and effective approach that can be implemented in schools to help students who are experiencing emotionally dysregulated behaviors. Some of the students receiving CSB-DBT may have Individualized Education Plans, while others may have been referred (via teacher or self) for needing additional support and strategies in coping with their emotion regulation. In needing to expand the reach of this important work further, with a focus on prevention for all, DBT STEPS-A (Mazza et al., 2016) was developed as a universal upstream social emotional learning (SEL) curriculum for middle and high school students that focuses on emotion regulation skills and coping strategies.

Development of dialectical behavior therapy skills in schools: skills training for emotional problem solving for adolescents

The development of DBT STEPS-A was designed at the universal level as an evidence-based prevention/intervention SEL curriculum that is grounded in the efficacy and effectiveness of comprehensive DBT. The development of DBT STEPS-A expanded the reach of DBT skills, especially within a multitiered system of support framework, to address the needs of all students, not just those who are at-risk (Tier 2) or those who have engaged in self-harming behaviors (Tier 3). Thus the complementary synergies of DBT STEPS-A and CSB-DBT cover the vast array of students' emotion regulation needs, from promotion of mental wellness to intervention of high-risk behaviors.

DBT STEPS-A incorporates the four basic modules of skills that are found in comprehensive DBT (Linehan, 1993, 2014) and DBT for adolescents (Miller et al., 2007; Rathus & Miller, 2015): core mindfulness, distress tolerance, emotion regulation, and interpersonal effectiveness. There are 30 DBT STEPS-A lessons that are designed to be delivered in

50-minute periods. Each lesson is structured similarly, with a beginning mindfulness activity, followed by homework review, the teaching of the new DBT skill/strategy, and ending with a summary and homework assignment. The majority of the skills selected, the handouts, and the homework activities were purposely aligned (i.e., content and structure) with the original adolescent DBT skills manual (Rathus & Miller, 2015) to provide a seamless transition from CSB-DBT services to DBT STEPS-A and vice-versa. It should be noted that the CSB-DBT and the adolescent skills manual include a fifth module called *Middle Path* that is not included in the DBT STEPS-A curriculum.

Dialectical behavior therapy skills in schools: skills training for emotional problem solving for adolescents: outcome data

The implementation of DBT STEPS-A is fairly recent, with the first implementation in 2013. The publication of the DBT STEPS-A curriculum is 2016, thus allowing a 3-year window into collecting research in the natural setting with the published curriculum. The data that has been collected by a few school-based settings, both qualitative and quantitative, has been promising. There are three different datasets that we are aware of regarding the effectiveness of DBT STEPS-A.

The first set of data was collected from an alternative middle school in Battle Ground, WA (Mazza & Hanson, 2015). The instructor had attended a formal training on DBT STEPS-A and began to implement the curriculum with his eighth-grade students. He taught only three of the four modules: core mindfulness, distress tolerance, and interpersonal effectiveness. He asked his students a single question: *Do you think the DBT STEPS-A program can help you and others?* The data is shown in Table 10.3.

He also examined his students' data from the Washington State Healthy Youth Survey, an annual self-report assessment measure focused on mental health issues, struggles, and strengths. As a part of

TABLE 10.3 Dialectical behavior therapy skills in schools: skills training for emotional problem solving for adolescents (DBT STEPS-A) single question outcome (Jones et al., 2015).

Question	Yes	No	Sometimes
($n = 72$)			
Do you think the DBT STEPS-A program can help you and others?	69 (96%)	3 (4%)	0 (0%)

TABLE 10.4 Self-harm reports from Washington State Healthy Youth Survey (Jones et al., 2015).

Examining cutting behavior	Winter 2011–14 (avg. = 500)	Winter 2014–15 (n = 497)	Winter 2015–16 (n = 485)
Number of students who have cut in the past year	10–12/year	3	0

TABLE 10.5 Dialectical behavior therapy skills in schools: skills training for emotional problem solving for adolescents (DBT STEPS-A) versus controls in high school settings in Cork, Ireland: outcomes.

Groups	DBT skill use	Dysfunctional coping	Emotion Symptom Index (BASC-2)	Internalizing Problems (BASC-2)
DBT STEPS-A	3.27	− 3.05	− 7.56*	− 6.91*
Controls	3.48	31	− 2.32	− 1.92

**Higher scores on the BRIEF denotes worse functioning.*
BASC-2, Behavioral Assessment System for Children—second edition.

this assessment, questions about self-harm are asked. Table 10.4 examines the cross-sectional data over time (Jones et al., 2015).

It should be noted that 2014 was the first year he implemented the curriculum at his school. Although this data does not represent causation, the significant drop in self-harming behavior is correlational and is going in the right direction.

A second study that took place in Cork, Ireland, used a quasiexperimental design to examine the effectiveness of DBT STEPS-A versus controls in high school settings (Flynn et al., 2018). Because the school structure is different than it is in the United States, they modified the curriculum into 22 weeks taught by 13 different teachers across eight different high schools. Due to dosage differences across some schools and other schools being gender specific, the treatment versus control sample ended up being 72 female adolescents ages 15–16 years old. Measures in this study included the DBT Ways of Coping Checklist (Neacsiu, Rizvi, Vitaliano, Lynch, & Linehan, 2010) and the BASC-2 (Reynolds & Kamphaus, 2004). The results are reported in Table 10.5 with scores being change scores (pretest–posttest) during one academic year. As shown in the table, two of the four outcome measures were significant, with reductions on the emotion symptom index and the internalizing problems composite scales of the BASC-2, both at the $p < .02$ level. Given the small sample size, examining the effect sizes is important, and in this case the results were very supportive, showing large effect sizes including a Cohen's *d* of 0.65 for the emotion symptom index and 0.83 for the internalizing problems. Interestingly, there were no differences found in the area of dysfunctional coping. From these results, it appears that DBT STEPS-A is effective in reducing the symptoms associated with emotion dysregulation and internalizing mental health issues.

A third study has recently been completed at a charter school in Staten Island, NY, examining 344 freshmen in high school, 67 who received DBT STEPS-A in seventh and eighth grade, compared to 277 peer controls who attended the same high school in ninth grade but did not receive DBT STEPS-A. The study was designed to examine the long-term impact of receiving DBT STEPS-A in the two prior years compared to peer controls. The outcome measure was the self-report Behavior Rating Inventory for Executive Functioning (BRIEF) (Gioia, Isquith, Guy, & Kenworthy, 2000). Table 10.6 provides the means for each subscale of the BRIEF.

TABLE 10.6 Means scores on the Behavior Rating Inventory for Executive Functioning (BRIEF) for ninth graders at a Staten Island charter school.

*BRIEF subscale	Ninth graders who received DBT STEPS-A ($n = 67$)	Ninth graders who were NON DBT STEPS-A peers ($n = 277$)
Emotional control	19.1**	21.2
Organization of materials	11.4**	13.0
Plan/organize	24.2**	25.7
Inhibit	20.1**	21.2
Initiate	15.2**	16.8
Self-monitor	15.6**	17.0
Shift	15.7**	17.5
Working memory	19.3**	21.2
Behavior regulation index	56.6**	59.9
Metacognition index	87.0**	93.6
Global executive composite	140.6**	153.4

DBT STEPS-A, DBT Skills in Schools: Skills Training for Emotional Problem Solving for Adolescents.
* Higher scores on the BRIEF denotes worse functioning.
** Indicate significant better scores at the $p < .05$ level.

Overall, the results from these three DBT STEPS-A studies are encouraging and yet more needs to be done. The next steps in evaluating DBT STEPS-A are pilot implementation studies followed by large randomized control trials.

Future directions

DBT is the leading evidence-based psychosocial intervention for suicidal multiproblem adolescents. Clinical and school psychologists have been adapting DBT for school settings over the past 17 years to address the myriad therapeutic needs of the students while also providing an SEL toolkit for every child. Thus DBT STEPS-A and CSB-DBT have shown promise based on pilot data and anecdotal reports by school staff who continues to recommend that more of the schools in their districts and neighboring districts get trained. Moreover, in NY State, there is new legislation requiring mental health education and literacy in schools, and DBT is one of the recommended interventions by the NY State Department of Education. Adopting and adapting treatments while conducting dissemination and implementation research take years. More research is necessary on both CSB-DBT and DBT STEPS-A to be able to verify the efficacy and effectiveness of DBT in schools.

References

Andrade, L. H., Alonso, J., Mneimneh, Z., Wells, J. E., Al-Hamzawi, A., Borges, G., ... Florescu, S. (2014). Barriers to mental health treatment: results from the WHO World Mental Health surveys. *Psychological Medicine, 44*(6), 1303–1317.

Bitsko, R. H., Holbrook, J. R., Ghandour, R. M., Blumberg, S. J., Visser, S. N., Perou, R., & Walkup, J. T. (2018). Epidemiology and impact of health care provider–diagnosed anxiety and depression among US children. *Journal of Developmental and Behavioral Pediatrics, 39*(5), 395–403.

Blackorby, J., & Cameto, R. (2004). Changes in school engagement and academic performance of students with disabilities. In *Wave 1 Wave 2 overview (SEELS)*. Menlo Park, CA: SRI International.

Dadd, A.C. (2016). *The effectiveness of dialectical behavior therapy in treating multiproblem adolescents in a school setting* (unpublished doctoral dissertation). New York: Fordham University.

Erskine, H. E., Moffitt, T. E., Copeland, W. E., Costello, E. J., Ferrari, A. J., Patton, G., ... Scott, J. G. (2015). A heavy burden on young minds: the global burden of mental and substance use disorders in children and youth. *Psychological Medicine, 45*(7), 1551–1563.

Försterling, F., & Binser, M. J. (2002). Depression, school performance, and the veridicality of perceived grades and causal attributions. *Personality and Social Psychology Bulletin, 28*(10), 1441–1449.

Flynn, D., Joyce, M., Weihrauch, M., & Corcoran, P. (2018). Innovations in practice: Dialectical behaviour therapy–skills training for emotional problem solving for adolescents (DBT STEPS-A): Evaluation of a pilot implementation in Irish post-primary schools. *Child and Adolescent Mental Health, 23*(4), 376–380.

Ghandour, R. M., Sherman, L. J., Vladutiu, C. J., Ali, M. M., Lynch, S. E., Bitsko, R. H., & Blumberg, S. J. (2019). Prevalence and treatment of depression, anxiety, and conduct problems in US children. *The Journal of Pediatrics, 206*, 256–267.

Gioia, G. A., Isquith, P. K., Guy, S. C., & Kenworthy, L. (2000). *BRIEF: Behav. Rat. inventory executive Funct.* Psychological Assessment Resources.

Graling, K., & Miller, A. L. (2017). *DBT in schools - feasibility survey*. White Plains, NY: The DBT in Schools Strategic Planning Meeting.

Hanson, J.B. (2016). School-based DBT: Merging mental health and behavioral supports for high school students at tiers II & III: Dialectical behavioral therapy in the public schools. In *Presented at the Georgia Association for positive behavior support conference*.

Hanson, J.B. (2019). *Lincoln High School MTSS Program evaluation 2018-19 school-based dialectical behavior therapy program (SB-DBT)* (unpublished data). Retrieved at <https://www.pps.net/Page/6853>.

Humensky, J., Kuwabara, S. A., Fogel, J., Wells, C., Goodwin, B., & Voorhees, B. W. V. (2010). Adolescents with depressive symptoms and their challenges with learning in school. *Journal of School Nursing, 26*(5), 377–392.

Mazza, J. J. & Hanson, J. B. (2015). Implementing DBT emotion regulation skills for tier II-III students. In *Invited workshop presented at the national conference of the National Association of School Psychologists*. February 2015, Orlando, FL. Jones, R.

Juszczak, L., Melinkovich, P., & Kaplan, D. (2003). Use of health and mental health services by adolescents across multiple delivery sites. *Journal of Adolescent Health, 32*(6), 108–118.

Kann, L., McManus, T., Harris, W. A., Shanklin, S. L., Flint, K. H., Queen, B., ... Lim, C. (2018). Youth risk behavior surveillance—United States, 2017. *MMWR Surveillance Summaries, 67*(8), 1.

Kessler, R. C., Berglund, P. A., Bruce, M. L., Koch, J. R., Laska, E. M., Leaf, P. J., ... Wang, P. S. (2001). The prevalence and correlates of untreated serious mental illness. *Health Services Research, 36*(6), 987.

Klonsky, E. D. (2007). The functions of deliberate self-injury: a review of the evidence. *Clinical Psychology Review, 27*, 226–239.

Kristensen, T. S., Borritz, M., Villadsen, E., & Christensen, K. B. (2005). The Copenhagen Burnout Inventory: A new tool for the assessment of burnout. *Work & Stress, 19*(3), 192–207.

Linehan, M. M. (1993). *Cognitive-behavioral treat. borderline personality disorder*. Guilford Publications.

Linehan, M. M. (2014). *DBT skills train. manual*. Guilford Publications.

Mason, P.M., Catucci, D., Lusk, V., & Johnson, M. (2011). An initial program evaluation of modified dialectical behavior therapy skills training in a school setting. In *Poster accepted for presentation at the International society for the improvement and teaching of dialectical behavior therapy (ISIT DBT)*. November 2011, Toronto, Canada.

Mazza, J. J., Dexter-Mazza, E. T., Miller, A. L., Rathus, J. H., & Murphy, H. E. (2016). *DBT Skills Schools: Skills Train. Emotional Probl. Solving Adolesc. DBT STEPS-A*. Guilford Press.

McCauley, E., Berk, M. S., Asarnow, J. R., Adrian, M., Cohen, J., Korslund, K., ... Linehan, M. M. (2018). Efficacy of dialectical behavior therapy for adolescents at high risk for suicide: a randomized clinical trial. *JAMA Psychiatry, 75*(8), 777–785.

Mehlum, L., Tørmoen, A. J., Ramberg, M., Haga, E., Diep, L. M., Laberg, S., ... Grøholt, B. (2014). Dialectical behavior therapy for adolescents with repeated suicidal and self-harming behavior: a randomized trial. *Journal of the American Academy of Child and Adolescent Psychiatry, 53*(10), 1082–1091.

Merikangas, K. R., He, J. P., Brody, D., Fisher, P. W., Bourdon, K., & Koretz, D. S. (2010). Prevalence and treatment of mental disorders among US children in the 2001–2004 NHANES. *Pediatrics, 125*(1), 75.

Miller, A.L., Graling, K., & Dadd, A. (2019). DBT in schools: Strategic planning and implementation. In *Presented at the DBT in schools strategic planning and implementation meeting, cognitive & behavioral consultants*. May 2019, White Plains, NY.

Miller, A. L., Rathus, J. R., & Linehan, M. M. (2007). *Dialect. Behav. Ther. Suicidal Adolesc.* New York: Guilford Press.

Miller, A. L., & Smith, H. L. (2008). Adolescent non-suicidal self-injurious behaviour: The latest epidemic to assess and treat. *Applied & Preventive Psychology, 12*, 178–188.

Mojtabai, R., Olfson, M., Sampson, N. A., Jin, R., Druss, B., Wang, P. S., … Kessler, R. C. (2011). Barriers to mental health treatment: Results from the National Comorbidity Survey Replication. *Psychological Medicine, 41*(8), 1751–1761.

Muehlenkamp, J. J., Claes, L., Havertape, L., & Plener, P. L. (2012). International prevalence of adolescent non-suicidal self-injury and deliberate self-harm. *Child and Adolescent Psychiatry and Mental Health, 6*(10), 10.

Murphy, S. L., Xu, J. Q., Kochanek, K. D., & Arias, E. (2018). *Mortality in the United States, 2017. NCHS data brief, number 328*. Hyattsville, MD: National Center for Health Statistics.

National Association of School Psychologists (NASP). (2014). *Prevention and wellness promotion* (Position statement). Bethesda, MD: NASP.

National Association of School Psychologists (NASP). (2015). *The importance of mental and behavioral health services for children and adolescents* (Position statement). Bethesda, MD: NASP.

Neacsiu, A. D., Rizvi, S. L., Vitaliano, P. P., Lynch, T. R., & Linehan, M. M. (2010). The dialectical behavior therapy ways of coping checklist: development and psychometric properties. *Journal of Clinical Psychology, 66*(6), 563–582.

New York State Education Department (NYSED). *Mental health education literacy in schools: Linking to a continuum of well-being*. (2018). Retrieved from <http://www.nysed.gov/common/nysed/files/programs/curriculum-instruction/continuumofwellbeingguide.pdf>.

Perou, R., Bitsko, R.H., Blumberg, S.J., Pastor, P., Ghandour, R.M., Gfroerer, J.C., … Huang, L.N. (2013). *Mental health surveillance among children – United States, 2005-2011*. Retrieved from <https://www.cdc.gov/mmwr/preview/mmwrhtml/su6202a1.htm>.

Rathus, J. H., & Miller, A. L. (2002). Dialectical behavior therapy adapted for suicidal adolescents. *Suicide and Life-Threatening Behavior, 32*(2), 146–157.

Rathus, J. H., & Miller, A. L. (2015). *DBT® skills Man. Adolesc.* Guilford Publications.

Reynolds, C. R., & Kamphaus, R. W. (2004). *BASC-2: Behav. Assess. Syst. Children: Man.* Circle Pines, MN: AGS Publishing.

Reynolds, C.R. & Kamphaus, R.W. (2015). *Behavior assessment system for children* (3rd ed.) [Assessment instrument]. Bloomington, MN: Pearson.

Ritschel, L., Miller, A. L., & Taylor, V. (2013). Dialectical behavior therapy for emotion dysregulation. In J. Ehrenreich-May, & B. Chu (Eds.), *Transdiagnostic mechanisms and treatment for youth psychopathology*. New York, NY: Guilford Press.

Rushton, J. L., Forcier, M., & Schectman, R. M. (2002). Epidemiology of depressive symptoms in the National Longitudinal Study of Adolescent Health. *Journal of the American Academy of Child and Adolescent Psychiatry, 41*(2), 199–205.

Schwartz, L., Gerardi, N., Garcia, J., Courtney-Seidler, E.A., McGinn, L., & Miller, A. (2017). The effect of training and implementation of DBT in schools on staff burnout. In *Poster accepted for presentation at the 51st annual convention of the association for behavioral and cognitive therapies (ABCT)*. November 2017, San Diego, CA.

Taliaferro, L. A., Muehlenkamp, J. J., Borowsky, I. W., McMorris, B. J., & Kugler, K. C. (2012). Risk factors, protective factors, and co-occurring health-risk behaviors distinguishing self-harm groups: A population-based sample of adolescents. *Academic Pediatrics, 12*(3), 205–213.

The Centers for Disease Control and Prevention. *Suicide*. (2019). Retrieved from <https://www.nimh.nih.gov/health/statistics/suicide.shtml>.

United States Government Accountability Office. (2008). Young adults with serious mental illness. In *Report to congressional requesters GAO report number GAO-08-678*. Washington, DC: United States Government Accountability Office.

Waddell, C., Shepherd, C., Schwartz, C., & Barican, J. (2014). *Child and youth mental disorders: Prevalence and evidence-based interventions*. Vancouver, BC: Children's Health Policy Centre, Simon Fraser University.

CHAPTER

11

Dialectical behavior therapy in college counseling centers

Carla D. Chugani[1], *Kristin P. Wyatt*[2] *and Rachael K. Richter*[1]

[1]Department of Pediatrics, University of Pittsburgh, Pittsburgh, PA, United States, [2]Department of Psychiatry & Behavioral Sciences, Duke University Medical Center, Durham, NC, United States

Introduction

Issues related to college student mental health and deaths by suicide on campuses across the nation continue to be a serious public health issue. College counseling centers (CCCs) are often at the fore of managing suicidality, which is now the second leading cause of college student death (Turner, Leno, & Keller, 2013). In addition, college students report mental health concerns at alarmingly high rates. The American College Health Association (AHCA) (2016) survey shows that within the previous 12 months, 35% of students reported that they felt so depressed that it was difficult to function, 58% felt overwhelming anxiety, and nearly 10% seriously considered suicide. One-third of first-year students has screened positive for at least one mood, anxiety, or substance disorder (Auerbach et al., 2018). Research has also demonstrated that mental health problems among college students are persistent over time, with 60% of students reporting that their mental health problem persisted over a 2-year period (Zivin, Eisenberg, Gollust, & Golberstein, 2009).

Unfortunately, student need and demand for counseling services often exceeds the resources available on campus. Counseling center directors have continued to report that students are seeking services in increased numbers and that those who present for treatment do so with

The Handbook of Dialectical Behavior Therapy
DOI: https://doi.org/10.1016/B978-0-12-816384-9.00011-7

more serious psychological problems (Gallagher, 2014). While some students needing specialized care can be referred off-campus to specialty providers, this is not always an option if local resources are inaccessible due to location or cost. In the case of rural campuses, off-campus mental health resources may not be available at all. With suicidal ideation being one of the top four concerns reported by college students (Reetz, Krylowicz, Bershad, Lawrence, & Mistler, 2015), innovative methods of effectively stabilizing and treating college students with heterogeneous mental health concerns are sorely needed.

One response to the landscape of college mental health described previously has been the implementation and adaptation of dialectical behavior therapy (DBT; Linehan, 1993a) programs within CCCs. While DBT was originally developed to treat chronically suicidal and self-injurious behavior, DBT programs are particularly well suited to address college mental health problems because the treatment has demonstrated utility as a transdiagnostic treatment, focusing on constructs underlying many different mental health disorders, such as emotion dysregulation (Neacsiu, Eberle, Kramer, Wiesmann, & Linehan, 2014). Thus a single DBT treatment program has the potential to address myriad student demands, ranging from the most severe and suicidal cases, to any concern where emotion dysregulation may be an underlying factor. However, DBT is a comprehensive and sophisticated mental health treatment and as such, there are numerous barriers to implementation of DBT in CCCs, including time, expertise, funds for training, and poor fit with CCC scope of services, which may not always include provision of such comprehensive mental health treatment (Chugani & Landes, 2016). Given these challenges, research has been dedicated to the development of DBT programs that can effectively meet the needs of students, while being realistic and feasible for CCC implementation. This chapter will review the current literature related to DBT in CCCs, by focusing first on the most comprehensive approaches and their outcomes, second, on adapted approaches and outcomes, and third, on additional research related to DBT with college students for specific populations outside of those traditionally treated with DBT [i.e., attention deficit hyperactivity disorder (ADHD), and students with text anxiety]. The chapter will conclude with a discussion of the future of DBT for college students, with a focus on highlighting emerging initiatives and future directions for research.

Comprehensive dialectical behavior therapy in college counseling centers

Comprehensive DBT programs are those that provide all four modes of the standard DBT model: individual therapy, group skills training, therapist consultation team, and between-session telephone coaching (Linehan, 1993a). The standard DBT model is a time-intensive approach involving several hours per week of therapy for a year or longer and as such, is often considered to be beyond the resources or scope of services for CCCs, which typically operate on a brief treatment model. However, efforts have been made to examine the effectiveness of comprehensive DBT implemented in CCCs. The most rigorous examination of comprehensive DBT in CCCs to date was conducted by Pistorello, Fruzzetti, MacLane, Gallop, and Iverson (2012) at the University of Nevada, Reno.

Pistorello et al. (2012) conducted a randomized controlled trial (RCT) with 63 suicidal college students who received 7–12 months of either standard DBT with minimal modifications or an optimized treatment as usual (TAU) condition, with variations in time in treatment being governed by whether or not students remained on campus year-round or left for breaks. Students in the DBT condition received all modes of standard DBT, with the following modifications: (1) the distress tolerance skills module was shortened somewhat and combined with a module on validation that had been used in other studies during that time period (see Iverson, Shenk, & Fruzzetti, 2009); (2) the four-miss rule was modified to state that students who missed four scheduled appointments in a row were considered to have dropped out of treatment, thus allowing students to leave for breaks typical during the college year during which appointments were not scheduled; (3) skills groups ran for 1.5 hours rather than the standard 2 hours; and (4) 8-week skills training modules followed the semester schedule, with one 8-week module being offered each fall, spring, and summer, beginning whenever enough participants had been recruited for a group to form. Adherence to DBT was assessed by having 10% of videotaped sessions rated for adherence by an independent coder. These authors found that compared with those receiving TAU, students who received DBT demonstrated significantly greater improvement in terms of suicidality, depression, nonsuicidal self-injury (NSSI), borderline personality disorder (BPD) symptoms, psychotropic medication use, and social adjustment. Moderation analyses also revealed that DBT was particularly efficacious for students who were more acute at baseline. This rigorous investigation provides strong evidence supporting the efficacy of DBT delivered via a CCC to treat suicidal college students, with strategic adaptations made only to increase the feasibility of the treatment within this clinical setting.

Engle, Gadischkie, Roy, and Nunziato (2013) conducted a small pilot trial of comprehensive DBT compared with a brief (8–10 sessions) psychodynamic treatment approach at Sarah Lawrence College with students who were diagnosed with BPD. As with Pistorello et al.'s (2012) study, these authors made strategic adaptations to the standard DBT model to increase feasibility of delivery within a CCC. These adaptations included

60–90 minute skills training group (as opposed to the typical 2 or 2.5 hours), commitment to treatment by the semester rather than by the year, modifying the four-miss rule such that students were considered to have dropped out if they missed four *unexplained* sessions over the course of a semester (rather than four *consecutive* sessions), and declining to offer telephone coaching during winter and summer breaks when therapists do not have access to the consultation team. These authors were particularly interested in psychiatric and substance-related hospitalizations as well as medical leaves as outcomes of their program. The authors provide data on these variables for students who engaged with the DBT program versus those who did not over a period of four semesters. They found that those who received DBT did not have any psychiatric or substance use related hospitalizations, and there was only one medical leave. In comparison, among those who received the brief psychodynamic treatment, there were 9 psychiatric hospitalizations, 4 substance-related hospitalizations, and 13 medical leaves.

While the data offered by Engle et al. is encouraging, substantial limitations related to the study design and presentation of the data hinder generalizability. These limitations include a lack of clarity about the comparability of the treatment conditions and lack of information about what skills were taught during DBT groups during the course of the program. Notably, there is also no information about the total number of participants in the study. While they provide a total number of students involved in the program at each semester, the program description indicates that students returned to the DBT program on a semester-by-semester basis, making it difficult to determine not only the number of total subjects involved in each treatment condition but also the dose of treatment received per treatment condition. For example, students receiving DBT could have received DBT for four consecutive semesters, while those in the comparison conditions only received 8–10 weeks of treatment—this difference in treatment dose may account for the substantial difference in outcomes between groups. Despite these significant limitations, which impede conclusions about the dose of DBT needed to achieve these outcomes, this study is the only one reviewed to provide evidence that DBT can reduce hospitalizations and medical leaves from school in college students. This is a noteworthy finding as these outcomes may carry more weight with campus administrators relative to improvements in skills use or symptom reduction.

Finally, Chugani (2017) provides a clinical guide to adapting DBT for delivery in a CCC. This clinical practice paper describes the growth of a DBT program (originally reported in Chugani, Ghali, & Brunner, 2013) over time and provides a variety of practical suggestions (e.g., recommended inclusion and exclusion criteria), as well as recommendations for consideration related to program and team development, and adapting the standard DBT treatment model. As this paper does not present data, it is not reviewed further here, but we wish to direct readers wishing for a more practical guide to implementing DBT in CCCs to this paper, as well as two clinically focused chapters on DBT in CCCs in *The Oxford Handbook of Dialectical Behavior Therapy* (2018) and the forthcoming second edition of *Dialectical Behavior Therapy in Clinical Practice.*

Dialectical behavior therapy skills training groups in college counseling centers

Despite the efficacy of comprehensive DBT across settings, including one CCC study (Pistorello et al., 2012), comprehensive DBT (Linehan, 1993a) is a high-resource treatment. Limited staff and financial resources of CCCs coupled with practical needs for mental health service access in a population with documented growing needs (e.g., Benton, Robertson, Tseng, Newton, & Benton, 2003) make implementation of full model DBT difficult in CCCs. Given that several studies point to the value of DBT skills specifically and that group therapy has been put forward as a solution to the growing demands of CCCs (e.g., Smith et al., 2007), DBT group skills training (DBT-ST), without full integration of the other modes, represents a promising solution.

Empirically, prior studies of comprehensive DBT have found that skills training accounts for significant variance in symptom improvement, including suicidality and depression (Linehan et al., 2015; Neacsiu, Rizvi, & Linehan, 2010). Further, Neacsiu et al. (2014) used DBT-ST alone for transdiagnostic emotion dysregulation. While RCTs of DBT (e.g., Linehan et al., 1999, 2006; Linehan, Armstrong, Suarez, Allmon, & Heard, 1991) use a 24-week skills training schedule to teach skills in mindfulness, distress tolerance, emotional regulation, and interpersonal effectiveness (Linehan, 2015), repeated to yield 48 weeks of skills training, Neacsiu et al. (2014) used a shorter protocol of 16 weeks. The authors found that skills use mediated significant improvements in emotion dysregulation, further supporting the rationale for emphasizing the skills training mode of DBT. Further, Valentine, Bankoff, Poulin, Reidler, and Pantalone (2015) found 17 studies examining DBT-ST without other modes of DBT in a systematic review of the literature, with various clinical populations. Despite methodological limitations of the studies reviewed, the authors concluded studies provide preliminary support for use of DBT-ST alone. As such, there is empirical basis to argue that DBT skills alone may yield meaningful symptom improvement in a college population.

While decreasing the number of therapy modes offered eliminates some barriers to implementation in a college setting, the 16-week duration of college semesters is too short to allow for delivery of the standard

DBT model on which the majority of Linehan's original research was based (Linehan et al., 1991, 1999, 2006). Standard DBT uses a 24-week skills training schedule, in which each skill is taught two times over the course of 1 year of skills training. Therefore studies of DBT-ST in a college population have used abbreviated interventions designed to fit the semester schedule. These DBT-ST interventions fall into two broad categories: (1) those that offer a condensed version of a skills training group and include all four core skills training modules (mindfulness, distress tolerance, emotion regulation, and interpersonal effectiveness) and (2) those that offer skills from selected (but not all) modules. Here, we first review research related to DBT-ST providing all modules and next review research focused on delivering partial content from the DBT skills. Of note, while the following studies examining DBT-ST in CCCs reviewed do not provide comprehensive DBT, several studies use additional modes of DBT (e.g., phone coaching, therapist consultation team; Chugani et al., 2013; Panepinto, Uschold, Olandese, & Linn, 2015), though often not uniformly.

All skills modules

Five studies to date have examined the application of abbreviated forms of DBT-ST that include material from all modules, with two using open trials and three using comparison groups.

In an uncontrolled pilot trial, Meaney-Tavares and Hasking (2013) applied an abridged DBT-ST group to college students with BPD, who were also attending weekly individual therapy. The abbreviated skills group covered condensed material from all four DBT modules (mindfulness, emotion regulation, distress tolerance, and interpersonal effectiveness) over the course of eight 2-hour weekly group sessions. Authors did not note availability of other modes of DBT and adherence ratings were not used. Materials were modified to appeal to the college student demographic by tailoring skill complexity, language, and examples. The authors found that depression and BPD symptoms significantly decreased from pretreatment to posttreatment, while 4 of 18 coping skills measured significantly improved: solving problems, self-blame, constructive self-talk, and seeking professional help. Anxiety did not change significantly over treatment, though the authors note that this may be due to the cooccurrence of posttreatment assessment with the end of the semester, which is typically a stressful period for students.

Extending beyond students with BPD, Panepinto et al. (2015) used a 12-week skills training schedule with college students demonstrating coping skill deficits, suicidal ideation, NSSI, substance use, disordered eating, risky sexual practices, or impulsive behaviors. Groups included

3 consecutive weeks of mindfulness, followed by 3 weeks each of distress tolerance and emotion regulation, 2 weeks of interpersonal effectiveness, and 1 week of wrap-up, though groups were at times shortened in total length (range: 6–13 weeks), depending on the time required for group recruitment. Students were required to be in concurrent individual therapy (although not necessarily DBT individual therapy), in which therapists agreed to facilitate skills strengthening and generalization. Phone coaching was provided, and group therapists sat on a biweekly DBT consultation team; adherence coding was not rated. From pre- to posttreatment, participants demonstrated significant reductions in self-reported overall distress, intensity of distress, and number of symptoms, including improvements in depression, anxiety, interpersonal sensitivity, and somatization, though not hostility. Further, significant reductions in four core BPD problem areas: confusion about self, impulsivity, emotion dysregulation, and interpersonal chaos were observed.

Three studies have elaborated on these promising findings using comparison groups, with two using RCTs (Lin et al., 2018; Uliaszek, Rashid, Williams, & Gulamani, 2016) and one using nonrandomized design (Chugani et al., 2013). Chugani et al. (2013) implemented an 11-week DBT-ST group adjunctive to individual therapy as compared to a nonrandomized TAU individual therapy in a sample of emotionally dysregulated college students with cluster B traits or personality disorders. Students needed to be in individual therapy to access the group, and some individual therapists provided DBT-informed individual therapy and sat on a DBT consultation team, though students could also be referred by other therapists in the CCC who were not involved with the DBT program. Phone coaching was offered, though only during business hours, with some variation by individual therapist in terms of how and when coaching was offered in the service of honoring therapist limits. Group sessions were 90 minutes in length and consisted of 2 weeks of mindfulness, 5 weeks of integrated distress tolerance and emotion regulation, and 4 weeks of interpersonal effectiveness; adherence coding was not rated. Both treatment groups yielded significant reductions in self-reported emotion dysregulation over the course of treatment. From pre- to posttreatment, DBT yielded significant reductions in dysfunctional coping and significant increases DBT skills use, while no significant changes were observed in TAU. When treatments were directly compared, DBT yielded significantly greater improvements in coping skill use, with those in the DBT skills group reporting significantly less use of dysfunctional coping strategies and significantly more use of adaptive strategies than those in TAU. In addition, DBT-ST nearly reduced emotion dysregulation more than TAU.

Two RCTs have examined variants of DBT-ST in college students, compared to alternative group psychotherapies. Uliaszek et al. (2016)

implemented a 12-week DBT-ST group, with 3 consecutive weeks each of distress tolerance, emotion regulation, and interpersonal effectiveness skills, and 1 week of mindfulness skills preceding each other module. Fifty-four college students with a range of symptoms, including anxiety, depression, and BPD, were referred for a group targeting emotion dysregulation. Students were randomized to two 12-week psychotherapy groups: DBT-ST and positive psychotherapy (PPT), where PPT focused on increasing pleasant emotions, meaning, and engagement. Unlike other studies in this literature, authors specify that each 2-hour DBT group session comprised mindfulness practice, home practice review, training of new skills, and homework assignment, consistent with standard DBT-ST (Linehan, 1993b, 2015), though no adherence ratings were used. Concurrent individual treatment was allowed but not required, and no other modes of DBT were noted by authors. Symptom improvement was observed across time for both groups on measures of depression, anxiety, and BPD symptoms and core problem areas. Participants in both groups demonstrated significant improvements in emotion dysregulation, mindfulness skills, distress tolerance, and increased DBT skills use. PPT demonstrated mainly small effect sizes (i.e., effect sizes were in the small range on five of the nine outcomes, range: $d = 0.26-1.29$), with DBT demonstrating medium to large effect sizes ($d = 0.61-1.23$) on all outcomes except overall happiness ($d = 0.32$). Further, the DBT condition yielded significantly more life satisfaction, less dropout, and stronger therapeutic alliance than PPT.

In a more specific sample of depressed college students referred from the CCC with recent suicide attempts and BPD in Taiwan, Lin et al. (2018) compared DBT-ST to cognitive group therapy (CGT; adapted from Free, 2007), which emphasized training in cognition identification, monitoring, and reappraisal strategies. Eighty-two students were randomized to receive 8 weeks of either CGT or DBT-ST, each of which met weekly for 2 hours. All participants in both conditions engaged in monthly case management meetings with a psychologist. While all DBT skills modules were included, the number of weeks allocated to each was not specified, nor was the availability of other DBT modes, and no adherence ratings were used. Both groups were found to reduce suicide attempts and depression. Emotion regulation strategies, as measured by a questionnaire based on the emotion regulation process model (Gross, 1998), were observed to improve across time, both groups improving attentional deployment equally. CGT yielded superior results to DBT on reducing cognitive errors and increasing cognitive reappraisal. DBT yielded more acceptance, less suppression, and at follow-up, significantly less suicidal ideation and BPD symptoms.

Taken together, abbreviated DBT-ST that includes mindfulness, distress tolerance, emotion regulation, and interpersonal effectiveness skills can yield significant reductions in psychopathology, including BPD symptoms, suicidality, and emotion dysregulation, as well as improvements in adaptive skills use. Despite these operationalizations of DBT-ST lasting for 50% or less of the duration of the standard adult 24-week DBT-ST schedule (Linehan, 2015), meaningful improvements in symptoms and behavioral skills were observed. These three studies benefit from controlled and/or randomized conditions, though they are limited by lack of adherence ratings and follow-up data.

Specific skills modules

Given the limited resources of CCCs and time constraints of typical university semesters, investigators have also attempted to improve efficiency of DBT skills provision through decreasing the breath of content. Specifically, some studies have examined skills training in only one module or some but not all modules, while others have condensed the timeline further to just 4 weeks.

In an open trial within a CCC, Muhomba, Chugani, Uliaszek, and Kannan (2017) examined the effectiveness of a mindfulness and distress tolerance skills group in a sample of 22 students demonstrating three or more areas of dysregulation (emotion, cognitive, self, interpersonal, and behavioral) identified as germane to pervasive emotional dysregulation by Linehan (1993a). The group was 7–10 weeks in duration (duration depended on how long it took to fill groups), though each time it ran, all materials were taught despite lessened length. Three weeks were spent on mindfulness skills, with 4–7 weeks on distress tolerance skills, including both crisis survival and reality acceptance skills; no adherence ratings were used. Group participants demonstrated significant reductions in emotional dysregulation and dysfunctional coping, as well as significant increases in adaptive skills use.

Rizvi and Steffel (2014) examined emotion regulation skills with and without mindfulness training in emotionally dysregulated university students with the aim of investigating the extent to which mindfulness skills provided an additive benefit over emotion regulation skills alone. While services were performed in a university setting by doctoral students with referrals from the CCC, skills training group services were provided in the university-based psychology training clinic, not by the CCC. Twenty-four participants in this study were assigned to treatment conditions based on availability (i.e., not randomized) and received either 8 weeks of emotion regulation skills only or 2 weeks mindfulness skills followed by 6 weeks of emotion regulation; no adherence ratings were used. Both groups demonstrated significant reductions in self-reported emotion dysregulation, depression, anxiety, stress, negative affect, and functional impairment, and increases in positive affect. Both groups also reported significant increases in skills use, across DBT skills categories and specifically mindfulness. Students who received emotion regulation skills only noted significantly less stress at follow-up than those who also learned mindfulness skills.

Finally, Lee and Mason (2018) implemented the shortest intervention observed in this literature, at 4 weeks in duration, with one overarching content area (e.g., thought, emotions) per week. Further, content of the group was DBT-informed and adapted from Linehan's (2015) skills training manual, with the aim of increasing resilience. Thirty-seven university students presenting to the CCC with various mental health problems were referred for participation, with 18 of the referred students participating in DBT-informed skills training and the remaining students serving as a reference group. Ninety-minute groups each began with a mindfulness practice, followed by psychoeducation and discussion. Sequentially, group sessions were titled: mindfulness, thought as thought, emotion as emotion, and interpersonal effectiveness. Mindfulness (week 1) consisted of group orientation, mindfulness skills, sleep hygiene and relaxation. Thought as a thought (week 2) covered "building a life worth living, ways to increase positive emotions, pleasurable activities, life values and goals, observing and describing thoughts, [and] common thinking traps" (pp. 6). Emotion as emotion (week 3) taught functions of emotion, wise, mind, model of emotions, observing and describing emotions, and attended to primary versus secondary emotions. Interpersonal effectiveness (week 4) included content relevant to most of the DBT interpersonal effectiveness skills, including factors reducing interpersonal effectiveness, skills for objective, relationship and self-respect effectiveness, and clarifying goals in interpersonal situations. No adherence ratings were used and this activity would be difficult given that the skills protocol investigated is "DBT-informed" rather than consistent with the standard DBT protocol. Notably, in 4 weeks, significant improvements in self-reported resilience and global mental health were observed from pre- to posttreatment.

Summary: dialectical behavior therapy group skills training

The collective literature on DBT-ST in college samples is not without limitations. Samples were often small, with heavy reliance on self-report measures and only a few studies using therapist rating scales. Several studies lacked control groups and/or randomization, postintervention follow-up, and control of adjunctive treatment components, including other modes of DBT, was limited. Further, none of the studies reviewed included adherence ratings, limiting conclusions about DBT fidelity and attribution of outcomes to DBT-ST. These limitations make it difficult to confidently attribute observed outcomes to DBT-ST alone. Further, length and content of interventions varied, which make it difficult to draw conclusions about content-specific mechanisms of change and dose required for meaningful change.

Despite these limitations, DBT-ST studies in CCCs demonstrate that group skills training is feasible with and acceptable to college populations when delivered with or without adjunctive treatment. Further, given that populations varied from more severe with recent suicidal behavior (e.g., Lin et al., 2018) to transdiagnostic (e.g., Uliaszek et al., 2016), this literature suggests that DBT-ST can be helpful to a diverse range of students presenting for care at CCCs. However, more research is needed to elucidate which specific skills or skills training modules are most effective overall as well as for specific clinical populations within CCCs.

Other dialectical behavior therapy research with college students

While early research related to DBT in CCCs focused primarily on BPD, suicidality, and emotion dysregulation, more recent research has investigated applications of DBT skills for distinct populations, such as students with ADHD, adjustment, and those with test anxiety. Such research is important not only because it investigates novel applications of DBT but also because, on a practical level, when DBT is demonstrated to be effective for increasingly diverse student populations, the upfront investment of time and cost to learn the treatment model may be viewed as less problematic due to the increasingly broad applicability of the skills CCC clinicians will learn.

Üstündağ-Budak, Özeke-Kocabaş, and Ivanoff (2019) used an 8-week group with 14 Turkish university students. While authors do not specify if services were provided in a CCC or equivalent, Üstündağ-Budak et al. (2019) provided a two-phase skills training intervention in a nonclinical population, wherein students reported adjustment problems and were excluded if receiving medication or presenting with current mental health diagnosis. In the first phase ($n = 14$), which occurred during the fall semester, 8 weeks of 2-hour long group skills training groups were provided, which included 4 weeks of mindfulness, followed by 2 consecutive weeks each of interpersonal effectiveness and emotion regulation skills. In the second phase ($n = 10$), which occurred during the spring semester, follow-up skills training was offered over the course of 12 weeks, with three monthly in-person meetings, with each attending to one of the three modules: mindfulness, interpersonal effectiveness, and emotion regulation, with homework delivered electronically between meetings to reinforce learning. Participants reported significant reductions in composite depression, anxiety, and stress ratings following the initial skills intervention, with continued significant improvements during the follow-up intervention.

Lothes and Mochrie (2017) sought to investigate the effectiveness of DBT mindfulness skills (specifically, the "what" and "how" skills, followed by discussions about how these skills could be used specifically to reduce test anxiety) with 16 undergraduate college students who self-identified as experiencing text anxiety and self-selected into a study to reduce test anxiety through mindfulness. Students were next screened with a test anxiety inventory and only those with scores in the high range were enrolled. Participants received 6 weeks of DBT mindfulness skills training, with each group session lasting about 1 hour, and homework assignments being provided to encourage practice between sessions. An introduction to the content and pretest assessment was conducted prior to the 6-week intervention, and postassessment and a brief mindfulness practice was conducted after the final week of the intervention, for a total of 8 weeks of participant contact. Participants demonstrated significant reductions in test anxiety from pre- to postintervention. Mindfulness was also found to have a significant effect on decreasing overall test anxiety (including the test anxiety subdomains of emotionality and worry) overall anxiety, state anxiety, and trait anxiety.

Finally, Fleming, McMahon, Moran, Peterson, and Dreessen (2015) conducted a pilot randomized trial comparing 8 weeks of DBT-ST to skills handouts from a treatment manual for ADHD only over the 8-week intervention phase for 33 undergraduate students with ADHD. This study is described as having been conducted at an outpatient psychology clinic on campus, and thus it is not clear whether this was a CCC, a training clinic, or another type of campus clinic. The DBT intervention consisted of a selection of DBT skills assessed as having the highest relevance to ADHD and each group met for 90 minutes. Participants also received one 90-minute booster session during the first week of the following quarter to encourage maintenance of skills use. Students who received DBT showed greater treatment response rates, improvement on ADHD symptoms, executive functioning, and quality of life, when compared to those who received skills handouts only.

Future directions for dialectical behavior therapy with college students

The research reviewed here demonstrates the acceptability, feasibility, and effectiveness of DBT interventions for college students. It is also evident that one trend in this literature is a shift from focusing on use of DBT to treat students with high risk of suicide, BPD, NSSI, and/or serious emotion dysregulation, to use of DBT skills to assist students with a variety of more mild presenting concerns, such as need for building more healthy coping skills or test anxiety. As an example of this trend toward use of DBT skills as prevention or for delivery at the universal level, we note the recent publication of *Dialectical Behavior Therapy Skills Training for Emotional Problem Solving for Adolescents* or DBT STEPS-A (Mazza, Dexter-Mazza, Miller, Rathus, & Murphy, 2016), which provides a manualized protocol of 30 DBT skills lessons meant to be delivered by general education teachers to middle and high school students as universal mental health promotion. While only one study to date has evaluated the DBT STEPS-A protocol, preliminary findings are encouraging (Flynn, Joyce, Weihrauch, & Corcoran, 2018) and thus we believe it is likely that the trend of increasingly using DBT skills for mild issues as well as for prevention and health promotion will continue. As evidence of this, we also note the course currently being offered at the University of Washington entitled, "Wellness and Resilience for College and Beyond." This course, developed by Dr. James Mazza, is based on the teaching notes associated with his DBT STEPS-A manual and is heavily grounded in DBT skills as well as evidence-based skills from other similar therapies, including acceptance and commitment therapy (Hayes, Strosahl, & Wilson, 2012) and the field of positive psychology (Seligman, Steen, Park, & Peterson, 2005). At the time of this writing, it is considered to be one of the most popular elective courses on campus, with more than 900 students enrolling each year. While no research has yet been conducted examining the health outcomes of this course, such a project is currently underway and being led by this writer (CDC) in collaboration with Dr. Mazza.

The use of specific modules of DBT skills training in isolation (Muhomba et al., 2017; Rizvi & Steffel, 2014) also demonstrates a potential trend in this literature. Given the aforementioned difficulties with timing, resources, and substantial barriers to accessing mental health care (e.g., Eisenberg, Golberstein, & Gollust, 2007), offering isolated skills training modules CCCs may offer a feasible, efficient, and targeted opportunity for empirically supported care. While it is likely that all of the modules of DBT skills will be beneficial for treatment seeking college students, future research should investigate the extent to which specific skills modules may be used to target different types of presenting problems such that students receive a more time-limited and streamlined treatment approach with higher relevance to their presenting concerns (e.g., students with relationship problems may only need interpersonal effectiveness skills). Similar to the DBT literature more broadly, adaptations for DBT for CCCs would benefit from mechanistic studies to aid in determining the most effective methods to distill down the imperative components of resource-heavy comprehensive DBT. Given the variable and notably shorter doses of DBT observed in this literature, dosing studies would be beneficial to aid in efficient service provision.

Research on DBT in CCCs is expected to continue to grow, as there has been increased attention in recent years to emerging adulthood (e.g., Arnett, 2000), the developmental stage during which typical college attendance falls. Efforts are being made to apply DBT to the specific needs of emerging adults, as the standard adult and adolescent applications of DBT (Linehan, 1993a; Miller, Rathus, & Linehan, 2007) do not necessarily account for the unique needs of this stage of life. Preliminary examinations of DBT for 18–25 year-olds demonstrate promising results and may offer valuable lessons germane to DBT in CCCs regarding the importance of peers in skills training.

Lyng, Swales, Hastings, Millar, and Duffy (2019) found that a young adult only (ages 18–25) DBT skills group yielded better outcomes for BPD symptoms and general psychopathology than young adults who pursued DBT skills training in a varied age group (18 +). This finding highlights the value of on-campus DBT resources, where skills training groups are likely to be comprised peers, unlike community skills groups, often varied in age (18 +). These findings suggest possible advantages of CCC DBT groups to mixed age community DBT skills for college students and may provide helpful data to CCCs deciding whether to allocate resources to on-campus DBT or not.

In sum, we conclude that the future of DBT for college students is bright, and, whether DBT is offered through a CCC or via other means of delivery on campus, it is likely that research and implementation in this area will continue.

References

American College Health Association (AHCA). (2016). *American College Health Association—National College Health Assessment II: Reference Group Executive Summary Fall 2015*. Hanover, MD: American College Health Association.

Arnett, J. J. (2000). Emerging adulthood: A theory of development from the late teens through the twenties. *American Psychologist, 55*(5), 469–480.

Auerbach, R. P., Alonso, J., Axinn, W. G., Cuijpers, P., Ebert, D. D., Green, J. G., ... Bruffaerts, R. (2018). Mental disorders among college students in the World Health Organization World Mental Health Surveys. *Psychological Medicine, 46*(14), 2955–2970.

Benton, S. A., Robertson, J. M., Tseng, W.-C., Newton, F. B., & Benton, S. L. (2003). Changes in counseling center client problems across 13 years. *Professional Psychology: Research and Practice, 34*(1), 66–72. Available from https://doi.org/10.1037/0735-7028.34.1.66.

Chugani, C. D. (2017). Adapting dialectical behavior therapy for college counseling centers. *Journal of College Counseling, 20*(1), 67–80. Available from https://doi.org/10.1002/jocc.12059.

Chugani, C. D., Ghali, M. N., & Brunner, J. (2013). Effectiveness of short term dialectical behavior therapy skills training in college students with cluster B personality disorders.

Journal of College Student Psychotherapy, 27(4), 323–336. Available from https://doi.org/10.1080/87568225.2013.824337.

Chugani, C. D., & Landes, S. J. (2016). Dialectical behavior therapy in college counseling centers: Current trends and barriers to implementation. *Journal of College Student Psychotherapy, 30*(3), 176–186. Available from https://doi.org/10.1080/87568225.2016.1177429.

Eisenberg, D., Golberstein, E., & Gollust, S. E. (2007). Help-seeking and access to mental health care in a university student population. *Medical Care, 45*(7), 594–601. Available from https://doi.org/10.1097/MLR.0b013e31803bb4c1.

Engle, E., Gadischkie, S., Roy, N., & Nunziato, D. (2013). Dialectical behavior therapy for a college population: Applications at Sarah Lawrence College and beyond. *Journal of College Student Psychotherapy, 27*(1), 11–30. Available from https://doi.org/10.1080/87568225.2013.739014.

Fleming, A. P., McMahon, R. J., Moran, L. R., Peterson, A. P., & Dreessen, A. (2015). Pilot randomized controlled trial of dialectical behavior therapy group skills training for ADHD among college students. *Journal of Attention Disorders, 19*(3), 260–271. Available from https://doi.org/10.1177/1087054714535951.

Flynn, D., Joyce, M., Weihrauch, M., & Corcoran, P. (2018). Innovations in practice: Dialectical behaviour therapy – Skills training for emotional problem solving for adolescents (DBT STEPS-A): Evaluation of a pilot implementation in Irish post-primary schools. *Child and Adolescent Mental Health, 23*(4), 376–380. Available from https://doi.org/10.1111/camh.12284.

Free, M. L. (2007). *Cognitive therapy in groups: Guidelines and resources for practice* (*2nd ed.*). New York: John Wiley & Sons Ltd.

Gallagher, R. (2014). *National survey of college counseling centers 2014*. Retrieved from <http://d-scholarship.pitt.edu/28178/1/survey_2014.pdf>.

Gross, J. J. (1998). The emerging field of emotion regulation: An integrative review. *Review of General Psychology, 2*(3), 271–299. Available from https://doi.org/10.1037/1089-2680.2.3.271.

Hayes, S. C., Strosahl, K. D., & Wilson, K. G. (2012). *Acceptance commitment therapy: The process and practice of mindful change* (2nd ed.). New York: The Guilford Press.

Iverson, K., Shenk, C., & Fruzzetti, A. (2009). Dialectical behavior therapy for women victims of domestic abuse: A pilot study. *Professional Psychology: Research and Practice, 40*, 242–248.

Lee, S., & Mason, M. (2018). Effectiveness of brief DBT-informed group therapy on psychological resilience: A preliminary naturalistic study. *Journal of College Student Psychotherapy, 33*(1), 25–37. Available from https://doi.org/10.1080/87568225.2018.1425646.

Lin, T.-J., Ko, H.-C., Wu, J. Y.-W., Oei, T. P., Lane, H.-Y., & Chen, C.-H. (2018). The effectiveness of dialectical behavior therapy skills training group vs. cognitive therapy group on reducing depression and suicide attempts for borderline personality disorder in Taiwan. *Archives of Suicide Research, 23*(1), 82–99. Available from https://doi.org/10.1080/13811118.2018.1436104.

Linehan, M. M. (1993a). *Cognitive-behavioral treatment of borderline personality disorder*. New York: Guildford Press.

Linehan, M. M. (1993b). *Skills training manual for treating borderline personality disorder*. New York: Guilford Press.

Linehan, M. M. (2015). *DBT® skills training manual* (2nd ed.). New York: The Guilford Press.

Linehan, M. M., Armstrong, H. E., Suarez, A., Allmon, D., & Heard, H. L. (1991). Cognitive-behavioral treatment of chronically parasuicidal borderline patients. *JAMA Psychiatry, 48*(12), 1060–1064. Available from https://doi.org/10.1001/archpsyc.1991.01810360024003.

Linehan, M. M., Comtois, K. A., Murray, A. M., Brown, M. Z., Gallop, R. J., Heard, H. L., ... Lindenboim, N. (2006). Two-year randomized controlled trial and follow-up of dialectical behavior therapy vs therapy by experts for suicidal behaviors and borderline personality disorder. *Archives of General Psychiatry*, *63*(7), 757–766. Available from https://doi.org/10.1001/archpsyc.63.7.757.

Linehan, M. M., Korslund, K. E., Harned, M. S., Gallop, R. J., Lungu, A., Neacsiu, A. D., ... Murray-Gregory, A. M. (2015). Dialectical behavior therapy for high suicide risk in individuals with borderline personality disorder: A randomized clinical trial and component analysis. *JAMA Psychiatry*, *72*(5), 475–482. Available from https://doi.org/10.1001/jamapsychiatry.2014.3039.

Linehan, M. M., Schmidt, H., Dimeff, L. A., Craft, J. C., Kanter, J., & Comtois, K. A. (1999). Dialectical behavior therapy for patients with borderline personality disorder and drug-dependence. *The American Journal on Addictions*, *8*(4), 279–292. Available from https://doi.org/10.1080/105504999305686.

Lothes, J. E., II, & Mochrie, K. (2017). The "what" and "hows" of mindfulness: using DBT's mindfulness skills to reduce test anxiety. *Building Healthy Academic Communities Journal*, *1*(2), 10–20. Available from https://doi.org/10.18061/bhac.v1i2.6029.

Lyng, J., Swales, M. A., Hastings, R. P., Millar, T., & Duffy, D. J. (2019). Outcomes for 18 to 25-year-olds with borderline personality disorder in a dedicated young adult only DBT programme compared to a general adult DBT programme for all ages 18+. *Early Intervention Psychiatry*, *0*(0). Available from https://doi.org/10.1111/eip.12808.

Mazza, J., Dexter-Mazza, E., Miller, A., Rathus, J., & Murphy, H. (2016). *DBT skills in schools: Skills training for emotional problem solving for adolescents (DBT STEPS-A)*. New York: Guilford Press.

Meaney-Tavares, R., & Hasking, P. (2013). Coping and regulating emotions: A pilot study of a modified dialectical behavior therapy group delivered in a college counseling service. *Journal of American College Health*, *61*(5), 303–309. Available from https://doi.org/10.1080/07448481.2013.791827.

Miller, A. L., Rathus, J. H., & Linehan, M. (2007). *Dialectical behavior therapy with suicidal adolescents*. New York: Guilford Press.

Muhomba, M., Chugani, C. D., Uliaszek, A. A., & Kannan, D. (2017). Distress tolerance skills for college students: A pilot investigation of a brief DBT group skills training program. *Journal of College Student Psychotherapy*, *31*(3), 247–256. Available from https://doi.org/10.1080/87568225.2017.1294469.

Neacsiu, A. D., Eberle, J. W., Kramer, R., Wiesmann, T., & Linehan, M. M. (2014). Dialectical behavior therapy skills for transdiagnostic emotion dysregulation: A pilot randomized controlled trial. *Behaviour Research and Therapy*, *59*, 40–51. Available from https://doi.org/10.1016/j.brat.2014.05.005.

Neacsiu, A. D., Rizvi, S. L., & Linehan, M. M. (2010). Dialectical behavior therapy skills use as a mediator and outcome of treatment for borderline personality disorder. *Behaviour Research and Therapy*, *48*(9), 832–839. Available from https://doi.org/10.1016/j.brat.2010.05.017.

Panepinto, A. R., Uschold, C. C., Olandese, M., & Linn, B. K. (2015). Beyond borderline personality disorder: Dialectical behavior therapy in a college counseling center. *Journal of College Student Psychotherapy*, *29*(3), 211–226. Available from https://doi.org/10.1080/87568225.2015.1045782.

Pistorello, J., Fruzzetti, A., MacLane, C., Gallop, R., & Iverson, K. (2012). Dialectical behavior therapy (DBT) applied to college students: A randomized clinical trial. *Journal of Consulting and Clinical Psychology*, *80*(6), 982–994.

Reetz, D., Krylowicz, B., Bershad, C., Lawrence, J., & Mistler, B. (2015). *The association for university and college counseling directors annual survey*. Retrieved from <https://www.aucccd.org/assets/documents/Governance/2017%20aucccd%20survey-public-apr26.pdf>.

Rizvi, S. L., & Steffel, L. M. (2014). A pilot study of 2 brief forms of dialectical behavior therapy skills training for emotion dysregulation in college students. *Journal of American College Health*, *62*(6), 434–439. Available from https://doi.org/10.1080/07448481.2014.907298.

Seligman, M. E. P., Steen, T. A., Park, N., & Peterson, C. (2005). Positive psychology progress: Empirical validation of interventions. *American Psychologist, 60*(5), 410–421. Available from https://doi.org/10.1037/0003-066X.60.5.410.

Smith, T. B., Dean, B., Floyd, S., Silva, C., Yamashita, M., Durtschi, J., & Heaps, R. A. (2007). Pressing issues in college counseling: A survey of American College Counseling Association members. *Journal of College Counseling, 10*(1), 64–78. Available from https://doi.org/10.1002/j.2161-1882.2007.tb00007.x.

Turner, J., Leno, E., & Keller, A. (2013). Causes of mortality among American college students: A pilot study. *Journal of College Student Psychotherapy, 27*(1), 31–42.

Uliaszek, A. A., Rashid, T., Williams, G. E., & Gulamani, T. (2016). Group therapy for university students: A randomized control trial of dialectical behavior therapy and positive psychotherapy. *Behaviour Research and Therapy, 77*, 78–85. Available from https://doi.org/10.1016/j.brat.2015.12.003.

Üstündağ-Budak, A. M., Özeke-Kocabaş, E., & Ivanoff, A. (2019). Dialectical behaviour therapy skills training to improve Turkish college students' psychological well-being: A pilot feasibility study. *International Journal for the Advancement of Counselling*, 1–18. Available from https://doi.org/10.1007/s10447-019-09379-5.

Valentine, S. E., Bankoff, S. M., Poulin, R. M., Reidler, E. B., & Pantalone, D. W. (2015). The use of dialectical behavior therapy skills training as stand-alone treatment: A systematic review of the treatment outcome literature. *Journal of Clinical Psychology, 71*(1), 1–20. Available from https://doi.org/10.1002/jclp.22114.

Zivin, K., Eisenberg, D., Gollust, S., & Golberstein, E. (2009). Persistence of mental health problems and needs in a college student population. *Journal of Affective Disorders, 117*(3), 180–185.

Further reading

Dimeff, L. A., & Koerner, K. (Eds.). (in press). *Dialectical behavior therapy in clinical practice* (2nd ed.). New York: The Guildford Press.

Swales, M. A. (Ed.), (2018). *The Oxford handbook of dialectical behavior therapy*. Oxford, UK: Oxford University Press.

CHAPTER

12

Dialectical behavior therapy research and program evaluation in the Department of Veterans Affairs

Sara J. Landes[1,2], *Suzanne E. Decker*[3,4], *Sacha A. McBain*[1,2], *Marianne Goodman*[5,6], *Brandy N. Smith*[7], *Sarah R. Sullivan*[5], *Angela Page Spears*[5] *and Laura L. Meyers*[8]

[1]Central Arkansas Veterans Healthcare System, Little Rock, AR, United States, [2]University of Arkansas for Medical Sciences, Little Rock, AR, United States, [3]VA Connecticut Health Care System, West Haven, CT, United States, [4]Yale School of Medicine, New Haven, CT, United States, [5]James J. Peters Veterans Administration Medical Center, The Bronx, NY, United States, [6]Icahn School of Medicine at Mount Sinai, New York, NY, United States, [7]VA Palo Alto Veterans Health Care System, Menlo Park, CA, United States, [8]Orlando VA Medical Center, Orlando, FL, United States

Introduction

The Department of Veterans Affairs (VA) Veterans Health Administration is the nation's largest integrated health-care system and it serves more than 9 million veterans annually. The VA is divided into 18 networks of care that are referred to as Veteran Integrated Service Networks (VISNs). Each VISN includes several VA medical center

The Handbook of Dialectical Behavior Therapy
DOI: https://doi.org/10.1016/B978-0-12-816384-9.00012-9

facilities. These facilities include large medical hospital campuses as well as satellite community–based outpatient clinics that offer fewer and less intensive services (e.g., primary care).

Within VA facilities, a number of mental health options are available. This usually includes a general mental health clinic and specialty clinics to treat diagnoses such as posttraumatic stress disorder (PTSD) and substance use disorders. VA also offers support for military sexual trauma; this care is often housed within the PTSD clinic. Given the variety of mental health clinics available at the VA, dialectical behavioral therapy (DBT) programs or components are offered in different services, such as one of the clinics listed previously. Some departments have created cross-clinic programs to increase access to DBT (Landes, Rodriguez, et al., 2017).

DBT is associated with reduced suicide attempt and nonsuicidal self-directed violence in metaanalyses (DeCou, Comtois, & Landes, 2019). This makes it a potentially attractive option for VA treatment providers given the increase in suicide among veterans and the greater suicide risk among veterans relative to nonveteran adults (Office of Mental Health and Suicide Prevention & Department of Veterans Affairs, 2018). DBT also directly targets emotion regulation skills, which have been identified as a key component of effective treatments for reducing suicide attempt (Rudd, Williams, & Trotter, 2008). The clinical practice guidelines for the assessment and management of patients at risk for suicide, published by the Department of Veterans Affairs (VA) and Department of Defense (2019), identify DBT as an evidence-based psychotherapy (EBP) for individuals with borderline personality disorder and recent self-directed violence. Beyond its utility in reducing suicide attempt and nonsuicidal self-directed violence, DBT may also be indicated for treating complex trauma in veterans (Landes, Garovoy, & Burkman, 2013), and new studies have examined DBT for treating PTSD in individuals who might not be candidates for other evidence-based PTSD therapies due to suicide attempt or nonsuicidal self-directed violence (Harned, Korslund, & Linehan, 2014), borderline personality disorder symptoms (Meyers et al., 2017), or treatment-resistant PTSD with cooccurring mental health disorder or borderline personality disorder features (Bohus et al., 2013).

While DBT is endorsed as an EBP, it has not been rolled out nationally in the VA with training, consultation, and other resources. Despite this, DBT can be found at multiple VAs across the country (Landes et al., 2016). A DBT virtual community of practice was created to provide a repository for resources, a platform for discussion among clinicians doing DBT, and to facilitate referrals through a list of sites offering DBT (Landes, Smith, & Weingardt, 2019). According to the list of sites offering components of DBT, as of May 2019, 34 sites offered full programs, 36 sites offered skills group only, and 10 sites offered a combination of DBT components (e.g., skills group and individual).

Dialectical behavioral therapy efficacy research in Department of Veterans Affairs

Efficacy of dialectical behavioral therapy for female veterans with BPD

Research supporting the use of DBT in a VA setting has been explored over the past 18 years. One of the first efficacy trials of DBT conducted independent of treatment developer Marsha Linehan was conducted by Koons et al. (2001) with a sample of female veterans ($N = 20$) diagnosed with borderline personality disorder (BPD). Koons et al. (2001) compared a 6-month course of standard DBT to treatment as usual (TAU). Standard DBT included weekly individual therapy, weekly skills group, weekly therapist consultation team, and phone coaching as needed. Two-way repeated measures ANOVAs were run on all outcome variables to determine significant differences pre/posttreatment and between groups. Veterans in the DBT group experienced a greater statistically significant decrease in suicidal ideation (SI), hopelessness, depression, and anger compared to TAU. The DBT group showed a significant improvement across the three time points in parasuicides and dissociation, but these differences were not statistically significant when compared to TAU.

Jacobson and Truax's (1991) Reliable Change Index (RCI) method was additionally used by Koons et al. (2001) to evaluate clinically significant and reliable changes in outcomes among both groups. This statistic explored if there was clinically significant change in individual's scores pre/post in DBT, as well as if these changes were statistically significant. Three times as many patients in DBT (e.g., 60% of DBT patients and 20% of TAU patients) reported a clinically and statistically significant decrease in SI. Seventy percent of DBT patients and 20% of TAU patients reported a clinically and statistically significant decrease in hopelessness. Lastly, twice as many DBT patients (80%) demonstrated clinically, but not statistically, significant changes in dissociation compared to TAU (40%). Overall, results from Koons et al. (2001) suggest that DBT is an effective treatment for female veterans with BPD.

Efficacy of dialectical behavioral therapy for veterans at high risk of suicide

While providing valuable information about the efficacy of DBT within a specific population of veterans, Koons et al.'s (2001) study represented a small proportion of veterans with unclear generalizability to other veteran populations. In addition, little DBT research was conducted within the VA in the years following this study. In the context of recent high rates of suicide among veterans and limited knowledge of effective suicide treatments within this population, Goodman et al. (2016) conducted a DBT efficacy trial to assess the effectiveness of a 6-month course of standard DBT compared to TAU with a transdiagnostic population of veterans at high risk of suicide ($N = 91$). Adherence to DBT was monitored by review of individual session tapes by members of Dr. Linehan's research team. Goodman et al.'s (2016) study was the first DBT efficacy trial within VA to include male veterans, which is especially notable as males represented the majority of the sample (67%).

Results from this study concluded that participants in DBT and TAU improved across outcomes of SI, depression, and hopelessness with no statistically significant difference between treatment arms. While both DBT and TAU improved, changes between groups were not significantly different. However, a post hoc analysis noted a statistically significant difference of 6 months in improvement in anxiety between DBT compared to TAU with DBT patients showing significantly more improvement. Survival analyses using Fisher's exact test for suicide attempts (DBT 3/46; TAU 5/45) and hospitalizations (about 35% in both groups) did not differ between treatment arms. However, veterans who received DBT ($M = 28.5$; $SD = 19.6$) utilized significantly more individual mental health services compared to TAU ($M = 14.7$; $SD = 10.9$).

Goodman et al.'s (2016) findings were consistent with the literature regarding the efficacy of DBT in improving SI and depression. Nevertheless, while studies of DBT in civilian women suggest DBT is superior to TAU, Goodman et al. (2016) in contrast found there was no significant difference between DBT and TAU. The lack of significantly larger improvements among veterans receiving DBT compared to TAU was hypothesized to be related to several aspects of this population. The VA possesses unique contextual factors, unlike other health-care settings, that may contribute to differences in DBT efficacy trials. Unlike many efficacy trials, the highly structured and robust nature of the existing TAU services available within VA (e.g., suicide prevention coordinators, 24-hour hotline services, mandated treatment monitoring for those at high risk) used for comparison within the study may have been more effective than traditional TAU conditions. Further, Goodman et al. adapted DBT by utilizing VA suicide-screening measures and lowering the threshold for psychiatric admission, to be consistent with VA policy, which may have impacted the efficacy of DBT in a VA context. The population served by VA, include patients with higher rates of homelessness, comorbid medical illnesses, substance use, and combat-related PTSD, which may further impact efficacy of DBT when compared to civilian populations.

Given Goodman et al.'s (2016) findings that veterans may respond equally to DBT and TAU, Stich (2017) sought to examine the patient-related predictors of DBT treatment success to inform treatment selection for veterans at high risk of suicide utilizing the same data set. The Beck Anxiety Inventory (BAI) and Beck Depression Inventory (BDI) were used to explore these outcomes in Goodman et al.'s (2016) original paper. Twenty-nine veterans who completed the DBT arm of the original study were further analyzed. Two regression models were run (one for BAI and one for BDI) with predictive variables indicating demographics, number of suicide attempts, baseline BAI and BDI scores, and combat exposure.

Veterans with greater suicidality (i.e., greater number of suicide attempts) and higher levels of education were most likely to experience reductions in anxiety due to DBT. Goodman et al. (2016) had hypothesized that the presence of combat-related PTSD may have compromised the efficacy of DBT within a VA population in comparison to civilian DBT trials. However, contrary to Goodman et al.'s (2016) hypothesis, Stich (2017) found that greater combat exposure was predictive of reductions in depressive symptoms due to DBT. Stich's (2017) findings suggest DBT may be well suited to the population's unique experience of combat and the resulting depressive reactions associated with this type of trauma exposure. Stich (2017) further hypothesized that this positive finding may be attributable to a lessening of moral injury (i.e., the guilt and shame associated with war-related activities such as combat and killing). While the construct of moral injury was not directly assessed in the current study, the emotional experience of moral injury is particularly negative and painful. If DBT were to prove effective for this type of injury in future studies, it would be a valuable contribution to lessen the burden of veterans with moral injury.

Adaptations of dialectical behavioral therapy skills group

Within VA, the majority of sites that offer components of DBT offer DBT skills group only (Landes, Rodriguez, et al., 2017). In addition, the majority of VA clinics that offer DBT do not systematically evaluate treatment outcomes, as they are not resourced for significant program evaluation. However, a few sites and researchers have collected outcomes. These outcomes are described here.

Dialectical behavioral therapy skills group for transdiagnostic sample

Dismantling trial data from DBT's developer (Linehan et al., 2015) suggests that DBT skills group, with rigorous safety planning, may be as effective as comprehensive DBT in reducing suicide attempt and nonsuicidal self-directed violence. In other controlled trials, DBT skills group was associated with reduction in SI (Soler et al., 2009), suicide attempt and nonsuicidal self-directed violence (McMain, Guimond, Barnhart, Habinski, & Streiner, 2017), and emotion dysregulation (McMain et al., 2017; Neacsiu, Eberle, Kramer, Wiesmann, & Linehan, 2014). DBT skills group has the added benefit of being less resource-intensive than comprehensive DBT and potentially efficacious in transdiagnostic samples beyond those diagnosed with borderline personality disorder (Neacsiu et al., 2014).

To test the feasibility, acceptability, and preliminary efficacy of 26-week DBT skills group for a transdiagnostic sample of veterans with emotion dysregulation and suicide risk factors, Decker et al. (2019) recruited 17 veterans with SI in the past 3 months (Suicidal Behaviors Questionnaire; Addis & Linehan, 1989) and emotion dysregulation (Difficulties in Emotion Regulation Scale; Gratz & Roemer, 2004) who were receiving some form of VA mental health care and willing to participate in safety planning using a six-step safety plan (Stanley & Brown, 2012). The open trial was reviewed and approved by the local institutional review board. Veterans with psychotic disorder, bipolar I, antisocial personality disorder, or thought disorder were excluded. Skills trainers were the lead author and advanced psychology trainees. All trainers participated in weekly 60-minute skills trainer peer consultation team supervision using the DBT structured peer consultation team meeting format (Linehan, 1993).

The trial sample included 11 men (65% of the sample) and 6 women (35% of the sample) and was largely Caucasian (76%). Mental health diagnoses included major depressive disorder (71%), PTSD (47%), and substance use disorder (29%). The intervention was feasible, in that 76% of participants completed the group (i.e., missed no more than three consecutive sessions). Participants and their primary mental health providers rated the treatment as highly acceptable (above 5.0 on a 7-point Likert-type scale created for the study) at mid-treatment, posttreatment, and 3-month follow-up. In paired sample *t*-tests adjusted for multiple comparisons, SI reduced significantly on the Suicidal Behaviors Questionnaire at mid-, post-, and 3-month follow-up ($d = 1.30$, 1.88, and 2.08, respectively, all $P < .01$) and on the Beck Scale for SI (Beck, Steer, & Rainieri, 1988) at posttreatment and follow-up ($d = 1.63$, 1.90, both $P < .05$). Emotion dysregulation reduced significantly at all three time points ($d = 2.06$, 2.75, and 2.59, respectively, all $P < .01$). Skillful coping on the DBT Ways of Coping Checklist (Neacsiu, Rizvi, Vitaliano, Lynch, & Linehan, 2010) increased at posttreatment ($d = 0.85$) and gains were maintained at follow-up ($d = 0.91$), although unskillful coping did not change significantly until 3-month follow-up ($d = 0.78$; all $P < .02$). There were no suicide attempts or deaths during the trial.

Authors concluded that although data from this small open trial must be interpreted with caution, they suggest DBT skills groups with safety planning are feasible and acceptable to veterans with emotion dysregulation and suicide risk factors and show promise for reducing SI and emotion dysregulation, while boosting coping skills. Data provide preliminary support for extending the study of DBT skills groups to veterans experiencing emotion dysregulation across several mental health diagnostic categories, rather than limiting its study to those with borderline personality disorder. The intervention's high feasibility and acceptability to participants and providers also indicate support for further testing and examination of DBT skills groups with safety planning at VA.

Dialectical behavioral therapy skills group for depression

Nappi, Ferriter, Campos, Wilkins, and Davis (2012) conducted an open-label DBT skills group with rolling enrollment within VA to examine efficacy and acceptability within a sample of veterans diagnosed with clinical depression. Veterans were eligible if they were seeking services for depression and did not have a current substance use disorder or psychotic symptoms. Data were collected from 31 participants. Participants were predominantly male (84%), Caucasian (77%), and their ages ranged from 23 to 64 years ($M = 46.2 \pm 12.4$). Of those participants, 71% completed the 22 session DBT skills group, which occurred weekly for 2 hours. Mindfulness, emotion regulation, interpersonal effectiveness, and distress tolerance were skills covered in the group. Self-report measures included the BDI-II (Beck, Steer, & Brown, 1996), Quality of Life Enjoyment and Satisfaction Questionnaire (Endicott, Nee, Harrison, & Blumenthal, 1993), and the Client Satisfaction Questionnaire (Attkisson & Zwick, 1982) for treatment acceptability.

Results seem promising as depression decreased on average by 9.7 points. Quality of life had a pretreatment score averaging 2.9 (i.e., poor to fair); posttreatment scores increased to an average of 3.6 (i.e., fair to good). The average treatment acceptability score was 30.1 (range 23–32), suggesting high accessibility as the maximum score is 32. Although the sample size was small which compromises the power, the findings indicate that veterans' depression significantly reduced following the DBT skills group. In addition, veterans were satisfied with the group, which was evidenced not only by the Client Satisfaction Questionnaire but also qualitative data (e.g., "I am incredibly grateful for this experience. It has been most helpful"). Nappi et al. noted that future directions include a larger sample, evaluating DBT skills with a PTSD sample, and exploration of mediators (e.g., mindfulness) on treatment outcomes.

Drop-in dialectical behavioral therapy distress tolerance group

Denckla, Bailey, Jackson, Tatarakis, and Chen (2015) had a comprehensive DBT program in a VA setting and noted that many veterans at high risk for suicide were not engaging in comprehensive DBT. To offer the benefits of DBT skills training to these high-risk veterans, and to offer a same-day resource for care, the authors developed a drop-in DBT skills group.

This group was a 55-minute skills training with each session focused on one of four distress tolerance skills: ACCEPTS, IMPROVE, self-soothe, or pros and cons. Like a traditional DBT skills group, the drop-in group was taught by two group coleaders and focused on skills learning rather than group process. The drop-in group was distinct from standard DBT skills groups in several ways: (1) veterans could attend this drop-in group without making any commitment to treatment, and thus there was no "four-miss rule"; (2) no between-group assignments or homework was assigned or reviewed; (3) the duration of group (55 minutes) was substantially shorter than the typical 120–180 minute sessions, and (4) the group focused only on four skills from the distress tolerance module.

To evaluate the drop-in group, Denckla et al. conducted chart review for 65 veterans who attended. They identified eight (12.3%) veterans who attended eight or more drop-in sessions over a 1-year period and had at least one suicide-related crisis event (i.e., suicide-related emergency room visit; suicide-related psychiatric admission; suicide attempt) in the year prior to drop-in group. The study sample included eight male veterans of mean age 54 ($SD = 9.7$) who were predominantly African-American ($n = 4$, 50%). The sample was transdiagnostic, including veterans with mood disorder/episode ($n = 4$, 50%), schizophrenia or other psychotic disorder ($n = 2$, 25%), adjustment disorder ($n = 1$, 12.5%), or PTSD ($n = 1$, 12.5%). At baseline the veterans had a range of 1–9 crisis events. A paired samples t-test was used to compare occurrence of crisis events in the year prior to and after starting drop-in group. There was a significant reduction in crisis events (pre–post $d = 1.06$). While the authors noted that results should be interpreted with caution, these data provide preliminary support for a drop-in adaptation of DBT skills for a particularly high-risk and difficult-to-engage sample in VA settings.

Affirmative dialectical behavioral therapy skills training for emotion dysregulation and minority stress

Cohen and Yadavaia developed another DBT skills group adaptation to address minority stress in sexual minority veterans. Minority stress, such as the stress of concealing one's identity under the former "Don't Ask, Don't Tell" policy, has been associated with increased depression or PTSD in sexual minority veterans (Cochran, Balsam, Flentje, Malte, & Simpson, 2013). Following recommendations from the American Psychological Association (2012) to adapt evidence-based interventions to meet the needs of sexual minority individuals, Cohen and Yadavaia (2017) adapted DBT skills group to address emotion dysregulation and minority stress in sexual minority veterans.

The resulting 10-session, 90-minute "Affirmative DBT Skills Training" group included new teaching handouts on minority stress, identified how "Don't Ask, Don't Tell" created an invalidating environment, and emphasized the dialectic of accepting that discrimination exists and engaging in social advocacy to increase fairness and equity (see Table 12.1 for content and Cohen & Newman, 2019 for clinical examples).

Authors conducted a pilot test of the intervention with four veterans (two male and two female) with anxiety and/or depression. Two identified as lesbian, one as gay, and one as bisexual. Veterans were middle-aged ($M = 51.0$, $SD = 17.8$). All veterans were receiving ongoing mental health care at VA. There was a statistically significant reduction in emotion dysregulation ($P = .02$, delta $= 19.6$). Changes were also reported in anxiety, depression, rejection sensitivity, internalized stigma, and concealment, although significance testing was not reported. Authors concluded that the approach had preliminary support and more study is indicated.

TABLE 12.1 Content of affirmative dialectical behavioral therapy skills training.

Week	Content
1	Minority stress/wise mind
2	Mindfulness what and how skills
3	Model of emotions
4	Check the facts
5	Opposite action
6	Problem solving
7	Accumulating positive emotions—short-term
8	Accumulating positive emotions—long-term
9	PLEASE
10	Mindfulness of current emotion

Dialectical behavioral therapy for BPD and PTSD

Past research has noted a large overlap between PTSD and BPD. Specifically, 76% of combat veterans with BPD also meet criteria for PTSD (Southwick, Yehuda, & Giller, 1993). Trauma-focused therapy (TFT) is a first-line intervention according to VA treatment guidelines. However, due to the comorbid diagnosis of BPD, many veterans with PTSD are excluded from TFT because clinicians and researchers often fear that patients would be unable to tolerate these treatments and TFT may have negative outcomes such as increased risk of suicide and/or self-harm (Becker, Zayfert, & Anderson, 2004; Feeny, Zoellner, & Foa, 2002).

Given research by Harned et al. (2014) that PTSD can be effectively treated through integration of DBT and prolonged exposure (PE) and the VA's emphasis on the paramount importance of the treatment of PTSD, VA clinicians created a 12-week intensive outpatient program that combined DBT with PE (Meyers et al., 2017) for veterans who were unable to complete TFT without integration of DBT skills. The program included weekly individual DBT and three DBT skills groups so that all skills were covered twice. PE began in Week 2 and included twice weekly 90-minute individual PE sessions. Other treatment components included a weekly mindfulness practice in groups, two community outings, two community meetings, and an interpersonal skills practice group. Community outings served the function of behavioral activation and engagement in enjoyable activities (i.e., Enjoying Live group) and in vivo exposure (i.e., Facing Life group). The program offered unstaffed (nontherapeutic) lodging for veterans who lived too far from a VA that provided DBT.

Meyers et al. (2017) conducted program evaluation of this 12-week intensive outpatient program combining DBT and PE. The targeted sample was those excluded from outpatient TFT or those who previously dropped out of TFT. Of the 33 veterans enrolled, 22 successfully completed the program and no dropouts occurred during the PE therapy portion of the program. To further examine completers versus noncompleters, a comparison of baseline assessment data and demographic data found no significant differences between the two groups. Meyers et al. examined pre- and postdifferences in the 22 program completers. The RCI was used to analyze if any data had clinically significant and reliable change. A majority of veterans (90.9%) experienced a reliable reduction in symptoms. In addition, 63.6% of completers no longer met the criterion for PTSD (i.e., had less than a score of 50 on the PTSD Checklist List; Weathers, Litz, Herman, Huska, & Keane, 1993) at posttreatment.

These pilot results are evidence that cooccurring PTSD and BPD can be safely and effectively treated in intensive outpatient settings, and it is the first demonstration of the DBT–PE protocol within VA settings. This data is especially encouraging as the sample included veterans who previously had been excluded or had dropped out of TFT, and no veterans dropped out during PE. Given the VA's emphasis on the importance of the treatment of PTSD, this initial study provides promising evidence that PTSD can be treated among high-risk populations. Meyers et al. note limitations of a small sample with only one arm. Future directions may include a randomized controlled trial where long-term efficacy can also be examined.

Cost of dialectical behavioral therapy

Little has been published on the cost-effectiveness of DBT. Some studies in the United Kingdom found the cost of DBT was higher, but not significantly when compared to TAU (Priebe et al., 2012). However, another study by Amner compared pre-and posttreatment service cots with 1 year of DBT and found £36,000 savings by the end of post year (Amner, 2012). Research on the cost-effectiveness of DBT in VA may help those considering implementation of this treatment.

Meyers, Landes, and Thuras (2014) evaluated the service utilization and associated costs of DBT for male and female veterans with symptoms of BPD. Using data from an existing full DBT program in VA, this program evaluation included veterans who had completed at least 6 months of DBT. Of the 41 participants, 54% were male and the average age was 47.1. Diagnoses included depression or dysthymia (100% of participants), PTSD (81%), substance abuse (70%), and personality disorder (95%). The evaluation compared the use of physical and mental health services during the year prior and the year following DBT. Pre- and post-DBT treatment costs were analyzed using cost data on mental health, emergency department, and primary care appointments.

Results showed a significant decrease in mental health services usage; the average number of mental health visits in the year before DBT was 92.8 and it was reduced to an average of 48.2 visits in the year after DBT. Psychiatric hospitalization admissions were significantly reduced by half (34.1% pre, 17.1% post) and for those who were hospitalized, the length of stay was shorter (5.2–1.6 days). The decline in primary care visits was modest and not significant. Use of the emergency department was also not significant and revealed a downward trend (1.95–1.34 visits).

Direct costs associated with all health-care appointments were significantly reduced in the 1-year following DBT when compared to 1 year prior to DBT ($21,182.73–$15,215.84). This led to a 28.2% savings per patient. Within mental health treatment, there was also a significant decrease from an average of $8888.98–$5219.44 which was a reduction of 41.3%. For inpatient costs there was a reduction of 71.2% ($2712.57–$781.40).

In summary, this study demonstrated the decrease in high-cost inpatient services following DBT; hospitalizations were halved, the length of stay was almost 70% shorter post-DBT compared to pre-DBT, and primary care services and emergency department visits declined but were not significant. The total decrease was $244,642.49 across the enrolled 41 patients. Meyers et al. calculated the average cost to deliver DBT in an outpatient VA clinic finding the cost was $183.55 per patient per week, which totaled to $8443.30 per patient over the entire treatment. Therefore even though DBT may seem expensive, there was long-term cost benefits that support further implementation of this treatment throughout VA hospitals.

Evaluation of implementation of dialectical behavioral therapy in Department of Veterans Affairs

Landes et al. (2016) conducted a sequential mixed methods evaluation of DBT implementation in VA that included self-report surveys (one per site, $N = 59$). The survey queried what modes of treatment (e.g., skills group) and strategies (e.g., diary cards) had been implemented at each site and to what extent, information on the setting where DBT was implemented, provider training received, resources desired, barriers and facilitators to implementation, and benefits of implementation. From survey participant sites a subsample of eight high adopter sites (i.e., implementing at least three of the four DBT modes) and eight low adopter sites (i.e., implementing two or less of the four DBT modes) were recruited for semistructured qualitative interviews. Interviews were conducted with one administrator in a leadership position and one clinical provider at each site. Interviews focused on the process of how DBT was implemented.

Less than half of all sites surveyed offered all four modes of DBT. While skills group was identified as the mode of DBT offered the most (98%), therapist consultation team was offered the least (56%), with individual therapy (75%) and phone coaching (61%) falling in between. It is important to note that phone coaching included any amount offered; only four sites affirmed that they offered it 24/7, as is recommended in the DBT manual. Site identified the following diagnoses and/or patient problems as appropriate for receiving DBT in their setting: BPD, emotion regulation problems, interpersonal problems, nonsuicidal self-injury, and suicidal behavior.

The researchers found that just 33% of sites reported that staff had received formal DBT training, consisting of two, 5-day workshops broken up by 6 months of self-study in between. This type of formal DBT training has been recognized as the gold standard for adoption of DBT in health-care settings. Less intensive instruction, specifically shorter DBT workshops such as 1- or 2-day trainings, was endorsed by 74% of sites. The majority of sites (97%) indicated that they had staff that had received low-intensity training categorized primarily as self-study (e.g., reading the DBT manual). When sites were asked to rank in order their preferences for DBT resources out of a list of 10 potential options, intensive DBT training was ranked as the number one desired resource. While the findings of this project evaluation demonstrate that VA clinicians desire more training, it also denotes that less intensive training can be a facilitating factor in initiating DBT components (Landes, Rodriguez, et al., 2017).

Further evaluation of the data gathered from the program evaluation previously outlined by Landes et al. (2016) resulted in the identification of barriers and facilitators to the implementation of DBT in VA settings (Landes, Rodriguez, et al., 2017). Prior to this work, very little was known about how providers were implementing this treatment in VA, what barriers they faced, and what facilitated implementation. The survey, distributed to the 59 sites as previously described, included a modified version of the DBT Barriers to Implementation Scale (BTI-S; Chugani, Mitchell, Botanov, & Linehan, 2017) questionnaire, routinely used to aid trainers with understanding team specific barriers to DBT during trainings, and a checklist to identify facilitators that was created by the study team based on prior DBT research. To obtain more information on the difficulty of barriers encountered, the BTI-S was modified by changing the response options from "yes" and "no" to "not a barrier/problem," "a problem we overcame," "a problem we are currently working on," "a problem we could not overcome," or "not applicable."

The most frequently endorsed "difficult" barrier items were identified as those that were endorsed as a barrier that at least one-third of sites was "working on" or "could not overcome." These most difficult to overcome barriers included number or availability of therapists, ability to meet as a team, difficulty with policies or lack of resources, and clients' expectations. Of note, 4 of the 13 most difficult barriers to overcome were regarding phone coaching. Facilitators to implementation that were endorsed the most included staff interest, knowledge, experience, and administrative or leadership support.

Initial analysis of qualitative data identified that a number of sites had solved barriers creatively. Clinicians and administrators interviewed frequently identified that logistical, structural, and local policy changes enhanced or facilitated implementation (Landes, Matthieu, Smith, & Rodriguez, 2017).

Future directions for dialectical behavioral therapy research in Department of Veterans Affairs

To date, DBT research in VA has examined the efficacy of comprehensive DBT in two distinct samples: female veterans with BPD (Koons et al., 2001) and transdiagnostic male and female veterans with suicide risk factors (Goodman et al., 2016). The efficacy of comprehensive DBT in other veteran samples, such as male and female veterans with recent suicide attempt or male veterans with BPD, is not yet known.

Future research should evaluate the efficacy and effectiveness of DBT adaptations in real-world VA settings. Mixed methods evaluation indicates that most VA sites implement a DBT skills group or some DBT components rather than comprehensive DBT (Landes, Rodriguez, et al., 2017). It is critical to evaluate the efficacy and effectiveness of these adaptations in VA settings to determine whether they are indeed effective for reducing veteran suicide attempt or nonsuicidal self-directed violence, reducing quality-of-life-interfering behaviors such as substance use or avoidance, increasing coping skills, and improving functioning. High priority should be placed on evaluating adaptations common in VA settings (e.g., DBT skills groups, DBT with limitations placed on telephone coaching), as well as further research into adaptations that target veterans with marginalized identities like the work of Cohen and Yadavaia (2017).

Notably, Stich (2017) was the first study to examine DBT outcomes in a veteran sample consisting primarily of men of color (75.8% of the sample identified as Black or Latinx). There was no significant relationship between racial or ethnic identity and change scores; therefore race was not included in the regression model. However, further research into the impact of race and ethnicity on DBT outcomes and adaptations to target intersectional identities is indicated.

Given initial promising findings of concurrent DBT and PE (Meyers et al., 2017) and VA's emphasis on the treatment of PTSD, further research into adaptations that address PTSD symptoms and BPD is warranted. Initial research indicates that concurrent DBT and PE can safely and effectively treat veterans who previously dropped out or were deemed inappropriate for TFT alone. Dedicating resources to studying the addition of DBT to TFT may be effective in furthering the VA's mission of the treatment of both PTSD and suicidality.

A final future direction for DBT research in VA settings includes further implementation studies. Landes' et al. (2016); Landes, Rodriguez, et al. (2017) mixed method evaluation identified barriers, facilitators, and desired resources for DBT in VA settings. These data can be used to generate hypotheses to test in hybrid effectiveness-implementation design trials (Curran, Bauer, Mittman, Pyne, & Stetler, 2012) or to select implementation strategies to use in starting DBT programs in new VA settings.

Acknowledgments

The ideas presented here are those of the authors and do not represent the views of the Department of Veterans Affairs (VA), Veterans Health Administration (VHA), or the United States Government. Writing of this chapter was supported by the VA Office of Academic Affiliations Advanced Fellowship Program in Mental Illness Research and Treatment; the Medical Research Service of the Central Arkansas Veterans Healthcare System; the VA South Central Mental Illness Research, Education, and Clinical Center (MIRECC); the VA New England MIRECC; the VA Pain Research, Informatics, Multimorbidities, and Education (PRIME) Center; the VISN 2 MIRECC; and a Clinical and Translational Science Award (CTSA) program from the NIH National Center for Advancing Translational Sciences (NCATS) awarded to the University of Arkansas for Medical Sciences (grant UL1TR003107).

Dr. Decker is a trainer-in-training with Behavioral Tech, LLC, which provides training in evidence-based therapies, and works to manage any potential conflict of interest. Dr. Goodman is a consultant for Boehringer Ingelheim Pharmaceuticals. We report no conflict of interest.

References

Addis, M., & Linehan, M. M. (1989). Predicting suicidal behavior: Psychometric properties of the Suicidal Behaviors Questionnaire. In Paper presented at the *Annual meeting of the Association for the Advancement of Behavior Therapy*. Washington, DC.

American Psychological Association. (2012). Guidelines for psychological practice with lesbian, gay, and bisexual clients. *American Psychologist*, *67*, 10–42. Available from https://doi.org/10.1037/a0024659.

Amner, K. (2012). The effect of DBT provision in reducing the cost of adults displaying the symptoms of BPD. *British Journal of Psychotherapy*, *28*, 336–352. Available from https://doi.org/10.1111/j.1752-0118.2012.01286.x.

Attkisson, C. C., & Zwick, R. (1982). The client satisfaction questionnaire. Psychometric properties and correlations with service utilization and psychotherapy outcome. *Evaluation and Program Planning*, *5*, 233–237.

Beck, A. T., Steer, R. A., & Brown, G. K. (1996). *Beck Depression Inventory* (2nd ed.). San Antonio, TX: Psychological Corporation.

Beck, A. T., Steer, R. A., & Rainieri, W. F. (1988). Scale for suicidal ideation: Psychometric properties of a self-report version. *Journal of Clinical Psychology*, *44*, 499–505. Available from https://doi.org/10.1002/1097-4679(198807)44:4%3C499::AID-JCLP2270440404%3E3.0.CO;2-6.

Becker, C. B., Zayfert, C., & Anderson, E. (2004). A survey of psychologists' attitudes towards and utilization of exposure therapy for PTSD. *Behaviour Research and Therapy*, *42*, 277–292. Available from https://doi.org/10.1016/S0005-7967(03)00138-4.

Bohus, M., Dyer, A. S., Priebe, K., Kruger, A., Kleindienst, N., Schmahl, C., … Steil, R. (2013). Dialectical behaviour therapy for post-traumatic stress disorder after childhood sexual abuse in patients with and without borderline personality disorder: A randomised controlled trial. *Psychotherapy and Psychosomatics*, *82*, 221–233. Available from https://doi.org/10.1159/000348451.

Chugani, C. D., Mitchell, M. E., Botanov, Y., & Linehan, M. M. (2017). Development and initial evaluation of the psychometric properties of the Dialectical Behavior Therapy Barriers to Implementation Scale (BTI-S). *Journal of Clinical Psychology*, *73*, 1704–1716. Available from https://doi.org/10.1002/jclp.22478.

Cochran, B. N., Balsam, K., Flentje, A., Malte, C. A., & Simpson, T. (2013). Mental health characteristics of sexual minority veterans. *Journal of Homosexuality*, *60*, 419–435. Available from https://doi.org/10.1080/00918369.2013.744932.

Cohen, J. M., & Newman, M. G. (2019). Group-based cognitive-behavioral therapies with sexual minority clients. In J. E. Pachankis, & S. A. Safren (Eds.), *Handbook of evidence-based mental health practice with sexual and gender minorities*. New York: Oxford University Press.

Cohen, J. M., & Yadavaia, J. E. (2017). Affirmative dialectical behavior therapy skills training as a transdiagnostic treatment for emotional disorders and minority stress. In Paper presented at the *Association for Behavioral and Cognitive Therapies*. San Diego, CA.

Curran, G. M., Bauer, M., Mittman, B., Pyne, J. M., & Stetler, C. (2012). Effectiveness-implementation hybrid designs: Combining elements of clinical effectiveness and implementation research to enhance public health impact. *Medical Care*, *50*, 217–226. Available from https://doi.org/10.1097/MLR.0b013e3182408812.

Decker, S. E., Adams, L., Watkins, L. E., Sippel, L. M., Presnall-Shvorin, J., Sofuoglu, M., & Martino, S. (2019). Feasibility and preliminary efficacy of dialectical behaviour therapy skills groups for Veterans with suicidal ideation: Pilot. *Behavioural and Cognitive Psychotherapy*, *47*, 616–621. Available from https://doi.org/10.1017/S1352465819000122.

DeCou, C. R., Comtois, K. A., & Landes, S. J. (2019). Dialectical behavior therapy is effective for the treatment of suicidal behavior: A meta-analysis. *Behavior Therapy*, *50*, 60–72. Available from https://doi.org/10.1016/j.beth.2018.03.009.

Denckla, C. A., Bailey, R., Jackson, C., Tatarakis, J., & Chen, C. K. (2015). A novel adaptation of distress tolerance skills training among military veterans: Outcomes in suicide-related events. *Cognitive and Behavioral Practice*, *22*, 450–457. Available from https://doi.org/10.1016/j.cbpra.2014.04.001.

Department of Veterans Affairs (VA), & Department of Defense. (2019). *VA/DoD clinical practice guideline for the assessment and management of patients at risk for suicide. Version 2.0*. Available from <https://www.healthquality.va.gov/guidelines/MH/srb/VADoDSuicideRiskFullCPGFinal5088212019.pdf>.

Endicott, J., Nee, J., Harrison, W., & Blumenthal, R. (1993). Quality of life enjoyment and satisfaction questionnaire: A new measure. *Psychopharmacology Bulletin*, *29*, 321–326.

Feeny, N. C., Zoellner, L. A., & Foa, E. B. (2002). Treatment outcome for chronic PTSD among female assault victims with borderline personality characteristics: A preliminary examination. *Journal of Personality Disorders*, *16*, 30–40. Available from https://doi.org/10.1521/pedi.16.1.30.22555.

Goodman, M., Banthin, D., Blair, N. J., Mascitelli, K. A., Wilsnack, J., Chen, J., … New, A. S. (2016). A randomized trial of dialectical behavior therapy in high-risk suicidal veterans. *The Journal of Clinical Psychiatry*, *77*, e1591–e1600. Available from https://doi.org/10.4088/JCP.15m10235.

Gratz, K. L., & Roemer, L. (2004). Multidimensional assessment of emotion regulation and dysregulation: Development, factor structure, and initial validation of the difficulties in emotion regulation scale. *Journal of Psychopathology and Behavioral Assessment*, *26*, 41–54. Available from https://doi.org/0882-2689/04/0300-0041/0.

Harned, M. S., Korslund, K. E., & Linehan, M. M. (2014). A pilot randomized controlled trial of Dialectical Behavior Therapy with and without the Dialectical Behavior Therapy Prolonged Exposure protocol for suicidal and self-injuring women with borderline personality disorder and PTSD. *Behaviour Research and Therapy, 55*, 7–17. Available from https://doi.org/10.1016/j.brat.2014.01.008.

Jacobson, N. S., & Truax, P. (1991). Clinical significance: A statistical approach to defining meaningful change in psychotherapy research. *Journal of Consulting and Clinical Psychology, 59*, 12–19. Available from https://doi.org/10.1037//0022-006x.59.1.12.

Koons, C. R., Robins, C. J., Tweed, J. L., Lynch, T. R., Gonzalez, A. M., Morse, J. Q., ... Bastian, L. A. (2001). Efficacy of dialectical behavior therapy in women veterans with borderline personality disorder. *Behavior Therapy, 32*, 371–390. Available from https://doi.org/10.1016/S0005-7894(01)80009-5.

Landes, S. J., Garovoy, N. D., & Burkman, K. M. (2013). Treating complex trauma among veterans: Three stage-based treatment models. *Journal of Clinical Psychology, 69*, 523–533. Available from https://doi.org/10.1002/jclp.21988.

Landes, S. J., Matthieu, M. M., Smith, B. N., & Rodriguez, A. L. (2017). Strategies to overcome barriers to implementing dialectical behavior therapy in the Department of Veterans Affairs: Perspective from a national program evaluation. *Behavioural Therapist, 40*, 251–255.

Landes, S. J., Matthieu, M. M., Smith, B. N., Trent, L. R., Rodriguez, A. L., Kemp, J., & Thompson, C. (2016). Dialectical behavior therapy training and desired resources for implementation: Results from a national program evaluation in the Veterans Health Administration. *Military Medicine, 181*, 747–752. Available from https://doi.org/10.7205/MILMED-D-15-00267.

Landes, S. J., Rodriguez, A. L., Smith, B. N., Matthieu, M. M., Trent, L. R., Kemp, J., & Thompson, C. (2017). Barriers, facilitators, and benefits of implementation of dialectical behavior therapy in routine care: Results from a national program evaluation survey in the Veterans Health Administration. *Translational Behavioral Medicine: Practice, Policy, Research, 7*, 832–844. Available from https://doi.org/10.1007/s13142-017-0465-5.

Landes, S. J., Smith, B. N., & Weingardt, K. R. (2019). Supporting grass roots implementation through an online community of practice: A case study in the Department of Veterans Affairs. *Cognitive and Behavioral Practice, 26*, 453–465. Available from https://doi.org/10.1016/j.cbpra.2019.02.002.

Linehan, M. M. (1993). *Cognitive-behavioral treatment of borderline personality disorder*. New York: Guilford Press.

Linehan, M. M., Korslund, K. E., Harned, M. S., Gallop, R. J., Lungu, A., Neacsiu, A. D., ... Murray-Gregory, A. M. (2015). Dialectical behavior therapy for high suicide risk in individuals with borderline personality disorder: A randomized clinical trial and component analysis. *JAMA Psychiatry, 72*, 475–482. Available from https://doi.org/10.1001/jamapsychiatry.2014.3039.

McMain, S. F., Guimond, T., Barnhart, R., Habinski, L., & Streiner, D. L. (2017). A randomized trial of brief dialectical behaviour therapy skills training in suicidal patients suffering from borderline disorder. *Acta Psychiatrica Scandinavica, 135*, 138–148. Available from https://doi.org/10.1111/acps.12664.

Meyers, L., Voller, E. K., McCallum, E. B., Thuras, P., Shallcross, S., Velasquez, T., & Meis, L. (2017). Treating Veterans with PTSD and borderline personality symptoms in a 12-week intensive outpatient setting: Findings from a pilot program. *Journal of Traumatic Stress, 30*, 178–181. Available from https://doi.org/10.1002/jts.22174.

Meyers, L. L., Landes, S. J., & Thuras, P. (2014). Veterans' service utilization and associated costs following participation in dialectical behavior therapy: A preliminary investigation. *Military Medicine, 179*, 1368–1373. Available from https://doi.org/10.7205/MILMED-D-14-00248.

Nappi C. M., Ferriter C., Campos M., Wilkins K. and Davis K., Dialectical behavior skills group for depression among veterans: A pilot effectiveness study. Poster presented at the annual meeting of the association of behavioral and cognitive therapies, National Harbor, MD, 2012.

Neacsiu, A. D., Eberle, J. W., Kramer, R., Wiesmann, T., & Linehan, M. M. (2014). Dialectical behavior therapy skills for transdiagnostic emotion dysregulation: A pilot randomized controlled trial. *Behaviour Research and Therapy, 59*, 40–51. Available from https://doi.org/10.1016/j.brat.2014.05.005.

Neacsiu, A. D., Rizvi, S. L., Vitaliano, P. P., Lynch, T. R., & Linehan, M. M. (2010). The dialectical behavior therapy ways of coping checklist: Development and psychometric properties. *Journal of Clinical Psychology, 66*, 563–582. Available from https://doi.org/10.1002/jclp.20685.

Office of Mental Health and Suicide Prevention, & Department of Veterans Affairs. (2018). *VA national suicide data report, 2005–2015*.

Priebe, S., Bhatti, N., Barnicot, K., Bremner, S., Gaglia, A., Katsakou, C., ... Zinkler, M. (2012). Effectiveness and cost-effectiveness of dialectical behaviour therapy for self-harming patients with personality disorder: A pragmatic randomised controlled trial. *Psychotherapy and Psychosomatics, 81*, 356–365. Available from https://doi.org/10.1159/000338897.

Rudd, M. D., Williams, B., & Trotter, D. (2008). The psychological and behavioral treatment of suicidal behavior: What are the common elements of treatments that work? In W. D. Oxford (Ed.), *Oxford textbook of suicidology*. Oxford, United Kingdom: Oxford University Press.

Soler, J., Pascual, J. C., Tiana, T., Cebria, A., Barrachina, J., Campins, M. J., ... Perez, V. (2009). Dialectical behaviour therapy skills training compared to standard group therapy in borderline personality disorder: A 3-month randomised controlled clinical trial. *Behaviour Research and Therapy, 47*, 353–358. Available from https://doi.org/10.1016/j.brat.2009.01.013.

Southwick, S. M., Yehuda, R., & Giller, E. L., Jr. (1993). Personality disorders in treatment-seeking combat veterans with posttraumatic stress disorder. *The American Journal of Psychiatry, 150*, 1020–1023. Available from https://doi.org/10.1176/ajp.150.7.1020.

Stanley, B., & Brown, G. K. (2012). Safety planning intervention: A brief intervention to mitigate suicide risk. *Cognitive and Behavioral Practice, 19*, 256–264. Available from https://doi.org/10.1016/j.cbpra.2011.01.001.

Stich, C. (2017). *Predicting dialectic behavioral treatment outcomes in veterans at high risk for suicide*. Smith College. Retrieved from <https://scholarworks.smith.edu/theses/1923> (1923).

Weathers, F.W., Litz, B.T., Herman, D.S., Huska, J.A., & Keane, T.M. (1993). The PTSD checklist: Reliability, validity, and diagnostic utility. In Paper presented at the *Annual meeting of the International Society for Traumatic Stress Studies*. San Antonio, TX.

CHAPTER

13

Dialectical behavior therapy stepped care for hospitals

Kalina N. Babeva[1,3], *Olivia Fitzpatrick*[2] and *Joan R. Asarnow*[3]

[1]Psychiatry and Behavioral Medicine, Seattle Children's Hospital, Seattle, WA, United States, [2]Psychology Department, Harvard University, Cambridge, MA, United States, [3]Psychiatry and Biobehavioral Sciences, UCLA, Los Angeles, CA, United States

Stepped care: definition and literature review

Stepped care is a health service delivery model aimed at enhancing the cost-effectiveness of and access to care for a range of health domains (Bower & Gilbody, 2005). The defining feature of stepped care is that patients are initially assigned to receive the lowest level of care still expected to yield therapeutic benefits, with an emphasis on repeatedly monitoring patient progress and accordingly adjusting the intensity of care throughout the course of treatment (Bower & Gilbody, 2005). As such, stepped care models offer opportunities to simultaneously personalize care and serve a greater number of patients. This approach is particularly suitable for chronic health concerns that are widespread, highly variable in prognosis and outcome, and for which services are difficult to access (Paris, 2013). With this in mind, the stepped care model has been increasingly recognized as a potential strategy for improving the delivery of mental health care (Andrews, Gavin, & WHO, 2006) and has been continually promoted by the National Institute for Health and Clinical Excellence (NICE) guidelines as a recommended therapeutic approach for several psychological disorders [e.g., NICE, 2019, 2011].

The Handbook of Dialectical Behavior Therapy
DOI: https://doi.org/10.1016/B978-0-12-816384-9.00013-0

Within the stepped mental health-care framework, early detection of and screening for psychiatric disorders is the critical starting point for appropriate triage (NICE, 2019). Given that primary care settings tend to be the first point of contact for mental health services, it is unsurprising that stepped care for psychiatric health was originally developed within the context of primary care. Over the years, this model has continued to be tested and shown to be effective within primary care settings worldwide (e.g., Rollman et al., 2017; Salomonsson et al., 2018). Despite its popularity in primary care, this efficient and cost-effective approach is suitable for and advantageous within any service delivery setting in which resources are limited, such as university counseling centers and community mental health clinics (Reetz, Barr, & Krylowicz, 2014).

In published studies of stepped care models, even those applied to just cognitive behavioral therapy (CBT; van Straten, Hill, Richards, & Cuijpers, 2015), there is significant variability in the number and duration of intervention steps, the specific treatments offered, the number and type of professionals involved, and the criteria for stepping up to higher levels of care. The number and forms of services offered within a stepped care model depend on several key factors, including health-care system parameters, the number of available evidence-based interventions, and levels of treatment intensities for a given disorder. Although stepped care models were originally proposed and developed within publicly funded health-care systems (i.e., in the United Kingdom), this approach can be successfully applied within any system, as long as system-specific characteristics are appropriately taken into account (Espie, 2009). Of particular importance, the standard amount of resources input into mental health services within a system, such as the number, type, and length of sessions typically offered for a given disorder, should be considered when developing the number and content of levels within a stepped care model (Bower & Gilbody, 2005). Broadly speaking, there tend to be four unique steps within such a model: self-help strategies, therapist-guided self-help and/or group therapy, brief individual therapy, and long-term individual therapy (Bower & Gilbody, 2005). Although this structure is generally accepted, the specifics within it can vary substantially across settings and research studies examining stepped care models.

Within the context of treatments for psychological concerns, the differing steps of care can be achieved through several approaches: (1) adjusting the dose of the originally assigned intervention, (2) shifting to a different intervention approach, or (3) supplementing the initial intervention with an additional treatment strategy (Bower & Gilbody, 2005). The most common psychotherapeutic approach used within a stepped care framework is CBT, a well-studied intervention that has been adapted for a wide range of disorders (e.g., Kopelovich, Strachan, Sivec, & Kreider, 2019; Salloum, Scheeringa, Cohen, & Storch, 2014; van Der

Leeden et al., 2011; van Straten et al., 2015). CBT is particularly suitable for stepped care models because it comprises structured components that can be extracted and modified for varying treatment intensities, allowing for similarities and consistency across levels of care within the framework (Bower & Gilbody, 2005). Despite these benefits, there may also be advantages to shifting between (e.g., nontheoretical bibliotherapy to intensive CBT; Ollendick, Öst, & Farrell, 2018) or combining different interventions as service level is increased (e.g., combining psychotherapy with medication during the highest intensity care level; Gelenberg, 2010). Notably, some patients, diagnoses, and/or specific features of a given patient's clinical presentation may be more responsive to a particular treatment approach (Newman, 2000), which would not be discovered unless multiple strategies are employed. Given the diversity within and across psychiatric disorders, it is important to consider and accordingly modify stepped care models to address the challenges specific to a given mental health domain.

The stepped care model has been proposed, adapted, and tested for a variety of psychiatric diagnoses and clinical populations (e.g., Espie, 2009; Kopelovich et al., 2019; Salloum et al., 2014; van Der Leeden et al., 2011; van Straten et al., 2015). Given that depression is highly prevalent and the leading cause of disability worldwide (Friedrich, 2017), it has been the most commonly targeted disorder within stepped care initiatives. Overall, evidence suggests that stepped care approaches produce moderate improvements in symptoms of depression (Firth, Barkham, & Kellett, 2015; van Straten et al., 2015). Randomized controlled trials (RCTs) comparing stepped care to treatment as usual (TAU)/enhanced TAU for depression generally yield significant effects in favor of stepped care, with benefits maintaining over time (e.g., Araya et al., 2003; Ell et al., 2010; Härter et al., 2018). Stepped care has also been shown to be an acceptable form of treatment for depression and better than usual care according to patients, suggesting that it may not only be an effective approach but also a preferred one among those receiving care (Haugh et al., 2019). Taken together, these findings implicate that stepped care is a promising approach for improving the early detection of and access to cost-effective treatments for depression, ultimately reducing the global burden of this disease.

Although depression has been a primary focus within stepped mental health-care models, this approach has been increasingly adapted and proposed for other psychiatric disorders as well. Findings from studies assessing stepped care models for anxiety have been mixed, with some showing that stepped care yields significantly greater therapeutic benefits than TAU (Rollman et al., 2017; van der Aa, van Rens, Bosmans, Comijs, & van Nispen, 2017), and others suggesting comparable results across treatment approaches (Nordgreen et al., 2016; Rapee et al., 2017). Despite this uncertainty, there is strong evidence for the cost-effectiveness of stepped care for anxiety (Ho, Yeung, Ng, & Chan, 2016; Ollendick, Öst, & Farrell, 2018). Similarly, there has been promising support for the therapeutic benefits and cost-effectiveness of stepped care models addressing posttraumatic stress (Salloum et al., 2014, 2016; Zatzick et al., 2015) and OCD (Gilliam, Diefenbach, Whiting, & Tolin, 2010; Tolin, Diefenbach, & Gilliam, 2011). Although there has been less research conducted on stepped care models adapted for domains outside of anxiety and related disorders, it has been explored as a promising approach for expanding access to mental health services for a range of mental health concerns, including substance abuse (Edelman et al., 2019; Kidorf, Neufeld, King, Clark, & Brooner, 2007), insomnia (Espie, 2009; Vincent & Walsh, 2013), psychosis (Kopelovich et al., 2019), and eating disorders (Tasca et al., 2019; Wilson, Vitousek, & Loeb, 2000). Considered together, this array of research suggests the potential for stepped care models in terms of improving access to and cost-efficiency of mental health services across a range of health systems.

Within the United States specifically, stepped care has been integrated as a key component of collaborative care programs for depression in patients with medical illness (e.g., diabetes) (Katon, Unützer, Wells, & Jones, 2010). Collaborative care models, originally developed by Wagner, Austin, and Von Korff (1996) to target depression, have evolved to include the following elements: patient self-management assistance to promote more active involvement in care (e.g., patient education with materials such as brochures/handouts, books, and videos); low level interventions supporting prevention/early intervention efforts; use of standardized measures (e.g., the Patient Health Questionnaire-9) to track progress and outcomes and give feedback to medical providers; implementation of care managers (e.g., allied health or mental health professionals supervised by a psychiatrist/psychologist), who in some cases, deliver brief evidence-based psychotherapy; and treatment decision guidelines and increases in treatment for patients who do not respond to lower levels of care (Katon & Seelig, 2008). Nesting stepped mental health-care models within primary/medical care settings has many advantages, including, but not limited to, improving access to specialty care for a larger portion of the patient population and thus also decreasing some of the disparities in mental health care; provision of close patient follow-up and monitoring of symptoms and side effects if medication (antidepressant) is utilized; decreasing stigma associated with mental health treatment; and, last but not least, overall medical care cost savings (Katon et al., 2010). Indeed, in a recent meta-analysis, integrated medical-behavioral primary care was found to have benefits in terms of improving rates of care and behavioral health outcomes (e.g., Asarnow, Rozenman, Wiblin, & Zeltzer, 2015).

Stepped care applied to dialectical behavior therapy

Dialectical behavior therapy (DBT) is a comprehensive, evidence-based intervention for Borderline Personality Disorder in adults that aims to aid patients in building a life worth living. This CBT-based treatment has gained significant popularity and has empirical support for other clinical populations, including adults with substance abuse problems (e.g., Linehan et al., 2002), adults with eating disorders (e.g., Safer, Telch, & Agras, 2001), adolescents with bipolar disorder (Goldstein et al., 2015), adolescents with emotion dysregulation and suicidality (McCauley et al., 2018; Mehlum et al., 2014) and children with disruptive mood dysregulation (Perepletchikova et al., 2017). In the context of treating suicidality, DBT has been found to be effective in terms of both patient outcomes and financial costs compared to other treatments (e.g., Haga, Aas, Groholt, Tormoen, & Mehlum, 2018). Nevertheless, it is a complex treatment typically requiring more than one clinician and incorporating multiple components, such as individual and group therapy as well as in-the-moment phone coaching available 24 h/day. Thus, providing full-model DBT, which typically lasts at least 6–12 months, to all patients with suicide risk/emotion dysregulation is unlikely to be feasible or to be the most efficient or cost-effective approach.

As previously highlighted, stepped care approaches providing the most effective yet least resource intensive treatment first, in conjunction with a move to more intensive services as needed, are a cost/time/resource effective solution and are gaining support and popularity in mental health. This approach can also be adapted for suicide prevention, with the highest risk patients receiving full-model DBT. However, to the authors' knowledge, no published studies of stepped care specifically applied to DBT exist yet. We thus summarize some research on alternate ways of DBT delivery, suggesting a possible stepped-care model for patients with suicidality/emotion dysregulation. We conclude by describing an ongoing RCT testing such a stepped care model for adolescents and young adults within the Kaiser Permanente Northwest (KPNW) system.

Building on the framework described by Bower and Gilbody (2005), the following four steps are proposed as part of a DBT stepped-care model: (1) self-guided strategies with the possibility of limited/brief contact with a mental health provider, (2) in-person group skills training paired with the lower level self-guided strategies, (3) briefer (e.g., 6 months) full-model DBT, and (4) longer term full-model DBT (12 months). Each of these steps is described in more detail later.

An important point to be emphasized here is that stepped care models vary in terms of whether the lowest level of treatment is first provided to all patients or whether level of treatment is based on current symptoms severity. For patients presenting with suicidality, it is particularly important to conduct a careful, comprehensive assessment of risk and then match treatment to current suicide risk. The rationale for this is that adverse consequences in terms of suicidal/self-harm behavior could result from providing a lower level intervention to a higher risk patient or from a patient experiencing a "treatment failure" at a lower step that could then influence motivation to continue with treatment. Furthermore, in some cases, intensive earlier intervention can be more effective in terms of clinical outcome and financial cost than initially providing lower level intervention. For example, providing full-model DBT, which has been found to be associated with a decrease in emergency department (ED) visits and psychiatric hospitalization (Linehan et al., 2015), to a high-risk patient is likely to be more clinically and financially efficacious than providing less intensive therapy that could result in suicidal behavior and higher use of crisis and medical services.

Lowest stepped-care level

The lowest level of any stepped-care model, incorporating self-guided intervention, can be provided through written resources (such as handouts and books), videos, and/or computerized/electronic intervention. Treatment dose can be adjusted within this level by varying frequency and duration of contact with a clinician, as well as number of self-guided services provided. Books describing DBT skills for lay audiences have been published (e.g., McKay, Wood, & Brantley, 2007) and publicly available videos teaching DBT skills also exist (e.g., nowmattersnow.org). However, to the authors' knowledge, no published studies examining the efficacy of DBT bibliotherapy exist, and it is therefore unknown how beneficial this would be as a stand-alone approach.

Advances in and accessibility of technology have also allowed for the computerized delivery of evidence-based treatment. Pocket skills, a mobile web application created by Microsoft to teach DBT skills, has been tested with a sample of adults and shown to have benefits in terms of self-reported decreases in symptoms of depression and anxiety, as well as increases in DBT skills use (Schroeder et al., 2018). Of note, for ethical reasons and due to risk levels, the adult patients in this study were concurrently enrolled in individual psychotherapy and were selected to have some familiarity with DBT. Thus, the effect of using pocket skills in a self-guided manner without the assistance of a clinician or with limited professional support still needs to be tested.

There have also been other initial efforts to create self-guided computerized/online versions of DBT. For example, a preliminary RCT conducted by Wilks et al. (2018) tests an 8-week internet-delivered DBT Skills

Training program for adults with suicidality and heavy episodic drinking. This computerized DBT (cDBT) is described as including four mindfulness, six emotion regulation, two distress tolerance, and four addiction-specific skills. This didactic intervention retains important features of in-person DBT by following a predetermined agenda, which incorporates homework review and specific skills to be taught each week; provides modeling of skills through video vignettes; incorporates practice exercises; and assigns practice to be completed between sessions. Participants in this study reported a significant reduction in suicidal ideation, alcohol use, and emotion dysregulation over the 4-month study period. These encouraging findings suggest that cDBT may be a useful resource that can be incorporated into stepped-care models, especially at lower levels of risk.

Intermediate stepped-care level

At the next intermediate level of intervention in a stepped-care model, in-person DBT skills group can be offered in addition to self-guided resources. Indeed, there is evidence that DBT skills group plus case management yields effects similar to standard DBT (Linehan et al., 2015). Specifically, based on a component analysis study by Linehan et al. (2015), compared to full-model DBT, DBT skills group plus case management was found to yield comparable decreases in suicidal ideation and behavior as well as in crisis service use (ED visits and psychiatric hospitalizations) due to suicidality. In this study, treatment for all participants incorporated the Linehan Risk Assessment and Management Protocol (LRAMP; Linehan, Comtois, & Ward-Ciesielski, 2012). Case management, which was reported to be based on the WA King County crisis and suicide management policies (King County Mental Health, Chemical Abuse and Dependency Services, 2015, as cited in Linehan et al., 2015), occurred weekly and included a strengths-based needs assessment, assistance with finding resources, management of suicidal crises, and support with problem-solving. Other studies have also documented positive effects of DBT skills group (adapted in some cases) for various presenting problems including mood disorders (Harley, Sprich, Safren, Jacobo, & Fava, 2008; Van Dijk, Jeffrey, & Katz, 2013), transdiagnostic emotion dysregulation (Neacsiu, Eberle, Kramer, Wiesmann, & Linehan, 2014), eating disorders (Safer, Robinson, & Jo, 2010), and attention-deficit/hyperactivity disorder symptoms (Fleming, McMahon, Moran, Peterson, & Dreessen, 2015). In these studies, DBT skills group was generally a stand-alone treatment augmented by medication (e.g., Harley et al., 2008) or brief/single-session individual contact with a clinician (e.g., Neacsiu et al., 2014). Taken together, these studies suggest that DBT skills training is an acceptable intervention that may be equivalent to full-model DBT for some patients, allowing for savings in patient and clinician time and financial costs.

Furthermore, within this intermediate step, the background and credentials of the individuals delivering treatment can be varied based on the risk level of the patients being served and the availability of resources/staff. For example, especially when resources are limited and mental health disparities are present in underserved communities, components of DBT (e.g., skills group or individual skills training) could be delivered by trained lay providers. While no studies testing treatment by trained lay DBT providers have been conducted, research supports that evidence-based mental health interventions, including CBT, can be effectively delivered by trained bachelor-level providers (e.g., Stanley et al, 2014) and community health workers, who do not have a formal mental health background (for a review, see Barnett, Gonzalez, Miranda, Chavira, & Lau, 2018).

Based on the characteristics of the specific health system, it is also possible for additional services to be offered in this intermediate step, such as computerized intervention (CBT, DBT, or other), check-ins or individual risk management sessions with a clinician, and/or medication management.

Highest stepped-care level

Finally, the highest levels in the stepped-care model provide full-model DBT (6 vs 12 months) with its multiple components. A possible way to structure these two levels is to enroll all patients in treatment for a 6-month period and then allow those needing additional intervention to continue for another 6-month course (or longer). For example, as is the case in some existing RCTs (e.g., McCauley et al., 2018), the DBT Skills Training Group curriculum can be consolidated to be delivered over the course of 6 months and then patients needing to continue treatment can complete a second cycle of group. Alternatively, repetition of DBT Skills Training Group without the individual therapy component can also be used as a step-down for those patients needing additional, less intensive support after 6 months of full-model DBT (e.g., a DBT "Graduate" group as described by Lopez & Chessick, 2013). These graduate groups can be facilitated by one clinician, with "graduates" taking a more active role and helping to colead the group, which would allow for savings in terms of clinician time.

Randomized Trial of Stepped Care for Suicide Prevention in Teens and Young Adults (Step2Health)

A collaborative stepped care model for adolescents and young adults based on DBT is currently being tested in a RCT funded by the National

Institute of Mental Health (NIMH). This trial is a collaborative effort between researchers at the University of California, Los Angeles (UCLA) and KPNW. The stepped-care model being tested incorporates the following key components:

1. An initial in-person risk assessment conducted over two sessions aimed at providing a behavioral assessment of imminent suicide attempt risk and enhancing protective processes for suicide prevention such as environmental support and protection, safety planning and emotion/distress regulation strategies, and decreasing access to lethal means. These two sessions also focus on increasing motivation for outpatient care and addressing barriers to participating in such care.
2. Triage algorithms to match youths to appropriate care level. More specifically, based on all of the behaviorally assessed suicide risk information gathered during the initial in-person sessions, appropriate level of care is determined for each patient based on standardized rules. For example, a teen having engaged in suicidal behavior in the past month and reporting ongoing suicidal ideation would be triaged to the highest level of outpatient care the model provides. On the other hand, a youth having engaged in suicidal behavior 1 year ago and reporting passive thoughts of death would be triaged to a lower level of care, with suicidal ideation and behavior being monitored closely over the course of treatment.
3. Integration of evidence-based treatments for depression and suicide prevention (namely, CBT and DBT) into three steps of care, with intervention components being delivered online, over the phone, and/or in person.
4. Ongoing symptom and risk monitoring in order to both guide care but also offer additional services/increase level of care provided if risk increases.
5. Phone check-ins and email/text message caring contact from care managers once active treatment has ended (or if youth has dropped out of treatment).

In this model the first level of care, which is intended for low risk patients, provides low intensity eCBT and DBT skills videos. A care manager (clinician) orients patients to these electronic resources and checks in with patients over the phone approximately once per month to monitor risk, help with use of resources, and answer questions related to material covered in the online interventions. The intermediate level of care offers a 16-week in-person DBT skills group (multifamily group for adolescents and patient-only groups for young adults >18 years of age) in addition to the lower level services (eCBT and DBT videos). Finally, the third level of care adds individual DBT-informed therapy sessions to the DBT skills group and lowest level services. Once this trial is completed, results will undoubtedly guide future implementations of DBT stepped care models.

Conclusion

There is convincing national and international data that DBT is an effective treatment for those with suicidality and emotion dysregulation and modifications of DBT for various other presenting problems are being created and tested. In this chapter, we propose a stepped-care model comprising four levels of treatment based on existing research on DBT and pragmatic considerations. There are numerous benefits of stepped-care models, including flexible clinical triage, efficiency of resource allocation, and population-wide improvements in access to care. Nevertheless, there is considerable research that still needs to be conducted on stepped-care models and on their application to DBT in particular to determine effectiveness. The process of testing and revising stepped-care DBT should be iterative and informed by measurement-based care and adaptive intervention research, with special attention given to the specification of algorithms/clinical decision rules for both initial level determination and subsequent movement between levels. Stepped-care models would ideally also incorporate research on mediators and moderators of treatment outcome to help better match individuals to the type and level of treatment they are most likely to benefit from. In this time of technological advances, innovation, integrated medical-behavioral care, and zero suicide initiatives in health-care systems, stepped-care DBT models nested within medical settings such as hospitals hold promise as a scalable, sustainable approach that will improve rates of care and behavioral health outcomes for patients.

References

Andrews, G., & Tolkein II Team. (2006). *A needs-based, costed stepped-care model for mental health services*. Sydney: CRUFAD, University of New South Wales.

Andrews, Gavin & World Health Organization. (2006). Collaborating Centre for Classification in Mental Health. *Tolkien II : a needs-based, costed, stepped-care model for mental health services : recommendations, executive summaries, clinical pathways, treatment flowcharts, costing structures*. World Health Organization, Collaborating Centre for Classification in Mental Health, Sydney, N.S.W.

Araya, R., Rojas, G., Fritsch, R., Gaete, J., Rojas, M., Simon, G., & Peters, T. J. (2003). Treating depression in primary care in low-income women in Santiago, Chile: A randomised controlled trial. *Lancet, 361*(9362), 995–1000. Available from https://doi.org/10.1016/S0140-6736(03)12825-5.

Asarnow, J. R., Rozenman, M., Wiblin, J., & Zeltzer, L. (2015). Integrated medical-behavioral care compared with usual primary care for child and adolescent behavioral health: A meta-analysis. *JAMA Pediatrics, 169*(10), 929–937. Available from https://doi.org/10.1001/jamapediatrics.2015.1141.

Barnett, M. L., Gonzalez, A., Miranda, J., Chavira, D. A., & Lau, A. S. (2018). Mobilizing community health workers to address mental health disparities for underserved populations: A systematic review. *Administration and Policy in Mental Health and Mental Health Services Research, 45*(2), 195–211. Available from https://doi.org/10.1007/s10488-017-0815-0.

Bower, P., & Gilbody, S. (2005). Stepped care in psychological therapies: Access, effectiveness and efficiency: Narrative literature review. *British Journal of Psychiatry, 186*(1), 11–17. Available from https://doi.org/10.1192/bjp.186.1.11.

Edelman, E. J., Maisto, S. A., Hansen, N. B., Cutter, C. J., Dziura, J., Deng, Y., ... Fiellin, D. A. (2019). Integrated stepped alcohol treatment for patients with HIV and alcohol use disorder: A randomised controlled trial. *Lancet HIV*. Available from https://doi.org/10.1016/S2352-3018(19)30076-1, Advance online Publ.

Ell, K., Katon, W., Xie, B., Lee, P. J., Kapetanovic, S., Guterman, J., & Chou, C. P. (2010). Collaborative care management of major depression among low-income, predominantly Hispanic subjects with diabetes: A randomized controlled trial. *Diabetes Care, 33*(4), 706–713. Available from https://doi.org/10.2337/dc09-1711.

Espie, C. A. (2009). "Stepped care": A health technology solution for delivering cognitive behavioral therapy as a first line insomnia treatment. *Sleep, 32*(12), 1549–1558. Available from https://doi.org/10.1093/sleep/32.12.1549.

Firth, N., Barkham, M., & Kellett, S. (2015). The clinical effectiveness of stepped care systems for depression in working age adults: A systematic review. *Journal of Affective Disorders, 170*, 119–130. Available from https://doi.org/10.1016/j.jad.2014.08.030.

Fleming, A. P., McMahon, R. J., Moran, L. R., Peterson, A. P., & Dreessen, A. (2015). Pilot randomized controlled trial of dialectical behavior therapy group skills training for ADHD among college students. *Journal of Attention Disorders, 19*, 260–271. Available from https://doi.org/10.1177/1087054714535951.

Friedrich, M. J. (2017). Depression is the leading cause of disability around the world. *The Journal of the American Medical Association, 317*(15), 1517. Available from https://doi.org/10.1001/jama.2017.3826.

Gelenberg, A. J. (2010). A review of current guidelines for depression treatment. *The Journal of Clinical Psychiatry, 71*(07). Available from https://doi.org/10.4088/JCP.9078tx1c.

Gilliam, C. M., Diefenbach, G. J., Whiting, S. E., & Tolin, D. F. (2010). Stepped care for obsessive-compulsive disorder: An open trial. *Behaviour Research and Therapy, 48*(11), 1144–1149. Available from https://doi.org/10.1016/j.brat.2010.07.010.

Goldstein, T. R., Fersch-Podrat, R. K., Rivera, M., Axelson, D. A., Merranko, J., Yu, H., ... Birmaher, B. (2015). Dialectical behavior therapy for adolescents with bipolar disorder: Results from a pilot randomized trial. *Journal of Child and Adolescent Psychopharmacology, 25*, 140–149. Available from https://doi.org/10.1089/cap.2013.0145.

Haga, E., Aas, E., Groholt, B., Tormoen, A., & Mehlum, L. (2018). Cost-effectiveness of dialectical behaviour therapy vs. enhanced usual care in the treatment of adolescents with self-harm. *Child and Adolescent Psychiatry and Mental Health, 12*(22). Available from https://doi.org/10.1186/s13034-018-0227-2.

Harley, R., Sprich, S., Safren, S., Jacobo, M., & Fava, M. (2008). Adaptation of dialectical behavior therapy skills training group for treatment-resistant depression. *The Journal of Nervous and Mental Disease, 196*, 136–143. Available from https://doi.org/10.1097/NMD.0b013e318162aa3f.

Härter, M., Watzke, B., Daubmann, A., Wegscheider, K., König, H.-H., Brettschneider, C., ... Steinmann, M. (2018). Guideline-based stepped and collaborative care for patients with depression in a cluster-randomised trial. *Sci. Rep., 8*(1), 9389. Available from https://doi.org/10.1038/s41598-018-27470-6.

Haugh, J. A., Herbert, K., Choi, S., Petrides, J., Vermeulen, M. W., & D'Onofrio, J. (2019). Acceptability of the stepped care model of depression treatment in primary care patients and providers. *Journal of Clinical Psychology in Medical Settings*. Available from https://doi.org/10.1007/s10880-019-09599-2.

Ho, F. Y., Yeung, W., Ng, T. H., & Chan, C. S. (2016). The efficacy and cost-effectiveness of stepped care prevention and treatment for depressive and/or anxiety disorders: A systematic review and meta-analysis. *Scientific Reports*, *6*(1), 29281. Available from https://doi.org/10.1038/srep29281.

Katon, W., & Seelig, M. (2008). Population-based care of depression: Team care approaches to improving outcomes. *Journal of Occupational and Environmental Medicine*, *50*(4), 459–467. Available from https://doi.org/10.1097/JOM.0b013e318168efb7.

Katon, W., Unützer, J., Wells, K., & Jones, L. (2010). Collaborative depression care: History, evolution and ways to enhance dissemination and sustainability. *General Hospital Psychiatry*, *32*(5), 456–464. Available from https://doi.org/10.1016/j.genhosppsych.2010.04.001.

Kidorf, M., Neufeld, K., King, V. L., Clark, M., & Brooner, R. K. (2007). A stepped care approach for reducing cannabis use in opioid-dependent outpatients. *Journal of Substance Abuse Treatment*, *32*(4), 341–347. Available from https://doi.org/10.1016/j.jsat.2006.09.005.

Kopelovich, S. L., Strachan, E., Sivec, H., & Kreider, V. (2019). Stepped care as an implementation and service delivery model for cognitive behavioral therapy for psychosis. *Community Mental Health Journal*, *55*(5), 755–767, https://doi.org/10.1007s10597-018-00365-6.

Linehan, M. M., Comtois, K. A., & Ward-Ciesielski, E. F. (2012). Assessing and managing risk with suicidal individuals. *Cognitive and Behavioral Practice*, *19*(2), 218–232. Available from https://doi.org/10.1016/j.cbpra.2010.11.008.

Linehan, M. M., Dimeff, L., Reynolds, S., Comtois, K. A., Welch, S., Heagerty, P., & Kivlahan, D. R. (2002). Dialectical behavior therapy versus comprehensive validation therapy plus 12-step for the treatment of opioid dependent women meeting criteria for borderline personality disorder. *Drug and Alcohol Dependence*, *67*(1), 13–26. Available from https://doi.org/10.1016/S0376-8716(02)00011-X.

Linehan, M. M., Korslund, K. E., Harned, M. S., Gallop, R. J., Lungu, A., Neacsiu, A. D., ... Murray-Gregory, A. M. (2015). Dialectical behavior therapy for high suicide risk in individuals with borderline personality disorder: A randomized clinical trial and component analysis. *JAMA Psychiatry*, *72*(5), 475–482. Available from https://doi.org/10.1001/jamapsychiatry.2014.3039.

Lopez, A., & Chessick, C. A. (2013). DBT graduate group pilot study: A model to generalize skills to create a "life worth living". *Social Work in Mental Health*, *11*(2), 141–153. Available from https://doi.org/10.1080/15332985.2012.755145.

McCauley, E., Berk, M. S., Asarnow, J. R., Adrian, M., Cohen, J., Korslund, K., ... Linehan, M. M. (2018). Efficacy of dialectical behavior therapy for adolescents at high risk for suicide: A randomized clinical trial. *JAMA Psychiatry*, *75*(8), 777–785. Available from https://doi.org/10.1001/jamapsychiatry.2018.1109.

McKay, M., Wood, J. C., & Brantley, J. (2007). *The dialectical behavior therapy skills workbook*. Oakland: N. Harbinger.

Mehlum, L., Tormoen, A. J., Ramberg, M., Haga, E., Diep, L. M., Laberg, S., ... Groholt, B. (2014). Dialectical behavior therapy for adolescents with repeated suicidal and self-harming behavior: a randomized trial. *Journal of the American Academy of Child and Adolescent Psychiatry*, *53*(10), 1082–1091. Available from https://doi.org/10.1016/j.jaac.2014.07.003.

National Institute for Health and Clinical Excellence (2011). *Generalized anxiety disorder and panic disorder in adults: management*. Retrieved from <https://www.nice.org.uk/guidance/cg113>.

National Institute for Health and Clinical Excellence (2019). *Depression in children and young people: identification and management*. Retrieved from <https://www.nice.org.uk/guidance/ng134>.

Neacsiu, A. D., Eberle, J. W., Kramer, R., Wiesmann, T., & Linehan, M. M. (2014). Dialectical behavior therapy skills for transdiagnostic emotion dysregulation: A pilot randomized controlled trial. *Behaviour Research and Therapy*, *59*, 40–51. Available from https://doi.org/10.1016/j.brat.2014.05.005.

Newman, M. G. (2000). Recommendations for a cost-offset model of psychotherapy allocation using generalized anxiety disorder as an example. *Journal of Consulting and Clinical Psychology*, *68*(4), 549–555.

Nordgreen, T., Haug, T., Öst, L.-G., Andersson, G., Carlbring, P., Kvale, G., ... Havik, O. E. (2016). Stepped care versus direct face-to-face cognitive behavior therapy for social anxiety disorder and panic disorder: A randomized effectiveness trial. *Behavior Therapy*, *47*(2), 166–183. Available from https://doi.org/10.1016/j.beth.2015.10.004.

Ollendick, T. H., Öst, L.-G., & Farrell, L. J. (2018). Innovations in the psychosocial treatment of youth with anxiety disorders: Implications for a stepped care approach. *Evidence-Based Mental Health*, *21*(3), 112–115. Available from https://doi.org/10.1136/eb-2018-102892.

Paris, J. (2013). Stepped care: An alternative to routine extended treatment for patients with borderline personality disorder. *Psychiatric Services*, *64*(10), 1035–1037. Available from https://doi.org/10.1176/appi.ps.201200451.

Perepletchikova, F., Nathanson, D., Axelrod, S., Merrill, C., Walker, A., Grossman, M., ... Walkup, J. (2017). Randomized clinical trial of dialectical behavior therapy for preadolescent children with disruptive mood dysregulation disorder: Feasibility and outcomes. *Journal of the American Academy of Child and Adolescent Psychiatry*, *56*, 832–840. Available from https://doi.org/10.1016/j.jaac.2017.07.789.

Rapee, R. M., Lyneham, H. J., Wuthrich, V., Chatterton, M. L., Hudson, J. L., Kangas, M., & Mihalopoulos, C. (2017). Comparison of stepped care delivery against a single, empirically validated cognitive-behavioral therapy program for youth with anxiety: A randomized clinical trial. *Journal of the American Academy of Child and Adolescent Psychiatry*, *56*(10), 841–848. Available from https://doi.org/10.1016/j.jaac.2017.08.001.

Reetz, D. R., Barr, V., & Krylowicz, B. (2014). Assoc. Univ. Coll. Counseling Cent. Dir. Annu. Surv. Retrieved from <http://files.cmcglobal.com/AUCCCD_Monograph_Public_2013.pdf>

Rollman, B. L., Belnap, B. H., Mazumdar, S., Abebe, K. Z., Karp, J. F., Lenze, E. J., & Schulberg, H. C. (2017). Telephone-delivered stepped collaborative care for treating anxiety in primary care: A randomized controlled trial. *Journal of General Internal Medicine*, *32*(3), 245–255. Available from https://doi.org/10.1007/s11606-016-3873-1.

Safer, D. L., Telch, C. F., & Agras, W. S. (2001). Dialectical behavior therapy for bulimia nervosa. *The American Journal of Psychiatry*, *158*, 632–634. Available from https://doi.org/10.1176/appi.ajp.158.4.632.

Safer, D. L., Robinson, A., & Jo, B. (2010). Outcome from a randomized controlled trial of group therapy for binge eating disorder: Comparing dialectical behavior therapy adapted for binge eating to an active comparison group therapy. *Behavior Therapy*, *41* (1), 106e120. Available from https://doi.org/10.1016/j.beth.2009.01.006.

Salloum, A., Scheeringa, M. S., Cohen, J. A., & Storch, E. A. (2014). Development of stepped care trauma-focused cognitive-behavioral therapy for young children. *Cognitive and Behavioral Practice*, *21*(1), 97–108. Available from https://doi.org/10.1016/j.cbpra.2013.07.004.

Salloum, A., Wang, W., Robst, J., Murphy, T. K., Scheeringa, M. S., Cohen, J. A., & Storch, E. A. (2016). Stepped care versus standard trauma-focused cognitive behavioral therapy for young children. *Journal of Child Psychology and Psychiatry*, *57*(5), 614–622. Available from https://doi.org/10.1111/jcpp.12471.

Salomonsson, S., Santoft, F., Lindsäter, E., Ejeby, K., Ljótsson, B., Öst, L.-G., ... Hedman-Lagerlöf, E. (2018). Stepped care in primary care – guided self-help and face-to-face cognitive behavioural therapy for common mental disorders: A randomized controlled trial. *Psychological Medicine*, *48*(10), 1644–1654. Available from https://doi.org/10.1017/S0033291717003129.

Schroeder, J., Wilks, C., Rowan, K., Toledo, A., Paradiso, A., Czerwinski, M., et al. (2018). Pocket skills: A conversational mobile web app to support dialectical behavioral therapy. In *Presented at the SIGCHI conference on human factors in computing systems (CHI 2018)*. Montreal, Canada.

Stanley, M. A., Wilson, N. L., Amspoker, A. B., Kraus-Schuman, C., Wagener, P., Calleo, J. S., ... Kunik, M. E. (2014). Lay providers can deliver effective cognitive behavior therapy for older adults with generalized anxiety disorder: A randomized trial. *Depression Anxiety*, *31*(5), 391–401. Available from https://doi.org/10.1002/da.22239.

Tasca, G. A., Koszycki, D., Brugnera, A., Chyurlia, L., Hammond, N., Francis, K., ... Balfour, L. (2019). Testing a stepped care model for binge-eating disorder: A two-step randomized controlled trial. *Psychological Medicine*, *49*(4), 598–606. Available from https://doi.org/10.1017/S0033291718001277.

Tolin, D. F., Diefenbach, G. J., & Gilliam, C. M. (2011). Stepped care versus standard cognitive-behavioral therapy for obsessive-compulsive disorder: A preliminary study of efficacy and costs. *Depression Anxiety*, *28*(4), 314–323. Available from https://doi.org/10.1002/da.20804.

van der Aa, H. P. A., van Rens, G. H. M. B., Bosmans, J. E., Comijs, H. C., & van Nispen, R. M. A. (2017). Economic evaluation of stepped-care versus usual care for depression and anxiety in older adults with vision impairment: Randomized controlled trial. *BMC Psychiatry*, *17*(1), 280. Available from https://doi.org/10.1186/s12888-017-1437-5.

van der Leeden, A. J. M., van Widenfelt, B. M., van der Leeden, R., Liber, J. M., Utens, E. M. W. J., & Treffers, P. D. A. (2011). Stepped care cognitive behavioural therapy for children with anxiety disorders: A new treatment approach. *Behavioural and Cognitive Psychotherapy*, *39*(1), 55–75. Available from https://doi.org/10.1017/S1352465810000500.

Van Dijk, S., Jeffrey, J., & Katz, M. R. (2013). A randomized, controlled, pilot study of dialectical behavior therapy skills in a psychoeducational group for individuals with bipolar disorder. *Journal of Affective Disorders*, *145*, 386–393. Available from https://doi.org/10.1016/j.jad.2012.05.054.

van Straten, A., Hill, J., Richards, D. A., & Cuijpers, P. (2015). Stepped care treatment delivery for depression: A systematic review and meta-analysis. *Psychological Medicine*, *45*(2), 231–246. Available from https://doi.org/10.1017/S0033291714000701.

Vincent, N., & Walsh, K. (2013). Stepped care for insomnia: An evaluation of implementation in routine practice. *Journal of Clinical Sleep Medicine*. Available from https://doi.org/10.5664/jcsm.2484.

Wagner, E. H., Austin, B. T., & Von Korff, M. (1996). Organizing care for patients with chronic illness. *The Milbank Quarterly*, *74*(4), 511–544.

Wilson, G. T., Vitousek, K. M., & Loeb, K. L. (2000). Stepped care treatment for eating disorders. *Journal of Consulting and Clinical Psychology*, *68*(4), 564–572.

Wilks, C. R., Lungu, A., Ang, S. Y., Matsumiya, B., Yin, Q., & Linehan, M. M. (2018). A randomized controlled trial of an Internet delivered dialectical behavior therapy skills training for suicidal and heavy episodic drinkers. *Journal of Affective Disorders*, *232*, 219–228. Available from https://doi.org/10.1016/j.jad.2018.02.053.

Zatzick, D., O'Connor, S. S., Russo, J., Wang, J., Bush, N., Love, J., ... Van Eaton, E. (2015). Technology-enhanced stepped collaborative care targeting posttraumatic stress disorder and comorbidity after injury: A randomized controlled trial. *Journal of Traumatic Stress*, *28*(5), 391–400. Available from https://doi.org/10.1002/jts.22041.

CHAPTER

14

DBT–ACES in a multicultural community mental health setting: implications for clinical practice

Lisa S. Bolden[1], *Lizbeth Gaona*[2], *Lynn McFarr*[3] *and Kate Comtois*[4]

[1]UCLA David Geffen School of Medicine Health Sciences at Harbor UCLA Medical Center, Torrance, CA, United States, [2]California Baptist University, College of Behavioral and Social Sciences, Riverside, CA, United States, [3]UCLA David Geffen School of Medicine at Harbor-UCLA Medical Center, Torrance, CA, United States, [4]Department of Psychiatry and Behavioral Sciences, University of Washington, WA, United States

Dialectical behavior therapy—accepting the challenges of exiting the system

Dialectical behavior therapy—accepting the challenges to exiting the system (DBT–ACES) is a program developed in 1999 by Harborview Mental Health Services as a second-year treatment program post clients' successful completion of standard DBT (SDBT) (Comtois, Kerbrat, Atkins, Harned, & Elwood, 2010). The aims of DBT–ACES are targeted at supporting clients in continuing to aspire for a life worth living, improve their quality of life and strive toward recovery, ultimately breaking free from psychiatric disability. From the end of SDBT toward the end of DBT–ACES, clients have demonstrated substantial gains. Clients have shown significant odds of being employed or going to

The Handbook of Dialectical Behavior Therapy
DOI: https://doi.org/10.1016/B978-0-12-816384-9.00014-2

school, working at least 20 hours a week and reporting a higher subjective quality of life (Comtois et al., 2010). Findings have illustrated how DBT–ACES has successfully aided clients in continuing to break free from dependence of public social systems and the bondage associated with psychiatric disability.

Although the outcomes of DBT–ACES have been positive, it has also been documented that some clients have struggled to complete the program due to barriers such as fear, competing obligations, the lack of interest, or willfulness (Carmel, Comtois, Harned, Holler, & McFarr, 2016). Contingency management has been illustrated as a successful means toward helping clients in DBT–ACES successfully complete the program (Carmel et al., 2016). Still there are other challenges that arise which hinder individuals from successfully completing DBT–ACES and/or make it a more challenging experience to meet the program's treatment goals. These issues may be related to issues related to diversity, being a minority and of low socioeconomic status. Therefore it is important to summarize the literature on the importance of considering diversity in general for the delivery of DBT.

This chapter will expand on the dialectic between the desires to successfully complete DBT–ACES and barriers that may arise among clients of diverse multicultural backgrounds. Examples from clinical practice from a DBT–ACES program based in urban Los Angeles made up of heterogeneous clients from diverse ethnics group and cultures will aid in illustrating possible issues to completing DBT–ACES from clients of multicultural backgrounds. Implications for clinical practice will be provided.

Diversity in DBT: why focus on diversity in DBT?

Numerous studies have demonstrated that culture and ethnicity have an impact on mental health (Hall, Ibaraki, Huang, Marti, & Stice, 2016; Hwang, Myers, Abe-Kim, & Ting, 2008) and that cultural factors are important in the treatment and diagnosis of borderline personality disorder (McFarr et al, 2014; DSM-V, American Psychiatric Association, 2013). Borderline personality disorder has more recently been noted in research as a psychological syndrome worthy of study across cultures and countries (Huang et al., 2009; McFarr et al., 2014). Preliminary, research shows that DBT has been shown to be effective in the reduction of borderline personality disorder symptoms across cultures, but additional study is needed (Hall et al., 2016; Loranger et al., 1994). For example, one study found that randomized controlled trials of dialectical behavior therapy have overwhelmingly consisted of females of

Caucasian descent relative to ethnic minorities and persons of diverse gender (Gaona & Amaro, 2017).

Both research- and practice-based evidence has shown DBT to be favorable in the treatment of minorities such as Latinos diagnosed with BPD (Germán et al., 2015; McFarr et al., 2014), South Asians in Nepali (Ramaiya, Fiorillo, Regmi, Robins, & Kohrt, 2017), African Americans diagnosed with eating disorders, and American Indians (Beckstead, Lambert, DuBose, & Linehan, 2015; Kinsey & Reed, 2015). There remains, however, a dearth of research in this area. Additional research would benefit by focusing on the relationship between the application of dialectical behavior therapy and multicultural factors as it relates to ethnic groups in the United States and internationally (Cardemil, 2010; Gaona & Amaro, 2017). Fortunately, DBT–ACES has gained ground in the area of recruiting clients of various ethnic groups in intervention research as will be discussed further in this chapter.

Multiculturalism and treatment

Historically, cultural differences have been viewed as deficits (Bolton-Brownlee, 1987; Boyd-Franklin, 1989). Multicultural counseling, however, seeks to rectify this imbalance by acknowledging cultural diversity, appreciating the value of the culture and using it to aid the client. Counselors cannot adopt their clients' ethnicity or cultural heritage, but they can become more sensitive to these things and to their own and their clients' biases. Clinical sensitivity toward client expectation, attributions, values, roles, beliefs, and themes of coping and vulnerability is always necessary for effective outcomes (LaFromboise, 1985). It is also important to be culturally response to clients' unique differences and needs. To be culturally responsive is to take an active stance in working with culturally specific ideas or meanings expressed or referred to by a client, which are viewed by the client and therapist together as relevant to the therapeutic task of specific modalities.

The dialectic: DBT is culturally competent and may be culturally enhanced

Several aspects of DBT lend it to be as culturally competent as many psychotherapies, particularly in the hands of a culturally competent therapist. As noted earlier, a few studies have demonstrated that cultural adaptations of the treatment were effective (Beckstead et al., 2015; Kinsey & Reed, 2015). In a study of DBT with an adolescent American Indian and Alaska Native population, Becksted et al. (2015) found improvement in mood symptoms when DBT was incorporated with traditional cultural and spiritual practices. Similarly, a cultural adaptation of DBT utilizing a toolkit for cultural modification of evidence-based treatments (Samuels, Schudrich, & Altschul, 2009) increased community engagement and access to DBT (Kinsey & Reed, 2015).

DBT is especially suited for cultural adaptations in several ways. First, DBT emphasizes client expectations, attributions, values, roles, beliefs, coping styles, and emotional vulnerability (Linehan, 1993; McFarr et al., 2014), which are all important for culturally competent clinical outcomes (LaFromboise, 1985). Second, DBT has a pretreatment period, which allows for engagement and assessment of the client, including information pertinent to the client's culture (Linehan, 1993). Third, DBT weaves phenomenological empathy and validation throughout treatment to strategically aid the therapist with conceptualization and communication in the therapeutic dyad. Fourth, the therapist is directed to conceptualize contextually which squarely places the client in their social and sociocultural context. The therapist can then use validation and a dialectical perspective to share their understanding of the client who is seen as the greater partner in deciding if the understanding is useful and meaningful. Fifth, DBT supports the therapist in being culturally sensitive through its collaborative style of treatment planning. Most of the interventions, such as chain analysis help the therapeutic dyad understand the context surrounding target behaviors. Lastly, DBT is culturally competent as it helps the clinician think dialectically by seeing the client as an equal partner in the treatment and focusing on the client's unique cultural strengths in case formulation and treatment (Linehan, 1993).

The DBT consultation team

In addition, the DBT (or DBT–ACES) consultation team has elements that strive toward cultural competence as it helps the therapist embrace a mindfulness approach of observation and description (rather than standard clinical interpretation) and a nonjudgmental stance when discussing the client. The DBT–ACES consultation team, which is generally part of the context of the SDBT team, assists the therapist with maintaining the balance of contextualism through validation, core strength–based assumptions about the client, and mindfulness skills of observation, description, nonjudgmental stance, and effectiveness. Further, as DBT therapists consult on cases, they are challenged to explore diversity aspects intertwined with clinical issues (McFarr et al., 2014). The DBT consultation team assists the therapist with maintaining the balance by keeping the team focused on the therapists' needs and skills (not the clients) and using the consultation team agreements to promote positive, strength-based, and accurate understanding of the clients and each other (Linehan, 1993).

What is missing?

In DBT, when a dialectical dilemma or tension arises, a DBT therapist is encouraged to conduct a dialectical assessment by considering "what is missing?" To this end, although we have highlighted a number of examples as to why and how DBT is culturally competent, we have also asked what may be missing. Based on practice-based evidence and literature, we posit that DBT–ACES treatment may be further enhanced by more explicitly adopting the use of multicultural competency models and being mindful to address employment and self-sufficiency cultural dialectics that are likely to arise. Using examples from clinical practice gained while providing DBT–ACES treatment to the diverse sample of clients from Harbor-UCLA Medical Center in Los Angeles County, California (Harbor-UCLA), this chapter will highlight the importance of using multicultural competency models and being mindful of cultural dialectics while providing DBT–ACES treatment.

DBT–ACES: state of the evidence

The goal of DBT–ACES is to achieve and maintain a living wage employment, self-sufficiency, and a life worth living outside of social services without the need for psychiatric disability payments or other dependency. DBT–ACES was developed within a community mental health center and has demonstrated feasibility and acceptability across three sites but has not been examined in a controlled trial. The first program evaluation was for psychiatrically disabled patients on Medicaid or Medicare at Harborview Mental Health and Addiction Services (Harborview), Seattle, WA. Published in 2010 (Comtois et al., 2010), the study compared outcomes during their year of SDBT to their year of DBT–ACES to the year following DBT–ACES (when they were discharged from the program and no longer receiving DBT). After completion of SDBT, participants were more likely to be employed in school and working at least 20 hours per week. Participants also reported significant improvements in their quality of life and fewer inpatient admissions. At 1 year follow-up following the completion of DBT–ACES, 36% of DBT–ACES clients were receiving public health services. In addition, clinical outcomes (e.g., self-harm, psychiatric admissions, quality of life) were retained.

Since the original paper, two additional sites—Harbor-UCLA and a clinic in Lengerich, Germany—have adopted DBT–ACES and all three sites conducted a coordinated program evaluation. Results of this evaluation are obtained with 45 clients—21 from Harborview, 8 from Harbor-UCLA, and 16 from Germany. The Harborview program was 95% female and 5% Latinex, 14% mixed ethnicity, and 81% white. The Harbor-UCLA sample was 100% female, 13% black, 13% Latinex, and 75% white. The German program was 88% female and 100% white. The program evaluation across three sites found, compared to the year before starting SDBT, participants significantly increased their hours of competitive employment and/or enrolled schooling by 7.96 h/week in the year of SDBT and by 16.65 h/week in the following year of DBT–ACES. The estimated net monetary benefit of SDBT was $16,491, driven primarily by a decrease in inpatient care, which remained low during DBT–ACES. The value of school and workplace productivity more than doubled during the DBT–ACES program to $546 compared to $246 during SDBT. Results were comparable across all three sites.

The Harbor-UCLA program, a community mental health clinic located in a suburban area of Los Angeles, was further expanded on given the cultural diversity of the clients. The program evaluation was conducted at Harbor-UCLA and included 23 clients enrolled in DBT–ACES over the past 6 years. The clients were fairly diverse in age and ethnicity (see Table 14.1). The mean age was 38.5 with a range of 29–55 years of age. Just over half of the clients were Caucasian, followed by Hispanic/Latina. Asian American clients made up 8% of the sample followed by 4% African American and 4% mixed Latina/Hispanic. Harbor-UCLA's richly diverse client sample allowed for lessons learned from clinical practice. Although the majority of the clients (47%) to date have graduated from DBT–ACES successfully, at times cultural dialectics arose during treatment, which appeared to hinder and influence the course of treatment.

Multicultural community mental health clinic and barriers to completing DBT–ACES treatment

Barriers related to cultural dialectics

We will refer to the term of cultural dialectic as a means of describing a dialectical dilemma in which a client is struggling to adhere to a value or norm associated with their culture and the tension of a divergent or opposing value. Although it is not exhaustive, Table 14.2 outlines some of the cultural dialectics that arose during DBT–ACES treatment of diverse clients. As illustrated, some clients shared that they experienced

TABLE 14.1 Demographic of clients receiving dialectical behavior therapy—accepting the challenge of exiting the system at Harbor-UCLA ($N = 23$).

	Mean	Range
Age	38.5	29–55
Gender	*n*	(%)
Female	23	(100)
Ethnic identity		
Latina/Hispanic	6	(26)
African American	1	(4)
Asian American	2	(8)
Caucasian	12	(52)
Mixed African American and Latina	1	(4)
Not reported	1	(4)
ACES program exit status		
Graduated successfully	11	(47)
Dropped out	3	(13)
Suspended	3	(13)
Not reported	6	(26)

TABLE 14.2 Cultural dialectics in dialectical behavior therapy—accepting the challenge of exiting the system (DBT–ACES) at Harbor-UCLA.

Dialectical tension	DBT–ACES treatment goal
Familism/parenting role versus self-sufficiency	Career activities (10 h a week by 4 months of treatment, 20 h a week by 8 months)
Caregiver versus pursuing grand ambition	
Traditional gender roles versus pursuing grand ambition	Work as therapy
Education or training versus W2 employment	

challenges with placing their families' needs and prioritizing family agenda items above all else, which we refer to as familism, in a tension with the desire to reach self-sufficiency. These clients shared the challenges of participating in career activities as part of the DBT–ACES treatment goals while having to negotiate family agenda items such as preparing daily fresh cooked meals or completing family and household chores. Another cultural dialectic is that of fulfilling their traditional gender role versus pursuing their grand ambition. Some female Latino DBT–ACES clients felt torn between their cultural traditional gender roles of staying at home and relying on a partner for financial stability versus their dreams of pursuing their grand ambition. Similarly, in one DBT graduate group pilot program that was influenced by DBT–ACES curriculum, one participant shared that her partner was not supportive of her returning to school (Lopez & Chessick, 2013). In this case the client's feelings were validated and the client used interpersonal effectiveness skills to solve problems (Lopez & Chessick, 2013).

In line with traditional gender roles, according to Falcón (2013) some clients of Latino backgrounds may hold values associated with *machismo* or *marianismo*. Falcón (2013) describes Machismo as male behavior that may appear as being dominant or patriarchal. At the same time, *machismo* as described by Arce (2013) may be associated with positive traits such as a man who works long hours to provide and meet familial obligations as the head of household, whereas *marianismo*, which derived from the worship of the Virgin Mary, is associated with behavior that emulates the conceptualization of the Virgin Mary as a woman who is seen as docile, subservient, self-sacrificing (Falcón, 2013). Further, *marianismo* is associated with a nurturing woman who is not only a caregiver but must also engage herself in self-sacrificial behaviors and express endless love and prioritize the care of her children (Falcón, 2013). In such cases, these clients may be faced with the dialectic of wanting to successfully complete DBT–ACES while at the same time struggling to also uphold their cultural values.

As mentioned, it may be possible that clients may feel hesitant to disclose valuing such gender roles as they may believe that they will be judged as being counter-mainstream culture, or for fear of disappointing their DBT–ACES therapist because their values are opposed to some of the work as therapy requirements of DBT–ACES. Given our practice-based evidence, we call attention to the importance of DBT–ACES clinicians to be mindful of cultural dialectics that may arise in treatment. It is key that early in treatment, clinicians encourage open dialogue with their clients on the possibility that these dialectical tensions may arise. Encouraging nonjudgmental dialogues on cultural dialectics may help clients avoid failing to disclose that they may be experiencing such tensions. Further, it may improve the course of treatment as clients may feel comfortable disclosing if they experience these tensions and have a greater opportunity to problem solve versus engage in behavior that may lead to suspension.

To this end, we suggest some practical tools that may assist clinicians in further strengthening their cultural sensitivity and humility skills. The American Psychological Association (APA) website www.apa.org offers a free search option in which one can search for publications, videos, books, and other databases on the topics of multicultural competence and multicultural provision of care. One of the few suggested books is *Cultural humility: Engaging diverse identities in therapy* by Hook, Captari, Davis, DeBlaere, and Owen (2017). The book highlights the stance of culturally humility in which one acknowledges that they have limitations in their ability to understand their clients' cultural experience and background. Another is *Multicultural care: A clinician's guide to cultural competence*, by Comas-Díaz (2012). This book offers practical suggestions for ways in which one can provide multicultural care in treatment.

Barriers related to intersectionality

Noteworthy, other barriers to successfully completing DBT–ACES may be related to the compounding effects of intersectionality. Broadly speaking, intersectionality can be described as the interaction of various individual and social factors that may affect a person's life (Gopaldas, 2013; Hankivsky et al., 2010; Vera & Feagin, 2007). One example is the compounding effects of being of minority gender status, being a member of a minority ethnic group, being poor and holding cultural values that may conflict with mainstream values or as with our previous examples, with the tenants of DBT–ACES. For example, for poor, single, African American mothers on welfare/public benefits, seminal work has illustrated how their values of familism and good parenting may be in conflict with the strains of low paying or unfavorable jobs (Jarrett, 1994). In their study, Jarrett (1994) found that poor single African American mothers felt conflicted with the desire to get off public benefits, but the fear of losing medical benefits for their children and/or torn by having to travel on public transportation for lengthy periods of time for low paying wages and feeling conflicted with only being home with their children late in the evening.

To this end, we emphasize the importance of considering a discussion with DBT–ACES clients on how intersectionality may factor into clients' progress in treatment. This can be done by integrating Hays' (2001) model. For example, the clinician can conceptualize the client based on their age, gender, indigenous heritage and national origin, sexual orientation, socioeconomic, and religious and spiritual characteristics during the assessment and intervention phases of DBT–ACES treatment; particularly while helping clients navigate a job search.

This dialogue with clients may engender much needed validation of the compounding factors that may bear weight on their experiences with the difficulties of finding work. Further, conceptualizing their clients' case using Hays' model may help clinicians better understand the dialectic between the DBT–ACES goals of diligently looking for work and their clients' experience of possibly feeling punished by the lack of response on the job market from employers who shy away from offering them interviews. In turn, therapist may be better equipped to validate their clients' experience, highlight the cultural dialectical tension, and help their client navigate building a bridge between their cultural experience, values, and DBT–ACES treatment goals despite the challenges of intersectionality.

Recommendations for clinical practice

Multicultural competence of clinicians

Given some of the barriers mentioned, we encourage continued emphasis and growth in the area of multicultural competence of DBT–ACES clinicians. Clients are influenced by a number of combined factors such as race, ethnicity, national origin, life stage, educational level, social class, and sex roles (Ibrahim, 1985). Consequently, therapists can improve their effectiveness from viewing the identity and development of culturally diverse people in terms of multiple, interactive factors, rather than a strictly cultural framework (Romero, 1985). A pluralistic counselor considers all facets of the client's personal history, family history, and social and cultural orientation (Arcinega & Newlou, 1981). Basic cultural competence involves self-assessment regarding matters of cultural identity, including issues of privilege (Johnson & Williams, 2015). We recommend that DBT–ACES therapists routinely adopt the use of multicultural competency models, including transtheoretical approaches to conceptualization (Hays, 2001) and the use of cultural adaption toolkits (Kinsey & Reed, 2015; Samuels et al., 2009) to aid them in providing multicultural competent treatment.

For instance, Model 1 highlights how the use of multicultural models in DBT–ACES may also increase clinicians' awareness of how intersectionality is experienced by the client, awareness of cultural dialectics the client may be experiencing, and multicultural humility. As illustrated in Model 1, we propose that assisting the DBT–ACES clinician to gain strength in these valuable concepts will help them to better address the dialectical tensions between DBT–ACES goals and expectations of clients' performance and the cultural values and other issues such as lived experiences of stereotypes and biases the clients may be experiencing.

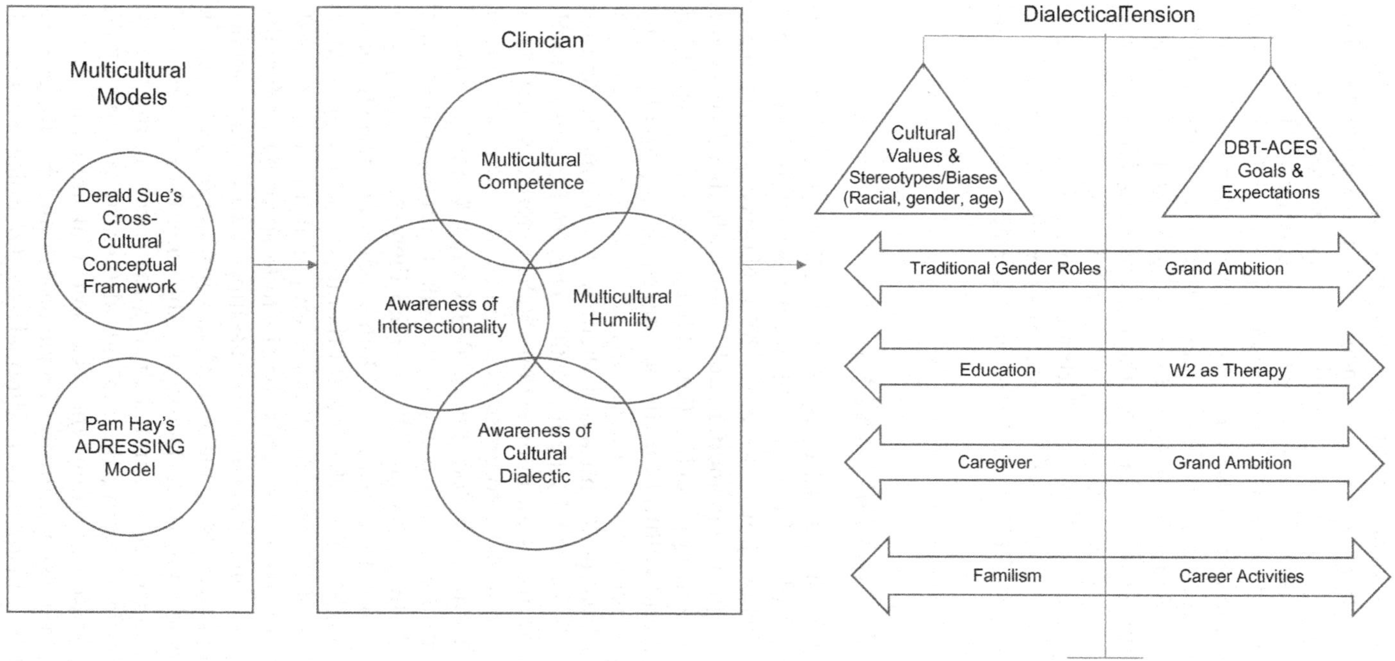
Multicultural Models
Derald Sue's Cross-Cultural Conceptual Framework
Pam Hay's ADRESSING Model
Clinician
Multicultural Competence
Awareness of Intersectionality
Multicultural Humility
Awareness of Cultural Dialectic
DialecticalTension
Cultural Values & Stereotypes/Biases (Racial, gender, age)
DBT-ACES Goals & Expectations
Traditional Gender Roles
Grand Ambition
Education
W2 as Therapy
Caregiver
Grand Ambition
Familism
Career Activities

MODEL 1

In addition to exploring clients' cultural values in treatment, we believe it is critical to explore their lived experiences related to stereotypes and biases related to factors such as race/ethnic group, gender, and age. Research related to African American women receiving DBT showed that they reported a lack of trust in the system and people in the system as a key factor that hindered their recovery (Creswell, 2014). This said, we underscore the importance of increasing clinician awareness of the client's experience compared side-by-side with DBT–ACES goals and expectations. The simple act of having these frank, humble conversations with clients may aid in problem-solving and reaching a synthesis, which in turn may help to decrease hindrances to recovery and treatment goals. Next, we will provide overviews of multicultural seminal models that we suggest DBT–ACES clinicians consider adopting into practice.

Multicultural models and DBT–ACES

First, in terms of multicultural competency models, it is valuable to assess the process of cultural conceptualization versus therapeutic process models (Huey, Tiley, Jones, & Smith, 2014; Nagayma et al., 2016). Many training and supervision models utilize individualized conceptualization and assessment approaches (Tao, Owen, Pace, & Imel, 2015). Cultural assessment and cultural functional analysis help provide a clinical understanding of ethnically and racially diverse clients to prevent their dropout from treatment and assist them with meeting functional outcomes (Okazaki & Tanaka-Matsumi, 2006). The application of models that approach culture as an intersection of characteristics that make up a client's identity may lead to greater outcomes in treatment (Bernal, Jiménez-Chafey, & Domenech Rodríguez, 2009; Griner & Smith, 2006).

Although there are numerous models, we will highlight two seminal multicultural models that may aid DBT–ACES therapists as they provide multicultural competent treatment. Both models are transtheoretical and can be applied by the DBT–ACES therapist and group leaders to the various modes of the treatment. For example, in individual treatment, collaboration on recovery goals that include securing and maintaining competitive employment, goal-setting, and contingency management around weekly achievement toward these goals can be framed around socio-contextual factors in the client's environment. These cultural factors can be integrated during the check-in and review of the DBT–ACES diary during the individual therapy portion of the treatment. During phone coaching the assessment around the client's experience of microagressions during the job search and hiring process and the effect of familism and traditional gender roles should be considered. For example, for African American clients, the DBT–ACES therapist should be mindful of the intersection of gender and racial issues when providing phone coaching around securing and maintaining employment, particularly the challenges for African American men to secure work due to a historical context of racism dating back to segregation and slavery (Brief, Dietz, Cohen, & Pugh, 2000). During skills training class, DBT–ACES skills group leaders should conceptualize these factors when engaging in contingency management as part of the group check-in.

Derald Sue's Cross-Cultural Conceptual Framework

Sue, Arredondeo, and McDavis (1992) highlight the Cross-Cultural Counseling Competencies Conceptual Framework, which is based on a tripartite model of awareness, knowledge, and skills. Awareness involves therapist's personal awareness of his or her own worldview. Knowledge refers to the therapist's understanding of other cultural groups norms and traditions, which can be gained in consultation, training, and dialogue with clients. Skills are techniques learned to work effectively with clients from diverse cultural populations. These skills are learned in formal training and maintained through supervision and consultation. At Harbor-UCLA the DBT–ACES consultation team functions in this regard and helps the ACES therapist exercise multicultural competence. Still, we recommend that the DBT–ACES consultation team intentionally consider routinely incorporating the use of awareness, knowledge, and skills during team meetings, including team mindfulness exercises, including interpersonal effectiveness mindfulness exercises to increase cultural awareness. For example, a mindfulness exercise in which the experience of being rejected for a job interview based on race, gender, or sexual orientation may be read aloud in an effort to increase clinician awareness of client's experience.

Pam Hay's ADRESSING Model

The ADRESSING Model (Hays, 2001) aids the therapist with conceptualizing cultural explanations for a client's behavior. The ADRESSING Model identifies the following factors as important when considering clients' treatment: (1) age and generational influences, (2) disability, (3) religion, (4) ethnicity, (5) social status, (6) sexual orientation, (7) indigenous heritage, (8) national origin, and (9) gender. We suggest that clinicians consider utilizing the ADRESSING Model as a means to assess and understand the role these factors may play in hindering or helping DBT–ACES clients with meeting employment and career contingencies as well as impacting their commitment to the program (Comtois et al., 2010). Furthermore, the DBT–ACES consultation team may utilize this model to help the therapist maintain a dialectical, nonjudgmental approach to problem-solving around a client's behavioral targets and therapy-interfering behaviors. For example, the DBT–ACES team observer and colleagues can ask the clinician what is missing in their conceptualization and intervention by asking them to discuss each of the previous cultural competencies that might be contributing to the client's behavioral avoidance. Furthermore, as part of the team's role of being therapy to the therapist (Linehan, 1993), the team acts as observer by pointing out the clinician's possible cultural bias, limits of multicultural competency, and how this might negatively affect the therapeutic relationship. In general, the DBT–ACES consultation team incorporates intersectionality as part of conceptualization and treatment with the ultimate of goal of supporting the clinician's treatment of the client and assisting their progress toward the goal of economic self-sufficiency.

The cultural dialectic and intersectionality

Lastly, we recommend that DBT–ACES clinicians be aware of clients' cultural values and how they may possible influence treatment. Although clients may have the best of intentions to complete DBT–ACES successfully, they may equally be struggling, in silence, with a cultural value or norm that is opposed to treatment goals. We also encourage a discussion on how intersectionality may play a role in the lives of clients, in terms of influencing their odds and/or experiences in participating in career activities such as job seeking and/or job interviews. It may be possible that clients may be actively searching for a job and engaged in career activities, yet still have a harder time finding employment due to the compounding factors of gender, ethnicity, age, and sexual identity. In addition to aiding these clients in using DBT skills to manage their experiences, a conversation about such factors may serve as both validating and encouraging to clients who are doing the best they can.

Summary

DBT–ACES has shown promising results as successful second-stage DBT program for individuals who desire to become independent of relying on social services. This chapter extended this promising work by introducing a multicultural DBT–ACES program and illustrated cultural dialectics that arose with clients of diverse ethnic backgrounds. This chapter encourages clinicians' use of intersectionality as a means to both educate and empower clients in their pursuit of successfully graduation from DBT–ACES; and although DBT–ACES is a culturally competent treatment, recommendations for clinical practice include the use of incorporating multicultural competence models such as Derald Sue's Cross-Cultural Conceptual Framework (Sue, 2001) and Pam Hay's ADRESSING Model (Hays, 2001).

Conclusion

As with any psychotherapy, it is essential that we acknowledge our own basic tendencies, the way we comprehend other cultures, and the limits our culture places on our comprehension. Elements of basic cultural competence involve self-assessment in regards to matters of cultural identity, including issues of privilege (Johnson & Williams, 2015). Further, it is essential to understand our own cultural heritage and worldview before we set about understanding and assisting other people (Sue, 2001). As previously mentioned, a strength of DBT is that it encourages clinicians to think dialectically and utilize an individual's unique cultural strengths in case formulation and treatment. Moreover, DBT therapists are to practice mindfulness skills, which incorporate awareness of judgment toward clients, DBT treatment team members, and the self. Nevertheless, as a DBT therapist, it is also important to ask, "What am I missing?"—in hopes to continue to cultivate and foster the cultural competence of DBT. We have suggested the consideration of cultural dialectics, intersectionality, and dialectical multicultural models in the delivery of DBT–ACES to multicultural clients.

References

Arcinega, M., & Newlou, B. J. (1981). A theoretical rationale for cross-cultural family counseling. *The School Counselor, 28*, 89–96.

Arce, W. (2013). Machismo. In C. E. Cortés (Ed.), *Multicultural America: A multimedia encyclopedia* (Vol. 1, pp. 1390–1391). Thousand Oaks, CA: SAGE Publications, Inc. Available from http://dx.doi.org/10.4135/9781452276274.n542.

Beckstead, J. D., Lambert, M. J., DuBose, A. P., & Linehan, M. (2015). Dialectical behavior therapy with American Indian/Alaska Native adolescents diagnosed with substance use disorders: Combining an evidence based treatment with cultural, traditional, and spiritual beliefs. *Addictive Behaviors, 51*, 84–87.

Bernal, G., Jiménez-Chafey, M. I., & Domenech Rodríguez, M. M. (2009). Cultural adaptation of treatments: A resource for considering culture in evidence-based practice. *Professional Psychology: Research and Practice, 40*(4), 361–368. Available from https://doi.org/10.1037/a0016401.

Bolton-Brownlee, A. (1987). Module 9 cultural competency, sensivity to diversity, and culturally specific treatment issues cultural competency and culturally specific issues eric identifier: ed279995 publication date: 1987-00-00.

Boyd-Franklin, N. (1989). *Black families therapy: A multisystemic approach.* Guilford Publishers.

Brief, A. P., Dietz, J., Cohen, R. R., & Pugh, S. D. (2000). Just doing business: Modern racism and obedience to authority as explanations for employment discrimination. *Organizational Behavior and Human Decision Processes*, *81*(1), 72–97.

Cardemil, E. V. (2010). Cultural adaptations to empirically supported treatments: A research agenda. *The Scientific Review of Mental Health Practice: Objective Investigations of Controversial and Unorthodox Claims in Clinical Psychology, Psychiatry, and Social Work*, *7* (2), 8–21.

Carmel, A., Comtois, K., Harned, M. S., Holler, R., & McFarr, L. (2016). Contingences create capabilities: Adjunctive treatments in dialectical behavior therapy that reinforce behavior change. *Cognitive and Behavioral Practice*, *23*, 110–120.

Comas-Díaz, L. (2012). *Psychologists in independent practice (Div. 42). Multicultural care: A clinician's guide to cultural competence*. American Psychological Association. Available from https://doi.org/10.1037/13491-000.

Comtois, K., Kerbrat, A. H., Atkins, D. C., Harned, M. S., & Elwood, L. (2010). Recovery from disability for individuals with borderline personality disorder: A feasibility trial of DBT-ACES. *Psychiatric Services*, *61*(11), 1106–1111.

Creswell, L. M. (2014). A critical feminist ethnography of treatment for women with co-occurring disorders in the psychiatric hospital. *The Journal of Behavioral Health Services & Research*, *41*, 167–184.

Diagnostic and Statistical Manual of Mental Disorders (5th ed.; DSM–5; American Psychiatric Association, 2013.

Falcón, K. (2013). Marianismo. In C. E. Cortés (Ed.), *Multicultural America: A multimedia encyclopedia* (Vol. 1, p. 1408). Thousand Oaks, CA: SAGE Publications, Inc. Available from http://dx.doi.org/10.4135/9781452276274.n550.

Gaona, L., & Amaro, H. (2017). Efficacy of dialectical behavior therapy for Latinos with borderline personality disorder: State of the evidence. In Poster presented at the *Association of Cognitive and Behavioral Therapy Annual Conference*, November 2017, San Diego, CA.

Germán, M., Smith, H. L., Rivera-Morales, C., González, G., Haliczer, L. A., Haaz, C., & Miller, A. L. (2015). Dialectical behavior therapy for suicidal latina adolescents: Supplemental dialectical corollaries and treatment targets. *American Journal of Psychotherapy*, *69*(2), 2015.

Gopaldas, A. (2013). Intersectionality 101. *Journal of Public Policy & Marketing*, *32*(1_Suppl.), 90–94.

Griner, D., & Smith, T. B. (2006). Culturally adapted mental health intervention: A meta-analytic review. *Psychotherapy: Theory, Research, Practice. Training*, *43*(4), 531–548. Available from https://doi.org/10.1037/0033-3204.43.4.531.

Hall, G. C., Ibaraki, A. Y., Huang, E. R., Marti, C. N., & Stice, E. (2016). A meta-analysis of cultural adaptations of psychological interventions. *Behavior Therapy*, *47*, 993–1014.

Hankivsky, O., Reid, C., Cormier, R., Varcoe, C., Clark, N., Benoit, C., & Brotman, S. (2010). Exploring the promises of intersectionality for advancing women's health research. *International Journal for Equity in Health*, *9*(1), 5.

Hays, P. A. (2001). *Addressing cultural complexities in practice: A framework for clinicians and counselors*. Washington, DC: American Psychological Association.

Hook, J. N., Captari, L. E., Davis, D. E., DeBlaere, C., & Owen, J. (2017). Cultural humility: A therapeutic framework for engaging diverse clients. *Practice Innovations*, 2(4), 221–233. Available from https://doi.org/10.1037/pri0000055.

Huang, Y. L., Yates, P., & Prior, D. (2009). Accommodating the diverse cultural needs of cancer patients and their families in palliative care. *Cancer Nursing*, *32*, E12–E21.

Huey, S. J., Tiley, J. L., Jones, E. O., & Smith, C. A. (2014). The contribution of cultural competence to evidence-based care for ethnically diverse populations. *Annual Review of Clinical Psychology*, *10*, 305–338.

Hwang, W. C., Myers, H. F., Abe-Kim, J., & Ting, J. (2008). A conceptual paradigm for understanding culture's impact on mental health: The cultural influences on mental health (CIMH) model. *Clinical Psychology Review, 28*(2), 212–228.

Ibrahim, F. A. (1985). *Effective cross-cultural counseling and psychotherapy: A framework, 13*(4), 625–638.

Jarrett, R. (1994). Living poor: Family life among single parent, African-American women. *Social Problems, 41*(1). Retrieved from <http://search.proquest.com/docview/1301548000/>.

Johnson, A., & Williams, D. J. (2015). White racial identity, color-blind racial attitudes, and multicultural counseling competence. *Cultural Diversity and Ethnic Minority Psychology, 21*(3), 440–449.

Kinsey, K., & Reed, P. G. (2015). Linking Native American tribal policy to practice in mental health care. *Nursing Science Quarterly, 28*(1), 82–87.

LaFromboise, T. D. (1985). The role of cultural diversity in counseling psychology. *The Counseling Psychologist, 13*(4), 649–655.

Linehan, M. (1993). *Cognitive-behavioral treatment of borderline personality disorder*. New York: Guilford Press.

Lopez, A., & Chessick, C. (2013). DBT graduate group pilot study: A model to generalize skills to create a "life worth living.". *Social Work in Mental Health, 11*(2), 141–153. Available from https://doi.org/10.1080/15332985.2012.755145.

Loranger, A. W., et al. (1994). The international personality disorder examination: The World Health Organization/Alcohol Drug Abuse, and Mental Health Administration international pilot study of personality disorders. *Archives Of General Psychiatry, 51*(3), 215–224.

McFarr, L., Gaona, L., Barr, N., Ramirez, U., Henriquez, S., Farias, A., & Flores, D. (2014). Cultural competency and dialectical behavior therapy. In A. Masuda (Ed.), *Cultural issues acceptance-mindfulness-based approaches*. New Harbinger.

Nagayma Hall, G. C., Ibaraki, A. Y., Huang, E. R., Marti, C. N., & Stice, E. (2016). A meta-analysis of cultural adaptations of psychological interventions. *Behavior Therapy, 47*(6), 993–1014.

Okazaki, S., & Tanaka-Matsumi, J. (2006). Cultural considerations in cognitive–behavioral assessment. In P. A. Hyes, & G. Y. Iwanasa (Eds.), *Culturally-sensitive cognitive-behavioral therapy: Assessment, practice, and supervision* (pp. 247–266). American Psychological Association.

Ramaiya, M. K., Fiorillo, D., Regmi, U., Robins, C. J., & Kohrt, B. A. (2017). A cultural adaptation of dialectical behavior therapy in Nepal. *Cognitive and Behavioral Practice, 24*(4), 428–444.

Romero, D. (1985). Cross-cultural counseling: Brief reactions for the practitioner. *The Counseling Psychologist, 13*, 665–671.

Samuels, J., Schudrich, W., & Altschul, D. (2009). *Toolkit for modifying evidence-based practice to increase cultural competence*. Orangeburg, NY: Research Foundation for Mental Health.

Sue, D. W. (2001). Multidimensional facets of cultural competence. *Counseling Psychologist, 29*(6), 790–821.

Sue, D. W., Arredondeo, P., & McDavis, R. J. (1992). Multicultural counseling competencies and standards: A call to the profession. *Journal of Multicultural Counseling and Development, 20*(2), 64–88.

Tao, K. W., Owen, K., Pace, B. T., & Imel, Z. E. (2015). A meta-analysis of culture of multicultural competencies and psychotherapy process and outcome. *Journal of Counseling Psychology, 62*(3), 337–350.

Vera, H., & Feagin, J. R. (Eds.), (2007). *Handbook of the sociology of racial and ethnic relations*. New York: Springer.

Further reading

Cardemill, E. V., & Battle, C. Y. (2003). Guess who's coming to therapy? Getting comfortable with conversations about race and ethnicity in psychotherapy. *Professional Psychology: Research and Practice, 34*(3), 278–286.

Comtois, K. A. (2013). Dialectical behavior therapy–accepting the challenges of exiting the system (DBT-ACES). In Presented at the *Annual conference of the Society for Dialectical Behaviour Therapy*. London, England.

Comtois, K. A., Hendricks, K. E., McFarr, L. M., Carmel, A., & Hoschel, K. A. (2017). DBT-accepting the challenges of employment and self-sufficiency (DBT-ACES) effectiveness: A re-evaluation in three settings. In Presented at the *DBT strategic planning meeting*. Seattle, WA.

Collins, P. Y., Patel, V., et al. (2011). Grand challenges in global mental health. *Nature, 475* (7354), 27–30.

Jones, E., Huey, S. J., & Rubenson, M. (2018). *Cultural competence in therapy with african americans. Cultural competence in applied psychology* (pp. 557–573). Cham: Springer.

Pieterse, A. L., Todd, N. R., Neville, H. A., & Carter, R. T. (2012). Perceived racism and mental health among Black American adults: A meta-analytic review. *Journal of Counseling Psychology, 59*(1), 1–9.

Sansone, R., & Sansone, L. (2012). Employment in borderline personality disorder. *Innovations in Clinical Neuroscience, 9*(9), 25–29.

Sue, D. W., Capodilupo, C. M., & Holder, A. M. B. (2008). Racial Microaggressions in the life experience of Black Americans. *Professional Psychology: Research and Practice, 39*, 329–336.

Sue, S., Nolan, Z., Nagayama Hall, G. C., & Berger, L. K. (2009). The case for cultural competency in psychotherapeutic interventions. *Annual Review of Psychology, 60*, 525–548.

Thompson, K., Mashhood, A., Nesci, J., & Rao, S. (2013). Where should the borders of psychiatry training be? The need for more emphasis on borderline personality disorder. *Australasian Psychiatry, 21*(2), 183–184.

CHAPTER

15

A review of the empirical evidence for DBT skills training as a stand-alone intervention

Sarah E. Valentine[1,2], *Ashley M. Smith*[2] *and Kaylee Stewart*[2]

[1]Department of Psychiatry, Boston University School of Medicine, Boston, MA, United States, [2]Boston Medical Center, Boston, MA, United States

Dialectical behavior therapy (DBT), a cognitive behavioral therapy (CBT), was originally designed to treat individuals diagnosed with borderline personality disorder (BPD; Linehan, 1993a). In order to address the motivational issues and skill deficits typically experienced by this population, the full program of DBT includes weekly individual therapy, weekly group skills training, phone coaching, and therapist consultation (Linehan, 1993b). While individual therapy focuses on maintaining safety and increasing motivation, skills training teaches clients strategies and exercises to improve behavior through (1) core mindfulness (CM), (2) emotion regulation (ER), (3) interpersonal effectiveness (IE), and (4) distress tolerance (DT; Linehan, 1993b).

Preliminary evidence suggests that skills training is a mechanism of change in DBT treatment (Linehan et al., 2015; Neacsiu, Rizvi, & Linehan, 2010); however, randomized controlled trials (RCTs) examining skills training as a stand-alone treatment are scarce and range in terms of treatment targets. Despite only preliminary empirical support, DBT skills training is often implemented as a stand-alone treatment for not only BPD, but a range of other psychiatric disorders in clinical practice (e.g., Dimeff & Koerner, 2007). As such, a new line of treatment outcome research on DBT skills training as a stand-alone intervention has emerged.

The Handbook of Dialectical Behavior Therapy
DOI: https://doi.org/10.1016/B978-0-12-816384-9.00015-4

Findings from our previous systematic review of DBT skills training as a stand-alone intervention suggest that skills training may be effective in addressing a range of mental health and behavioral issues (Valentine, Bankoff, Poulin, Reidler, & Pantalone, 2014). Participants of previously reviewed studies included adults in inpatient, outpatient, or correctional settings; youth in outpatient or correctional settings; and nonclinical samples such as caregivers. At the time of the review (Feb 2000–June 2013), there were only 17 published studies, including nine RCTs. Recommendations from the previous review highlighted the need for (1) standardized treatment manuals to assist with cross-study comparison, (2) component analysis studies, (3) RCTs comparing manualized DBT skills training to other active therapies (including standard DBT), and (4) naturalistic studies replicating findings across populations and settings (Valentine et al., 2014).

This chapter presents an updated review of DBT skills training implemented as stand-alone interventions. We have taken care to replicate methodology of our previous review paper and have only included studies published since the past review (June 2013–January 2019). We will characterize DBT interventions across studies and provide an overview of treatment outcomes (and effect sizes) by study design and by clinical outcome.

Method

We followed the Preferred Reporting Items for Systematic Reviews and Meta-Analyses (PRISMA) guidelines (Liberati et al., 2009).

Inclusion and exclusion criteria

We included peer-reviewed articles on treatment outcomes for DBT skills training modules, delivered in either individual or group format. We excluded studies where participants received additional DBT-focused therapeutic contact (i.e., individual DBT therapy and phone coaching) but included studies with consultation team support for therapists. We included studies where participants had ongoing ancillary treatment that was non-DBT (e.g., non-DBT individual therapy). We excluded studies where the unit of analysis was not the individual (i.e., couples or families). We excluded studies where the intervention was "DBT-style" but did not include formal DBT skills training (i.e., DBT-style case management). Studies that did not report treatment outcome data or studies where group-level outcome data were not presented (e.g., case studies) were also excluded. We excluded articles that were unavailable in English. When necessary, authors were contacted to gather missing eligibility information.

Article identification and data extraction

We searched various combinations of the terms "skills," "skills group," "DBT," "dialectical behavior therapy," and "empirical studies" in PsychInfo, PubMed, and CINHAL for articles published between June 2013 and January 2019. As seen in Fig. 15.1, we identified 517 records through our searches. Based on the relevance of the titles, we examined 255 abstracts and 73 full-text articles. A total of 33 articles were included in this review. We developed a data extraction table summarizing the major content of each article in the present review. Reviewers (authors) extracted data from assigned articles. After the initial phase of data extraction, two of the reviewers cross-checked the accuracy of the data.

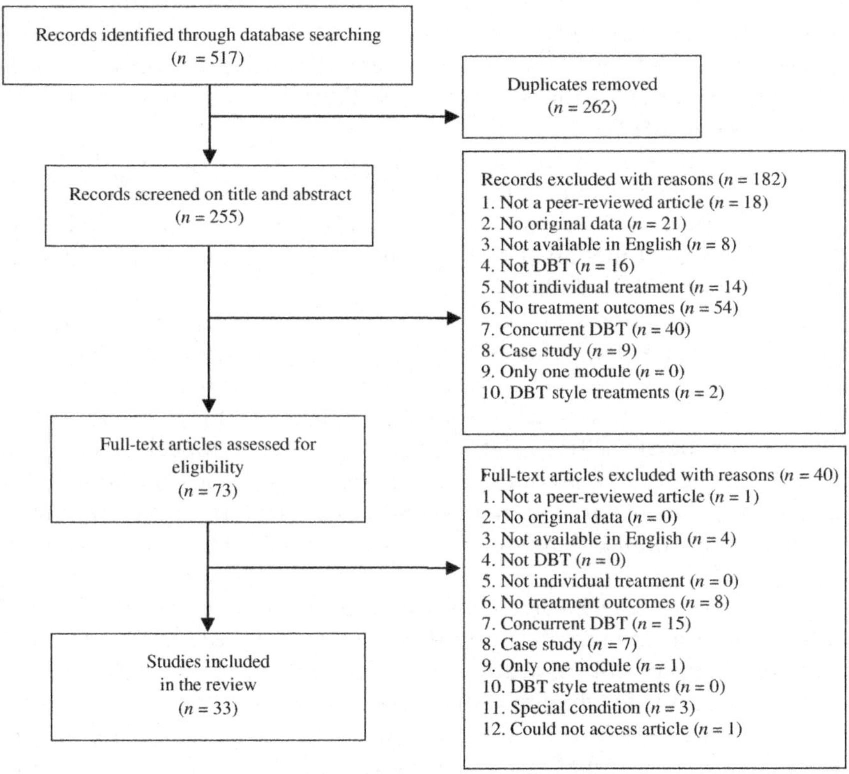

FIGURE 15.1 PRISMA flow diagram. *PRISMA*, Preferred Reporting Items for Systematic Reviews and Meta-Analyses.

When possible, we calculated effect sizes (Cohen's *d*; Cohen, 1988) for studies that did not report these in text.

Results

Extracted data regarding the study participants, treatment protocol, and main outcomes are presented in Table 15.1. There were two instances where articles reported data from the same study (Kramer et al., 2016 and Kramer, 2017; Neacsiu, Eberle, Kramer, Wiesmann, & Linehan, 2014 and Neacsiu, Rompogren, Eberle, & McMahon, 2018). Thus our findings pertain to the results of 31 original research studies.

Dialectical behavioral therapy implementation

Of the 31 reviewed studies, 20 (64.5%) employed all four modules of DBT skills training, while 11 (35.5%) omitted at least one module. The most commonly omitted module was IE (7, 22.6%). Four studies conducted a head-to-head comparison of skills modules (Carmona i Farrés et al., 2018; Dixon-Gordon, Chapman, & Turner, 2015; Elices et al., 2016; Rizvi & Steffel, 2014).

Various treatment manuals were cited in the reviewed studies. A total of 24 (77.4%) studies cited one of Marsha Linehan's skills training manuals. Fifteen (48.4%) studies cited Linehan's original DBT skills training manual (Linehan, 1993b), eight (25.8%) studies cited Linehan's second edition DBT skills manual (Linehan, 2014), and four (12.9%) studies cited Linehan's et al. (2015) component analysis of DBT skills training. Nine (29.0%) studies cited an additional manual along with one by Linehan. Three (9.7%) studies cited an alternative published protocol or manual without citing one by Linehan (Bihlar Muld, Jokinen, Bölte, & Hirvikoski, 2016; Edel, Hölter, Wassink, & Juckel, 2014; Flynn, Joyce, Weihrauch, & Corcoran, 2018) Three (9.7%) studies did not cite a published protocol or manual (Ben-Porath, Federici, Wisniewski, & Warren, 2014; Conrad, Sankaranarayanan, Lewin, & Dunbar, 2017; Quinn & Hymas, 2017).

Seven studies (22.6%) noted adaptations to improve applicability of skills training to the targeted population. Types of adaptations included revising examples for relevance to eating pathology (Cancian, Souza, Liboni, Machado, & Oliveira, 2017; Delparte, et al., 2019; Mushquash & McMahan, 2015), adolescent developmental level (Zapolski & Smith, 2017), classroom or correctional settings (Justo, Andretta, & Abs, 2018; Moore et al., 2018), and cultural relevance for Nepali women (Ramaiya et al., 2018). Four (12.9%) studies added non-DBT components to their

TABLE 15.1 Treatment outcome research for dialectical behavior therapy (DBT) skills training as stand-alone intervention.

Article, population	Sample	Assessments, modules, therapist contact (min)	Primary outcomes and effect sizes (Cohen's *d* or equivalent)
		I. Single Group Designs	
Beaulac et al. (2018)	$N = 18$	Pre–post, 3-month follow-up	Improvements in mindfulness skills ($\eta^2 = 0.43$), emotion regulation (*DERS*[a]: $\eta^2 = 0.45$), and emotional overeating ($\eta^2 = 0.43$) pre–post and follow-up
Weight loss clinic patients with BPD symptoms and emotional eating	Analysis: $N = 15$ (8–10)	DBT modules: ALL	Null findings for life difficulties, including personal distress, relationships, and responsibilities
	17% Male	1260 min	
	Ethnicity not specified		
	M age: 46.3		
	Canada		
Ben-Porath et al. (2014)	$N = 65$	Pre–post	Improvement in emotion regulation (*DERS*[a]: $d = 0.29$)
Patients enrolled in ED day treatment program	Analysis: $N = 47$ (37–65)	DBT modules: ALL	Improvement in healthy weight ($d = 0.67$)
	0% Male	1560 min	Improvements in ED behaviors: binging, purging, restriction, excessive exercise ($d = 0.36$–0.59); restraint, weight and eating concerns, and global concerns ($d = 0.39$–0.75)
	7% Racial or ethnic minority		
	M age: 23.4 ($SD = 6.7$)		
	United States		
Bihlar Muld et al. (2016)	$N = 40$	Pre–post	Improvements in self-reported ADHD ($d = 0.77$[b]) and psychiatric symptoms ($d = 0.54$[b])

(Continued)

TABLE 15.1 (Continued)

Article, population	Sample	Assessments, modules, therapist contact (min)	Primary outcomes and effect sizes (Cohen's *d* or equivalent)
Patients with ADHD diagnosis in compulsory care for substance abuse	Analysis: $N = 28$ (27–28) 100% Male Ethnicity not specified *M* age: 27.5 ($SD = 8.0$) Sweden	DBT modules: ALL + modules on ADHD, depression, anxiety 1440 min	Improvement in general well-being ($d = 1.04^{b}$)
Booth et al. (2014) Inpatients with a history or strong ideation/high risk of deliberate self-harm	$N = 167$ Analysis: $N = 114$ 19% Male Ethnicity not specified *M* age: 35.2 ($SD = 11.1$) Ireland	Pre–post, 3-month follow-up DBT modules: CM, DT, ER 480 min	Reduction in deliberate self-harm ($\eta_p^2 = 0.16$) pre–post and follow-up Improvement in DT ($\eta_p^2 = 0.59$) pre–post and follow-up
Conrad et al. (2017) Mental health service clients with less than four self-harm episodes in the last 12 months	$N = 58$ Analysis: $N = 38$ 16% Male Ethnicity not specified *M* age: 35.1 Australia	Pre–post DBT modules: ALL 600 min	Improvements in hopelessness ($d = 0.05^{b}$), impulsivity ($d = 0.63^{b}$), suppression of unwanted thoughts ($d = 0.53^{b}$), and quality of life ($d = 0.87^{b}$)

(*Continued*)

TABLE 15.1 (Continued)

Article, population	Sample	Assessments, modules, therapist contact (min)	Primary outcomes and effect sizes (Cohen's d or equivalent)
Justo et al. (2018)	$N = 55$	Pre–post, 2-month follow-up	Increase in difficulty engaging in goal-directed behavior when experiencing a negative emotion (*DERS*[a]—*Goals subscale*: $d = 0.44$[b]) pre–post and follow-up
Elementary school teachers	Analysis: $N = 27$	DBT modules: ALL	Increase in the lack of emotional awareness (*DERS*[a]—*Awareness subscale*: $d = 0.65$[b]) at follow-up, but not pre–post
	4% Male	900 min	
	Ethnicity not specified		
	M age: 45.0 ($SD = 9.7$)		
	Brazil		
Maffei et al. (2018)	$N = 244$	Pre–post	Improvements in emotion regulation (*DERS*[a]: $d = 1.14$)
Alcohol use disorder	Analysis: $N = 157$	DBT modules: CM, DT, ER	Improvements in number of consecutive days of abstinence ($d = 3.57$)
	61% Male	6480 min	Reduction in alcohol use severity measured by biomarker ($d = 0.73$)
	Ethnicity not specified		
	M age: 47.1 ($SD = 9.1$)		
	Italy		
Moore et al. (2018)	$N = 28$	Pre–post	Null findings for BPD symptoms and use of effective coping strategies
Jail inmates engaged in educational programming	Analysis: $N = 16$	DBT modules: ALL	
	100% Male	600 min	

(Continued)

TABLE 15.1 (Continued)

Article, population	Sample	Assessments, modules, therapist contact (min)	Primary outcomes and effect sizes (Cohen's *d* or equivalent)
	70% Racial or ethnic minority *M* age: 34.8 ($SD = 8.5$) United States		
Murphy et al. (2018) Patients with "very severe and complex, nonpsychotic" mental health difficulties	$N = 66$ Analysis: $N = 26$ 27% Male Ethnicity not specified *M* age: 38.3 ($SD = 10.4$) United Kingdom	Pre–post DBT modules: ALL 2850 min	Improvements in frequency of thoughts and feelings ($d = 1.42^b$), positive behaviors ($d = 1.10^b$), negative behaviors ($d = 1.51^b$), and suicidal thoughts/behaviors ($d = 1.13^b$) experienced by people with BPD
Mushquash and McMahan (2015) Patients with BED seeking bariatric services	$N = 11$ Analysis: $N = 10$ 9% Male Ethnicity not specified Age *M*: 44.6 ($SD = 16.3$) Canada	Pre–post DBT modules: ALL 1200 min	Improvement in binge eating ($d = 0.87$) Null findings for emotional eating, negative mood regulation, self-esteem, depressive symptoms, and generalized anxiety

(Continued)

TABLE 15.1 (Continued)

Article, population	Sample	Assessments, modules, therapist contact (min)	Primary outcomes and effect sizes (Cohen's *d* or equivalent)
Quinn and Hymas (2017)	$N = 17$	Pre–post	Null findings for anxiety and depressive symptoms, anger, disruptive behaviors, self-concept, and life functioning
Adolescents experiencing moderate to severe self-harm	Analysis: $N = 13$	DBT modules: ALL	
	8% Male	1440 min	
	Ethnicity not specified		
	M age: 15.8		
	United Kingdom		
Ramaiya et al. (2018)	$N = 10$	Pre–post, 1- and 4-week follow-up	Improvements in emotion regulation (*DERS*[a]: $r = 0.89$), depressive symptoms ($r = 0.89$), resiliency ($r = 0.89$), use of coping skills ($r = 0.89$), and suicidal ideation ($r = 0.89$) at pre–post (follow-up NR)
Women with suicide or self-harm attempt within the last 2 years or current suicidal ideation	Analysis: $N = 9$	DBT modules: ALL + "self-forgiveness/encouragement"	Null findings for anxiety symptoms
	0% Male	1800 min	Change in proportion above PTSD clinical cutoff, 100% at pre versus 25% at post (follow-up NR)
	Ethnicity not specified		
	M age: 30.8 ($SD = 8.8$)		
	Nepal		

(Continued)

TABLE 15.1 (Continued)

Article, population	Sample	Assessments, modules, therapist contact (min)	Primary outcomes and effect sizes (Cohen's *d* or equivalent)
Wilks et al. (2017)	$N = 38$	Pre–post	Improvements in emotion regulation (*DERS*[a]: $d = 1.51$), interpersonal problems ($d = 1.14$), and stress reactivity ($d = 1.39$)
Caregiver of a friend or family member with a chronic mental or physical health problem	Analysis: $N = 20$	DBT modules: ALL	Null findings for anxiety and depressive symptoms
	40% Male	2160 min	
	5% Racial or ethnic minority		
	M age: 54.8 ($SD = 10.3$)		
	United States		
Zapolski and Smith (2017)	$N = 80$	Pre–post	Improvement in intentions to engage in risky behaviors due to positive mood ($d = 0.40^{b}$)
Students enrolled in seventh or eighth grade with behavioral or academic problems	Analysis: $N = 53$	DBT modules: DT, ER, IE	
	49% Male	405 min	
	58% Racial or ethnic minority		
	M age: 12.7		
	United States		

(Continued)

TABLE 15.1 (Continued)

Article, population	Sample	Assessments, modules, therapist contact (min)	Primary outcomes and effect sizes (Cohen's *d* or equivalent)
		II. Nonrandomized Controlled Trials	
Delparte et al. (2019)	$N = 112$	Pre–post, 4-month follow-up	Greater improvements in emotional eating ($\eta_p^2 = 0.043$) in DBT + TAU (vs TAU) pre–post and follow-up
Bariatric surgical candidates	Analysis: $N = 95$	DBT + TAU (bariatric presurgery program) group versus TAU	Significant improvement in emotional eating for both conditions ($\eta_p^2 = 0.325$) across time points
	20% Male	DBT modules: ALL	Greater improvements in binge eating ($\eta_p^2 = 0.042$) and eating pathology ($\eta_p^2 = 0.041$) in the DBT + TAU (vs TAU) at follow-up, but not pre–post
	14% Racial or ethnic minority	840 min (DBT) versus NR min (TAU)	Improvements in binge eating ($\eta_p^2 = 0.447$) and eating pathology ($\eta_p^2 = 0.094$) in both conditions across time points
	M age: 44.4 (*SD* = 10.1)		Clinical impairment ($\eta_p^2 = 0.290$) improved in both conditions across time points
	Canada		
Edel et al. (2014)	$N = 91$	Pre–post	No differences between groups in ADHD symptoms, mindfulness, or self-efficacy
ADHD diagnosis (adults)	60% Male	MBTG versus DBT	Greater number of treatment responders (ADHD symptoms) in MBTG (vs DBT)
	Race or ethnicity not specified	DBT modules: ALL + modules on ADHD, depression, anxiety	Improvements in ADHD symptoms ($d = 0.26–0.49$), mindfulness ($d = 0.33–0.56$), and self-efficacy ($d = 0.23–0.26$) in both groups
	M age: 33.8 (*SD* = 10.1) versus 36.7 (*SD* = 10.1) (MBTG vs DBT)	1560 min	
	Germany		

(Continued)

TABLE 15.1 (Continued)

Article, population	Sample	Assessments, modules, therapist contact (min)	Primary outcomes and effect sizes (Cohen's *d* or equivalent)
Flynn et al. (2018)	$N = 72$	Pre–post	Greater improvements in emotional symptoms ($F^2 = 0.65$) and internalizing problems ($F^2 = -0.83$) for DBT (vs control)
High school students (nonclinical)	0% Male	DBT versus matched controls	Null findings for dysfunctional coping and DBT skills use
	Race or ethnicity not specified	DBT modules: ALL	
	M age: 15.3 ($SD = 0.5$)	880 min	
	Ireland		
Gibson et al. (2014)	$N = 103$	*Pre–post, 3-month follow-up*	*Greater improvements in self-harm* ($d = 0.27$), *ability to* engage in goal-directed behavior (*DERS*[a]: $d = 0.62$)/access to emotion regulation strategies (*DERS*[a]: $d = 0.55$), and cognitive coping strategies ($d = 0.50–0.74$) in DBT + TAU (vs TAU) pre–post (follow-up NR)
Individuals who engaged in deliberate self-harm within 6 weeks prior to intervention or met diagnostic criteria for BPD	Analysis: $N = 58\text{-}70$	DBT + TAU versus TAU	No differences between groups in depressive and anxiety symptoms
	21% versus 43% male (active vs control)	DBT modules: CM, DT, ER	Improvements in depressive symptoms ($d = 0.50^b$), anxiety symptoms ($d = 0.46^b$), emotion clarity (*DERS*[a]: $d = 0.38^b$)/ nonacceptance (*DERS*[a]: $d = 0.37^b$), and cognitive coping strategies ($d = 0.32–0.45^a$) for DBT + TAU pre–post (follow-up NR)

(Continued)

TABLE 15.1 (Continued)

Article, population	Sample	Assessments, modules, therapist contact (min)	Primary outcomes and effect sizes (Cohen's *d* or equivalent)
	Race or ethnicity not specified	240 min (DBT) + NR min (TAU) versus NR min (TAU)	Reduction in self-harm ($\eta_p^2 = 0.29$) for both groups at follow-up
	M age: 38.1 (*SD* = 10.3) versus 31.5 (*SD* = 11.2) (active vs control)		
	Ireland		
Ricard et al. (2013)	*N* = 303	Pre–post	Improvement in total behavioral symptoms for both groups ($\eta^2 = 0.02$)
Student enrolled in the disciplinary alternative education program	56% versus 67% Male (active vs control)	DBT + TAU versus TAU	Greater improvements in aggression ($\eta^2 = 0.013$) and conduct ($\eta^2 = 0.014$) for DBT + TAU (vs TAU)
	80% versus 83% Racial or ethnic minority (active vs control)	DBT modules: ALL	
	Adolescents	400 min (DBT) versus NR min (TAU)	
	United States		
Rizvi and Steffel (2014)	*N* = 24	Pre–post, 1-month follow-up	No differences between groups
Undergraduate students with emotion regulation difficulties	13% Male	DBT-ER versus DBT-ER + DBT-CM	Improvements in emotion regulation (*DERS*[a]: *d* = 1.52), depressive symptoms (*d* = 0.74), stress symptoms (*d* = 0.64), coping skills use (*d* = 1.26), mindfulness (*d* = 1.97), and functioning (*d* = 1.32) for both groups pre–post and follow-up

(Continued)

TABLE 15.1 (Continued)

Article, population	Sample	Assessments, modules, therapist contact (min)	Primary outcomes and effect sizes (Cohen's *d* or equivalent)
	29% Racial or ethnic minority Age: 18–29 United States	960 min	Increase in general positive affect ($d = 1.08$) and decrease in general negative affect ($d = 0.89$) for both groups pre–post and follow-up Null findings for anxiety symptoms for both groups
III. Randomized Controlled Trials			
Burckhardt et al. (2018) High school students (nonclinical)	$N = 96$ Analysis: $N = 79–89$ 0% Male Race or ethnicity not specified *M* age: 15.5 Australia	Pre–post, 6-month follow-up DBT versus waitlist DBT modules: ALL 300 min (DBT) versus 0 min (waitlist)	No differences between groups in emotion regulation, depressive symptoms, anxiety symptoms, or anger pre–post or follow-up (within group findings NR)
Cancian, et al. (2017)	$N = 79$	Pre–post	Greater improvements in binge eating severity ($d = 0.80$), depressive symptoms ($d = 0.82$), and emotion regulation ($d = 0.55$) in DBT (vs waitlist)

(*Continued*)

TABLE 15.1 (Continued)

Article, population	Sample	Assessments, modules, therapist contact (min)	Primary outcomes and effect sizes (Cohen's *d* or equivalent)
Weight management patients with BMI > 30	Analysis: $N = 31$ 0% versus 12% male (active vs control) Ethnicity not specified *M* age: 39.5 (*SD* = 9.2) versus 40.1 (*SD* = 11.2) (active vs control) Brazil	DBT versus waitlist DBT modules: CM, DT, ER 1200 min (DBT) versus 0 min (waitlist)	No differences between groups in emotional eating, intuitive eating, mindful eating, or anxiety and stress symptoms
Carmona i Farrés et al. (2018)	$N = 70$	Pre–post	Greater improvements in impulsivity ($\eta_p^2 = 0.21$), decentering ($\eta_p^2 = 0.09$), and mindfulness ($\eta_p^2 = 0.24$) in the DBT-CM (vs DBT-IE)
BPD	Analysis: $N = 50$ 10% Male Race or ethnicity not specified *M* age: 30.5 (*SD* = 6.9) versus 33.3 (*SD* = 8.5) (DBT-CM vs DBT-IE) Spain	DBT-CM versus DBT-IE 1500 min	Improvements in BPD symptoms ($\eta_p^2 = 0.09$), emotion clarity (*DERS*[a]: $\eta_p^2 = 0.25$), and nonacceptance (*DERS*[a]: $\eta_p^2 = 0.16$) for both groups

(Continued)

TABLE 15.1 (Continued)

Article, population	Sample	Assessments, modules, therapist contact (min)	Primary outcomes and effect sizes (Cohen's d or equivalent)
Dixon-Gordon et al. (2015)	$N = 19$	Pre–post, 7-week follow-up	Significant improvements in emotion regulation ($d = 0.48$), self-reported emotional reactivity ($d = 1.10$), social problem solving ($d = 0.67$), DT ($d = 1.04$), BPD symptoms ($d = 0.85$), and depressive symptoms ($d = 0.32$) in DBT-ER, but not DBT-IE or psychoeducation. No significant group differences
BPD	0% Male	DBT-ER versus DBT-IE versus psychoeducation group	Significant reductions in biomarker emotional reactivity ($d = 0.66$) in DBT-ER, but no changes in DBT-IE or psychoeducation. No significant group differences
	37% Racial or ethnic minority		Greater improvement in inappropriate interpersonal problem solving ($d = 0.91$) in DBT-IE (vs DBT-ER and psychoeducation)
	M age: 34.5 ($SD = 11.8$)	840 min	Greater improvement in mindfulness ($d = 1.10$) in DBT-ER (vs DBT-IE and psychoeducation)
	Canada		
Elices et al. (2016)	$N = 64$	Pre–post	Greater improvement in BPD symptoms ($d = 1.32$) and decentering ($d = 1.06$) for DBT-CM (vs DBT-IE)
BPD	Analysis: $N = 44$	DBT-CM versus DBT-IE	Greater improvements in mindful describing ($d = 0.69$) and nonjudging ($d = 0.84$) for DBT-CM (vs DBT-IE)
	16% Male	900 min	
	0% Racial or ethnic minority		
	M age: 31.6 ($SD = 7.3$)		
	Spain		

(Continued)

TABLE 15.1 (Continued)

Article, population	Sample	Assessments, modules, therapist contact (min)	Primary outcomes and effect sizes (Cohen's *d* or equivalent)
Elices et al. (2017)	$N = 75$	Pre–post, bimonthly follow-up for 1 year	Greater improvements in depressive symptoms ($d = 0.51$) and general psychiatric symptoms ($d = 0.55$) for DBT (vs psychoeducation) pre–post (not assessed at follow-up)
MDD in partial or complete remission	Analysis: $N = 57$	DBT versus psychoeducation	Null findings for mindfulness in both groups
	21% Male	DBT modules: CM, ER	
	Ethnicity not specified	1200 min (DBT) versus 450 min (psychoeducation)	
	M age: 52		
	Spain		
Kramer (2017)	$N = 41$	Pre–post	Greater improvement in overall coping functioning ($d = 0.70$) for DBT + TAU (vs TAU)
BPD	Analysis: $N = 31$	DBT + TAU versus TAU	Improved BPD symptoms in both groups ($d = 0.35$). No significant group differences
	13% Male	DBT modules: ALL	
	Ethnicity not specified	1800 min (DBT) versus NR min (TAU)	
	M age: 34.5 ($SD = 9.6$)		
	France		

(Continued)

TABLE 15.1 (Continued)

Article, population	Sample	Assessments, modules, therapist contact (min)	Primary outcomes and effect sizes (Cohen's d or equivalent)
Kramer et al. (2016)	$N = 41$	Pre–post, 3-month follow-up	Greater improvements in symptom distress, interpersonal relationships, social role ($d = 0.15–0.25$), and healthy assertive anger ($d = 0.78$) in DBT + TAU (vs TAU) pre–post, but not follow-up
BPD	Analysis: $N = 31$	DBT + TAU versus TAU	
	5% versus 20% Male (active vs control)	DBT modules: ALL	
	Ethnicity not specified	1800 min (DBT) versus NR min (TAU)	
	M age: 35.1 ($SD = 9.7$) versus 33.60 ($SD = 8.6$) (active vs control)		
	France		
McMain et al. (2017)	$N = 84$	Pre–post, 3-month follow-up	Greater improvements in BPD symptoms ($d = 0.32$), symptom distress ($d = 0.41$), and social performance ($d = 0.45$) in DBT (vs waitlist) pre–post, but not follow-up
BPD	21% Male	DBT versus waitlist	Greater reductions in suicidal and self-harm episodes in DBT (vs waitlist) at follow-up, but not pre–post
	Ethnicity not specified	DBT modules: ALL	Greater improvements in negative anger expression ($d = 0.80$), emotion regulation (DERS[a]: $d = 0.50$), and DT ($d = 0.56$) for DBT (vs waitlist) pre–post, and follow-up
	M age: 29.7 ($SD = 8.6$)	2490 min (DBT) versus 0 min (waitlist)	Null findings for impulsivity, depressive symptoms, and mindfulness
	Canada		

(*Continued*)

TABLE 15.1 (Continued)

Article, population	Sample	Assessments, modules, therapist contact (min)	Primary outcomes and effect sizes (Cohen's *d* or equivalent)
Neacsiu, Eberle, Kramer, Wiesmann, and Linehan (2014)	$N = 44$	Pre–post, 2-month follow-up	Greater improvements in emotion regulation (DERS[a]: $d = 1.86$) and anxiety symptoms ($d = 1.37$) for DBT (vs ASG) pre–post, but not follow-up
Non-BPD adults with high emotion dysregulation who met criteria for at least one anxiety or depressive disorder	32% versus 36% Male (active vs control)	DBT versus ASG	Greater improvements in coping abilities ($d = 1.02$) in DBT (vs ASG) pre–post, but not follow-up
	5% versus 9% racial or ethnic minority (active vs control)	DBT modules: ALL	Improvements in depressive symptoms ($d = 0.73$) for both groups pre–post, and follow-up for ASG but not DBT. No significant group differences
	M age: 32.3 ($SD = 10.5$) versus 38.8 ($SD = 13.6$) (active vs control)	1920 min	
	United States		
Neacsiu et al. (2018)	$N = 44$	Pre–post, 2-month follow-up	Greater and faster reductions in anger suppression ($d = 0.93$) and distress ($d = 1.04$) in DBT (vs ASG) pre–post and follow-up
Non-BPD adults with high emotion dysregulation who met criteria for at least one anxiety or depressive disorder	34% Male	DBT versus ASG	Improvements in shame ($d = 0.38–0.58$[b]), disgust propensity ($d = 0.43–0.62$[b]), and disgust sensitivity ($d = 0.38–0.82$[b]) for both groups pre–post and follow-up. No significant group differences
	7% Racial or ethnic minority	DBT modules: ALL	Null findings in anger expression for both groups
	M age: 35.6 ($SD = 12.4$)	1920 min	
	United States		

(Continued)

TABLE 15.1 (Continued)

Article, population	Sample	Assessments, modules, therapist contact (min)	Primary outcomes and effect sizes (Cohen's *d* or equivalent)
Uliaszek et al. (2016)	$N = 54$	Pre–post	Improvements in depressive symptoms ($d = 0.94$–1.00), BPD symptoms ($d = 0.76$), suicidality ($d = 1.23$), anxiety symptoms ($d = 0.61$), mindfulness skill use ($d = 1.07$), emotion regulation (*DERS*[a]: $d = 1.16$), and DT ($d = 0.71$) for both groups pre–post. No significant group differences
General outpatients referred by counselor based on emotion regulation difficulties	22% Male	DBT versus PPT	
	72% Racial or ethnic minority	DBT modules: ALL	
	M age: 22.2 ($SD = 5.0$)	1440 min	
	Canada		
Wilks, et al. (2018)	$N = 59$	Pre–post, 3- and 4-month follow-up	No differences between groups for suicidal ideation, hazardous alcohol consumption, or emotion regulation
Suicidal ideation in the past month, heavy drinking, and emotion regulation difficulties	Analysis: $N = 48$	Internet-delivered DBT versus waitlist	Greater improvements in alcohol use quantity and frequency for DBT (vs waitlist) pre–post (follow-up NR)
	31% Male	DBT modules: CM, DT, ER	Improvements in suicidal ideation ($d = 0.81$), hazardous alcohol consumption ($d = 0.75$), alcohol use quantity and frequency, and emotion regulation (*DERS*[a]: $d = 0.42$) for DBT pre–post and follow-up
	18% Racial or ethnic minority	400 min (DBT) versus 0 min (waitlist)	Improvement in suicidal ideation ($d = 0.25$) in waitlist pre–post
	M age: 38.0 ($SD = 10.4$)		
	United States		

[a]*Gratz and Roemer (2004).*
[b]*Calculated for this review paper based on available data.*
ADHD, Attention deficit hyperactivity disorder; *ASG*, activities-based support group; *BED*, binge eating disorder; *BMI*, body mass index; *BPD*, Borderline personality disorder; *CM*, core mindfulness; *DERS*, difficulties in emotion regulation scale; *DT*, distress tolerance; *ED*, eating disorder; *ER*, emotion regulation; *IE*, interpersonal effectiveness; *MBTG*, mindfulness-based training group; *MDD*, major depressive disorder; *NR*, not reported; *PPT*, positive psychotherapy; *PTSD*, posttraumatic stress disorder; *TAU*, treatment as usual.

interventions (Bihlar Muld et al., 2016; Edel et al., 2014; Ramaiya et al., 2018; Ricard, Lerma, & Heard, 2013).

The amount of therapist contact varied widely across studies, ranging from 4 to 108 hours across interventions ($M = 22.7$ hours [$SD = 20.0$], $Mode = 20$ hours). The majority (29, 93.5%) of the studies reviewed had less contact hours than the amount provided in standard DBT skills training (i.e., 60 hours; Linehan, 1993a; Linehan, Armstrong, Suarez, Allmon, & Heard, 1991). Three studies did not specify the length or number of sessions, and authors were contacted for clarification (Bihlar Muld et al., 2016; Flynn, et al., 2018; Quinn & Hymas, 2017).

Studies used a range of comparison conditions, with nearly half using no comparison group at all (14, 45.2%). Five (16.1%) studies used a non-active comparison group, including waitlist (Burckhardt et al., 2018; Cancian, et al., 2017; McMain, Guimond, Barnhart, Habinski, & Streiner, 2017; Wilks et al., 2018) and matched control groups (Flynn et al., 2018). Eight (25.8%) studies used an active comparison group (e.g., comparison DBT module, psychoeducation, and positive psychotherapy), and four (12.9%) compared DBT to treatment as usual (TAU).

Treatment outcomes by design

DBT skills training interventions were used to address mental health symptoms and problematic behaviors across a range of populations. These include individuals with BPD, major depressive disorder (MDD), eating pathology, past or current suicidality or self-injury, problematic alcohol or substance use, attention deficit hyperactivity disorder (ADHD), and problems with general emotional and behavioral functioning.

Single group designs

Fourteen (45.2%) studies were single group design. Of these 14, 12 (85.7%) found significant improvements in at least one clinical outcome.

Clinical outcomes

In these single group design studies, small-to-large effect sizes were found across eating pathology outcomes, including emotional eating (Beaulac, Sandre, & Mercer, 2018), eating disorder behaviors (Ben-Porath et al., 2014), and binge eating (Mushquash & McMahan, 2015). In terms of alcohol use outcomes, Maffei, Cavicchioli, Movalli, Cavallaro, and Fossati (2018) found medium-to-large effect sizes for number of consecutive days of abstinence and biomarker-based alcohol use severity. A study focused on ADHD and substance use disorder outcomes found medium-to-large effect sizes for ADHD and psychiatric symptoms, and overall well-being (Bihlar et al., 2016). Four (28.6%) of the

14 single group designs measured suicidality or self-injury (Booth, Keogh, Doyle, & Owens, 2014; Murphy, Hostick, Louise Skitt, & Turner, 2018; Quinn & Hymas, 2017; Ramaiya et al., 2018), and three (75.0%) of those four found improvements with large effect sizes (Booth et al., 2014; Murphy et al., 2018; Ramaiya et al., 2018).

Dialectical behavioral therapy module–related outcomes

Of the 14 single group design studies, six (42.9%) measured ER, assessed by the Difficulties in Emotion Regulation Scale (DERS; Gratz & Roemer, 2004). Five of these (83.3%) found improvements in ER with small-to-very-large effect sizes (Beaulac et al., 2018; Ben-Porath et al., 2014; Maffei et al., 2018; Ramaiya et al., 2018; Wilks et al., 2017). In addition to ER, large effect sizes were found in studies examining mindfulness abilities (Beaulac et al., 2018), interpersonal problem solving (Wilks et al., 2017), and DT (Booth et al., 2014) as treatment outcomes.

Nonrandomized controlled trials

Six (19.4%) studies were non randomized controlled trials. Five studies (83.3%) found significant between-group differences on clinical outcomes. The one study that did not find between-group differences had compared two DBT conditions head-to-head, finding that both conditions evidenced similar within-group improvements (Rizvi & Steffel, 2014).

Clinical outcomes

In terms of eating pathology, Delparte et al. (2019) found greater improvement in emotional eating and binge eating for the DBT condition compared to TAU with small effect sizes. Gibson, Booth, Davenport, Keogh, and Owens (2014) found greater decreases in the frequency of self-injury in the DBT condition compared to TAU with a small effect size. Edel et al. (2014) found within-group improvements in ADHD symptoms for the DBT-CM condition with a smalleffect size, but no significant differences when comparing DBT-CM to a mindfulness-based training group.

Dialectical behavioral therapy module–related outcomes

Of the two nonrandomized controlled trials that measured ER using the DERS (Gratz & Roemer, 2004), only one found significant between-group differences. Gibson et al. (2014) found greater improvements in the DERS subscales of ability to engage in goal-directed behavior and access to ER strategies for the DBT condition compared to TAU with medium effect sizes. While Rizvi and Steffel (2014) did not find between-group differences in ER when comparing DBT-ER to DBT-ER + CM, they did find improvements in ER within each condition with a very large effect size. The two studies that measured mindfulness as an outcome found significant within-group improvements in the DBT conditions, with small-to-medium (Edel et al., 2014) and very large (Rizvi & Steffel, 2014) effect sizes, but no between-group differences.

Randomized controlled trials

Eleven studies (35.5%) were RCTs. Nine (81.8%) found significant between-group differences in main outcomes. Of the two studies that did not find between-group differences, Uliaszek, Rashid, Williams, and Gulamani (2016) found within-group differences for the DBT condition and Burckhardt et al. (2018) did not report within-group findings.

Clinical outcomes

In terms of eating pathology, Cancian et al. (2017) found within-group improvements in binge eating severity and emotional eating with medium-to-very-large effect sizes, and within-group *decreases* in mindful eating with a medium effect size in the DBT condition, but no significant group differences when comparing DBT to waitlist.

Seven RCTs (63.6%) measured depressive symptoms. Two (28.6%) RCTs found between-group improvements favoring DBT conditions (DBT > waitlist: Cancian et al., 2017; DBT > psychoeducation: Elices et al., 2017). Three of the five studies (70.0%) that did not find between-group differences compared DBT skills training to active control treatments (DBT-ER vs DBT-IE vs psychoeducation: Dixon-Gordon et al., 2015; activities-based support group: Neacsiu, Eberle, et al., 2014; positive psychotherapy: Uliaszek et al., 2016). Also, three of the five studies that did not find between-group differences found within-group improvement in depressive symptoms in the DBT condition with small-to-large effect sizes (Dixon-Gordon et al., 2015; Neacsiu, Eberle, et al., 2014; Uliaszek et al., 2016).

In terms of alcohol use outcomes, greater improvements in alcohol use quantity and frequency were found for the DBT skills condition compared to the waitlist with a small effect size (Wilks et al., 2018). Of the three (27.3%) RCTs that assessed for suicidality or self-injury, only one found between-group differences (DBT > waitlist: McMain et al., 2017) with a medium effect size. Of the studies that did not find between-group differences, both Uliaszek et al. (2016) and Wilks et al. (2018) found within-group improvements for the DBT condition with large effect sizes.

Dialectical behavioral therapy module–related outcomes

Eight RCTs (72.7%) used the DERS (Gratz & Roemer, 2004) to measure ER. Only three (37.5%) of the eight RCTs measuring ER found significant differences between groups with medium-to-very-large effect sizes when comparing DBT skill training to waitlist controls (Cancian et al., 2017; McMain et al., 2017) and an activities-based support group (Neacsiu, Eberle, et al., 2014). Of the studies that did not find between-group differences in ER, three (60.0%) were comparing DBT to an active treatment condition, and four (80.0%) reported within-group improvements in the DBT conditions with small-to-very-large effect sizes (Dixon-Gordon et al., 2015; Uliaszek et al., 2016; Wilks et al., 2018; Carmona i Farrés et al., 2018). Dixon-Gordon et al. (2015) found within-group improvement in the DBT-ER condition, but not for DBT-IE or psychoeducation.

Of the six (45.5%) RCTs that measured mindfulness as an outcome, three (50.0%) found between-group differences with medium-to-large effect sizes, when comparing DBT modules head-to-head (DBT-CM > DBT-IE: Carmona i Farrés et al., 2018; DBT-ER > DBT-IE: Dixon-Gordon et al., 2015; Elices et al., 2016). One of the three RCTs that did not find between-group differences compared DBT to positive psychotherapy, and found within-group improvements in mindfulness in the DBT condition with a large effect size (Uliaszek et al., 2016).

All three (27.3%) RCTs that measured social and interpersonal functioning found significant between-group differences with small-to-large effect sizes. Kramer et al. (2016) found greater improvements in interpersonal relationships and social role in the DBT condition with a small effect size compared to TAU, and McMain et al. (2017) found greater improvements in social performance for the DBT condition compared to waitlist controls with a small effect size. Dixon-Gordon et al. (2015) found greater improvements in inappropriate interpersonal problem solving for DBT-IE (vs DBT-ER vs psychoeducation) with a large effect size.

Three RCTs measured DT, and only McMain et al. (2017) found between-group differences in DT for DBT compared to waitlist controls with a medium effect size. Of the studies that did not find between-group differences, both found within-group improvements in DBT conditions with medium (Uliaszek et al., 2016) and large (DBT-ER group only: Dixon-Gordon et al., 2015) effect sizes.

Findings by treatment outcome

Borderline personality disorder

Eight (25.8%) studies assessed for BPD symptoms; two were single group design and six were RCTs. Of the two single group design studies, only one found improvements in BPD symptoms with large-to-very-large effect sizes (Murphy et al., 2018).

Two (33.3%) of the six RCTs measuring BPD symptoms found significant between-group differences favoring the DBT condition. Three (75.0%) of the four studies that did not find between-group differences compared

DBT skills training to active control treatments (DBT-CM vs DBT-IE: Carmona i Farrés et al., 2018; DBT-ER vs DBT-IE vs psychoeducation: Dixon-Gordon et al., 2015; positive psychotherapy: Uliaszek et al., 2016). Of note, all RCTs that did not find between-group differences still found within-group improvements for DBT condition.

Three (50.0%) RCTs compared DBT skills modules head-to-head (Dixon-Gordon et al., 2015; Elices et al., 2016; Carmona i Farrés, et al., 2018). Carmona i Farrés et al. (2018) found improvements in BPD symptoms for both DBT-ER and DBT-IE skills training conditions with a medium effect size, with no group differences. In contrast, Elices et al. (2016) found greater improvement in BPD symptoms for the DBT-CM condition with a largeeffect size compared to the DBT-IE condition. One study comparing DBT-ER vs DBT-IE vs psychoeducation, found within-group improvements in BPD symptoms for the DBT-ER skills training condition with a large effect size (Dixon-Gordon et al., 2015). Another study comparing DBT skills training to a waitlist found greater improvements in the DBT condition with a small effect size (McMain et al., 2017). Two RCTs found within-group improvements in the DBT condition with small (Kramer, 2017) and medium (McMain et al., 2017) effect sizes.

Depressive symptoms

Thirteen (41.9%) studies assessed for depressive symptoms—four were single group design, two were nonrandomized controlled trials, and seven were RCTs. Of the studies using a single group design, only one (25.0%) study found significant improvements in depressive symptoms with a very large effect size (Ramaiya et al., 2018).

Of the nine controlled studies (RCTs and nonrandomized controlled trials) assessing for depressive symptoms, three (33.3%) found significant between-group differences favoring the DBT condition. Of six controlled studies that did not find between-group differences, four (80.0%) compared DBT skills training to active control treatments (DBT-ER vs DBT-ER + DBT-CM: Rizvi & Steffel, 2014; DBT-ER vs DBT-IE vs psychoeducation: Dixon-Gordon et al., 2015; activities-based support group: Neacsiu, Eberle, et al., 2014; positive psychotherapy: Uliaszek et al., 2016). Of the six controlled studies that did not find between-group differences, four (80.0%) found within-group improvements in the DBT condition. The remaining study did not report within-group improvements (Burckhardt et al., 2018).

The two nonrandomized controlled trials assessed for depressive symptoms and found improvements within the DBT condition with a medium effect size (Gibson et al., 2014) and within both a DBT-ER and DBT-ER + DBT-CM condition with a medium effect size (Rizvi & Steffel, 2014). Of the seven RCTs measuring depressive symptoms, two (28.6%) found between-group differences, Cancian et al. (2017) finding greater improvements in depressive symptoms in the DBT condition compared to waitlist with a large effect size and Elices et al. (2017) finding greater improvements in the DBT condition compared to psychoeducation with a medium effect size. One RCT's finding was null for depression within the DBT condition and when compared to waitlist for individuals with BPD (McMain et al., 2017).

Emotion regulation

In total, 16 (51.6%) studies assessed ER using the DERS (Gratz & Roemer, 2004)—six were single group design, two were nonrandomized controlled trial, and eight were RCTs. Of the six single group design studies, five (83.3%) found improvements in ER with effect sizes ranging from small to very large. In contrast, one study found reductions in ER in a nonclinical sample of teachers with a small effect size (Justo et al., 2018).

Of the 10 controlled studies (RCTs and nonrandomized controlled trials) assessing for ER, four (40.0%) found significant improvements between groups. Four (66.7%) of the six controlled studies that did not find between-group differences compared DBT skills training to active control treatments (DBT-ER vs DBT-ER + DBT-CM: Rizvi & Steffel, 2014; DBT-CM vs DBT-IE: Carmona i Farrés et al., 2018; DBT-ER vs DBT-IE vs psychoeducation: Dixon-Gordon et al., 2015; PPT: Uliaszek et al., 2016). Of the six studies that did not find significant between-group improvements, five (83.3%) found significant improvements within the DBT condition.

One of the two nonrandomized controlled trials found greater improvements in ER compared to TAU in individuals with a history of self-harm or BPD with a small effect size (Gibson et al., 2014). The second nonrandomized controlled trial found improvements for both a DBT-ER skills training condition and a DBT-ER + DBT-CM skills training condition in undergraduates with ER difficulties with a large effect size (Rizvi & Steffel, 2014). Of the eight RCTs measuring ER, three (37.5%) found significant improvements between groups in ER outcomes with medium-to-very-large effect sizes (Cancian, et al., 2017; McMain et al., 2017; Neacsiu, Eberle, et al., 2014). One RCT among nonclinical adolescent students (Burckhardt et al., 2018) did not find any effect of DBT skills training on ER outcomes.

Suicidality or self-injury

Seven (22.6%) studies assessed for suicidality—three were single group design, one was a nonrandomized controlled trial, and three were RCTs. This included interventions for individuals with a history of suicidality or self-injury (Booth et al., 2014; Ramaiya et al., 2018); individuals with BPD and a history of self-harm (Gibson et al., 2014; McMain et al., 2017); individuals with a history of suicidal ideation, heavy drinking, and emotion dysregulation (Wilks et al., 2018); individuals with severe and nonpsychotic mental health difficulties (Murphy et al., 2018); and individuals with ER difficulties (Uliaszek et al., 2016). The three single group design studies that assessed for suicidality and self-injury found improvements in self-harm with a large effect size (Booth et al., 2014), improvements in suicidal ideation with a very large effect size (Ramaiya et al., 2018), and improvements in the frequency of suicidal thoughts and behaviors with a large effect size (Murphy et al., 2018).

Of the four controlled studies (RCTs and nonrandomized controlled trials) measuring suicidality, two (50.0%) found significant between-group differences. McMain et al.'s (2017) RCT found greater reductions in suicidality and self-harm for the DBT condition compared to waitlist controls with a medium effect size, and Gibson et al.'s (2014) nonrandomized controlled trial found greater reductions in self-harm for the DBT skills condition compared to TAU with a small effect size post-treatment and a large effect size at follow-up (Gibson et al., 2014). Both studies that did not find between-group differences found significant improvements within the DBT condition. Specifically, Uliaszek et al.'s (2016) RCT found improvements in suicidality in the DBT condition with a large effect size, and Wilks et al.'s (2018) RCT found improvements in suicidal ideation in the DBT condition with a large effect size.

Eating pathology

Five (16.1%) studies assessed for eating pathology—three were single group design, one was a nonrandomized controlled trial, and one was a RCT. This included interventions for individuals seeking bariatric surgery (Delparte et al., 2019; Mushquash & McMahan, 2015), individuals who were overweight (Beaulac et al., 2018; Cancian et al., 2017), and individuals with anorexia or bulimia nervosa (Ben-Porath et al., 2014). The three single group design studies assessing eating pathology found improvements in emotional overeating (Beaulac et al., 2018), eating disorder behaviors (Ben-Porath et al., 2014), and binge eating (Mushquash & McMahan, 2015) with small-to-large effect sizes.

Both of the studies assessing for eating pathology with control groups (RCT and nonrandomized controlled trial) found significant between-group differences. Specifically, Cancian et al.'s (2017) RCT found greater improvements in binge eating severity in the DBT condition compared to a waitlist with a large effect size. In a nonrandomized controlled study, Delparte et al. (2019) found greater improvements in emotional eating, binge eating, and eating pathology for the DBT condition compared to TAU with small effect sizes.

Discussion

Our review included 31 original treatment outcome studies that implemented DBT skills training as a stand-alone treatment. Studies included 14 single group designs and 17 controlled trials (including 11 RCTs). It was difficult to compare across studies as there were large variations in therapist contact hours, manualized protocol content, sample characteristics (diagnosis, clinical severity, selected outcomes), and intervention setting (nonclinical, clinical, research). That said, the majority of single group studies (12, 85.7%) and controlled studies (14, 82.4%) found DBT skills training to be effective in improving at least one clinical outcome, although four (23.5%) controlled studies did not find the DBT condition superior to the comparison condition on any clinical outcome. These data suggest that DBT skills training may be helpful for a range of disorders and symptoms, and yet it remains unclear as to whether DBT skills training is more effective than other manualized treatments.

The literature examining stand-alone DBT skills training has tripled in volume since our last review (Valentine et al., 2014). The previous review identified only 17 studies, including eight single group designs and nine RCTs. Adding these studies to our current review, there is a total of 22 single group and 26 controlled trials. Although some studies in our review provided preliminary evidence that stand-alone DBT is superior to equivalent active treatment groups, none of these comparators represent gold-standard treatments for their respective clinical populations. As such, the lack of noninferiority trials precludes us from drawing conclusions regarding whether stand-alone DBT skills training is as effective as evidence-based treatments for various populations.

Both systematic reviews examined the effectiveness of DBT skills training for an array of populations and settings. Contrasting current totals to the past review, there are currently five (vs 1) studies that examine outcomes for BPD, 10 (vs 5) for eating pathology, three (vs 1) for ADHD, six (vs 1) for suicidality and self-harm behaviors, six (vs 1) for emotional and behavioral functioning in nonclinical populations, three (vs 2) for MDD, three (vs 0) for substance use, and six (vs 4) for various behavioral problems and disorders. Eating pathology remained a major focus of research, and researchers are increasingly examining the utility of stand-alone DBT skills training for transdiagnostic and nonclinical populations.

Whereas no studies compared DBT skill modules head-to-head in the previous review (Valentine et al., 2014), we were pleased to find that four studies in this updated review compared individual DBT skill modules. These studies found that DBT-CM (Carmona i Farrés et al.,

2018; Elices et al., 2016) and DBT-ER (Dixon-Gordon et al., 2015) were more effective for increasing mindfulness than DBT-IE and that there were no differences in mindfulness when comparing DBT-ER to DBT-ER + DBT-CM (Rizvi & Steffel, 2014). These preliminary data suggest the need for additional head-to-head comparisons, including dismantling studies of DBT skills training modules and components analysis.

Less than half of the studies across the two reviews included a follow-up assessment (8 of 17 in previous review; 15 of 31 in updated review), indicating the need for studies to examine whether treatment gains are sustained post-treatment. Follow-up can be particularly elucidating when utilized in controlled trials, as shown by several studies in the current review where group differences favoring DBT skills training became significant (Delparte et al., 2019; McMain et al., 2017) or null (Kramer et al., 2016; McMain et al., 2017; Neacsiu, Eberle et al., 2014) during follow-up.

Both reviews indicate a lack of standardized interventions, due in part to researchers' appropriate attempts to adapt the DBT skills training for their targeted populations or settings. Authors often did not report data-driven intervention adaptations, making the precise content of the intervention unclear. We encourage researchers to standardize and publish their manuals so they can be used in replication studies and allow for more generalizable findings. Reporting data on facilitator adherence to the chosen manual is also essential to ensure adequate delivery of DBT skills training—only three (9.8%) of the reviewed studies reported formal assessment of adherence for DBT interventions.

Findings of this review add to our understanding of the DBT literature more broadly. Over half (16, 51.6%) of the studies in this review measured ER. ER improved in the DBT condition in the majority of these studies (14, 87.5%) across a range of populations, supporting the recent promotion of DBT skills training as an effective intervention for transdiagnostic ER (Neacsiu, Bohus, & Linehan, 2014). It remains unclear whether DBT is superior to other active therapy conditions in improving ER, as only 40.0% of controlled studies found group differences. Although only one study in the current review (vs 2 in the previous review) targeted MDD, 13 (41.9%) studies in the current review (vs at least 5 in the previous review) measured depressive symptoms as a clinical outcome. Little evidence for the effectiveness of DBT for depression exists. The literature reports mixed findings for depressive symptoms (Harley, Sprich, Safren, Jacobo, & Fava, 2008; Lynch et al., 2007; Lynch, 2003). Only a third (3, 33.3%) of the controlled trials in this review found DBT skills training to be superior for improving depressive symptoms.

Five studies in this review assessed for the effect of DBT skills training on nonclinical populations, including students, teachers, and caregivers. Three (60.0%) of these studies found improvements in a clinical outcome but did not assess findings at follow-up. There is currently little to no evidence to support DBT as an effective nonclinical mental health prevention intervention, although, some researchers have found general improvements in nonclinical populations (Haskell et al., 2014; Hoffman et al., 2005; Hoffman, Fruzzetti, & Buteau, 2007).

Although the quality of research regarding DBT skills training has generally improved since the past review, limitations still remain. Heterogeneity within samples, especially for studies set in usual care with non-disorder-specific samples, led to difficulties in interpreting and generalizing findings. Although studying transdiagnostic samples may provide evidence for the broad helpfulness of DBT skills training, it limits our ability to pinpoint the symptoms targeted by DBT skills training. Analyzing diagnosis and symptom severity as mediators of improvement in DBT skills training may allow researchers to determine the effect of DBT skills training in heterogeneous samples.

Selected assessments varied widely in the present review making it difficult to compare findings across studies. An exception to this heterogeneity is use of the DERS (Gratz & Roemer, 2004) which was consistently used across all of the studies assessing ER in this review. Standardizing measures would increase the generalizability of findings and the ability to compare effects across populations. In addition, several studies targeted a specific population, but did not report treatment outcomes expected based on the study sample. For example, one study's sample included those with a history of deliberate self-harm, but did not include self-injury as a main outcome. We suspect that null findings may have been under-reported, which diminishes our ability to attribute the improvements reported by researchers to the effect of the intervention versus chance (Type I error).

There are several limitations to the present review. We excluded studies that reported concurrent individual DBT therapy, but allowed concurrent non-DBT individual therapy, leading to a reduced sample of articles and possible confounding effects. It is possible that there were errors in the data extraction process, but we attempted to reduce possible inaccuracies with multiple reviews of full-text articles and correspondence with authors for additional information when necessary. The lack of consistency in reported effect sizes is also a limitation. Since many articles did not report a generalizable effect size, we calculated Cohen's *d* for seven (21.2%) of the 33 articles included in the current review.

Future research could utilize several techniques to address these limitations and build upon the strengths of the studies presented in the current review. As evidence of the applicability of DBT skills training, it has been modified and implemented in a diverse array of populations and settings. To help apply these findings to practice and to better compare across studies, researchers also need to better characterize study samples and the adaptations made to Linehan's (2014) training manual for those populations. We also recommend a data-driven approach to adaptation wherein intervention protocols are iteratively adapted and tested systematically, rather than by investigator clinical judgment alone (Chambers & Wynne, 2016). Most importantly, future research should focus on comparing DBT skills training to the full package of DBT and other evidence-based treatments for specific disorders. Dismantling studies are also needed to determine active "core" components of DBT skills modules. Finally, by replicating protocols and procedures utilized by rigorous RCTs, researchers could conduct translational research to determine the effectiveness of DBT skills training implemented in usual care settings.

References

Beaulac, J., Sandre, D., & Mercer, D. (2018). Impact on mindfulness, emotion regulation, and emotional overeating of a DBT skills training group: A pilot study. *Eating and Weight Disorders—Studies on Anorexia, Bulimia and Obesity*, *24*(2), 373–377. Available from https://doi.org/10.1007/s40519-018-0616-9.

Ben-Porath, D., Federici, A., Wisniewski, L., & Warren, M. (2014). Dialectical behavior therapy: Does it bring about improvements in affect regulation in individuals with eating disorders? *Journal of Contemporary Psychotherapy*, *44*(4), 245–251. Available from https://doi.org/10.1007/s10879-014-9271-2.

Bihlar Muld, B., Jokinen, J., Bolte, S., & Hirvikoski, T. (2016). Skills training groups for men with ADHD in compulsory care due to substance use disorder: a feasibility study. *Attention Deficit and Hyperactivity Disorders*, *8*(3), 159–172. Available from https://doi.org/10.1007/s12402-016-0195-4.

Booth, R., Keogh, K., Doyle, J., & Owens, T. (2014). Living through distress: A skills training group for reducing deliberate self-harm. *Behavioural and Cognitive Psychotherapy*, *42*(2), 156–165. Available from https://doi.org/10.1017/S1352465812001002.

Burckhardt, R., Manicavasagar, V., Shaw, F., Fogarty, A., Batterham, P. J., Dobinson, K., & Karpin, I. (2018). Preventing mental health symptoms in adolescents using dialectical behaviour therapy skills group: A feasibility study. *International Journal of Adolescence and Youth*, *23*(1), 70–85. Available from https://doi.org/10.1080/02673843.2017.1292927.

Cancian, A. C., Souza, L. A., Liboni, R. P., Machado, W. D., & Oliveira, M. D. (2017). Effects of a dialectical behavior therapy-based skills group intervention for obese individuals: A Brazilian pilot study. *Eating and Weight Disorders—Studies on Anorexia, Bulimia and Obesity*, 1–13. Available from https://doi.org/10.1007/s40519-017-0461-2.

Carmona i Farrés, C., Elices, M., Soler, J., Domínguez-Clavé, E., Pomarol-Clotet, E., Salvador, R., & Pascual, J. C. (2018). Effects of mindfulness training on borderline personality disorder: Impulsivity versus emotional dysregulation. *Mindfulness*, 1–12. Available from https://doi.org/10.1007/s12671-018-1071-4.

Chambers, D. A., & Wynne, N. E. (2016). The adaptdome: Advancing the science of intervention adaptation. *American Journal of Preventive Medicine*, *51*(4S2), 124–131. Available from https://doi.org/10.1016/j.amepre.2016.05.011.

Cohen, J. (1988). *Statistical power analysis for the behavioral sciences* (2nd ed.). Hillsdale, NJ: Lawrence Earlbaum Associates.

Conrad, A. M., Sankaranarayanan, A., Lewin, T. J., & Dunbar, A. (2017). Effectiveness of a 10-week group program based on dialectical behaviour therapy skills among patients with personality and mood disorders: Findings from a pilot study. *Australasian Psychiatry, 25*(5), 466–470. Available from https://doi.org/10.1177/1039856217707393.

Delparte, C. A., Power, H. A., Gelinas, B. L., Oliver, A. M., Hart, R. D., & Wright, K. D. (2019). Examination of the effectiveness of a brief, adapted dialectical behavior therapy-skills training group for bariatric surgical candidates. *Obesity Surgery, 29*(1), 252–261. Available from https://doi.org/10.1007/s11695-018-3515-2.

Dimeff, L. A., & Koerner, K. (2007). *Dialectical behavior therapy in clinical practice: Applications across disorders and settings*. New York: Guilford Press.

Dixon-Gordon, K. L., Chapman, A. L., & Turner, B. J. (2015). A preliminary pilot study comparing dialectical behavior therapy emotion regulation skills with interpersonal effectiveness skills and a control group treatment. *Journal of Experimental Psychopathology, 6*(4), 369–388. Available from https://doi.org/10.5127/jep.041714.

Edel, M.-A., Hölter, T., Wassink, K., & Juckel, G. (2014). A Comparison of mindfulness-based group training and skills group training in adults with ADHD. *Journal of Attention Disorders, 21*(6), 533–539. Available from https://doi.org/10.1177/1087054714551635.

Elices, M., Pascual, J. C., Portella, M. J., Feliu-Soler, A., Martín-Blanco, A., Carmona, C., & Soler, J. (2016). Impact of mindfulness training on borderline personality disorder: A randomized trial. *Mindfulness, 7*(3), 584–595. Available from https://doi.org/10.1007/s12671-016-0492-1.

Elices, M., Soler, J., Feliu-Soler, A., Carmona, C., Tiana, T., Pascual, J. C., ... Alvarez, E. (2017). Combining emotion regulation and mindfulness skills for preventing depression relapse: a randomized-controlled study. *Borderline Personality Disorder and Emotion Dysregulation, 4*(13). Available from https://doi.org/10.1186/s40479-017-0064-6.

Flynn, D., Joyce, M., Weihrauch, M., & Corcoran, P. (2018). Innovations in practice: Dialectical behaviour therapy—Skills training for emotional problem solving for adolescents (DBT STEPS-A): Evaluation of a pilot implementation in Irish post-primary schools. *Child and Adolescent Mental Health, 23*(4), 376–380. Available from https://doi.org/10.1111/camh.12284.

Gibson, J., Booth, R., Davenport, J., Keogh, K., & Owens, T. (2014). Dialectical behavior therapy informed skills training for deliberate self-harm: A controlled trial with 3-month follow-up data. *Behaviour Research and Therapy, 60*, 8–14. Available from https://doi.org/10.1016/j.brat.2014.06.007.

Gratz, K. L., & Roemer, L. (2004). Multidimensional assessment of emotion regulation and dysregulation: Development, factor structure, and initial validation of the difficulties in emotion regulation scale. *Journal of Psychopathology and Behavioral Assessment, 26*(1), 41–54. Available from https://doi.org/10.1023/B:JOBA.0000007455.08539.94.

Harley, R., Sprich, S., Safren, S., Jacobo, M., & Fava, M. (2008). Adaptation of dialectical behavior therapy skills training group for treatment-resistant depression. *Journal of Nervous and Mental Disease, 196*(2), 136–143. Available from https://doi.org/10.1097/NMD.0b013e318162aa3f.

Haskell, I., Daly, B. P., Hildenbrand, A., Nicholls, E., Mazza, J. J., & Dexter-Mazza, E. T. (2014) Skills training for emotional problem solving for adolescent (STEPS-A); Implementation and programme evaluation. In *Paper presented at the annual conference on Advancing Mental health*, Pittsburgh, PA.

Hoffman, P. D., Fruzzetti, A. E., & Buteau, E. (2007). Understanding and engaging families: An education, skills and support program for relatives impacted by borderline personality disorder. *Journal of Mental Health, 16*(1), 69–82. Available from https://doi.org/10.1080/09638230601182052.

Hoffman, P. D., Fruzzetti, A. E., Buteau, E., Neiditch, E. R., Penney, D., Bruce, M. L., ... Struening, E. (2005). Family connections: A program for relatives of persons with borderline personality disorder. *Family Process, 44*(2), 217–225. Available from https://doi.org/10.1111/j.15455300.2005.00055.x.

Justo, A. R., Andretta, I., & Abs, D. (2018). Dialectical behavioral therapy skills training as a social-emotional development program for teachers. *Practice Innovations*, *3*(3), 168–181. Available from https://doi.org/10.1037/pri0000071.

Kramer, U. (2017). The role of coping change in borderline personality disorder: A process-outcome analysis on dialectical-behaviour skills training. *Clinical Psychology & Psychotherapy*, *24*(2), 302–311. Available from https://doi.org/10.1002/cpp.2017.

Kramer, U., Pascual-Leone, A., Berthoud, L., de Roten, Y., Marquet, P., Kolly, S., & Page, D. (2016). Assertive anger mediates effects of dialectical behaviour-informed skills training for borderline personality disorder: A randomized controlled trial. *Clinical Psychology & Psychotherapy*, *23*(3), 189–202. Available from https://doi.org/10.1002/cpp.1956.

Liberati, A., Altman, D. G., Tetzlaff, J., Mulrow, C., Gotzsche, P. C., Ioannidis, J. P. A., … Moher, D. (2009). The PRISMA statement for reporting systematic reviews and meta-analyses of studies that evaluate health care intervention: Explanation and elaboration. *PLoS Cognitive Neuroscience Channel*, *6*, e1000100. Available from https://doi.org/10.1371/journal.pmed.1000100.

Linehan, M. M. (1993a). *Cognitive-behavioral treatment of borderline personality disorder*. New York: Guilford Press.

Linehan, M. M. (1993b). *Skills training manual for treating borderline personality disorder*. New York: Guilford Press.

Linehan, M. M. (2014). *DBT skills training manual* (2nd ed.). New York: Guilford Press.

Linehan, M. M., Armstrong, H. E., Suarez, A., Allmon, D., & Heard, H. I. (1991). Cognitive-behavioral treatment of chronically parasuicidal borderline patients. *Archives of General Psychiatry*, *48*, 1060–1064. Available from https://doi.org/10.1001/archpsyc.1991.01810360024003.

Linehan, M. M., Korslund, K. E., Harned, M. S., Gallop, R. J., Lungu, A., Neacsiu, A. D., … Murray-Gregory, A. M. (2015). Dialectical behavior therapy for high suicide risk in individuals with borderline personality disorder: A randomized clinical trial and component analysis. *JAMA Psychiatry*, *72*(5), 475–482. Available from https://doi.org/10.1001/jamapsychiatry.2014.3039.

Lynch, T. R. (2003). Dialectical behavior therapy for depressed older adults: A randomized pilot study. *American Journal of Geriatric Psychiatry*, *11*(1), 33–45. Available from https://doi.org/10.1097/00019442-200301000-00006.

Lynch, T. R., Cheavens, J. S., Cukrowicz, K. C., Throp, S. R., Bronner, L., & Beyer, J. (2007). Treatment of older adults with co-morbid personality disorder and depression: a dialectical behavior therapy approach. *International Journal of Geriatric Psychiatry*, *22*(2), 131–143. Available from https://doi.org/10.1002/gps.1703.

Maffei, C., Cavicchioli, M., Movalli, M., Cavallaro, R., & Fossati, A. (2018). Dialectical behavior therapy skills training in alcohol dependence treatment: Findings based on an open trial. *Substance Use & Misuse*, *53*(14), 2368–2385. Available from https://doi.org/10.1080/10826084.2018.1480035.

McMain, S. F., Guimond, T., Barnhart, R., Habinski, L., & Streiner, D. L. (2017). A randomized trial of brief dialectical behaviour therapy skills training in suicidal patients suffering from borderline disorder. *Acta Psychiatrica Scandinavica*, *135*(2), 138–148. Available from https://doi.org/10.1111/acps.12664.

Moore, K. E., Folk, J. B., Boren, E. A., Tangney, J. P., Fischer, S., & Schrader, S. W. (2018). Pilot study of a brief dialectical behavior therapy skills group for jail inmates. *Psychological Services*, *15*(1), 98–108. Available from https://doi.org/10.1037/ser0000105.

Murphy, D., Hostick, M., Louise Skitt, S., & Turner, A. (2018). A practice-based evaluation of a dialectical behavioural therapy skills group intervention in a secondary care mental health service. *Mental Health Practice*, *21*(6), 20–25. Available from https://doi.org/10.7748/mhp.2018.e1254.

Mushquash, A. R., & McMahan, M. (2015). Dialectical behavior therapy skills training reduces binge eating among patients seeking weight-management services: Preliminary evidence. *Eating and Weight Disorders, 20*(3), 415–418. Available from https://doi.org/10.1007/s40519-015-0177-0.

Neacsiu, A., Rizvi, S., & Linehan, M. (2010). Dialectical behavior therapy skills use as a mediator and outcome of treatment for borderline personality disorder. *Behaviour Research and Therapy, 48*, 832–839. Available from https://doi.org/10.1016/j.brat.2010.05.017.

Neacsiu, A. D., Bohus, M., & Linehan, M. M. (2014). Dialectical behavior therapy: An intervention for emotion dysregulation. In J. J. Gross (Ed.), *Handbook of emotion regulation* (pp. 491–507). New York: Guilford Press.

Neacsiu, A. D., Eberle, J. W., Kramer, R., Wiesmann, T., & Linehan, M. M. (2014). Dialectical behavior therapy skills for transdiagnostic emotion dysregulation: A pilot randomized controlled trial. *Behaviour Research and Therapy, 59*, 40–51. Available from https://doi.org/10.1016/j.brat.2014.05.005.

Neacsiu, A. D., Rompogren, J., Eberle, J. W., & McMahon, K. (2018). Changes in problematic anger, shame, and disgust in anxious and depressed adults undergoing treatment for emotion dysregulation. *Behavior Therapy, 49*(3), 344–359. Available from https://doi.org/10.1016/j.beth.2017.10.004.

Quinn, M., & Hymas, R. (2017). Evaluation of a pilot dialectical behaviour therapy skills training group, in a child and adolescent mental health service team. *Mental Health Practice, 21*(4), 24–28. Available from https://doi.org/10.7748/mhp.2017.e1247.

Ramaiya, M. K., McLean, C., Regmi, U., Fiorillo, D., Robins, C. J., & Kohrt, B. A. (2018). A dialectical behavior therapy skills intervention for women with suicidal behaviors in rural Nepal: A single-case experimental design series. *Journal of Clinical Psychology, 74*(7), 1071–1091. Available from https://doi.org/10.1002/jclp.22588.

Ricard, R. J., Lerma, E., & Heard, C. C. C. (2013). Piloting a dialectical behavioral therapy (DBT) infused skills group in a disciplinary alternative education program (DAEP). *Journal for Specialists in Group Work, 38*(4), 285–306. Available from https://doi.org/10.1080/01933922.2013.834402.

Rizvi, S. L., & Steffel, L. M. (2014). A pilot study of 2 brief forms of dialectical behavior therapy skills training for emotion dysregulation in college students. *Journal of American College Health, 62*(6), 434–439. Available from https://doi.org/10.1080/07448481.2014.907298.

Uliaszek, A. A., Rashid, T., Williams, G. E., & Gulamani, T. (2016). Group therapy for university students: A randomized control trial of dialectical behavior therapy and positive psychotherapy. *Behaviour Research and Therapy, 77*, 78–85. Available from https://doi.org/10.1016/j.brat.2015.12.003.

Valentine, S. E., Bankoff, S. M., Poulin, R. M., Reidler, E. B., & Pantalone, D. W. (2014). The use of dialectical behavior therapy skills training as stand-alone treatment: A systematic review of the treatment outcome literature. *Journal of Clinical Psychology, 71*(1), 1–20. Available from https://doi.org/10.1002/jclp.22114.

Wilks, C. R., Lungu, A., Ang, S. Y., Matsumiya, B., Yin, Q., & Linehan, M. M. (2018). A randomized controlled trial of an internet delivered dialectical behavior therapy skills training for suicidal and heavy episodic drinkers. *Journal of Affective Disorders, 232*, 219–228. Available from https://doi.org/10.1016/j.jad.2018.02.053.

Wilks, C. R., Valenstein-Mah, H., Tran, H., King, A. M. M., Lungu, A., & Linehan, M. M. (2017). Dialectical behavior therapy skills for families of individuals with behavioral disorders: Initial feasibility and outcomes. *Cognitive and Behavioral Practice, 24*(3), 288–295. Available from https://doi.org/10.1016/j.cbpra.2016.06.004.

Zapolski, T. C. B., & Smith, G. T. (2017). Pilot study: Implementing a brief DBT skills program in schools to reduce health risk behaviors among early adolescents. *The Journal of School Nursing, 33*(3), 198–204. Available from https://doi.org/10.1177/1059840516673188.

SECTION IV

Future directions

CHAPTER

16

Recommendations and future directions for the scientific study of dialectical behavior therapy: emphasizing replication and reproducibility

Jamie D. Bedics

California Lutheran University, Thousand Oaks, CA, United States

> You cannot help dealing with the limited information you have as if it were all there is to know. You build the best possible story from the information available to you, and if it is a good story, you believe it. Paradoxically; it is easier to construct a coherent story when you know little, when there are few pieces to fit into the puzzle. Our comforting conviction that the world makes sense rests on a secure foundation: our almost unlimited ability to ignore our ignorance. ***Kahneman (2011, p. 201).***

> Considering how little we know, the confidence we have in our beliefs is preposterous – and it is also essential. ***Kahneman (2011, p. 209).***

In his book, *Thinking Fast, and Slow,* Kahneman (2011) summarizes decades of research examining how cognitive heuristics and biases can impact our decision-making, subjective judgments, and evaluations. Of the many heuristics reviewed, the idea of the narrative fallacy is particularly relevant to the goal of this edited volume. In describing the narrative fallacy, Kahneman discussed how we can place too much confidence in our beliefs through the compelling nature of a good story. The resulting sense of overconfidence can lead to inaccurate judgments and mistaken generalizations that go beyond the current evidence base,

The Handbook of Dialectical Behavior Therapy
DOI: https://doi.org/10.1016/B978-0-12-816384-9.00016-6

a phenomenon known as the halo effect. A sense of overconfidence in the field of psychotherapy is especially concerning for two reasons. First, therapists and clients can be motivated to participate in a treatment for which they are not well suited. Similarly, they can be misled with respect to their expectations for treatment outcomes. Second, the integrity of the treatment, for whom we know it works best, can be compromised. Although our confidence in a good story can be misleading, the absence of a story can make our ability to understand and advance our knowledge of the world impossible. In other words, the story is essential.

As scientific thinkers we are drawn to coherent narratives. These narratives are the theories we hold to explain the phenomenon of the world we care about most. Theories are comprised of our personal beliefs along with the evidence, or data, we acquire through the scientific method. The relationship between theory and data is an iterative one where theory informs our data collection and the results, in turn, shape our understanding of the world (Wampold, Davis, & Good, 1990). In the same vein, Popper (1959) described theories as "nets cast to catch what we call 'the world': to rationalize, to explain, and to master it. We endeavor to make the mesh ever finer and finer" (p. 831).

The theory of dialectical behavior therapy (DBT; Linehan, 1993), along with its model of understanding borderline personality disorder (BPD) (i.e., the biosocial model), is likely what attracted many of us to DBT. Comprehensive or standard-DBT (S-DBT) is a program of psychotherapy that carefully balances various treatment strategies of acceptance (e.g., Zen meditation) and change (e.g., cognitive-behavioral therapy), across multiple treatment modalities (i.e., individual therapy, skills training, telephone consultation, and team consultation), and within a larger, overarching framework informed by dialectical philosophy. Further, the specific treatment strategies, along with their careful balance, were specifically developed for the emotional, interpersonal, and cognitive experience of those meeting criteria for BPD.

It is clear that in DBT we have a strong and compelling theory for the conceptualization and treatment of BPD. We also have the benefit of three decades of accumulated research to review and improve our understanding of the theory. The purpose of this book is to highlight the various clinical and research innovations in the scientific thinking surrounding the study of DBT. The contributing authors shared their summaries of the literature examining the efficacy and effectiveness of DBT-based interventions across a variety of populations and settings. As stated in the opening preface, the authors have demonstrated "what we have done" and "how we have done it." In explicating this research the authors described the facts and details of each study allowing the reader to make their own informed judgments regarding the data. The results of these efforts do not, however, lend themselves to easy answers. Instead, each contributing author shared what has been done in their area of expertise with little fanfare as they stayed close to the data with precise and clear language. The results revealed just how much has been accomplished as well as how much has yet to be confirmed and understood in the study of DBT.

In this chapter, I provide a summary of the challenges faced in DBT research that could be considered threats to the overall interpretability and coherence of DBT science. These challenges are not related to any flaws in the methodological designs or statistical analyses in existing DBT research. Instead, these threats come from, in part, the success of the treatment. The widespread adoption of DBT has led to a variety of treatment modifications across a diversity of populations and settings. On the one hand, this speaks to the overall generalizability of DBT-based interventions and the potential transdiagnostic application of DBT (e.g., Neacsiu, Eberle, Kramer, Wiesmann, & Linehan, 2014). On the other hand, the various modifications pose a threat to the integrity of the treatment when researchers are not as cognizant or explicit with respect to the replicability and reproducibility of their efforts that allow for a coherent DBT science to be maintained. The following sections will highlight these threats along with proposed solutions.

Threats to the interpretability and coherence of dialectical behavior therapy science

The past decade has seen an increase in emphasis on how psychological science is being conducted with respect to the replicability and reproducibility of research. Although the majority of this work has been conducted within the fields of social and personality psychology [e.g., Open Science Collaboration (OSC), 2015], recent efforts have expanded this thinking to clinical science (Tackett et al., 2017). The renewed effort to improve psychological science has been referred to as "psychology's renaissance" (Nelson, Simmons, & Simonsohn, 2018), but the seeds of this renaissance have existed for decades. Commentaries on the prevalence of underpowered investigations (Cohen, 1962; Maxwell, 2004), the unaccountability of various post hoc methodological and statistical decision-makings (Kerr, 1998), and the failure to build a cumulative body of knowledge based upon adequate theory and hypothesis testing (Meehl, 1978; Wampold et al., 1990) are a few examples of this important work. The following section will extend this work by first describing the concepts of replication and reproducibility. The principles derived from these definitions will then be applied as tools to address threats to the interpretability of DBT research.

Replication in science

On the surface, replication appears to be a relatively simple concept where a study repeats a specific experimental procedure to confirm the results of a prior study. Such a definition, although broadly accurate, is misleading when considering the complexity of the concept of replication. In his discussion of replication, Schmidt (2009) takes a functional approach to understanding the benefits of replication by considering the balance of *sameness* and *difference* in repeated experimental designs (p. 93). Based on the work of Hendrick (1991), Schmidt described four broad classes of information or aspects of an experiment that can be varied to serve *five functions* of a replication. The four broad classes of information include (A) primary information (i.e., the instructions provided to participants, including treatment procedures and their method of delivery); (B) contextual background of the experiment (i.e., participant demographics and research history, the larger culture and historical context when the study is conducted, general physical setting and the research team that interacts with the participants); (C) procedures for the selection and allocation of participants; and (D) procedures that constitute the dependent variable.

The five functions of a replication consist of variations in the four classes mentioned previously. In Function 1, a new sample is collected (all classes are held constant, unchanged). The goal of Function 2 is to control for artifacts by running the same experiment in a new lab with separate investigators and research personnel (classes B and D are changed). Function 3 attempts to control for fraud and changes the research personnel only (only class B is changed). Function 4 prioritizes generalization to a larger or different population (e.g., a new country or state) and occurs when the same research team implements the same procedures but varies the sample with the goal of generalization (only class C changes). Lastly, Function 5 occurs when a researcher might, for example, test the bounds of the effect of a treatment on various operationalization of the dependent variable (classes B, D, and the material presentation of class A can change). Although there is no such thing as an exact replication, the first four functions can be considered *direct replications* while the fifth function is a *conceptual replication*. In all of these functions the *essential* primary information (i.e., class A) provided to the participants (i.e., the treatment) is held constant. The last point regarding the constancy of class A is critical and will be revisited below in reviewing the proliferation of DBT-based interventions.

Reproducibility in science

In contrast to replicability, reproducibility, also referred to as *analytic-reproducibility* (LeBel, McCarthy, Earp, Elson, & Vanpaemel, 2018), can be defined as the expectation that when an independent party uses the same statistical code and same data, they will reproduce the exact same numbers as originally published (Patil, Peng, & Leek, 2016). The minimum requirement for analytic-reproducibility is the sharing of statistical code and data in an online repository such as the Open Science Framework (Soderberg, 2018; https://osf.io). Such practices are not, however, typical of scientists for a variety of reasons (see Houtkoop et al., 2018) and also perhaps due to the existing cultural norms in science (Anderson, Martinson, & De Vries, 2007).

In addition to analytic-reproducibility, recent efforts have emphasized the importance of examining the *robustness of analytic findings* as a complement to analytic-reproducibility (LeBel et al., 2018; Steegen, Tuerlinckx, Gelman, & Vanpaemel, 2016). This refers to the idea that there are multiple, valid methods for the analysis of any given dataset. The variety of analytic decisions a research team can make are numerous and range from, for example, decisions on data transformations (e.g., log transformations, transformation of data to an ordinal scale), use of dichotomous versus continuous data values, the analysis of specific time points (e.g., pre- to posttreatment or the analysis of multiple intermediary points), the use of particular subscales, the application of specific statistical models (e.g., negative binomial vs logistic regression), the use of subsets of data as a test of moderators, and the various methods for the management of missing data. The variety of data analytic strategies, for the most part, will largely be a reflection of the personal preferences of the research team that is guided by the data itself.

Research has shown that such a variety of data analytic strategies can, however, lead to a diversity of outcomes. One study demonstrated this by providing 29 research teams with the exact same dataset for analysis to test one particular hypothesis (Silberzahn & Uhlmann, 2015). As would be expected, a variety of reasonable data analytic techniques were conducted across research teams resulting in a variety of outcomes with some, but not all, finding statistically significant results. The results were equally variable with respect to effect sizes. Although the results did, however, demonstrate an overall consensus in one direction, any one of these studies, reported independently, could have been very misleading. Based on these results, the authors of the study suggested multiple data analytic approaches are necessary to test one hypothesis in order to measure the robustness of a finding. The process of testing the robustness or sensitivity of any given finding is not unlike what researchers do when examining the effect of an outlier but in this case the process is generalized to the entire data analysis (Steegen et al., 2016).

As most researchers' can attest and as demonstrated above, data analysis begins with a set of particular techniques and ideas and then adjusts based on a review of the data. These analytic decisions and adjustments are often not planned and are instead part of a natural and organic process that is flexible and guided by the data. Although useful for maximizing the results for one dataset, such flexibility can present a unique challenge to the veracity of the scientific process when (1) there are a variety of valid data analytic strategies available; (2) the variety of data analytic strategies can change the statistical significance and magnitude of effect; and (3) we are not blinded to the hypothesis (Carp, 2012; Kerr, 1998; Simmons, Nelson, & Simonsohn, 2011). As research has shown, such flexibility can result in an increase in false-positive results as well as inflated effect sizes (Button et al., 2013; Ioannidis, 2005). These unreliable findings are even more likely to occur in underpowered statistical analyses where the slightest change in analytic strategy can drastically impact the results (Fraley & Vazire, 2014).

Replication and reproducibility: summary

The principles of replication and reproducibility, along with a compelling theoretical narrative, are the mainstays of science. The scientific principle of replication can serve five functions that systematically vary four aspects of an experimental procedure. The concepts of analytic-reproducibility and analytic-robustness refer to the process of conducting data analysis to confirm an individual study's findings. These principles not only hold research to a high degree of accountability but also allow for tests of the robustness of findings. The following section will highlight how the concepts of replication and reproducibility can enhance current DBT research.

Improving dialectical behavior therapy science with an emphasis on replication and reproducibility

It is clear from the chapters in this volume that the gold standard DBT intervention, with respect to both theoretical development and empirical evidence from carefully controlled randomized-controlled trials (RCTs), remains S-DBT for BPD. Although not always explicitly citing the function of replication, research on the efficacy of S-DBT for BPD has been well replicated. The majority of RCT research on S-DBT for BPD have met a variety of functions of replication as noted previously. Function 1 has been met through the work of multiple studies by Linehan (e.g., Linehan, Armstrong, Suarez, Allmon, & Heard, 1991; Linehan et al., 2006, 2015). Functions 2, 3, and 4 have been met through the investigations conducted in separate laboratories and populations (e.g., McMain et al., 2009; McMain et al., 2018; Verheul et al., 2003).

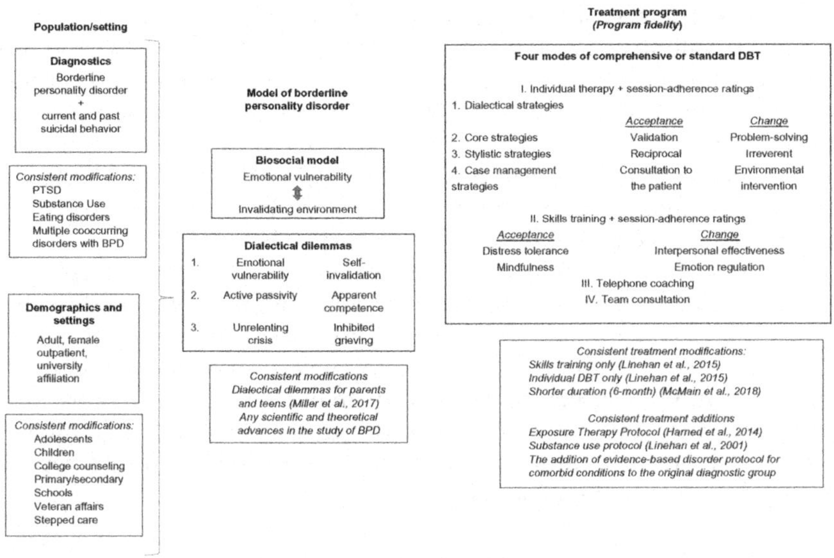

FIGURE 16.1 Treatment adaptations consistent with standard or comprehensive dialectical behavior therapy (DBT).

Function 5 has been completed in diverse populations such as those diagnosed with substance use (e.g., Linehan et al., 1999, 2002) among others. It is fair to say that the quality of this work, examining S-DBT for BPD, and its focus on replication has contributed greatly to the positive reputation of DBT in the research and clinical community.

In contrast to the abovementioned studies, the majority of treatment modifications reviewed in this textbook can vary in one of two ways. First, there are subsets of studies that remain largely consistent with the theoretical framework of S-DBT for BPD as defined in the main treatment manual (Linehan, 1993). Fig. 16.1 outlines three major areas were S-DBT has been modified while remaining consistent with S-DBT theory, including diagnostics and settings, an expanded understanding of the biosocial model of BPD, and variations in the treatment program itself. All of these modifications have two features in common allowing them to remain consistent with the theory of S-DBT. First, they stay within the larger context of treating BPD based on the biosocial model. Second, they do not fundamentally alter the core of the treatment itself (i.e., they maintain *program fidelity*; see Harned, 2019). These modifications include, for example, a shorter duration of outpatient treatment (McMain et al., 2018), the dismantling of the four major modules of S-DBT (Linehan et al., 2015), the addition of specific evidence-based protocols for the treatment of disorders that commonly co-occur with BPD, including substance abuse (Linehan et al., 1999, 2002) and PTSD (Harned, Korslund, & Linehan, 2014), the application of S-DBT for BPD in novel settings (e.g., university counseling centers; Pistorello, Fruzzetti, MacLane, Gallop, & Iverson, 2012), and the modification of S-DBT for children (Perepletchikova et al., 2011) and adolescents (McCauley et al., 2018; Mehlum et al., 2014; Rathus & Miller, 2002. All of these adaptations represent creative treatment modifications that broaden the scope of S-DBT for BPD while maintaining its theoretical coherence.

An important point when considering this work is that despite the theoretical coherence of many of these adaptations, each modification will have its own unique evidence base that requires a careful evaluation of its efficacy through replication. While the majority of the abovementioned modifications have served many of the functions of a replication, they have also modified the treatment itself (i.e., altering class "A" or primary information) making the need for future replications, of the same material, a priority.

The proliferation of dialectical behavior therapy–based interventions

In comparison to the studies reviewed previously, a second group of DBT-based interventions fall outside the theoretical coherence of S-DBT for BPD. These interventions have either applied the treatment to a population without BPD or they have significantly revised the treatment itself. These changes are often subtle. For example, in Chapter 6, Eating disorders, the authors provided a careful analysis revealing that of the 29 studies reviewed, 23 reported unique adaptations. Such adaptations, although reflective of the innovation and creativity of DBT researchers, require careful attention for three reasons. First, the majority of adaptations are no longer consistent with S-DBT for BPD and reflect unique and novel modifications that have likely not been evaluated in the empirical literature to date. Consequently, the majority of these studies, although having "DBT" in the title, will not serve the function of any replication, although often cited or reviewed as a homogenous set of treatments. Perhaps as a result of viewing all "DBT" interventions as relatively similar, systemic replication, as seen in S-DBT for BPD, has not been consistent. Relatedly, and unfortunately for the coherence of DBT science, these nonreplicated studies typically consist of small sample sizes and are thus the most vulnerable to false positives (i.e., spurious statistically significant findings that would likely not be significant with a larger sample size), unreliable and inflated effect sizes, and false negatives (i.e., nonstatistically significant findings that might have been significant with a larger sample size).

Session-rated adherence in dialectical behavior therapy

In addition to the variation in modes of delivering DBT-based interventions, the research literature on DBT has been equally challenged by the lack of consistent measurement of how sessions are being conducted. As can be seen from Fig. 16.1, S-DBT is a complex multimodal intervention requiring skill across a variety of treatment strategies. S-DBT also requires a great deal of responsivity and flexibility on the part of the therapist to effectively meet clients' needs. Therapist responsivity in S-DBT, however, has its limits. The extent to which DBT therapists act in accordance with principles from S-DBT theory during their sessions is referred to as treatment adherence.

As reviewed in Chapter 4, Accreditation, adherence, and training in dialectical behavior therapy: data review and practical applications, of this book, adherence in DBT is not a stable trait acquired through training or an attribute one can proclaim of oneself. Instead, adherence ratings quantify the degree to which the therapist *acts* in a way consistent with the principles of the treatment during *one* individual therapy or skills training session. The DBT adherence scale (Linehan, & Korslund, 2003) is an observer-rated scale used to measure session adherence in S-DBT. The measure contains multiple subscales that capture the essential qualities of the components underlying S-DBT, including problem assessment, validation, dialectics, and stylistic strategies among others. Historically, the DBT adherence scale is copyrighted and has not been open for public review. Interested researchers or therapists wanting to have sessions rated for adherence or learn how to code adherence would have to pay for the service through the University of Washington or receive the service through the DBT-certification process (https://dbt-lbc.org/). Currently, work is being done to demonstrate the reliability and validity of this measure along with additional, more readily available, measures for rating adherence in DBT (Harned, 2019).

The absence of a quantifiable metric of adherence in the majority of research reviewed in this book presents at least three challenges for the DBT research and clinical community. First, and perhaps most obvious, is that the internal validity of the studies reported without session-based adherence is compromised. In the absence of session-based adherence ratings, it is impossible to tell the extent to which the treatment is being delivered with adherence. The results from such studies are difficult to interpret in these cases. A researcher who fails to find significance for any given outcome can easily point to the lack of adherence as the cause. Conversely, although much less likely to be acknowledged, the positive results from a study could equally be attributed to the failure of therapists to conform to the treatment. A second concern related to the absence of adherence is the tendency for authors to appeal to authority as a method of verifying the integrity of the study. Authors can, for example, make an appeal to their level of training (e.g., "DBT-intensively trained" or "DBT-certified") or to the authority of the investigator, collaborators, or supervisors. Such a strategy is counter to the basic principles of science that value objective evaluation. Further, such a tendency can reinforce black-and-white thinking about DBT adherence rather than thinking of adherence as a quantifiable index that has an average, variance, and fluctuates across time and subscales of DBT strategies. Such black-and-white thinking about one's own competence is also antithetical to the philosophy of the treatment that values humility, vulnerability, and a continual desire to learn and grow on the part of the therapists. A third challenge related to the absence of adherence ratings lies in its impact on the development of treatment adaptations and replication. In the absence of adherence ratings, it is unclear how a researcher can adapt or replicate a treatment and know whether or not it remains within the spirit of the original treatment (e.g., maintains a careful balance of acceptance and change in strategies and therapist style, incorporates validation, etc.).

Empirical evidence has begun to underscore that session-rated adherence does matter. In a RCT of S-DBT for substance abuse (Linehan et al., 1999), a post hoc evaluation of a small subset of nonrandomly selected participants supported the importance of adherence for one of the outcomes assessed. In this study, four participants who received S-DBT from therapists who achieved consistent ratings of acceptable adherence had significantly more clean urinalysis tests compared to three participants who received treatment from therapists who did not achieve consistent session adherence (Linehan et al., 1999). The post hoc nature of these analyses, centered around a single outcome for seven participants, obviously limits this finding. However, more recent data from numerous trials of S-DBT for BPD suggests that increased adherence is related to less frequent treatment dropout as well as a decrease in mean number of suicide attempts (Harned, 2019).

Summary on treatment integrity. The multimodal nature of DBT lends itself easily to adaptation in order to meet the needs of unique populations and settings. At the same time, the frequent variation in treatment delivery (i.e., treatment modifications) along with the absence of in-session adherence ratings can present significant challenges for the overall coherence of DBT as well as the training and dissemination of DBT-based interventions. In addition, researchers should do their best to attend to the principles of replication in their work and highlight the various functions of replication being met in the study. In consuming novel research, clinicians can benefit from being particularly cognizant of the underlying evidence in support of the version of DBT they are implementing while remembering to avoid equating a unique body of evidence with the evidence of S-DBT for BPD (i.e., the halo effect).

Multiple outcomes as a challenge to research synthesis

The previous section highlighted the benefits of increased clarity and transparency in the delivery of DBT-based interventions with a focus on replication. An additional challenge in the synthesis of multiple studies is the lack of clarity and consistency in the measurement of the outcomes or dependent variables of the study (e.g., Mayo-Wilson et al., 2017). Outcome variables can vary in five ways, including the domain (i.e., hypothetical construct), measure (i.e., operationalization), metric (e.g., value at a particular time point such raw score, mean, median), method of aggregating data (i.e., continuous variable or dichotomous), and the timing of assessments (e.g., every 3 months, pre to post) (Mayo-Wilson et al., 2017). There are, of course, benefits to the intentional manipulation of these five outcome domains in research. In conducting clinical trials, variation in the outcome domain can demonstrate the breadth of a treatment's effect across multiple types of outcomes (e.g., suicidal behavior, BPD symptoms) and mechanisms (e.g., coping skills, emotion regulation). Similar to analytic-robustness, the intentional manipulation of the five aforementioned outcome domains can further test the sensitivity or robustness of a finding. Lastly, and as demonstrated in Chapter 5, Efficacy of dialectical behavior therapy in the treatment of suicidal behavior, of this text, meta-analytic research can be an effective statistical method for the quantitative synthesis of an individual outcome domain across variations in the other four domains.

Despite these strengths, the diversity of outcomes can present challenges in the synthesis and evaluation of a body of research. One of the main challenges faced is the simple fact that many of the aforementioned methods of manipulating outcomes are not conduced with purposeful, planned intent. Instead, and similar to the challenges faced in multiple data analytic methods noted earlier, the variety of ways an outcome is manipulated is likely due to the research team's preference and the organic process of attempting to understand the data. Although often unintended, such a process will likely result in a greater likelihood of false-positive findings (Mayo-Wilson et al., 2017), which cannot be corrected through metaanalytic techniques (Nelson et al., 2018).

As an example from DBT research, Table 16.1 presents a brief review of the variety of methods of analyzing nonsuicidal self-injury (NSSI) from 10 unique RCTs of S-DBT for adults with BPD (https://behavioraltech.org/research/evidence/efficacy-trials/#Standard). As can be seen in Table 16.1, the majority of outcomes are focused on the frequency of

TABLE 16.1 Operationalization of nonsuicidal self-injury (NSSI) in standard-dialectical behavior therapy for borderline personality disorder.[a]

NSSI	Any NSSI (yes/no)	Number of NSSI acts	Number of NSSI episodes	Percentage of participants with any NSSI acts	Number of NSSI acts: subset: when participants had more than 1 NSSI act	Number of NSSI episodes: subset: when participants had more than 1 NSSI episode	Number of NSSI acts: subset: median split of baseline NSSI lifetime	Ordinal cut points for overall weighted summary score of total acts	Five ordinal cut points of total NSSI acts
1	–	√	–	√	√	√	–	–	–
1a	–	–	√	–	–	–	–	–	–
2	–	–	√	–	–	–	–	–	–
3	–	–	√[b]	–	–	–	–	–	–
4	–	√[c]	–	–	–	–	√	–	–
5	–	–	–	–	–	–	–	–	√
6	–	–	–	–	–	–	–	–	–
7	–	–	–	–	–	–	–	√	–
8	–	–	√	–	–	–	–	–	–
8a	–	√[b]	√	√	–	–	–	–	–
9	√	–	√	√[d]	–	–	–	–	–
10	√	–	–	–	√	–	–	–	–

[a]*Check marks do not indicate that statistical significance was found in the study.*
[b]*Exact classification is unclear.*
[c]*Log-transformed.*
[d]*Episodes were rated, not acts.*
(1) Linehan et al. (1991); (1a) Linehan, Heard, and Armstrong (1993); (2) Linehan et al. (1999); (3) Linehan et al. (2002); (4) Verheul et al. (2003); (5) Linehan et al. (2006); (6) Clarkin et al. (2007); (7) Linehan et al. (2008); (8) McMain et al. (2009); (8a) McMain et al (2012); (9) Carter et al. (2010); (10) Linehan et al. (2015).

NSSI acts (i.e., number of individual acts) or episodes (i.e., number of events that could contain more than one act). It is also evident that there is great variability in the methods of understanding and thinking about NSSI across these studies of S-DBT for BPD. Of particular interest is the relative lack of consistency across studies, the tendency to incorporate unique modifying conditions, and the tendency to avoid using multiple methods to test the robustness of findings in one study. In addition, in the two studies that reported follow-ups, the exact metrics assessed from the first study to the second study were inconsistently measured, thus potentially increasing the likelihood of false-positive findings that would not be captured in a meta-analysis.

Summary and conclusion for the future of dialectical behavior therapy science

The goal of this chapter was to highlight the strengths and weaknesses in the scientific study of DBT-based interventions as reviewed throughout this text. The research on S-DBT for BPD remains the strongest evidence base for DBT-based interventions due to the high internal validity (i.e., program fidelity and session-rated adherence) and high degree of emphasis placed on replication. The interpretability of the studies, however, becomes less clear when one looks at the subtle changes in outcome measurement and data analysis that can have a significant impact on the results of any one individual study. Similar challenges were apparent in the review of the various DBT-based interventions that went beyond the theory of S-DBT for BPD. These studies were further hampered by a lack of emphasis on replication, inconsistent adaptations across studies, and an absence of session-rated adherence. The current chapter proposed a renewed emphasis on functions of replication and enhanced transparency through analytic-reproducibility and analytic-robustness as solutions to improve the interpretability of DBT science.

In a seminal research article published in 1990, Wampold et al. discussed the critical role of theory and hypothesis testing in psychological science. The authors coined the term "hypothesis validity" to define the extent to which research hypotheses reflected predictions made by theory as well as the quality of inferences made based upon the results from the study. The first pane of Fig. 16.2 reflects the model defined by Wampold where the iterative process of theory to results and vice versa is demonstrated. In addition to this model, Wampold provided several recommendations for the improvement of psychological science consistent with those made in this chapter. For example, the authors spoke of the diffusion of multiple statistical tests to capture a single hypothesis, the inclusion of extraneous independent variables

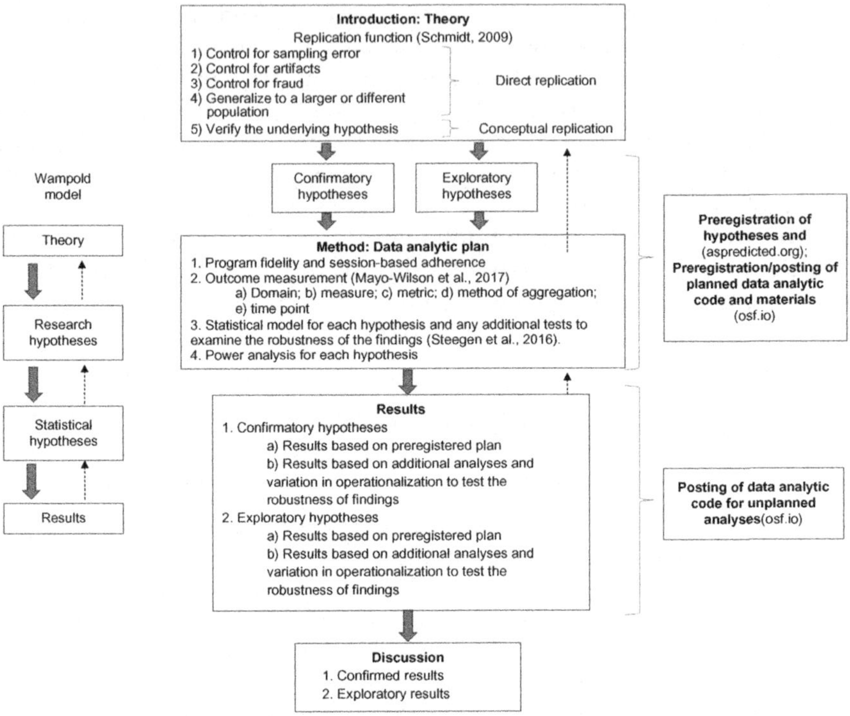

FIGURE 16.2 A model for replicable and reproducible science in the study of dialectical behavior therapy.

(e.g., unplanned or predicted moderators), and the ill consequences of low-powered studies.

In the second pane of Fig. 16.2, I attempted to expand upon the original model provided by Wampold in a manner consistent with the several threats to the interpretation of DBT research reviewed earlier. They are fairly straightforward, and I will elaborate on each point next.

1. *Theory replication.* The strength of a theory not only lies in the coherence of the narrative but also on the quality of the science from which it is comprised. The development of theory, to progress DBT science, would benefit by placing a greater emphasis on replication and the systematic manipulation of aspects of an experiment to confirm new and novel interventions in well-powered studies.
2. *Hypothesis development as confirmation or exploration.* In furthering Wampold's emphasis on hypothesis validity, the inclusion of replication as a core principle of science would then require that explicit attention be made to the distinction between confirmation and exploration in hypothesis generation.

3. *Preregistration of hypotheses.* Confirmatory and exploratory hypotheses can be preregistered through a variety of online websites (e.g., https://aspredicted.org; https://osf.io). The function of preregistration is to allow authors to state the original intentions of their research, which, in turn, would allow them to freely explore their data after the planned analysis is complete.
4. *Method and data analytic plan: outcome domain.* Given the complexity of an outcome, researchers would benefit from bringing greater attention to the exact definition of their outcome to improve replicability. The intentional inclusion of multiple methods of assessing and measuring a single outcome domain would further test the analytic-robustness of an individual finding.
5. *Method and data analytic plan: data analysis.* Researchers should plan a variety of methods of data analysis in order to test the analytic-robustness of a finding. Similar to DBT clinical team consultation, research teams can ask themselves, "What is being left out?", "Is there another way to approach this problem?", or "How can we make this significant finding and/or large effect disappear?" as a means to test the durability of the finding.
6. *Preregistration of method and data analysis.* The preregistration of the method and data analytic plan (syntax or statistical computing code) is an essential part of the research process that provides researchers with the flexibility to maximize the credibility of their findings. Although the preregistration plan provides a baseline from which researchers begin their analysis, it does not define its end. Instead, the incorporation of a pre-registered data analytic plan is the only way that a researcher can effectively explore and understand their data with freedom and creativity that does not sacrifice credibility. A preregistered data analytic plan, along with a revised or final data analytic plan, can also allow consumers of the research to transparently see how the process of a data analysis unfolds when complex data analytic problems are being solved. When a reader has the two plans to compare (preregistered and unplanned/actual), they can learn from the researchers' process of analysis which could, in turn, inform their own data analytic thinking in the future.
7. *Results: confirmation versus exploratory.* Consistent with Wampold, the results should be focused around the hypotheses and not the statistical models themselves. The current modification would require a distinction be made between confirmatory and exploratory hypotheses as noted in the introductory literature review of the research paper.
8. *Results: planned versus unplanned.* The completion of preregistration affords the researcher the opportunity to distinguish between planned (preregistered) and unplanned (organic data analytic

changes) results for both confirmatory and exploratory hypotheses. These data analytic scripts (planned and unplanned) can be freely shared with the scientific community using online repositories to enhance reproducibility and transparency.

9. *Discussion: confirmatory versus exploratory.* Lastly, the discussion of the results should maintain a consistent focus on the distinction between confirmatory and exploratory results as well as the functions of replication the study has met.

What is most encouraging about DBT science is the passion and commitment of the community to both the theory of DBT and to maintaining the integrity of the scientific method. These principles and this spirit have been evident since the inception of DBT and as exemplified by Linehan who would not publish her treatment manual prior to the publication of the first RCT. As research on DBT continues to grow and expand, it is the responsibility of the DBT scientific community to maintain the integrity of the treatment. In doing so, we can ensure the treatment remains effective and continues to impact and enhance the well-being of our clients whose lives we hope to improve for the better.

Acknowledgment

Thanks to Erin Ward-Ciesielski for comments on an earlier draft and Katie Patel for her assistance with this chapter.

References

Anderson, M. S., Martinson, B. C., & De Vries, R. (2007). Normative dissonance in science: Results from a national survey of US scientists. *Journal of Empirical Research on Human Research Ethics*, *2*(4), 3–14.

Button, K. S., Ioannidis, J. P. A., Mokrysz, C., Nosek, B. A., Flint, J., Robinson, E. S. J., & Munafò, M. R. (2013). Power failure: Why small sample size undermines the reliability of neuroscience. *Nature Reviews Neuroscience*, *14*(5), 365–376.

Carp, J. (2012). The secret lives of experiments: Methods reporting in the fMRI literature. *NeuroImage*, *63*(1), 289–300.

Carter G. L., Willcox C. H., Lewin T. J., Conrad A. M. and Bendit N. (2010). Hunter DBT Project: Randomized controlled trial of dialectical behaviour therapy in women with borderline personality disorder. *Australian and New Zealand Journal of Psychiatry 44*, 162–173.

Clarkin J. F., Levy K. N., Lenzenweger M. F. and Kernberg O. F. (2007). Evaluating three treatments for borderline personality disorder: A multiwave study. *American Journal of Psychiatry*, *164*, 922–928.

Cohen, J. (1962). The statistical power of abnormal-social psychological research: A review. *The Journal of Abnormal and Social Psychology*, *65*, 145–153. Available from https://doi.org/10.1037/h0045186.

Fraley, R. C., & Vazire, S. (2014). The N-pact factor: Evaluating the quality of empirical journals with respect to sample size and statistical power. *PLoS One*, *9*(10), e109019.

Harned, M. (2019). *Annual update on DBT research.* Atlanta, GA: International Society for the Improvement and Teaching of Dialectical Behavior Therapy.

Harned, M. S., Korslund, K. E., & Linehan, M. M. (2014). A pilot randomized controlled trial of Dialectical Behavior Therapy with and without the Dialectical Behavior Therapy Prolonged Exposure protocol for suicidal and self-injuring women with borderline personality disorder and PTSD. *Behaviour Research and Therapy, 55,* 7–17.

Hendrick, C. (1991). Replications, strict replications, and conceptual replications: Are they important? *Journal of Social Behavior & Personality, 5*(4), 41–49.

Houtkoop, B. L., Chambers, C., Macleod, M., Bishop, D. V. M., Nichols, T. E., & Wagenmakers, E.-J. (2018). Data sharing in psychology: A survey on barriers and preconditions. *Advances in Methods and Practices in Psychological Science, 1*(1), 70–85.

Ioannidis, J. P. A. (2005). Why most published research findings are false. *PLoS Med, 2* (8), e124.

Kahneman, D. (2011). *Thinking, fast and slow.* Farrar, Straus and Giroux.

Kerr, N. L. (1998). HARKing: Hypothesizing after the results are known. *Personality and Social Psychology Review, 2*(3), 196–217.

LeBel, E. P., McCarthy, R. J., Earp, B. D., Elson, M., & Vanpaemel, W. (2018). A unified framework to quantify the credibility of scientific findings. *Advances in Methods and Practices in Psychological Science, 1*(3), 389–402.

Linehan, M. (1993). *Cognitive-behavioral treatment of borderline personality disorder.* Guilford Press.

Linehan, M. M., Armstrong, H. E., Suarez, A., Allmon, D., & Heard, H. L. (1991). Cognitive-behavioral treatment of chronically parasuicidal borderline patients. *Archives of General Psychiatry, 48*(12), 1060–1064.

Linehan, M. M., Comtois, K. A., Murray, A. M., Brown, M. Z., Gallop, R. J., Heard, H. L., ... Lindenboim, N. (2006). Two-year randomized controlled trial and follow-up of dialectical behavior therapy vs therapy by experts for suicidal behaviors and borderline personality disorder. *Archives of General Psychiatry, 63*(7), 757–766.

Linehan, M. M., Dimeff, L. A., Reynolds, S. K., Comtois, K. A., Welch, S. S., Heagerty, P., & Kivlahan, D. R. (2002). Dialectical behavior therapy versus comprehensive validation therapy plus 12-step for the treatment of opioid dependent women meeting criteria for borderline personality disorder. *Drug and Alcohol Dependence, 67*(1), 13–26.

Linehan, M. M., Heard, H. L., & Armstrong, H. E. (1993). Naturalistic follow-up of a behavioral treatment for chronically parasuicidal borderline patients. *Archives of General Psychiatry, 50*(12), 971–974.

Linehan, M. M., & Korslund, K. E. (2003). *Dialectical behavior therapy adherence manual.* Seattle, WA: Department of Psychology, University of Washington, [Unpublished manuscript].

Linehan, M. M., Korslund, K. E., Harned, M. S., Gallop, R. J., Lungu, A., Neacsiu, A. D., ... Murray-Gregory, A. M. (2015). Dialectical behavior therapy for high suicide risk in individuals with borderline personality disorder: A randomized clinical trial and component analysis. *JAMA Psychiatry, 72*(5), 475–482.

Linehan, M. M., Schmidt, H., III., Dimeff, L. A., Craft, J. C., Kanter, J., & Comtois, K. A. (1999). Dialectical behavior therapy for patients with borderline personality disorder and drug-dependence. *The American Journal on Addictions, 8*(4), 279–292.

Linehan M. M., McDavid J. D., Brown M. Z., Sayrs J. H. and Gallop R. J. (2008). Olanzapine plus dialectical behavior therapy for women with high irritability who meet criteria for borderline personality disorder: A double-blind, placebo-controlled pilot study. *Journal of Clinical Psychiatry, 69,* 999–1005.

Maxwell, S. E. (2004). The persistence of underpowered studies in psychological research: Causes, consequences, and remedies. *Psychological Methods, 9,* 147–163. Available from https://doi.org/10.1037/1082-989X.9.2.147.

Mayo-Wilson, E., Fusco, N., Tianjing, L., Hong, H., Canner, J. K., & Dickersin, K. (2017). Multiple outcomes and analyses in clinical trials create challenges for interpretation and research synthesis. *Journal of Clinical Epidemiology, 86*, 39–50.

McCauley, E., Berk, M. S., Asarnow, J. R., Adrian, M., Cohen, J., Korslund, K., ... Linehan, M. M. (2018). Efficacy of dialectical behavior therapy for adolescents at high risk for suicide: A randomized clinical trial. *JAMA Psychiatry, 75*(8), 777–785.

McMain S. F., Guimond T., Streiner D. L., Cardish R. J. and Links P. S. (2012) Dialectical behavior therapy compared with general psychiatric management for borderline personality disorder: Clinical outcomes and functioning over a 2-year follow-up. *American Journal of Psychiatry, 169*, 650–661.

McMain, S. F., Chapman, A. L., Kuo, J. R., Guimond, T., Streiner, D. L., Dixon-Gordon, K. L., ... Hoch, J. S. (2018). The effectiveness of 6 versus 12-months of dialectical behaviour therapy for borderline personality disorder: The feasibility of a shorter treatment and evaluating responses (FASTER) trial protocol. *BMC Psychiatry, 18*.

McMain, S. F., Links, P. S., Gnam, W. H., Guimond, T., Cardish, R. J., Korman, L., & Streiner, D. L. (2009). A randomized trial of dialectical behavior therapy versus general psychiatric management for borderline personality disorder. *The American Journal of Psychiatry, 166*(12), 1365–1374.

Meehl, P. E. (1978). Theoretical risks and tabular asterisks: Sir Karl, Sir Ronald, and the slow progress of soft psychology. *Journal of Consulting and Clinical Psychology, 46*(4), 806–834.

Mehlum, L., Tørmoen, A. J., Ramberg, M., Haga, E., Diep, L. M., Laberg, S., ... Grøholt, B. (2014). Dialectical behavior therapy for adolescents with repeated suicidal and self-harming behavior: A randomized trial. *Journal of the American Academy of Child & Adolescent Psychiatry, 53*(10), 1082–1091.

Neacsiu, A. D., Eberle, J. W., Kramer, R., Wiesmann, T., & Linehan, M. M. (2014). Dialectical behavior therapy skills for transdiagnostic emotion dysregulation: A pilot randomized controlled trial. *Behaviour Research and Therapy, 59*, 40–51.

Nelson, L. D., Simmons, J., & Simonsohn, U. (2018). Psychology's Renaissance. *Annual Review of Psychology, 69*(1), 511–534.

Open Science Collaboration (OSC). (2015). Estimating the reproducibility of psychological science. *Science, 349*(6251), aac47161–aac47168.

Patil, P., Peng, R. D., & Leek, J. T. (2016). What should researchers expect when they replicate studies? A statistical view of replicability in psychological science. *Perspectives on Psychological Science, 11*(4), 539–544.

Perepletchikova, F., Axelrod, S. R., Kaufman, J., Rounsaville, B. J., Douglas, P. H., & Miller, A. L. (2011). Adapting dialectical behaviour therapy for children: Towards a new research agenda for paediatric suicidal and non-suicidal self-injurious behaviours. *Child and Adolescent Mental Health, 16*(2), 116–121.

Pistorello, J., Fruzzetti, A. E., MacLane, C., Gallop, R., & Iverson, K. M. (2012). Dialectical behavior therapy (DBT) applied to college students: A randomized clinical trial. *Journal of Consulting and Clinical Psychology, 80*(6), 982–994.

Popper, K. R. (1959). *The logic of scientific discovery*. New York: Basic Books.

Rathus, J. H., & Miller, A. L. (2002). Dialectical behavior therapy adapted for suicidal adolescents. *Suicide and Life-Threatening Behavior, 32*(2), 146–157.

Schmidt, S. (2009). Shall we really do it again? The powerful concept of replication is neglected in the social sciences. *Review of General Psychology, 13*(2), 90–100.

Silberzahn, R., & Uhlmann, E. L. (2015). Many hands make tight work. *Nature, 526*, 189–191.

Simmons, J. P., Nelson, L. D., & Simonsohn, U. (2011). False-positive psychology: Undisclosed flexibility in data collection and analysis allows presenting anything as significant. *Psychological Science, 22*, 1359–1366.

Soderberg, C. K. (2018). Using OSF to share data: A step-by-step guide. *Advances in Methods and Practices in Psychological Science*, *1*(1), 115–120.

Steegen, S., Tuerlinckx, F., Gelman, A., & Vanpaemel, W. (2016). Increasing transparency through a multiverse analysis. *Association for Psychological Science*, *11*(5), 702–712.

Tackett, J. L., Lilienfeld, S. O., Patrick, C. J., Johnson, S. L., Krueger, R. F., Miller, J. D., ... Shrout, P. E. (2017). It's time to broaden the replicability conversation: Thoughts for and from clinical psychological science. *Perspectives on Psychological Science*, *12*(5), 742–756.

Verheul, R., van den Bosch, L. M. C., Koeter, M. W. J., de Ridder, M. A. J., Stijnen, T., & van den Brink, W. (2003). Dialectical behaviour therapy for women with borderline personality disorder: 12-month, randomised clinical trial in The Netherlands. *The British Journal of Psychiatry*, *182*(2), 135–140.

Wampold, B. E., Davis, B., & Good, R. H., III. (1990). Hypothesis validity of clinical research. *Journal of Consulting and Clinical Psychology 58*, 360–367.

Index

Note: Page numbers followed by "*f*" and "*t*" refer to figures and tables, respectively.

C

D

Made in the USA
Coppell, TX
24 November 2025

63803097R00227